To:

I trust that as you lear[n] these marvelous hymns, and the devout men and w[omen] who have gifted us with them, your hearts may be inspired, your minds informed, and your spirits BLESSED by the One who gives us reason to sing!

In His Service,

Courtney A. Furman
M. Graham Clark Professor
of Christian Nurture
College of the Ozarks

A Surprising Light

A Surprising Light

*The Christian Hymn
in Contemporary Usage*

Courtney Albert Furman

Dedications

The author dedicates this work, together with the extensive studies that have preceded it, to these persons, whose encouragement and help have enabled him to complete it:

to the late Rev. Dr. Robert C. Rayburn, whose course in Reformed Liturgics reawakened the author's interest in hymnology and who provided generous praise as these studies were in process;

to the late Ralph Willoughby, the InterVarsity staff member who urged the author to make the reading and singing of great hymns a regular devotional practice;

to Professor Gunnar Urang, whose course in Church Music first introduced the author to the lives of hymn-writers over four decades ago;

to the members and friends of the Hollister Presbyterian Church for their long-suffering support and interest;

to Leonard and Edith Gittinger, loyal friends, for their generosity;

to a host of Christian women in the author's life:

Mary Elizabeth Furman, his mother, whose love for music of all types was infectious, and was promoted, enjoyably, in his childhood;

Jody, his wife, whose own love for music, beautiful voice, patience, and faithful prayers have been a source of strength;

Rosemary Wagnon and Gale Arnold, his secretaries, whose skills aided him in producing the critiques and papers necessary in his doctrinal program; and finally

Betty Gifford, his most capable, thorough, and conscientious typist, whose skill and dedication need no comment once one has perused this volume!

Contents

Introduction   1

1. Singing in Worship: The Witness of History   5

2. Singing in Worship: The Witness of Paul and Others   25

3. Singing in Worship: "As You Sing Psalms . . . "   40

     Luther "A Mighty Fortress Is Our God"   44
     Ken "All Praise to Thee, My God, This Night"   49
     Newton "Glorious Things of Thee Are Spoken"   54
     Williams "Guide Me, O Thou Great Jehovah"   59
     Montgomery "Hail to the Lord's Anointed"   63
     Watts "Jesus Shall Reign Where'er the Sun . . . "   68
     Watts "Joy to the World, the Lord Is Come"   73
     Grant "O Worship the King, All Glorious Above"   77
     Watts "Our God, Our Help in Ages Past"   81
     Lyte "Praise, My Soul, the King of Heaven"   86
     Anon "Praise the Lord, Ye Heavens Adore Him"   91
     Neander "Praise to the Lord, the Almighty, the King . . . "   96
     Keble "Sun of My Soul, Thou Savior Dear"   101
     Ellerton "The Day Thou Gavest, Lord, Has Ended"   106
     Baker "The King of Love My Shepherd Is"   111

4. Singing in Worship: "As You Sing Hymns . . . "   116

     Lyte "Abide with Me, Fast Falls . . . "   120
     Theodulph "All Glory, Laud and Honor"   127
     Heber "Brightest and Best of the Sons of the Morning"   131
     Wesley "Christ the Lord Is Risen Today"   136
     Wesley "Christ, Whose Glory Fills the Skies"   142

Bridges "Crown Him with Many Crowns"   147

How "For All the Saints, Who from Their Labors . . ."   152

Wesley "Hark, the Herald Angels Sing"   158

Heber "Holy, Holy, Holy"   163

Newton "How Sweet the Name of Jesus Sounds"   168

Lyte "Jesus, I My Cross Have Taken"   173

Wesley "Jesus, Lover of My Soul"   178

Bernard of Clairvaux "Jesus, the Very Thought of Thee"   186

Bernard of Clairvaux "Jesus, Thou Joy of Loving Hearts"   191

Elliott "Just as I Am, without One Plea . . ."   196

Wesley "Love Divine, All Loves Excelling"   203

Palmer "My Faith Looks Up to Thee"   209

Latin "O Come, O Come, Emmanuel . . ."   214

Brooks "O Little Town of Bethlehem"   219

Bernard of Clairvaux "O Sacred Head Now Wounded"   226

Milman "Ride On, Ride On in Majesty . . ."   232

Toplady "Rock of Ages"   237

Watts "When I Survey the Wondrous Cross . . ."   244

Caswell "When Morning Gilds the Skies . . ."   249

5. Singing in Worship: "As You Sing Spiritual Songs . . . "   254

Perronet "All Hail the Power of Jesus' Name"   256

Alford "Come, Ye Thankful People, Come"   263

Monsell "Fight the Good Fight with All Thy Might . . ."   268

Cowper "God Moves in a Mysterious Way . . ."   273

Bonar "I Heard the Voice of Jesus Say . . ."   280

Sears "It Came upon the Midnight Clear . . ."   286

Bernard of Cluny "Jerusalem the Golden"   292

Havergal "Like a River Glorious . . ."   299

Rinkart "Now Thank We All Our God . . ."   305

Anon "O Come, All Ye Faithful . . ."   311

Baring-Gould "Onward, Christian Soldiers . . ."   316

Stone "The Church's One Foundation"   324

Alexander "There Is a Green Hill Far Away . . ."   332

Conclusion   339

Bibliography   341

Index   345

A Surprising Light

Introduction

The Apostle Paul writes to Christians in Corinth, "I will sing with the spirit, and I will sing with the understanding also" (I Corinthians 14:15). As Moffatt and Patrick affirm,

> It is indeed possible to sing a hymn without knowing or caring very much who wrote it, or how it ever came into the use of the church. There are moods and moments when such knowledge is irrelevant, as the soul worships God with words and music which it can make instinctively its own expression of devotion. But such knowledge often adds to our appreciation, and, therefore, to our spiritual profit. Since a hymn gains by its associations, [with] these present to the mind of the worshipper, he will be likely to sing it with a quickened sense of its message and meaning. And it is ESPECIALLY the function of preachers and of teachers from time to time to convey this knowledge to their congregations and classes.[1]

Very early in my Christian experience I was encouraged by the late Ralph Willoughby, an InterVarsity Christian Fellowship staff member in our region, to use a hymnbook regularly in my personal devotional or quiet time. I have done this, "singing through" several hymnbooks over the years. (In fact, I still have and use my dog-eared copy of InterVarsity *Hymns,* edited by the late Paul Beckwith and first published in 1951, a veritable treasury of magnificent hymns—many of praise to Jesus Christ—which I have thoroughly memorized as a result of repeated singing.) Moreover, owning my own hymnal, I can heartily concur with Winfred Douglas's suggestion that *every* Christian ought to own his own hymnal as well as his own Bible! An authority on church music in his own right, he notes that "probably I should not now feel so intense an interest in the Hymns of the Church if my Presbyterian father had not, out of his poverty, provided a Hymnal for each of his children."[2]

This regular singing of hymns has proven to be a rich experience for me as it has nourished my soul, my inner man, and has been my instructor, teaching me solid biblical theology in the process. And of course, in those times when others have formulated, in beautiful language, the thoughts I

1

yearned to express to God but could not, I have made use of their words, in praise and in prayer.

This practice of hymn-singing has also contributed to my interest in learning about our hymns: the background of the authors' lives, the circumstances surrounding the writing of the hymns, the biblical texts from which they have been forged, the musical intentions of the tunes' composers, and the theological teaching that undergirds them.

However, such information is not readily available to busy pastors, church musicians, and others who have responsibility for preparing the liturgies (orders of worship) for their congregations week after week. As a result, congregations—and often their spiritual leaders as well—are ill-informed about the hymns they sing time and again, and their spiritual lives are thereby deeply impoverished.

Therefore, my intention in this book is to make the fruits of my intensive study of some fifty-two of the greatest Christian hymns readily available to all who will utilize them.

Each study will include the above details, and where available, interesting facts or anecdotes relating to past use of the hymns. In regard to this, incidentally, I have avoided the repetition of such details as are frequently cited by some authors when my research has discovered that they are at best of questionable historical accuracy. For while the focus of this book is practical rather than academic, I am concerned with accuracy and precision wherever possible. Were the late Erik Routley, himself an eminent church music authority, able to evaluate my labors, I would hope that he would laud them in words similar to these:

> In the field of Church music, what a blessing it is to have a work of such precise scholarship! Exactness of thought is not a quality in which church musicians commonly excel. Among us there is much opinion and conjecture, and probably less fastidiousness of intellect than there ought to be. . . . After this there will be no excuse for anybody's failure to go to the true source for the evidence he presents . . . [so that the] study of [hymns] will be made . . . more worthy of scholarly respect.[3]

Much of the material cited herein is available in one or more of the books included in the bibliography, but the information is scattered among them and many of them are out of print. Further, as a matter of fact, few authors have dealt with the biblical texts that have served as the basis for, or at least the inspiration of, the hymns themselves. And even fewer have examined (especially with any sympathetic treatment) the theological teachings contributing to or arising from them. If there is any current validity to an observation made by Louis Benson some years ago—that "in the mind of the plain, everyday Christian, where feeling conditions reflection so strongly, the hymns he loves do more to form his religious thinking than anything else except the Bible"[4]—it is important for leaders of God's people to encourage them to learn and to sing substantial truth, reinforced by great, heart-warming, and uplifting music! And the leaders' ability to enlarge congregations' understanding of the hymns they sing will contribute to that end, even as we have previously suggested.

Finally, let me describe the method used in selecting the hymns I have included in this study.

When John Julian finished his monumental *Dictionary of Hymnology* in 1892, he estimated that over four hundred thousand Christian hymns had been written by that time. By the present time, that number probably far exceeds a half million.[5] It would almost appear to be ludicrous to select one in ten thousand to study; however, only a small percentage of those hymns still exist, and an even smaller number are still being sung, at least with any frequency. Moreover, while authorities do not all agree on what all the greatest hymns are, there is, and has been, widespread agreement about those written over the past three centuries; and when we limit our study, by and large, to hymns originally written in or now translated into English, we narrow the scope of our investigation even farther.

My method of selection was as follows: I collated several lists of the most widely used hymns, which I found in books by Erik Routley (twelve hymnals cited),[6] Albert Bailey (ten hymnals cited),[7] and Harvey Marks (several different lists cited),[8] including a compilation from 107 hymnals, made by Louis Benson, who was considered "an excellent judge of hymn material, [evidencing] the broadest of catholic sympathies, and without sectarianism of any kind."[9]

The hymns included in this study ranked at or near the top of each of these compilations; moreover, further research on them individually has confirmed their eminence. Of those missing from these studies, one deserves a word of explanation, Sir John Bowring's "In the Cross of Christ I Glory," since it also ranks very high, consistently. My rationale for omitting it is rather obvious: it does not appear in the *Trinity Hymnal,* and I have chosen to utilize that hymnal since its selection of hymns is excellent, representing a broad spectrum of Christian hymn-writers and composers.

A word is in order as to how I envision the use of this study, if it is to be of any practical value. If I were selecting one of the more familiar of these hymns, I would prepare a brief statement telling my congregation some significant fact about either the author (of the words), or the composer (of the tune), knowing that people are always interested in finding out about other people (!) and their lives; or I would point out some scriptural truth that has been emphasized therein in beautiful poetic fashion.

If I chose one of the more unfamiliar of these hymns for use, I would probably call it a "Hymn of the Month," and I would share some of this information each week, following up the biographical or historical details with some emphasis on the Scripture passages as it illumines them; or the theology of the author as it unfolds, verse by verse; or, recalling Reynolds's considered judgment that "a hymn is not good because of the merit of its verse, or for the excellence of its tune, but for the felicitous union of both words and tune,"[10] I would seek to show how this text and this tune do happily complement each other. In this way I would seek to elevate both the scriptural and the musical awareness of my congregation.

Finally, it is my earnest desire and ongoing prayer that this study will have wide use by pastors of all ages and musical tastes, so that we, with Luther, might "praise God with the gift of language and the gift of song—with both word and music, proclaiming the Word of God through music, and providing sweet melodies with words."[11]

Notes

1. James Moffatt and Millar Patrick, eds., *Handbook to the Church Hymnary* (London: Oxford University Press, 1927), p. ix.

2. Winfred Douglas, *Church Music in History and Practice* (New York: Charles Scribners' Sons, 1962), p. 191.

3. Paul Yeats-Edwards, *English Church Music—A Bibliography* (London: White Lion, 1975), cited in the foreword.

4. Robert McCutchan, *Hymns in the Lives of Men* (Nashville: Abingdon-Cokesbury, 1945), p. 180.

5. James Sydnor, *The Hymn and Congregational Singing* (Richmond: John Knox, 1960), p. 43.

6. Erik Routley, *Christian Hymns Observed* (Princeton: Prestige, 1982), pp. 115ff.

7. Albert Bailey, *The Gospel in Hymns* (New York: Charles Scribners' Sons, 1952), pp. 585–596.

8. Harvey Marks, *The Rise and Growth of English Hymnody* (New York: Revell, 1938), pp. 39–45.

9. *Ibid.*, pp. 39–40.

10. William Reynolds, *A Survey of Christian Hymnody* (New York: Holt, Rinehart and Winston, 1963), p. 134.

11. Friedrich Blume, *Protestant Church Music* (New York: W. W. Norton, 1974), p. 9.

Singing in Worship:
The Witness of History

Biblical faith is, and has always been, a singing faith. While it can be and often has been used for base and unworthy purposes, music also has uplifting power: power to quicken the emotions, power to elevate the mind, power to inspire the spirit so that one can experience being "lost in wonder, love, and praise." It may have been this awesome power of music that prompted Charles Kingsley to say that

> Music has been called the speech of angels; I will go further and call it the speech of God Himself. All melody and all harmony on earth . . . is beautiful in as far as it is a pattern and type of the everlasting music, which was before all worlds, and shall be after them. Therefore music is sacred . . . and was given to [us] by Christ to lift up our hearts to God, and make us feel something of the glory and beauty of God, and all which God has made.[1]

It is hard to conceive of being a fully human being without some capacity to "make music," some capacity to express oneself musically; so it is not surprising to read of Jubal, very early in the pages of Scripture, as "the father of all who play the harp and flute" (Genesis 4:21); and it makes perfect sense that Moses, and later his sister Miriam—accompanied by tambourines and dancing—would sing a song to the Lord for delivering them from the hand of the pursuing Egyptian army (Exodus 15:1–21). Music in such and similar circumstances, and later in more formalized religious settings, was destined to become a most significant aspect of Israelite worship. It was David, the Lion of the tribe of Judah, the sweet singer of Israel, who was to set her worship in order, and music was a central feature of it. So we read:

> David told the leaders of the Levites to appoint their brothers as singers to sing joyful songs, accompanied by musical instruments: lyres, harps and cymbals. (I Chronicles 15:16)

Heman and Jeduthun were responsible for the sounding of the trumpets and cymbals and for the playing of the other instruments for sacred song. (I Chronicles 16:42)

Psalm-singing, or more likely, a form of antiphonal chanting, was regularly practiced in the liturgy of Jewish worship, both in the temple, and later on, in the services of the synagogue. The Psalter expressed the spirit of praise and adoration, of awe and reverence for God; it also gave expression to the deepest of human needs, desires, and longings. Thus we are not surprised to read that Jesus and His disciples "sang a hymn" at the conclusion of their celebration of the Passover feast (Matthew 26:30; Mark 14:26), noting that this was probably chosen from Psalms 115–118 as these were "among those customarily sung after the Passover meal."[2]

In addition to the Hebrew psalms, which continued to play an important role in the life of the early Christian community, there were apparently other early Christian hymns, composed by (now) unknown believers, which were sung in worship. As Phillips observes, it is probable that "several of the more rhythmical passages in Paul's letters were quotations from such hymns,"[3] listing Ephesians 5:14; I Timothy 1:15; 3:16; 6:15–16; and II Timothy 2:11–13. He later, also, cites several passages in Revelation: 4:8, "Holy, holy, holy . . . ," 4:11, "You are worthy, our Lord and God . . . ," 5:12, "Worthy is the Lamb, who was slain . . . ," and 5:13, "Blessing and honor and glory and power . . . ," referring to all of these as types of future hymnody.[4]

Paul's exhortation, sent both to the Christians in Colosse and to Christians in Ephesus and the surrounding communities (if the Letter to the Ephesians is rightly to be considered a circular letter), makes a strong case for the view that the early church did not limit its singing to materials found in the Psalter. Paul writes:

Let the word of Christ dwell in you richly as you teach and admonish one another with all wisdom, and as you sing psalms, hymns and spiritual songs with gratitude in your hearts to God. And whatever you do, whether in word or in deed, do it all in the name of the Lord Jesus, giving thanks to God the Father through him. (Colossians 3:16–17)

Be filled with the Spirit. Speak to one another with psalms, hymns and spiritual songs. Sing and make music in your heart to the Lord, always giving thanks to God the Father for everything, in the name of our Lord Jesus Christ. (Ephesians 5:18–20)

While we cannot be dogmatic about the precise nature of the distinctions among these three types or categories of music, it is obvious that early Christians used more than just psalms, and it would appear that the latter two categories might include those of someone's "human" composition, in addition to others, possibly from canonical Scripture. Moreover, such certainly could have been inspired by the same Holy Spirit, who (I believe) centuries later was to "inspire" Watts, the Wesleys, and others as they sought to compose hymns of praise to God that have indeed proven to be worthy of use in divine worship. So I concur with Erik Routley when he affirms that "it is everywhere agreed that Christians were singing hymns within a generation of Pentecost."[5]

Moreover, this practice of congregational singing continued well into the postapostolic age. Witnesses to this come from various sources: Pliny, a second-century Roman governor, wrote to Emperor Trajan regarding Christians whose practices he had been ordered to investigate, that "they were in the habit of meeting on a certain fixed day before it was light, when they sang in alternate verses [i.e., antiphonally] a hymn to Christ, as to a god";[6] Tertullian, a second-century Christian apologist, describes an agape feast, saying "each is asked to stand forth and sing, according to his ability, a hymn to God, either one from the holy Scriptures, or one of his own composing."[7] And more recently Erik Routley writes of the hymn *Phos Hilaron* ("Cheerful Light, or "O Gladsome Light"), which St. Basil (A.D. 370) described as "well known," indicating that as an ancient Latin poem, it may have been as many as two hundred years old by his time.[8]

The practice of composing one's own hymns was not without its dangers, however; even then heretics, such as the Arians, made up their own hymns, stressing their doctrines; and so the orthodox leaders, to propagate the truth, frequently favored singing only the Scriptures as "hymns," and tended to stress the singing of the psalms. Ambrose, the famous fifth-century bishop, even encouraged women "to sing their psalms well, as psalms are sweet for every age, and are becoming to every sex!"[9]

One further observation about hymnody as we know it today: it is probable, as Stulken points out, that it "originated during the fourth century . . . developing within the prayer offices [i.e., services]. By the end of that century, worship at the *3rd, 6th* and *9th* hours was established and the singing of hymns was enjoined";[10] since laity were encouraged to attend at least two of these (i.e., at dawn and at dusk) services, this could be considered as congregational singing in a worship context.

The tragedy of course is that during the next thousand years, as worship became more and more a spectator event, with the Mass becoming the focus of one's experience in church, congregational singing was replaced by chanting, done by trained choirs composed of men from the religious orders. Phillips has an amusing reference to the desire of Charlemagne, the Holy Roman Emperor, to introduce cantors and chants into Germany; but alas, as one John the Deacon says of his German pupils,

These mountainous bodies, whose voices roar like thunder, cannot imitate our sweet tones; for their barbarous and ever thirsty throats can only produce sounds like those of a loaded waggon passing over a rough road.[11]

According to Lightwood[12] and others, it was John Hus who gave the chief impetus to return singing to the congregation prior to the Reformation. Hus "believed that Church music should be *by* as well as *for* the people,"[13] and it was his followers, known later as the Bohemian Brethren, who published the first Protestant hymnal in 1501—a Czech songbook containing eighty-seven songs.[14] It is also interesting, although in an ominous way, that after Hus's martyrdom, the Council of Constance warned Hus's successor, Jacob of Misi, to cease the singing of hymns in the churches; it decreed

If laymen are forbidden to preach, and to interpret the Scriptures, much more are they forbidden to sing publicly in the Churches![15]

Is it not incredible that a church council could and would so openly contradict a clear teaching from the Apostle Paul? Of course, ignorance of Scripture was so widespread that few even realized what had happened, and probably fewer still really cared. It remained, then, for another priest to call the corrupt church back to its foundations, and when that proved to be impossible because of the cynicism and intransigence of its leaders, it remained for him to break the shackles of the ecclesiastical system that for so long had held much of the Western world in spiritual ignorance and bondage!

Chains, long forged, were broken when Martin Luther burst on the scene in the early sixteenth century; "articulate and energetic, he used words the way other leaders used armies."[16] His importance theologically and biblically may be familiar to my readers, but his role in the restoration of congregational singing, and his overall recognition of the importance of music for Christian worship, both corporate and private, need to be detailed. Friedrich Blume expresses it well when he writes:

For Luther, music was an essential ingredient for the life of the spirit and soul. His relationship to music was not incidental but part of his very existence. . . . When . . . Luther publicly began his work of reform, he apparently already had a comprehensive musical and liturgical education, comparable to that of the most significant intellectual figures of the time.[17]

Moreover, Luther united theology and music, saying, "after theology, I give music the highest place and highest honor."[18] Indeed, Luther's very reforms of the church grew from his view of church music as (1) the praise of

God, (2) a congregational offering to God, and (3) a means of Christian education—undergirded by the basic theological conviction that "everything should contribute to the bringing of the Word to the people."[19] So Luther can ringingly affirm:

> Next to the Word of God, music deserves the highest praise. She is a . . . governess of those human emotions . . . which govern, or more often overwhelm men. . . . For, whether you wish to comfort the sad, to terrify the happy, to encourage the despairing, to humble the proud, to calm the passionate, or to appease those full of hate . . . what more effective means than music could you find?[20]

But note, please: Luther gives music the "highest place after theology," the "highest praise next to the Word of God." His conception, and what was to become the new Protestant perspective—though, indeed, it was simply a return to the New Testament perspective—laid great stress on worship as an offering, worship as service given to God. This gave congregational singing a mighty impetus indeed, for Luther "taught the people that in singing praise they were performing a service that was well pleasing to God and was a necessary part of public communion with Him."[21]

Moreover, the principle of the believer having direct access to the Father through the mediating grace of Jesus Christ, His well-beloved Son, was symbolized and realized in congregational singing; the spirit of worship in this new church was thus advanced through their music. As Dickinson says,

> The popular hymns, in their own language set to familiar [but] appropriate melodies became at once the characteristic, official and liturgical expression of the emotions of the people in direct communion with God.[22]

It is, therefore, easy to see why an indignant Jesuit would declare that "Luther's songs have damned more souls than all his books and speeches,"[23] since they were so widely disseminated and so regularly used that they became part of the people's very understanding in matters religious! For their souls had indeed been thirsting for these truths, and his words, in language of extraordinary force, "sang the work of redemption and extolled the faith in the free, undeserved grace of God."[24]

The other of the great early Reformers was, of course, John Calvin, who "thought his way out of the Medieval Catholic Church," in contrast to Luther, who "fought his way out of it."[25] But we are not concerned here with style or polemics; we are concerned with music, especially with congregational singing, both in its practice and in its content. What, then, was

Calvin's view of this practice, and what did he consider as appropriate to be sung in corporate worship? It is with at least a grain of sarcasm that Erik Routley laments:

> Calvin saw the infinite possibilities of degeneracy in these new freedoms [i.e., congregational singing, but without instrumental accompaniment, and including naught but biblical words]; you might even say that he saw "The Old Rugged Cross" coming and did what he could to warn us against it. But he didn't win.[26]

What, then, was Calvin's view? In 1541, Calvin introduced congregational singing into the service of worship in Geneva's church; however, he had two basic and interrelated concerns. First, because he sought to stress the Word of God, which he identified with canonical Scripture, he permitted only the singing of the psalms—although he later also allowed one New Testament paraphrase and a metrical version of the Ten Commandments—[27]and rejected the singing of hymns, "since they did not come under his 'sole source of truth' criterion."[28] Second, because he recognized the "avowed power of music to seduce, as well as be a vehicle for man to invoke and praise God,"[29] he would permit nothing but the unaided human voice in worship.

But there is another, powerful, consideration here: as Werner points out, this controversy about whether Christians should sing only psalms in worship, or should be free to sing hymns (i.e., noncanonical compositions) as well, goes back to the days of the postapostolic church.[30] Calvin, following a saying of his master, St. Augustine, that "we have nothing worthy to sing to God but what we have received from Him," insisted—with some compelling logic—that "the Psalms were the only vehicle of praise that rose to the level of what the worship of God required."[31] It is perhaps unfortunate that Calvin did not extend his reverence for the words of the Fathers to include those of St. Ambrose, the Father of Church Music and the mentor of his beloved bishop of Hippo; for had he read and heeded St. Ambrose's wisdom, that "the hymns, the canticles and the psalms should be to us manifestations of God,"[32] he might have encouraged the Reformed branch of the Reformation in its willingness to sing what later came to be known, and loved, as "hymns of human composition"! In any event, if we are inclined to be critical of Calvin, lamenting his rigidity in this matter, we would be wise to temper that criticism, hearing with approval Hodgin's avowal that "he could count on the fingers of one hand all the men who lived in the last six centuries who could be as illy spared as could be John Calvin"[33]—and that praise from a Unitarian!

It is common knowledge that, given its strong impulse from Luther, who himself wrote at least thirty-seven hymns and many fine tunes, hymn-writing and hymn tune-composing proceeded steadily in Germany and in the other countries touched by Lutheranism; as Lang well notes,

> The further Protestant Church music developed, the more it became evident that music was the truest artistic expression of Protestantism; it corresponded to its doctrines and aspirations, and it was in this art that all that was missing in the fine arts was fully realized.[34]

As Liemohn agrees, "the music of the churches of the Reformation as a whole was a tremendous force in the culture of the western world."[35] Had Luther lived to see his impact on that culture as it so developed, he would have rejoiced and perhaps recalled his early words: "I would love to see all the arts, and especially music, in the service of Him who has given and created them."[36]

Meanwhile, in those countries most affected and influenced by the Reformed, or Calvinistic wing of the Reformation, psalmody was the chief vehicle for musical expression in worship—the Genevan system of metrical psalmody.[37] Louis Benson instructs us as to its merits:

> Metrical Psalmody . . . was a utilitarian device, based on devotion to the letter of God's word, aiming merely to cast it into measured and rhyming lines which plain people could sing to simple melodies, as they sang their ballads. The Swiss and French Calvinists, it is true, were able to make large use of the work of Clement Marot, the outstanding French poet, and so secured a version of one third of the Psalter which satisfied Calvin for its accuracy and the whole of France for its beauty. In England and Scotland it was otherwise. The men who made their Psalters were not poets, nor even good craftsmen, . . . their work (producing) metrical versions devoid of the grace or charm of poetry.[38]

Among those English psalters so unflatteringly described, two in particular need to be mentioned: the first (though not the first actually published in England) was published in 1562, and bore this impressive title:

> The whole Booke of Psalmes, collected into Englysh metre by T. Starnhold, I. Hopkins and others: conferred with the Ebrue, with apt Notes to sing them withal, Faithfully perused and alowed according to thordre appointed in the Quenes maiesties Iniunctions. Very mete to be used of all sortes of people privately for their solace and comfort: laying apart all ungodly songes and Ballades, which tende only to the norishing of vyce, and corrupting of youth. . . .[39]

This became known in later years as *Sternhold and Hopkins,* or the *Old Version.* While it did provide religious songs and doctrinal teachings—things desirable for the good English Christians to know—its use was clearly intended for outside the church, and it was not until 1566 that its title page claimed authorization for its use in church, stating:

> Newlye set foorth and allowed to bee soong of the people together, in Churches, before and after morning and evening prayer: as also before and after the Sermon, and moreover in private houses. . . .[40]

Before we consider the other psalter, mention must be made of Richard Baxter, the godly, influential, and sometimes outspoken leader of those English Presbyterians who were ejected in 1662, and for whom the following several decades were times of poverty and distress, if not actual persecution, since many of them were driven from their parsonages and their livings. Baxter, who paraphrased some of the psalms in meter and added other hymns of his own, apparently imposed on himself a strict literalness in paraphrasing the psalms, so that while he "durst make Hymns of his own, . . . he feared adding to God's Word, and thus 'making my own to pass for God's.' "[41] Moreover, he maintained that hymns had been sung from the very beginning of the New Testament era; that Paul

> doubtless meaneth not only David's Psalms, when he bids men sing with grace in their hearts, Psalms, Hymns and Spiritual Songs: yea it is past doubt that Hymns more suitable to Gospel-times, may and ought now to be used; and if used, they must be premeditated.[42]

The second of these psalters that we must consider was published in 1696 by two Irishmen, Nahum Tate, when England's Poet Laureate, and Nicholas Brady, a Royal Chaplain; entitled "A New Version of the Psalms of David, fitted to the tunes used in Churches. By N. Tate and N. Brady," it was, by command of King William III, "Allowed and permitted to be used in all Churches, Chappels, and Congregations, as shall think fit to receive the same." And, as if to head off those who might think it unfit to receive the same, the bishop of London in 1698 "heartily recommended the Use of this Version to all his Brethren within his Diocess."[43]

It is readily apparent that the psalms in this *New Version,* as it came to be known, were fluent, rhythmical, and eminently singable; but while they followed closely the sense of Scripture,[44] they were criticized as having far too many variations from the Hebrew (!) text, and as therefore being inferior to the *Old Version.* In fact, it is ironic that Brady's own church in London refused to accept this version because of the "feeling that Scriptural accuracy had been sacrificed for poetic beauty."[45] So, while it did supplant the *Old Version,* especially in some of the larger parish churches in London and other cities, it never dispossessed that version in the rural country and village parishes; and while both, in fact, continued to be used until replaced by modern hymnody in the nineteenth century, that development was actually encouraged as Christians used this *New Version* and its "Supplement."

One final note about metrical psalms: they were increasingly ridiculed as sheer doggerel by literary scholars, and Queen Elizabeth scorningly referred to their tunes as "Geneva jiggs"; another critic wrote that "two hammers on a smith's anvil would have made better music"; and then there are these famous lines, written by the Earl of Rochester after listening to psalm-singing in a church:

> Sternhold and Hopkins had great qualms
> when they translated David's psalms
> to make the heart right glad;
> But had it been King David's fate
> to hear thee sing and them translate
> by God! t'would set him mad![46]

We turn next to Isaac Watts, of whom Routley writes in his inimitable way, "he broke the log jam and caused the logs to come tumbling down the river."[47] To introduce the reader to this courageous and incredibly gifted man in a more formal fashion, we may say without fear of contradiction that Watts began a new epoch in English church music, that indeed he revolutionized church praise. As Frere writes,

> He was the creator of the modern English hymn; which is neither an Office Hymn like Wither's or Ken's or Austin's, nor . . . a metrical psalm, nor again a close paraphrase of Scripture, but a new species, evolved from the last named, and acquiring in the process a novel liberty of treatment and a balanced artistic form.[48]

The stories of Watts's versifying ventures as a child are legion, well-known, and many perhaps apocryphal; on one occasion as a young child, after being warned by his father to stop his incessant rhyming, and being threatened with corporeal punishment, he cried, "Oh Father, do some pity take, and I will no more verses make"!

His basic purpose was to revive congregational praise, which through both neglect and indifference had become the parody of music earlier mentioned. Moreover, he sought to both "Christianize" the psalms of David and to write hymns that would worthily express his own praise to God. In an essay he wrote to justify his position as being thoroughly consistent with the highest regard for the Bible's words and teachings, he declared

> *First:*   A Psalm properly translated for Christian use is no longer inspired as to form and language: only its materials are borrowed from God's word. It is just as lawful to use other Scriptural thoughts, and compose them into a spiritual song.
>
> *Second:*   The very ends and design of Psalmody demand songs that shall respond to the fullness of God's revelation of Himself. God's revelation in Christ, and our own devotions responding to it, require Gospel songs.
>
> *Third:*   The Scriptures themselves . . . command to sing and give thanks in the name of Christ. Why shall we pray and preach in that name, and sing under terms of the Law?
>
> *Fourth:*   The Book of Psalms does not provide for all occasions of Christian praise, or express all Christian experiences.
>
> *Fifth:*   The primitive "Gifts of the Spirit" covered alike preaching, prayer and song. [If] . . . under the present administration of Grace, ministers are by study and diligence to acquire the cultivate gifts of preaching and prayer, why shall they not also seek to acquire and cultivate the capacity of composing spiritual songs, and exercise it along with the other parts of worship, preaching and prayer?[49]

As Watts wrote his hymns, he consciously avoided the artificial poetical standards of his time, seeking ever to enable ordinary, everyday Christians to find in his words expressions that would enrich their spiritual lives; he published his *Hymns* in 1707. As he paraphrased the psalms, he sought to "make their language more agreeable to the clearer Revelations of the Gospel"[50] and his completed work, published in 1719, included versions (in whole or in part) of 138 psalms, some written in two or three meters for ease of singing. In the preface to these he spoke of his

> Pleasure of being the First who have brought down the Royal Author into the common Affairs of the Christian Life, and led the Psalmist of ISRAEL into the Church of CHRIST, without anything of a JEW about him.[51]

Thus completing *The Psalms of David Imitated* when he was forty-six and suffering from ill-health, the *System of Praise,* which he had envisioned from his youth and had carried steadily forward, was finished; of this two-part work, he wrote: "if an Author's own Opinion may be taken, he esteems it the greatest Work that ever he has publish'd or ever hopes to do, for the use of the Churches."[52]

But this was not the end of his labors, for he also wrote a book of *Divine Songs . . . for the use of Children . . .* , to be used in connection with catechet-

ical instruction, claiming that it was nonpartisan in its theological tone so
that

> children of high and low degree, of the Church of England or dissenters
> [Watts himself was a Nonconformist clergyman], whether baptized in in-
> fancy or not, may join together in these songs.[53]

This proved to be a worthy and influential forerunner of a long series of similar hymnbooks for children.

The reception that Watts's *Hymns and Psalms* received varied, from an enthusiastic usage of them, to an ever-so-slight suspicion; writing almost a century after they first appeared, Walter Wilson, a Dissenter, observes that

> the poetry of Watts was received but slowly into most of our congrega-
> tions. It is only of late years that it has acquired so general a patronage, and
> even in the present day there are many who prefer the rhyming of Brady
> and Tate, or the bald version of the Scotch. The reason is that mankind
> [is] afraid of innovation, and it is only by degrees that their prejudices are
> loosened.[54]

On the other hand, they sold by the thousands of copies, and were used
not only in church services but also widely in family devotional times; in
fact, in 1864, sixty thousand copies were sold! A letter to Watts from Dr.
Doddridge dated April 5, 1731, shows how deeply his hymns had touched
the hearts of the people:

> On Tuesday last, I was preaching to a large assembly of plain country peo-
> ple at a village a few miles off, when, after [my] sermon . . . we sang one
> of your hymns . . . and in that part of the worship I had the satisfaction to
> observe tears in the eyes of several of the people; and after the service was
> over, some of them told me that they were not able to sing, so deeply were
> their minds affected. . . . They were most of them poor people, who work
> for their living, yet, on the mention of your name, I found that they had
> read several of your books with great delight, and that your psalms and
> hymns were almost their daily entertainment; and when one of [them] said
> "What if Dr. Watts should come down to Northampton!" another replied,
> with remarkable warmth, "The very sight of him would be as good as an
> ordinance to me."[55]

Moreover, Watts's success encouraged others of equal—and alas, at times,
of lesser—poetic gifts to try their hand at writing hymns. Individuals too numerous to mention wrote, published, and in some instances sold hymnbooks, often modeling them after Watts, and frequently appending them to a

collection of his (in whole or in part) in order to get them sold! Neverthe-less, it is Watts's figure that stands out, not alone to be sure, but stands out as *the* writer who squarely raised the issue of hymn against psalm, and who, by his marvelous ability to adapt to the then current situation and change it for the better, most influenced the movement "which has transformed all but a comparatively insignificant minority of English-speaking Churches from psalm singing into hymn singing Churches."[56] And thus, of course, Watts paved the way for the prodigious labors and phenomenal success of the char-ter members of Oxford's "holy club," John and Charles Wesley. For, as Man-ning observes,

> No one can read Watts without having Wesley in mind, and nothing will enable a man to see the greatness of Watts' hymns so well as a thorough knowledge of Wesley's.[57]

It is perhaps necessary to be reminded that the impact of Watts was largely, at least at first, felt in the Nonconformist churches, and that he had little or no influence on either the Anglican churches or on the unchurched masses, the folk to whom the Wesleys would turn and to whom their music would especially minister.

Initially the Wesleys, especially John, were deeply troubled by the de-graded conditions of psalmody in the parish churches, one of which Samuel, their father, served as rector. He himself once attributed the preference of the common folk for the *Old Version* over the *New Version* to "their strange genius at understanding nonsense."[58] And John contributed as his scathing criticism of their psalmody, that it was

> miserable scandalous doggerel . . . at first droned out, two staves at a time, "by a poor humdrum wretch," and then "bawled out by a handful of poor, unawakened striplings who neither feel nor understand what they scream," while the congregation is "lolling at ease, or in the indecent pos-ture of sitting, drawling out one word after another."[59]

Contrast this with the impact made on both him and Charles by the Moravian colonists, their fellow passengers en route to their New World asy-lum; among the hymns they sang on board ship would have been those of Paul Gerhardt, which were "the foundation of evangelical hymnody—free ranging, poetically imaginative and intensely personal";[60] how far removed from the Wesleys' earlier singing experiences!

John Wesley, finding his mind challenged and his heart gripped by such music, began to translate and even try his hand at composing similar hymns;

indeed among the criticisms of his work that eventually led to his return to England, two related to this newfound love: (1) his alterations of the authorized metrical psalms, and (2) his use of such unauthorized psalms and hymns in divine worship! Before his return, however, he had published his first collection of some seventy-four pages in 1737—though without his name![61] Watts contributed half, and various others, including George Herbert and Joseph Addison, plus several from his family, and his own translations from the German, comprised the rest—none, incidentally, from Charles, who already had returned home. His contributions were to come later, and make him the chief rival of Watts as England's preeminent hymn-writer.

Both John and Charles experienced profound evangelical conversions within a few days of each other in London in 1738; it was this, and their growing awareness of living in obedience to God, which determined their future callings as itinerant preachers of the gospel. Hymn-singing became one of their chief means of nurturing the new converts, whom they gathered together in "classes" for fellowship, prayer, and testifying to the grace of God; these "classes" became the foundation of the Methodist Societies established in November 1739. This year is also memorable as it saw the publishing of Wesley's third hymn collection, *Hymns and Sacred Poems,* bearing both their names and containing several written by Charles, the first of a "stream uninterrupted until his death," numbering possibly as many as nine thousand, and definitely, 6,500.

Moreover, their hymns were not written in a cloister, but rather came out of the active life of traveling preachers, whose ministries continued to nurture a profound evangelical awakening especially among the working classes, but touching all classes to some extent. And it did not create a self-centered, individualistic pietism; rather, as Routley well says,

> With all the lofty spiritual emphasis of the Wesleyan revival—especially in the greatest of Charles Wesley's hymns—there went a thorough down-to-earth impulse to make [England] a better place. The teaching of the Wesleys inspired people to seek fulfillment in direct service to their . . . underprivileged fellows . . . to found great charity foundations [like] the Foundling Hospital, orphanages, and the Lock Hospital "for restoring unhappy wayward women . . ."; every movement of social reform: the education of the poor, the improvement of prisons, the change of attitude toward the sick and mentally handicapped, the abolition of slavery, had behind it an evangelical impulse.[62]

A telling demonstration of "the power that lies in popular song when inspired by conviction";[63] would that our record were as good and our concern as great today!

Later Wesleyan hymnals added to the increasingly rich store of hymnody that their followers could utilize; and, of course, they included many hymns intentionally "Methodist" in doctrinal content, including those lauding "Christian Perfection" and "Universal Redemption" (which opposed the Calvinist doctrine of election); some of these fanned the flames of dissention that eventually led to the

separation of the Revival forces into two camps, the Calvinistic under Whitefield, the Arminian under Wesley, and to the organization of Lady Huntington's Connection and of Calvinistic Methodism in Wales. . . . Soon hymn tracts were published, mingling tender appeals with scathing satire of the doctrines [they opposed] which were described as "hellish" and "satanic," and presented with little fairness—"Controversial" hymns, which for the good of the Evangelical cause did not survive, and yet which threatened to undo the positive aspects of the Revival Movement.[64]

Eventually, of course, this Methodist movement established Sunday as well as weekday services, and Wesley felt the necessity of providing hymnbooks that were inexpensive and yet sufficiently inclusive of a variety of hymns for the spiritual and doctrinal needs of his flocks. As these were published— some fifty-six in fifty-three years—they included more and more of their own hymns, so that the collection published in 1780, *A Collection of Hymns for the use of the People Called Methodists,* included 525 hymns, all but ten written by members of the Wesley family.[65] Wesley described it as "a little body of experimental and practical divinity" and it became the book of song in Methodist congregations; even though it later underwent several revisions, as late as 1904 when it appeared as *The Methodist Hymn Book,* nearly half of its thousand hymns were still those written by Charles. Of this 1780 *Collection of Hymns,* Manning says,

Wesley's confidence is rooted in the orthodox catholic, evangelical faith. . . . Nothing is more untrue than to represent the heart of Wesley's religion as personal experience or even personal feeling. The heart of Wesley's religion is sound doctrine. . . . There is the solid structure of historic dogma, . . . and the passionate thrill of present experience; but there is, too, the glory of a mystic sunlight coming directly from another world. This transfigures history and experience. This puts past and present into the timeless eternal NOW. . . . It is Wesley's glory that he united these three strains— dogma, experience, mysticism—in verse so simple that it could be understood, and so smooth that it could be used, by plain men.[66]

Finally, the matter of hymn-singing itself must be considered, since this was one of the chief contributions of Wesley and Methodism to the use of hymns in worship. Hymns were to be sung, by all the congregation, and sung acceptably—with joy and delight, but also with reverence. To facilitate this John gave specific directions for congregational singing—seven "canonical" rules. Here they are in "abridged" version:

> Learn *these* tunes before any others; sing them *exactly* as printed; sing all of them; sing lustily; sing modestly; sing in time; above all sing spiritually, with an eye to God in every word.[67]

And these instructions were taken quite seriously, so that at its best Methodist singing was spontaneous, expressing both fervor and gladness, without being raucous or shallow. For even those musically ignorant—and they were legion—were to be taught to sing acceptably and by note; to this end he also published helpful tractates. After all, as Benson so finely says,

> Refined, scholarly, of Anglican training and with Churchly sympathies, neither of [them] conceived or abetted congregational song that was vulgar in its literary contents or flippant in music or indecorous in expression. They cultivated a Hymnody that should be reverently and decently ordered without any sacrifice of its heartiness.[68]

It has been pointed out earlier that Watts took pains to write at the "level of meanest capacity," sacrificing, if necessary, the poetic niceties of language; Wesley on the other hand saw the hymn as a religious lyric, and argued "that the masses must be lifted up to the level of the Hymn, and be made to feel the beauty and inspiration of poetry."[69] It is for this reason that W. J. Courthope, a historian of English poetry, referred to Charles as "the most admirable devotional lyric poet in the English language."[70]

Another group of English hymn-writers needs to be mentioned, for they—though disparate in backgrounds and theological convictions—both continued their ministries within the established church; I refer to the Evangelical wing, and to those associated with the Oxford Movement, some of whom eventually found their way back into the Roman Catholic Church, but most of whom continued to be loyal to Anglicanism.

The Evangelical Party included persons like John Cennick; Martin Madan, who published a *Collection of Psalms and Hymns* in 1760; John Berridge, whose collection published in 1785 was "composed for . . . them who love and follow the Lord Jesus Christ in sincerity"; Richard Conyers, whose collection included two by Cowper; and Augustus Toplady, whose collection included many that developed, clearly, the Five Points of Calvinism. These constituted the first group of Church of England hymnbooks,[71] all of which sought to introduce and encourage hymn-singing in that Communion. To these were added the very important *Olney Hymns* in 1779 by

John Newton and William Cowper, one of England's finest poets; this volume's influence was remarkable, and its appeal, both immediate and permanent, as it became a "people's manual of evangelical doctrine and an instrument of spiritual discipline."[72]

As time went on, this Evangelical Party as it moderated its views and sought closer conformity to its Church's order, had an increasing impact on the entire church, attempting to draw the moderates from "the Prayer Book side" into its fellowship and expanding the number of parish churches and chapels that were committed to the congregational singing of both psalms and hymns.

However, the struggle continued, and many—still concerned with the integrity of the Prayer Book system—watched with dismay as hymn-singing spread from parish to parish. The issue came to a head when, in 1819, Thomas Cotterill, "who combined the piety of a saint, the tastes of a scholar, and the demeanor of an unaffected Christian gentleman," sought to enforce the use of the latest edition of his *Selection of Psalms and Hymns . . . adapted to the services of the Church of England* by his congregation at St. Paul's, Sheffield. In the lawsuit that followed, the chancellor, who lauded Cotterill's book and assumed that no one "could attack a practice—though irregular and without due authority—which was so general and so edifying,"[73] suggested that the archbishop mediate the controversy! He did, and a compromise was reached: Cotterill prepared a new and smaller book, and copies sufficient for his congregation were provided at the archbishop's expense (!) and with this inscription on each copy:

The gift of his Grace the Lord Archbishop of York.[74]

Thus hymn-singing in the Church of England had become substantially recognized, with hymns incorporated on an equal footing with psalms, and with those hymns reflecting their Evangelical origins and nonsectarian character.

The Oxford Movement, the second of the two groups now under consideration and which dominated the Church of England for some time, was a movement to restore the Prayer Book to a central place in worship and to return to the more liturgical hymn, especially the Ambrosian hymnody—those Latin hymns laid aside at the Reformation. Liturgical hymns were the voice of the worshipping church, rather than of the individual believer; and though they expressed common experience, they related it objectively to the hour of worship, the church season, and the sacraments.[75] Some of the hymns by Heber, Keble, Newman, and Edward Caswell are illustrative of this concern for liturgical order.

John Mason Neale, a classics scholar of the first rank, spent his life patiently researching the ancient church manuscripts and succeeded in translating many beautiful hymns from the Latin Fathers, including St. Ambrose, and the two St. Bernards, of Cluny and of Clairvaux—"thereby adding a wealth of medieval Hymnody to the actual resources of English speaking Churches."[76] (Three of these, incidentally, are included in this present study.) Moreover, he also pioneered the rediscovery of the hymns of the ancient Greek church, and has been credited with making a few of them—"Christian, Dost Thou See Them," "The Day of Resurrection," and "Art Thou Weary, Art Thou Languid"—also part of the standard hymnody of English-speaking churches.

During the mid-nineteenth century, the desire to get the hymnody back into the hands of the people and make it again congregational led to a proliferation of published collections of uneven quality. One of the best was Mercer's *Church Psalter and Hymn Book* (1854), with its hymn tunes edited by Sir John Goss. A group of men, many of Tractarian beliefs,

> shared Neale's . . . sense of the unique position of the hymns of the ancient and undivided Church, but . . . also realized that many modern hymns, including some by dissenters, were dear to the people and spiritually effective; and that a selection could be made of such, . . . and used without any real violation of liturgical propriety.[77]

However, they realized that if such a venture was to succeed, various publishers, then competing, would have to cooperate. Under the leadership of Sir Henry Baker, an editorial committee was formed and solicited contributions from all sides; it first published *Hymns Ancient and Modern* in 1861, a collection of 273 pieces, many of them by Baker himself. Its success was phenomenal, comparing favorably with that experienced by Watts and the Wesleys. over the next half century it was revised, edited, and enlarged many times; by 1912, its circulation had reached over 60 million copies.[78] It was considered "nothing less than a national institution,"[79] including as it did hymns of all periods and from many different countries—a remarkably comprehensive achievement.

Moreover, every important name among Anglican hymn-writers is represented in one or another of its editions; the list, sounding like a musical "Hall of Fame," includes Keble, Neale, Cecil Alexander, Dix, How, Osler, Baring-Gould, Stone (whose "The Church's One Foundation" is a "masterpiece of didactic Hymnody"[80]), Ellerton ("possibly the best of the Liturgical hymn writers"), Newman, Bode, Monsell, Faber, Oakeley, Caswall, Charlotte Elliott ("whose ministry in the sick room was beyond estimate"), Francis Ridley Havergal ("the most voluminous . . . and best loved of the Evangelical School, whose hymns reveal her supreme devotion to the spiritual life"), Dean Alford, Bishop Edward Bickersteth ("Peace, Perfect Peace"), J. Mountain, and Bishops J. C. Ryle and Hanley C. G. Moule.[81]

Add to this illustrious company of writers the names of these composers: John Dykes (one of the greatest), William Monk (its musical editor and a fine composer in his own right), Elvey, Richard Redhead, Reinagle, and others, and it is apparent why this hymnal, with Monk's choice arrangements,

> crystallized the musical tendencies of the time into a definite Anglican hymn tune, with restrained melodies and close harmonies wonderfully adapted to liturgical worship, and yet appealing to the taste of the people . . . not only within but beyond the bounds of the [Anglican Communion]; and finding their way into the books of the dissenting Churches and even into the Church of Scotland.[82]

As we bring this historical survey of the use of singing in worship to a close, having begun with the Old Testament Psalter and ended with the English hymn—the theme of this book—we cite the carefully crafted statement of Raymond Abba, who summarizes the place wherein we now stand:

> The Church today has thus a three-fold heritage of hymnody: it inherits the Catholic tradition of St. Ambrose and the Middle Ages . . . ; it is the heir to the Puritan tradition of Milton and Doddridge, exemplified supremely in Isaac Watts; and to it is bequeathed the Evangelical tradition of Zinzendorf and the Moravians which flowers so finely in John and Charles Wesley.[83]

As Cowper once observed, "sometimes a light surprises the Christian while he sings." But this should not surprise us, for when we sing, the door of our understanding is opened, through our emotions, to realities beyond the meaning of words. So then, let us frequently

> be filled with the freedom and the ecstacy of singing. The reward will be that we are numbered among the immortals who sing the never-beginning, the never-ending, the ever-old, the always-new song, to the praise of God![84]

Notes

1. Alfred Pike, *A Theology of Music* (Toledo: The Gregorian Institute of America, 1953), p. 5.

2. Marilyn Kay Stulken, *Hymnal Companion to the Lutheran Book of Worship* (Philadelphia: Fortress, 1981), p. xiii.

3. C. S. Phillips, *Hymnody Past and Present* (London: SPCK, 1937), p. 14.

4. *Ibid.*, p. 15.

5. Routley, *Christian Hymns Observed*, p. 7.

6. Edwin Liemohn, *The Singing Church* (Columbus: Wartburg, 1959), p. 9.

7. *Ibid.*

8. Routley, *op. cit.,* p. 8.

9. Liemohn, *op. cit.,* p. 16.

10. Stulken, *op. cit.,* p. xiii.

11. Phillips, *op. cit.,* p. 102.

12. James Lightwood, *The Music of the Methodist Hymn-Book* (London: Epworth, 1935), p. x.

13. William Rice, *A Concise History of Church Music* (Nashville: Abingdon, 1964), p. 20.

14. Blume, *op. cit.,* p. 593.

15. Lester Hostetler, *Handbook to the Mennonite Hymnary* (Elgin: Brethren Publishing House, 1949), p. xv.

16. Routley, *op. cit.,* p. 17.

17. Blume, *op. cit.,* p. 6.

18. *Ibid.,* p. 10.

19. *Ibid.,* p. 14.

20. *Ibid.,* p. 10.

21. Edward Dickinson, *Music in the History of the Western Church* (New York: Charles Scribners' Sons, 1953), p. 242.

22. *Ibid.,* p. 243.

23. *Ibid.,* p. 255.

24. *Ibid.,* p. 256.

25. Routley, *op. cit.,* p. 19.

26. *Ibid.,* p. 21.

27. Moffatt and Patrick, *op. cit.,* p. xii.

28. Liehmohn, *op. cit.,* p. 42.

29. Blume, *op. cit.,* p. 517.

30. Eric Werner, *The Sacred Bridge* (New York: Columbia University Press, 1959), p. 319.

31. Moffatt and Patrick, *op. cit.,* p. xii.

32. Werner, *op. cit.,* p. 320.

33. McCutchan, *Hymns in the Lives of Men,* p. 133.

34. Paul Henry Lang, *Music in Western Civilization* (New York: W. W. Norton, 1941), p. 321.

35. Liemohn, *op. cit.,* p. 54.

36. Dickinson, *op. cit.,* p. 16.

37. Louis Benson, *The English Hymn* (Richmond: John Knox, 1962), p. 26.

38. *Ibid.,* p. 46–47.

39. *Ibid.,* p. 28.

40. *Ibid.,* p. 30.

41. Douglas, *op. cit.,* p. 226.

42. *Ibid.*

43. Benson, *op. cit.,* p. 48.

44. *Ibid.,* p. 49.

45. Liemohn, *op. cit.,* p. 49.

46. Reynolds, *op. cit.*, p. 39.

47. Erik Routley, *A Short History of English Church Music* (London: Mowbrays, 1977), p. 31.

48. Raymond Abba, *Principles of Christian Worship* (London: Oxford University Press, 1957), p. 128.

49. Benson, *op. cit.*, pp. 112–113.

50. *Ibid.*, p. 118.

51. *Ibid.*, p. 120.

52. *Ibid.*

53. *Ibid.*, p. 121.

54. *Ibid.*, p. 123.

55. *Ibid.*, p. 125.

56. *Ibid.*, p. 218.

57. Abba, *op. cit.*, p. 129.

58. Benson, *op. cit.*, p. 222.

59. *Ibid.*

60. Routley, *A Short History* . . . , p. 36.

61. Benson, *op. cit.*, p. 226.

62. Routley, *op. cit.*, pp. 43–45.

63. Dickinson, *op. cit.*, p. 379.

64. Benson, *op. cit.*, pp. 232–233.

65. *Ibid.*, p. 236.

66. Abba, *op. cit.*, p. 130.

67. Benson, *op. cit.*, p. 241.

68. *Ibid.*, p. 242.

69. *Ibid.*, p. 253.

70. *Ibid.*

71. *Ibid.*, p. 335.

72. *Ibid.*, p. 338.

73. *Ibid.*, p. 355.

74. *Ibid.*, p. 356.

75. *Ibid.*, p. 498.

76. *Ibid.*, p. 502.

77. *Ibid.*, p. 509.

78. *Ibid.*, p. 511.

79. Kenneth Long, *The Music of the English Church* (New York: St. Martin's, 1971), p. 334.

80. Benson, *op. cit.*, p. 516.

81. *Ibid.*, pp. 516–520.

82. *Ibid.*, p. 521.

83. Abba, *op. cit.*, p. 131.

84. Reynolds, *op. cit.*, p. 134.

2

Singing in Worship:
The Witness of Paul and Others

Church music should focus the attention of the worshipper first and foremost on God. Whatever other feelings the worshipper may have, "a sense of awe and reverence as in the Presence of the divine holiness should never be absent."[1] And music that is best suited for worship can inspire this feeling, can create an atmosphere that fills the worshipping person with solemn, reverent thoughts, and makes of the sanctuary a house of prayer, a holy place indeed. Moreover, it is the conviction of this writer that there is a kind of music—a music that has dignity and gravity—which is particularly able to create this sense; an illustration of this is what Mendelssohn once said of Bach's music, that "it turned any room in which it was performed into a Church."[2]

However, this is not to urge that the proper mood in worship is to be that of gloom, as if we are sullenly carrying out the duty required of us. Far from it, for a spirit of joy and gladness is quite consistent with—if indeed not integral to—wonder and awe, for as sinners redeemed by God's grace and well acquainted with His mercy, we have much reason for joy. As Haydn, when asked why there was such a cheerful note in his church music, replied,

> When I think upon God, my heart is so full of joy that the notes dance and leap, as it were, from my pen; and since God has given me a cheerful heart, it will be pardoned me that I serve Him with a cheerful spirit.[3]

And this is not without biblical warrant, for we are admonished by Paul to "rejoice in the Lord always, and again I say rejoice" (Philippians 4:4); and by James, "Is any merry? Let him sing psalms" (i.e., songs of praise, James 5:13, NIV).

In addition to this joyful, reverent praise of God, church music has a second, and no less important function: to encourage and enrich the fellowship of the believing community at worship. For we are "members, one of another," parts of one body whose Head is Jesus Christ (I Corinthians 12), and in congregational singing it is one common song that we raise! As we unite our voices, it should be the aim of our singing to utilize the power of music to draw these individual hearts together, thus removing any feelings of isolation and deepening our sense of unity and harmony with God and with one another. Paul Cook expresses well this twofold function of church music, Godward and manward, when he writes,

> Our hymnody, as is the case with our theology, must begin with God, proceed in dependence upon Him, and redound to His glory. . . . However, psalms and hymns serve a deeper function than simply to state in true but objective fashion the glory of our God. . . . The God of the Bible is One who is graciously pleased to come down and to manifest His presence to His children. By His Spirit He sheds His love abroad in their hearts and causes them to rejoice with joy unspeakable and full of Glory.[4]

It is my judgment that Paul's exhortation—if not command[5]—given both in his Letter to the Colossians and in his circular letter to a wider group of Christians (perhaps centering in Ephesus) focuses on the second of these two functions of music in worship, the building up or edifying of the body of believers. While I cite both passages below, I will discuss primarily the former, since I believe that the Ephesians passage expresses essentially the same teaching.

> Let the word of Christ richly dwell within you, with all wisdom teaching and admonishing one another with psalms and hymns and spiritual songs, singing with thankfulness in your hearts to God. And whatever you do, in word or deed, do all in the name of the Lord Jesus, giving thanks through Him to God the Father." (Colossians 3:16–17, NASB)

> Be filled with the Spirit, speaking to one another in psalms and hymns and spiritual songs, singing and making melody with your heart to the Lord; always giving thanks for all things in the name of our Lord Jesus Christ to God, even the Father. (Ephesians 5:18–20, NASB)

I note, first, that the wisdom we need to "continue teaching and admonishing one another" comes to us as "The word of Christ richly dwells within us"; to what "word of Christ" was Paul referring here? Did Paul mean some definite body of oral written truth? Was he thinking of the messianic psalms? Or, as Lightfoot suggests, does this "word of Christ" simply denote "the presence of Christ in the heart as an inward monitor"?[6] Or again, as Guthrie argues, does "word of Christ" imply some specific teaching(s), either about Christ or which Christ Himself gave?[7] Without being dogmatic I incline to this latter suggestion—seeing the "word of Christ" as teaching given by Jesus Himself. Moreover, the fact that we are told in the parallel passage from Ephesians to be "filled with the Spirit" in order to effectively "speak to one another" would suggest the Holy Spirit's role as Illuminator—the One who reminds the believer of the truths Christ Himself taught (John 14:26). As F. F. Bruce summarizes,

> Christian teaching . . . based on the teaching of Jesus Himself . . . unmistakably "the word of Christ . . ." would "dwell richly" in their midst when they came together and in their hearts as individuals if they paid heed to what they heard, bowed to its authority, assimilated its lessons and translated them into daily life.[8]

Second, there is in both Epistles an emphasis on thankfulness; believers are commanded to have and to demonstrate an attitude of gratitude to God, who is both the Father of our Lord Jesus Christ and our Father. Regarding this grace, Simpson says:

> The obligation of thankfulness to God for "mercies countless as the sands" holds the premier place. That we exist . . . that our days are passed in comparative tranquility . . . that all our positive blessings . . . we owe to His loving kindness. Our very deprivations and trials . . . if we are His by grace as well as by nature, come to us as benedictions in disguise. . . . The Lord's sovereign dispensations are matter for gratitude, not for murmuring. . . . The mixed yarn of life, woven in the loom of heaven by the Father of mercies, traces a perfect design for those "in Christ," and their thanksgivings should reascend to Him through their mediatorial All-in-all.[9]

Third, Paul's exhortation emphasizes "teaching and admonishing one another," a witness to the fact that in these early Christian assemblies, the practical implications of the doctrine of the priesthood of all believers included mutual edification; the worship services of the Corinthian community coming to his mind may have occasioned this statement.[10] In any event, the use of music as an instructional medium certainly makes sense; as Clark points out, "in an age without printing, and when many would not read, and before catechisms had been worked out, singing the words was a good method of learning. It still is."[11] One further point: Douglas raises an interesting question. Did Paul have the antiphonal method of singing psalms in view here when he says "singing to one another"?[12] Certainly if these instructions are intended for corporate worship as well as for private devotions—which even Clark grudgingly allows[13]—this may well point to the continued use of that practice. As F. F. Bruce affirms, "Antiphonal praise or solo singing for

mutual edification in their church meetings is probably what the apostle rec-
ommends."[14]

Fourth, and here we consider the major concern of this passage for our
research, Paul's exhortation that with grace-filled hearts we do that teaching
and admonishing of one another by "singing psalms and hymns and spiritual
songs." The precise significance of these terms has probably been debated
ever since the first partisan of one or another of them—as different types of
"church music"—read Paul's instructions. Scholars have voiced varying
opinions, with different degrees of certitude. For example, Bruce argues that

> It is unlikely that any sharply demarcated division is intended, although
> the "psalms" may have been drawn from the OT Psalter (which has sup-
> plied a chief vehicle for Christian praise from primitive times), the
> "hymns" might be Christian canticles (e.g., the Magnificat and the Bene-
> dictus), and the "spiritual songs" might be unpremeditated words sung "in
> the Spirit," voicing holy aspirations (such as an early collection of Christ-
> ian hymns known as the "Odes of Solomon").[15]

Guthrie questions this identifying of hymns with the Lukan passages, saying
that "it seems more likely that 'hymns' are ascriptions to Christ"[16] on the
model of passages in Revelation 4–5. Ralph Martin says, regarding all three
of these categories, that "probably distinctively Christian compositions are
intended for all three types."[17] In these technical matters, Calvin's view is
similar to Lightfoot's, which I will cite for its comprehensiveness, below;
Calvin, expounding as a pastor, tells his parishioners/readers that

> Paul . . . means that all our words should be disposed to edification, that
> even those that serve cheerfulness may not be pointless. . . . Leave to un-
> believers that foolish delight which they get from ludicrous and frivolous
> jests and witticisms. Let your words, not merely those that are serious, but
> those also that are joyful and cheerful, contain something profitable. In
> place of their obscene, or at least barely modest and decent, songs, it be-
> comes you to sing hymns and songs that sound forth God's praise.[18]

Lightfoot's exposition deserves to be cited at length; he refers to a number
of postapostolic sources, including Hippolytus, Philo, Pliny, Eusebius,
Clement of Alexandria, and Tertullian, and cites also sources more contemporary with him. After pointing out that these three words—"psalms,"
"hymns," and "songs"—are demonstrated by Trench to be somewhat distin-
guishable, he writes:

In other words, while the leading idea of [psalms] is a musical accompaniment, and that of [hymns] praise to God, [songs] is the general word for a song, whether accompanied or unaccompanied, whether of praise or on any other subject. Thus it was quite possible for the same song to be at once psalm, hymn and song. In the text, psalms we may suppose are specially, though not exclusively, the Psalms of David which would early form part of the religious worship of the Christian brotherhood. . . . Hymns would . . . designate those hymns of praise which were composed by the Christians themselves on distinctly Christian themes. . . . The third word, songs, gathers up the other two and extends the precept to all forms of song with the limitation, however, that they must be spiritual. . . . St. Chrysostom treats [hymns] here as an advance upon [psalms], which in one aspect they are [i.e., as proper words for Christian worship; moreover,] the reference in this text is not solely . . . to public worship as such. Clement treats it as applying to social gatherings (of Christians), and Tertullian (apparently) relates it to the agape [i.e., the Communion celebration and its prior common meal].[19]

Arndt and Gingrich define these terms simply: psalms—(1) "a song of praise, psalm in accordance with OT usage, of the OT Psalms; (2) of Christian songs of praise";[20] hymns—"a hymn or song of praise";[21] and (spiritual songs—"in our literature only of a sacred song, a song of praise to God."[22]

(An interesting aside: Paul refers in this passage both to the intellect ["with all wisdom . . ."] and to the emotions [" . . . in your hearts"] as involved in the Christian's act of praising God and exhorting one's fellows. Breed, comparing Watts and Wesley, notes that "Watts is more reverential, Wesley more loving; Watts appeals profoundly to the intellect, while Wesley takes hold of the heart.")[23]

It is obvious that while Paul was urging Christians to consecrate their minds and hearts as they lifted their voices in "psalms, and hymns, and spiritual songs," types of music suitable both for worship and for other informal Christian gatherings—used even perhaps as Christians were employed at their daily workplace[24]—we cannot rigidly define the precise nature of those musical forms. But I believe we can be assured of one thing at least: they were offerings to God, and they were worthy! Anything otherwise the Apostle would not have tolerated in those congregations in and over which he labored, toiling in prayer for them until "they attained some measure of the stature of the fulness of Christ."

Finally, it is lamentable that many Christian congregations today—and this includes myriads who "believe the Bible from cover to cover"—do not in fact take this exhortation of Paul seriously. All too often their musical diets are highest in "spiritual songs," which they have translated as meaning "gospel songs," supplemented with a few of the great hymns ("A Mighty Fortress," "Holy, Holy, Holy," and selected others); rarely do psalms even appear on their menus, unless it be one of the more familiar settings of Psalm 23, 100, or 150—because "we learned them in our high school glee club"! Erik Routley's plea is quite to the point:

> I understand that in many parts of the United States . . . there is a marked resistance to the use of psalms in Christian worship. I must plead with those who thus set their faces against the Psalter. Nothing could so effectively dehumanize and damage Christian worship as the neglect of the Psalter. [For] . . . once one has admitted that we naturally live in the Old Testament, and constantly have to be recalled, like prodigals to our Father's house, what one finds is that the Psalter, through 90% of its length has a wisdom, a perceptiveness, and a sense of God's glory which lifts us from where we are toward the New Testament as nothing else in literature can. The Psalter prepares us to sing our hymns of faith.[25]

The reader will note that a serious effort is made in the following chapters to remedy this lamentable situation by including some of the finest examples of each of these three categories. For the author believes that this categorization into "psalms, hymns, and spiritual songs" is to be understood as referring to three distinctive types of church hymnody, with a twofold purpose: to exalt the Triune God and to edify the believing community. But then consider: Is this really a dual purpose? On the surface it may appear to be, but on more careful examination is there not just one purpose for church music—to exalt God? For is it not the case that even the edification itself of the believing community glorifies God? Is it not true that as God, the common focus of our worship, draws us to Himself, as we are "lost in wonder, love, and praise," at the same time we are indeed drawn more intimately toward one another? Would it not be quite consistent with the intention of John to read his familiar words from his first letter in this fashion: "what we have seen and heard we [sing] to you also, that you also may have fellowship with us [the horizontal plane of edification]; and indeed our fellowship is with the Father, and with His Son Jesus Christ [the vertical plane of worship]. And these things we [sing] that our joy may be made complete" (I John 1:3–4)? With this understanding in mind, I cite with approval Davison's words:

> There is, I am convinced, but one logical purpose for which church music may be employed, and that is to the glory of God; not for any of the psychological, social, opportunistic or utilitarian ends for which our worship

music is now tortured out of its true nature, but as an offering, a sacrifice, a return in kind of God's gift of beauty to man. The finest church music . . . is uniquely the music of worship.[26]

If, then, the ultimate and all-encompassing purpose of church music and hymnody is to bring glory to God, both directly as our singing ascribes worth to Him and indirectly as that common praise enriches the lives of the worshipping community, we must consider two or three related matters.

First, as regards the music itself, which we make the vehicle for our hymnodic praise, can we eliminate any styles, beats, rhythms, and the like as intrinsically worthy, or at least inappropriate, for the purpose of worship? Popular opinion would probably reject any such idea as "high brow prejudice," and perhaps even cite Scripture in its defense: for example, "make a joyful NOISE unto the Lord" (Psalm 100:1); "and WHATEVER you do in word or deed [i.e., sing] do it heartily, as unto the Lord" (Colossians 3:17, 23 conflated). Professor Berglund, in a superb discussion,[27] points out, to the contrary, that there are very important issues to be considered, especially the matter of what associations music has for the listener/participant, and whether or not certain types of music, because of their usual associations, are thereby inappropriate for use in worship. In his discussion that focuses on one contemporary style, "pop music," he points out that its usual associations do carry over into a "religious setting" and create a serious problem—the music still communicates the "meanings, feelings and moods of pop music," even though the text is religious. Therefore, he warns:

Church musicians must . . . be culturally aware. . . . They must . . . see and hear how various musical idioms are used. It quickly becomes apparent that WHAT SOME MUSIC STYLES MEAN IS DIAMETRICALLY OPPOSED TO THE VERBAL COMMUNICATION OF SPIRITUAL TEXTS. . . . The Church musician [must insure] that his musical values be consistent with and supportive of his theological views.[28]

It is an interesting historical fact that Sir F. A. Ouseley opposed the use, in his day, of secular tunes for hymns in a similar way. He writes:

How can such tunes—in 6-8 time, in tripping measure in secular style, with associations of secular and even amorous and questionable words . . . how can such tunes conduce to devotion? . . . How can they result in aught but the disgust and discouragement of all musical churchmen, the misleading of the unlearned, the abasement of sacred song, the falsification of public taste, and last but not least, the DISHONOR of God and His worship?[29]

He asks some good questions, does he not? However, there are those who would—if not directly contradict Ouseley—at least argue the point differently. Thus Erik Routley maintains that today the sacred/secular distinction in music has been obliterated, and that this is healthy for music itself. Moreover he asserts, "neither Purcell nor Bach made that distinction"; in fact, "all respectable composers have distinguished only between music that is, and music that is not, applied to sacred uses." But, he continues, we must bring back "the distinction between secular music considered as excellent, and secular music considered as vulgar."[30] While I applaud this latter statement, it seems to me that Routley's discussion presupposes the existence, imagined or real, of types of music that could be considered sacred or secular.

Stewart also discussed this issue of the sacred/secular distinctive in church music in his Baird Lectures in 1926;[31] he also refers to the power of associations that music possesses, and points out that music associated with the theater, the dancing saloon, the taverns, and the like—certainly "secular" contexts—is thereby inappropriate for the worship of Almighty God. However, he maintains, "the hard and fast line which we draw between the sacred and the secular in music has not much justification in history,"[32] and cites as evidence both early Catholic Church music and some, at least, of the early Lutheran chorale music, reminding us that Luther "thought that the devil should not have all the good tunes to himself!"[33] But associations do matter, and so Stewart continues, once a secular tune (e.g., a folk song) "has passed out of general use, . . . if it has the necessary dignity and merit (and that of course is a significant *if*) there is no reason why it should be denied admission to our Church praise."[34] In any event, whatever the music we offer to God, it should be the very best of its kind'; how dare we offer Almighty God anything else? We should begrudge no labor or care to make our offering worthy; it should be "solid, dignified . . . music with a strength and virility about it . . . fit to be presented as an offering to God."[35] One further note from Stewart: he is not here arguing that the elaborate is necessarily the most worthy; his view is quite balanced and realizable.

> The plain, unambitious music of a little country church may be musically as excellent in quality, and therefore as worthy of being presented as an offering to God, as the elaborate cathedral service. . . . What I contend . . . is that the praise should be the best possible in the circumstances, in respect both of the character of the music selected and the manner of its [rendering].[36]

Berglund also deals, as we might expect, with this distinction between the sacred and the secular in music, and especially with Luther's use of the popular tunes of his day, tunes that were, admittedly, used in the "pubs, where people socialized, caught up on current news, and sang folk songs."[37] Berglund points out that Luther's congregation, used to being spectators rather than participants in worship, would well resist any personal involvement in what had been the solemn service of the Mass. So Luther had to start where they were; yet even he soon "realized the incongruity of using tunes on Sunday mornings that had been sung the previous Saturday evening; he explicitly referred . . . to the paradox created by this mixture of associations, and . . . took steps to compose new tunes."[38]

Moreover, as Berglund shows, Luther took great pains to avoid using music that might in any way detract from the reverent worship of God. As Luther himself wrote to young people, regarding music as the gift of God, highest next to theology,

> And you, my young friend, let this noble, wholesome and cheerful creation of God be commended to you. By it you may escape shameful desires and bad company. At the same time you may by this creation accustom yourself to recognize and praise the Creator. Take special care to shun perverted minds who prostitute this lovely gift of nature and of art with their erotic rantings; and be quite assured that none but the devil goads them on to defy their very nature which would and should praise God its Maker with this Gift, so that these bastards purloin the gift of God and use it to worship the foe of God, the enemy of nature and of this lovely art. [Moreover he argued that young people need] something to wean them away from love ballads and carnal songs and to teach them something of value in their place, thus combining the good with the pleasing, as is proper for youth. . . . I would like to see . . . music used in the service of Him who gave and made [it]. . . . As it is, the world is too lax and indifferent about teaching and training the young for us to abet this trend.[39]

To answer my earlier question, whether or not there are musical styles, beats, and rhythms that are at least inappropriate for use in worship, I would say yes; associations with their past usage, it seems to me, would greatly reduce their ability to be effective vehicles for the praise of God; and therefore I would argue why use them at all when there are such magnificent tunes available. Moreover, why not make every effort to raise the level of musical taste and appreciation of our congregations rather than simply "giving them what they like, what they are used to, and therefore what they want." Of course, as Routley candidly points out, "Beauty [in music] can never be gotten at cut-rate; it must be paid for, not only in money, but in what money properly represents—the honorable labour of taking the trouble."[40] All too often it is simply too much trouble, for little apparent gain, to try to elevate and educate people to appreciate, to want, and to use the finest available in their public—and indeed in their private—worship of God.

Next, let us examine the practice of congregational singing as one of the most vital uses of church music. If Dickinson could write, with accuracy, at the turn of this century that

> English church music has never been in a more satisfactory condition than it is today. There is no other country in which religious music is so highly honored, is so much the basis of the musical life of the people, [and contributes so much] to the deep rooted religious reverence which enters into the substance of English society,[41]

this has not always been the case, especially in England, before his time or since. For, as Benson points out, the singing of hymns in the English-speaking world is a relatively modern practice, and a protracted and at times bitter struggle preceded their general acceptance as a necessary, let alone worthy, part of divine worship. For, "to love hymns in eighteenth century Scotland was to be accused of heresy; in England it was to be convicted of that worse thing, 'enthusiasm'";[42] thus it was not until the mid-nineteenth century that hymn-singing won the general esteem it had had in Germany from the earliest days of the Protestant Reformation.

It was really a threefold problem: the compositions to be sung, the musical ability of the average lay person, and the unavailability of hymnbooks (words, tunes, or both). Let us look at each of these, briefly, to see why music was neglected and congregational singing was often suspended, as sometimes "controversial."

First, metrical psalms and many of the earlier hymns had meters or rhymes that were difficult to sing, or were doggerel, and sometimes both; for example, one critic spoke thus of metrical psalm-singing:

> Could poor King David but for once
>   to Salem church repair
> And hear his psalms thus warbled out
>   Good Lord, how he would swear![43]

Another cites these lines, based on Song of Solomon 2:3:

> The tree of life my soul hath seen
> Laden with fruit and always green;
> the trees of nature fruitless be
> Compared with Christ, the Apple tree.[44]

and yet another describes fuging pieces:

> light and quick, they were sung by choirs as the congregation sat in be-
> wilderment listening to the voices chasing hither and yon in pursuit of
> snatches of text and melody.[45]

Thus, until at least the breakthrough occasioned by the beautiful, understandable, and eminently singable poetry in the hymns of Watts, the Wesleys,
and others, content was a problem.

The second problem, the limited musical abilities of the average lay person, was compounded by the third, the lack of available hymnbooks, especially those which supplied tunes as well as the words. Benson informs us
that

> In the lack of music books and the inability to sing by note, a very few
> tunes were sung from memory, "tortured and twisted as every unskillful
> throat saw fit," producing a medley of discordant noises, . . . something like
> five hundred different tunes, roared out at the same time . . . the singers
> often one or two words apart.[46]

And this condition was not limited to rural congregations, for he later mentions the "scholars at Princeton Chapel, singing as badly as the Presbyterians in New York,"[47] and those in Philadelphia, whose congregational singing
"seems rather to imitate the braying of Asses than the divine Melody so often
recommended in Scripture."[48]

One cause of this inability to participate well, and therefore frequent un-
willingness to even try, was the dependence at various times in our historical past on choirs or trained singers to sing for us; this of course was the
problem Luther faced initially, the spectator-at-Mass syndrome. He writes of
this:

> . . . in the Old Covenant (and by implication, under Romanism) divine
> service was tedious and tiresome. . . . And . . . they performed this service
> unwillingly. Now . . . with a heart unwilling as this, nothing good can be
> sung. Heart and mind must be cheerful and willing if one is to sing. . . .
> God has cheered our hearts and minds through His dear Son, who He
> gave for us to redeem us from sin, death and the devil. He who believes
> this earnestly cannot be quiet about it . . . but must gladly and willingly
> sing . . . about it so that others may come and hear it.[49]

Wienandt and Young speak to this same point:

Go into our churches on Sunday. . . . The music is going on. Observe the attitude and the appearance of the congregations assembled. Do they appear like persons engaged in a solemn act of devotion? . . . Is listening to music devotion? Is hearing a choir sing, worship? Is a *passive* state of *any* kind, worship? . . . It is difficult for . . . the mind to follow . . . the devotional thought of the hymn, with the unwandering attention of heart worship . . . unless the tongue *be itself uttering the words of devotion,* and thereby *nailing the mind* to the devotional thought.[50]

Again: as regards effective congregational singing when hymnbooks were unavailable, there was the abominable but necessary practice of lining out the hymns; as Liemohn demonstrates:

The Lord will come and He will not
   The Lord will come and He will not
Keep silence but speak out
   Keep silence but speak out[51]

Eventually, of course, when hymnbooks became available lining out was no longer necessary; yet it was still, as a hallowed practice, sometimes done. Billings, a self-taught musician and composer, voices his disgust: "as now all have books, and all can read, 'tis insulting to have the lines read in this way; for it is practically saying 'we men of letters, and you ignorant creatures'";[52] he had a point!

Lowell Mason and Thomas Hastings claimed that this neglect of congregational song was due to the ignorance and indifference of the laity. Hastings wrote, in 1829,

Go where we may into the place of worship . . . when the singing commences . . . the congregation are either . . . gazing at the select performers to admire the music or . . . expressing their dissatisfaction by general symptoms of restlessness. We observe everywhere . . . the appearance of restlessness or relaxation.[53]

But they did not just complain; they did something. They established singing schools for children and singing classes for congregations; perhaps most in advance of their time, they trained church choir leaders to see their role as leaders of congregational singing. They also wrote and published tune books, with everything they did characterized by a spirit of devoutness; their tunes, moreover, "were simple, and aptly gauged for the average capacity and feeling"[54] of the increasingly larger numbers of those who used them. Their work thus made a telling impact on both the spirit and practice of congregational singing.

All of this was certainly in the spirit of William Byrd (Birde), whose first published work in English in 1588 had, as its intention, to provide some reasons to persuade people to learn to sing. I quote these most interesting, and quaint, principles in full:

1. It is a knowledge easily taught, and quickly learned, where there is a good master and an apt SCOLLER.
2. The exercise of singing is delightful to Nature and good to preserve the health of Man.
3. It doth strengthen all parts of the breast, and doth open the pipes.
4. It is a singular good remedie for a stutting and stammering in the Speech.
5. It is the means best to procure a perfect pronunciation, and to make a good Orator.
6. It is the only way to know where Nature hath bestowed a good voyce; which gift is so rare as there is not one among a thousand that hath it; and in many that excellent gift is lost, because they want [lack] art to express nature.
7. There is not any musicke of instruments whatsoever comparable to that which is made of the voices of men; where the voyces are good and the same well sorted and ordered.
8. The better the voyce is, the meeter it is to honour and serve God therewith; and the voyce of man is chiefly to be employed to that ende. Omnis Spiritus laudet Dominum
   Since singing is so good a thing,
   I wish all men would learn to sing.[55]

Finally, to complete this examination of scriptural injunctions, and the urging of countless others for believers to participate, joyously, in congregational song, I cite John Wesley's "Rules for Methodist Singers" as still instructive, even for such a sophisticated religious culture as ours seems to consider itself to be:

1. Learn the tunes.
2. Sing them as printed.
3. Sing all. If it is a cross to you, take it up and you will find it a blessing.
4. Sing lustily and with a good courage.
5. Sing modestly, do not bawl.
6. Sing in time. Do not run before or stay behind.
7. Above all, sing spiritually. Have an eye to God in every word you sing. Aim at pleasing Him more than yourself or any other creature. In order to do this, attend strictly to the sense of what you sing, and see

that your *heart* is not carried away with the sound, but offered to God continually.[56]

Notes

1. G. W. Stewart, *Music in Church Worship* (London: Hodder and Stoughton, n.d.), p. 60.
2. *Ibid.*
3. *Ibid.*, p. 66.
4. Paul Cook and Graham Harrison, eds., *Christian Hymns* (Bryntirion: The Evangelical Movement of Wales, 1977), cited in the Preface.
5. J. B. Lightfoot, *St. Paul's Epistle to the Colossians and Philemon* (Grand Rapids: Zondervan, 1961), p. 224.
6. *Ibid.*
7. D. Guthrie and J. A. Motyer, eds., *The New Bible Commentary, Revised* (Grand Rapids: Eerdmans, 1970), p. 1151.
8. E. K. Simpson and F. F. Bruce, *The Epistles to the Ephesians and Colossians* (Grand Rapids: Eerdmans, 1957), p. 283.
9. *Ibid.*, p. 126.
10. Guthrie and Motyer, *op. cit.*, p. 1120.
11. Gordon H. Clark, *Colossians* (Phillipsburg: Presbyterian and Reformed, 1979), p. 121.
12. Douglas, *op. cit.*, p. 94.
13. Clark, *op. cit.*, p. 121.
14. Simpson and Bruce, *op. cit.*, p. 284.
15. *Ibid.*, pp. 284–285.
16. Guthrie and Motyer, *op. cit.*, p. 1151.
17. *Ibid.*, p. 1120.
18. T. H. L. Parker, ed., *Calvin's New Testament Commentaries . . . Colossians* (Grand Rapids: Eerdmans, 1965), p. 353.
19. Lightfoot, *op. cit.*, pp. 224–225.
20. William F. Arndt and F. Wilbur Gingrich, *A Greek-English Lexicon of the New Testament . . .* (Chicago: University of Chicago Press, 1952), p. 899.
21. *Ibid.*, p. 844.
22. *Ibid.*, p. 903.
23. David R. Breed, *The History and Use of Hymns and Hymn Tunes* (New York: Revell, 1903), p. 119.
24. Clark, *op. cit.*, p. 121.
25. Erik Routley, *Words, Music and the Church* (London: Herbert Jenkins, 1969), pp. 187–189, 191–192.
26. A. T. Davison, *Church Music* (Cambridge: Harvard University Press, 1952), pp. 129–130.
27. Robert Berglund, *A Philosophy of Church Music* (Chicago: Moody, 1985), pp. 15–36.

28. *Ibid.*, pp. 24–25, emphasis added.

29. Lightwood, *op. cit.*, pp. 377–378.

30. Erik Routley, *A Short History of English Church Music* (London: Mowbrays, 1977), p. 107.

31. Stewart, *op. cit.*, pp. 47–80.

32. *Ibid.*, p. 74.

33. *Ibid.*, p. 75.

34. *Ibid.*, p. 76.

35. *Ibid.*, p. 79.

36. *Ibid.*, p. 73.

37. Berglund, *op. cit.*, p. 78.

38. *Ibid.*, p. 79.

39. *Ibid.*

40. Routley, *op. cit.*, pp. 97–98.

41. Dickinson, *op. cit.*, pp. 356.

42. Benson, *op. cit.*, p. v.

43. Liemohn, *op. cit.*, p. 91.

44. Robert McCutchan, *Hymns in the Lives of Men* (Nashville: Abingdon-Cokesbury, 1945), p. 163.

45. Liemohn, *op. cit.*, p. 96.

46. Benson, *op. cit.*, pp. 161–162.

47. *Ibid.*, p. 184.

48. *Ibid.*, p. 185.

49. Berglund, *op. cit.*, p. 78.

50. Elwyn Wienandt and Robert Young, *The Anthem in England and America* (New York: The Free Press, 1970), p. 302.

51. Liemohn, *op. cit.*, p. 90.

52. *Ibid.*, p. 96.

53. Benson, *op. cit.*, p. 37.

54. *Ibid.*, p. 378.

55. William Barrett, *English Church Composers* (London: Sampson, Low, Marsten, 1900), p. 36.

56. Cook and Harrison, *op. cit.*, cited in the Preface.

3

Singing in Worship:
"As You Sing Psalms . . ."

As we have shown, the singing of the psalms in Israel's worship began, probably, in the days of the United Kingdom, when Israel under the leadership of King David—the Lion of the tribe of Judah—experienced her Golden Age, both territorially and in terms of her influence on other nations. Even David's desire to build a house for the Lord (II Samuel 7), which was to be realized by Solomon his son, was motivated in part, it appears, so that God might be magnified through being worshipped therein; and music played a significant role (I Chronicles 15–17, 22).

Moreover, the use of psalms in the worship of the early Christian community is a well-established fact. As time elapsed, however, controversy arose, concerned as they were with the use of other types of hymnody, including even the inspired utterances that apparently were accepted as praise in the Corinthian church.

Thus in the postapostolic period, as Werner points out,[1] the Church Fathers were divided; while Didymus attempted to draw a firm line between psalms and hymns, this was rejected by St. Augustine as but "vainly established." Chrysostom encouraged the common folk to sing psalms every day, whether traveling, at home, or at work; yet at the same time he apparently held hymns in higher esteem, attributing the miraculous escape of Paul and Silas (Acts 16:25ff.) to their hymn-singing in prison. He writes:

Behold the famous and efficient powers of hymns! . . . Not only did the Apostles not suffer any detriment, but more splendid, they escaped. . . . Everyone of their fellow captives was deeply impressed and reformed. . . . Do you now recognize the power of hymns, sung to God?[2]

On the other hand, the "penitential character of the Psalter was stressed . . . and apparently hymns were not considered conducive to either penitence or humility, as were the psalms." And a further problem arose when heretics like Marcion, "spurning the traditional Psalter, composed new hymns,"[3] substituting the words of men for the words of God. As we have seen, this latter problem, "substituting the words of men [i.e., hymns] for the words of God [i.e., psalms]," was to persist as an accusation for well over a millennium, and while it was never completely "laid to rest," continuing even into our day, it was finally effectively challenged by the work of Isaac Watts. Douglas also points out that in the early Middle Ages, Christian liturgies used the Gloria Patri, "singing it at the end of each psalm reading" and thus "confirming the seal of Christ upon the use of His Hymnal."[4]

In his Baird Lecture, Stewart includes an excellent chapter on psalmody,[5] and it would profit any reader to peruse his discussion with care. He writes:

> Perhaps the most precious inheritance that the Christian Church has received from Judaism is the Psalter, which touches some of the tenderest chords in the human heart. . . . No [other] book of the Bible . . . has so woven itself into the life of man . . . touching the deepest instincts of our nature, ministering to its most pressing needs. . . . In the presence of Him who has searched us and known us, the inmost secrets of the heart are laid bare, and the deepest feelings poured forth with frankness. . . . The whole gamut of human emotion is there: joy and sorrow, hope and despair, doubt and trustfulness, anxiety and confidence, chase one another across its pages like the shadows of the clouds upon the hills.[6] [For recall] it was in the words of a Psalm that the Saviour uttered that cry of despair . . . , and in the words of a Psalm that He committed His soul to God as He gave up the ghost. And throughout the ages the psalter has supplied the language in which saint and sinner, gentle and simple, the learned theologian and the unlettered peasant have found most appropriate expression for their religious feelings.[7] [Moreover, the Psalter] "must have contributed to . . . the spiritualizing of [Jewish] religion which reaches its culmination in Christianity . . . [so that] when the Master came He could speak of the Temple not as the place of sacrifice but as the house of prayer.[8]

So, while Thomas Hooker may have overstated his case when he said, "What is there necessary for man to know [of religion] which the Psalms are not able to teach?"[9] they have certainly—and should have—exerted a powerful influence on God's people.

We have already discussed the problems with the use of the metrical psalms, and have evaluated the *Old Version* by Sternhold and Hopkins, of which one critic wrote:

> . . . their piety was better than their poetry . . . ; with the best of intentions and the worst taste, they have degraded the spirit of Hebrew psalmody by flat and homely phraseology, and, mistaking vulgarity for simplicity, turned into bathos what they found sublime.[10]

We have also seen how difficult it was for the smoother and more elegant *New Version,* by Tate and Brady, to surmount the enormous prejudice against its use, a prejudice that succeeded in keeping alive the use of the *Old Version* until long after the days of Watts!

Moreover, it is important that we remember that one of the most critical reasons for Watts's protest against the continued restriction of congregational song to psalmody was not his aversion to the sacred Scriptures being read or even sung. It was, rather, the fact that many of the psalms were unsuited, in temper and teaching, as expressions of Christian devotion. He writes, in vigorous language, that

> Some of them are almost opposite to the Spirit of the Gospel. . . . When we are entering into an Evangelic Frame by some of the Glories of the Gospel presented in the brightest Figures of Judaism, yet the very next line . . . has something in it so extremely Jewish that it darkens our Sight of God the Saviour . . . and the Vail of Moses is thrown over our hearts.[11]

Furthermore, Watts did not want to eliminate metrical psalmody, in either form or substance; he wanted it carried on

> not as inspired Scripture but as a department of Christian song, whose "sense and materials" were taken from the Bible. And then, to this evangelized and modernized Psalter he added a body of hymns of purely human composure, representing our approximation of the Gospel through Christian experience; this represents the full terms of Watts' settlement of the relation of Christian song—Psalms and hymns, to the Bible.[12]

Speaking of Watts, in his paraphrases of the psalms, of which three are included in this book, and in the paraphrases of others—Luther, Ken, Lyte, Baker, Neander, and Grant, to name a few—the reader will notice that some follow rather closely the original metrical psalms on which they are patterned, while others are very free paraphrases, seeking only to "catch the spirit" or to "distill the essence" of the psalms on which they are based. An illustration of the former would be Lyte's "Praise, My Soul, the King of Heaven" (Psalm 103), and of the latter, Watts's "Jesus Shall Reign" (Psalm 72:8).

One final note before we proceed to our studies of the specific "psalms" that have given us some of our greatest musical sources of Christian devotion. Bishop Perowne suggests that their "unique universality gives them that excellence which has made them appeal to all classes of men throughout the centuries; . . . thus they were 'not of an age, but for all time.'"[13]

Notes

1. Werner, *op. cit.*, pp. 319–320.
2. *Ibid.*, p. 319.
3. *Ibid.*, p. 320.
4. Douglas, *op. cit.*, p. 153.
5. Stewart, *op. cit.*, pp. 81–129.
6. *Ibid.*, p. 83.
7. *Ibid.*, p. 84.
8. *Ibid.*, p. 90.
9. *Ibid.*, p. 103.
10. *Ibid.*, p. 109.
11. Armin Haeussler, *The Story of Our Hymns* (St. Louis: Eden, 1952), p. 966.
12. *Ibid.*
13. McCutchan, *Hymns in the Lives of Men,* p. 71.

Title/Date	*"A Mighty Fortress Is Our God"*
Author	*Martin Luther*
Composer/Tune	*Martin Luther "Ein Feste Burg"*
Scriptural Basis	*Psalm 46*

This, "the greatest hymn of the greatest man in the greatest period of German history,"[1] of which Carlyle wrote "There is something in it like the sound of Alpine avalanches, or the first murmur of earthquakes,"[2] was written at a critical time in the early days of the Protestant Reformation. Less than two years had elapsed since Leonard Kaiser, a Lutheran pastor and friend of Martin Luther (1483–1546), had been burned at the stake. Now Emperor Charles V had called a Reichstag at Speyer demanding that the Evangelical cities submit to the rule of the Roman Catholic bishops, reintroduce the Mass, and disown Luther and his teachings. The Evangelical princes met this ultimatum with a defiant protest, which gave rise to the word "Protest-ant" as a term of derision. It was at this time that Luther penned these immortal lines, seeking to emphasize the positive nature of his doctrines. As Hunecker aptly puts it, "this hymn thunders at the very gate of heaven in its magnificent affirmation of beliefs"[3] that were expressed in the clearest possible language, bringing profound biblical truth home to the hearts of the common people, in what Julian calls a "bold, confident joyful spirit of justifying faith which was the beating heart of his theology and piety."[4]

It spread like wildfire over Germany, being sung by both Protestants and even some who were still loyal to the Roman Catholic faith. Translated by the Englishman Miles Coverdale within a decade of its writing, it was nevertheless little known in the English-speaking world until the mid-nineteenth century. Its most spectacular use was in 1869, when it was sung in Boston by a chorus of ten thousand voices accompanied by a one thousand-piece orchestra led by the famous Irish American band master Patrick S. Gilmore![5] To date it has been translated into close to three hundred languages, plus about seventy-five English versions. Our *Trinity Hymnal*'s version is that by Frederick Hedge.

While the tunes for many of Luther's thirty-seven hymns—some five of which were entirely original—were at least in part adaptations from earlier

God is our refuge and strength, a very present help in trouble. Psalm 46:1

Martin Luther, 1529
Tr. by Frederick H. Hedge, 1853

EIN' FESTE BURG 8. 7. 8. 7. 6. 6. 6. 6. 7.
Martin Luther, 1529

1. A might - y For - tress is our God, A Bul-wark nev - er fail - ing;
2. Did we in our own strength con-fide, Our striv-ing would be los - ing;
3. And though this world, with dev - ils filled, Should threat-en to un - do us,
4. That Word a - bove all earth-ly powers, No thanks to them, a - bid - eth;

Our Help - er he a - mid the flood Of mor - tal ills pre - vail - ing.
Were not the right Man on our side, The Man of God's own choos - ing.
We will not fear, for God hath willed His truth to tri - umph through us.
The Spir - it and the gifts are ours Through him who with us sid - eth;

For still our an - cient foe Doth seek to work us woe; His craft and pow'r are
Dost ask who that may be? Christ Je - sus, it is he, Lord Sab - a - oth his
The prince of dark-ness grim, We trem-ble not for him; His rage we can en -
Let goods and kin-dred go, This mor-tal life al - so; The bod - y they may

great; And, armed with cru - el hate, On earth is not his e - qual.
Name, From age to age the same, And he must win the bat - tle.
dure, For lo! his doom is sure; One lit - tle word shall fell him.
kill: God's truth a - bid-eth still; His king-dom is for ev - er. A - MEN.

written music, this tune, "Ein feste Burg," seems to have been his own composition, and it certainly complements the rugged and powerful words. As mentioned earlier in this study, Luther was an accomplished musician and would lead his entire family—including students who boarded with them—in hymn-singing after supper in the evenings. He considered himself an artist as well as a teacher and preacher, and once wrote: "Our opponents cannot claim ignorance of the doctrine of the Gospel, since we have preached, written, painted and sung it."[6]

This hymn, a paraphrase of Psalm 46, takes its title and its spirit from these words of Scripture: "God is our refuge and strength, a very present help in trouble" (Psalm 46:1). And trouble there was—indeed, the gravest crisis, "the darkest hour in the history of this fateful movement."[7]

Stanza One: God is seen as our source of strength: a Fortress, Bulwark, Helper in the midst of a flood of swirling deadly evils, chief among which is His, and therefore our, foe, the ancient, treacherous adversary, Satan; crafty, cruel, and relentless, no human being can hope to stand against him. Moreover, in Luther's day Satan

> was incarnate in the worldly Pope Clement VII and in the ambitious, intriguing "Holy" Roman Emperor, Charles V, . . . constituting a triangle of hate and power such as the world had seldom seen.[8]

Stanza Two: With such an enemy, there is but one Person in whom we can trust; but He is sufficient—yea, more than sufficient, for He is God's Man, Jesus Christ, "the same yesterday, today and forever" (Hebrews 13:8), Lord Sabaoth, "the Lord of Hosts, the One who has wrought desolations in the earth" (vss. 7–8). This is indeed Protestant theology, "for our confidence is not in an infallible Church and its sacraments, but in an unconquerable Man, clothed with the authority and [power] of God Himself!"[9]

Stanza Three: While the psalm does not mention Satan, our archenemy, Luther certainly believed in his literal existence—indeed, he is reported to have hurled an inkwell at him while he was "confined" by his rescuer, Frederick the Elector of Saxony, in Wartburg Castle. In such times of treachery and deceit as Luther lived, he trusted in God's Truth, personified in Jesus (John 14:6), to ultimately win the day, and it did! Moreover, exorcism by that matchless Name was his defense, "for God has highly exalted Him, and bestowed on Him the name which is above every name, that at the name of Jesus every knee should bow . . . and every tongue should confess that [He] is Lord" (Philippians 2:9–11)—including the knee and the tongue of the Prince of darkness!

Stanza Four: "That little word . . ." (vs. 3) is "that Word" (vs. 4) "which stands above all earthly powers" (his religious and political enemies) and is triumphant; that Word and the Holy Spirit come to us through God, "Him who with us sideth" (vs. 4), and ministers to us with His gifts. We therefore need not fear the loss of goods, family, health—even life itself—for His Truth will abide and His Kingdom will last forever—a Kingdom Luther was certainly instrumental in extending! Thus he combines ideas from both Testaments in a moving and inspiring Christian hymn, a hymn the people of Halle sang with tear-filled eyes as they lined the streets in 1546 as his coffin passed through their city en route from Eisleben to Wittenberg, its final resting place.[10]

Louis Benson writes of this, the "Marseillaise of the Reformation":

> It was sung by poor Protestant emigrees on their way into exile, and by martyrs at their death. . . . Gustavus Adolphus ordered it sung by his army before the battle of Leipzig in 1631, and again . . . in Lutzen in 1632 where he was killed, but his army victorious. It has been sung in countless celebrations commemorating the men and events of the Reformation; its first line is engraved on the base of [his] monument at Wittenberg. . . . An imperishable hymn! Not polished and artistically wrought, but rugged and strong like Luther himself, whose very words seem like deeds.[11]

Finally, if it's true that institutions are often the lengthened shadow of the men or women who founded them, it is similarly true of this hymn. For Luther himself has been both vilified and adored, seen as both saint and syphilitic drunkard; however, on balance, his countless biographers reveal him as a man "who was a thorough scholar, a great preacher, a widely-read author, a capable musician, an affectionate husband and devoted father, a loyal friend, and a public-spirited citizen."[12] As one of the most noble and dominant personalities in the history of our sometimes most ignoble human race, Luther has been accorded this estimate by the great historian James A. Froude, writing in 1883, or thereabouts:

> That the Reformation was to establish itself in the form which it assumed, was due to the one fact that there existed at the crisis a single person of commanding mind. . . . The traces of this mind are to be seen today in the mind of the modern world. Had there been no Luther, the English, American and German peoples would be thinking differently, and would be altogether different men and women from what they are at this moment.[13]

Notes

1. Moffatt and Patrick, *op. cit.,* p. 179.
2. Haeussler, *op. cit.,* p. 313.

3. *Ibid.*, p. 312.

4. Dickinson, *op. cit.*, p. 17.

5. Haeussler, *op. cit.*, p. 313.

6. *Ibid.*, p. 772.

7. Bailey, *op. cit.*, p. 315.

8. *Ibid.*

9. *Ibid.*

10. Reynolds, *op. cit.*, p. 18.

11. Bailey, *op. cit.*, p. 316.

12. Haeussler, *op. cit.*, p. 768.

13. *Ibid.*

Title/Date	*"All Praise to Thee, My God, This Night"*
	(1695; text of 1709)
Author	*Thomas Ken*
Composer/Tune	*Thomas Tallis "Tallis' Evening Hymn"*
Scriptural Basis	*Psalms 4:8; 91:4*

This hymn, to be sung at eventide, is one of a trilogy of hymns ("Morning," "Evening," and "Midnight") written by Thomas Ken (1637–1711), which have appeared in every English-language hymnal published in the past three hundred years. Of this hymn-writer and nineteenth-century social reformer and newspaper publisher James Montgomery has written,

> Had [Ken] endowed three hospitals, he might have been less a benefactor to posterity. . . . The well known doxology "Praise God from Whom All Blessings Flow"—which comprises the last verse of this, and also of his morning hymn "Awake, My Soul and with the Sun"—is a masterpiece at once of amplification and compression.[1]

Moreover, few Englishmen had ever been held in higher esteem than this man—small in stature, but great in spiritual power—of whom Lord Macauley said, "His moral character seems to approach, as near as human infirmity permits, to the ideal perfection of Christian virtue."[2]

But if Ken attained this degree of genuine piety, and apparently he did, his was not an easy, flower-strewn pathway! Orphaned as a young child, he went to live with his older step-sister Ann and her husband, the famous fisherman Izaak Walton, author of the *Compleat Angler,* a home that proved congenial to him and which he sorely missed when he was sent, as a lad of fourteen, to Winchester College in London. A typical boarding school, with many unruly students and schoolmasters who were of necessity tough, it was "learn, leave or be licked,"[3] and "little Ken" apparently got his share of lickings although more from his larger, jealous peers than from his tutors. Returning there as chaplain some years later, after he had taken Holy Orders in the Anglican Communion, he labored faithfully to bring a genuinely spiritual ministry to the boys, writing for their use a *Manual of Prayers,* and these three hymns, to which he attached this exhortation:

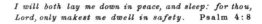

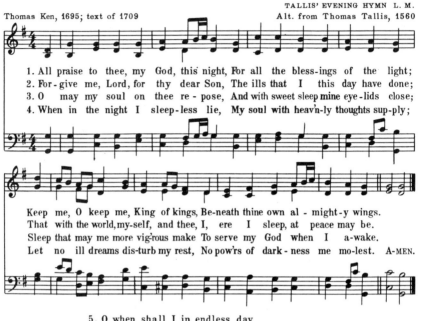

5. O when shall I in endless day
   For ever chase dark sleep away,
   And hymns with the supernal choir
   Incessant sing, and never tire!

6. Praise God from whom all blessings flow;
   Praise him, all creatures here below;
   Praise him above, ye heav'nly host:
   Praise Father, Son, and Holy Ghost.

Be sure to sing the Morning and Evening Hymn in your chamber de-
voutly, remembering that the Psalmist, upon happy experience, assures
you that it is a good thing to tell of the loving-kindness of the Lord early
in the morning and of his truth in the night season.[4] [One wonders how
often the "Midnight" hymn was sung!]

Ken's powerful preaching and his conscientious attention to his duties
won for him the respect, albeit grudging at times, of King Charles II. On
one occasion when the king visited the palace he was building in Winchester, he brought Nell Gwyn, his mistress, along with him, and proposed to
lodge her in Ken's home. Ken refused, had the workmen remove the roof
from his house "for necessary repairs," and vowed rather courageously

A woman of ill-repute ought not to be endured in the house of a clergy-man, least of all in that of the King's chaplain. . . . Not for his kingdom will I comply with the King's commands.[5]

Embarrassed, perhaps, but admiring Ken's pluck, soon after this incident King Charles bestowed the bishopric of Bath and Wells on "little black Ken"—one more instance of a servant of God who risked his career, if not his head, in refusing to be a "yes man" and whose principles were vindicated.

In this evening hymn, Ken focuses the attention of the singer on God, who alone can enable us to dwell in safety even as we lie helpless in our beds (Psalm 4:8); on God under whose wings we are protected and secure (Psalm 91:4), even as a chick with hits mother hen, or an eaglet, resting confident in its mother's comforting presence.

After all, nighttime is fearful: there are wild beasts, and thieves, burglars and evil spirits (witness the proliferation of locks, dead bolts, and alarms in our society); but there are also other dangers that can rob us of peace—anxieties, worries, cares, fretfulness—and therefore, of sleep. So he prays for God's peace-enabling forgiveness to cleanse him from the ills of his day (vs. 2).

Moreover, that he might serve God better on the morrow (vs. 3), or, if he lies awake with insomnia (vs. 4), that he might turn his thoughts God-ward with its obvious benefits, he also prays; heavenly thoughts can include those that are sane and sensible, those of truth and purity; and, of course, if when he should awake some tomorrow having slept the sleep of death (vs. 5), his heart's desire is to sing his hymns unwearied, forevermore!

Obviously, that kind of answer to his prayer should evoke the praise of the Triune God from all His creation since it is He who is, has been, and will be the source of every blessing in this life and in the life of the world to come! As Routley nicely has it, "the humble creature's prayer is, in the end, absorbed in universal praise."[6]

Thomas Tallis (1520–1585), the composer of the tune supplied for this hymn, has been called the "Father of English Cathedral music";[7] he was a composer of the highest rank, having produced motets and Masses almost as fine as those by Palestrina. His motet, "Spem in alium non habui," Patrick calls the "noblest achievement of the English nation in sacred music."[8] While he conformed to the changes in the liturgy for worship begun by King Henry VIII, he was probably more sympathetic to the older Roman Catholic musical forms, and was hardly ready "to be fettered by the regulations of [English] Reformed worship."[9] As an important link between pre-Reformation and post-Reformation church music, "professional musicians revere him especially as a thoroughgoing master of counterpoint,"[10] combining "rare genius, exquisite taste, technical mastery, and amazing versatility"; indeed, in his music "every Englishman may take the same pride as he feels in the achieve-ments of . . . Chaucer, . . . Shakespeare, Newton and Lister."[11]

Tallis was also a happily married man—unlike his sovereign—and has been immortalized in this epitaph:

> Enterred here doth ly a worthy wyght,
>   Who for long tyme in musick bore the bell:
> His name to shew, was Thomas Tallys hyght,
>   In honest vertuous lyff he dyd excell.
>
> He scru'd long tyme in chappel with grete prayse.
>   Fower sovcreygnes reygnes (a thing not often seene)
> I mean Kyng Henry and prynce Edward's dayes,
>   Quene Mary, and Elizabeth our quene.
>
> He maryd was, though children he had none,
>   He lyu'd in love ful thre and thirty yeres
> Wyth loyal spowse, whose name yclept was Jone,
>   Who here entomb'd, him company now bears.
>
> As he dyd lyue, so also did he dy,
>   In myld and quyet sort, O happy man!
> To God ful oft for mercy did he cry,
>   Wherefore he lyues, let Deth do what he can.[12]

One final note: This hymn was translated into the Maori language in New Zealand by a young missionary, Thomas Whytehead, who died a few months after he landed there in 1843. His was the first instance where a translation's meter and rhythm were identical with the English! As the young may lay dying, natives, who had just learned this hymn in their church and school, came and sang it under his window! Whytehead wrote to a friend:

> they call it the "new hymn of the sick minister"; . . . they seem pleased with it, and it is a comfort to think one has introduced Bishop Ken's beau-tiful hymn into [their] evening worship and left them this legacy when I could do no more for them.[13]

Notes

1. Haeussler, *op. cit.,* p. 741.
2. *Ibid.,* p. 744.

3. Bailey, *op. cit.,* p. 36.

4. Haeussler, *op. cit.,* p. 108.

5. Bailey, *op. cit.,* p. 36.

6. Erik Routley, *Hymns and the Faith* (Greenwich, Conn.: Seabury, 1956), p. 90.

7. Moffatt and Patrick, *op. cit.,* p. 514.

8. *Ibid.*

9. *Ibid.*

10. Haeussler, *op. cit.,* p. 932.

11. *Ibid.,* p. 931.

12. Barrett, *English Church Composers,* p. 26.

13. Haeussler, *op. cit.,* p. 108.

Title/Date	*"Glorious Things of Thee Are Spoken"* *(1779)*
Author	*John Newton*
Composer/Tune	*Franz Josef Haydn "Austrian Hymn" (1797)*
Scriptural Basis	*Psalm 87:3; Isaiah 33:20–21; Exodus 13:22*

This hymn, wedded to one of Haydn's greatest tunes—written initially for the newly composed Austrian national anthem and first sung for the emperor's birthday in 1797—is found in practically all hymnbooks, and is regarded as one of the greatest of Newton's hymns.[1]

The details of the life of John Newton (1725–1807) are well known. After the death of his devout mother when he was seven, and some years under a boarding school's harsh master, whose cruelty he scarcely endured, he went to sea with his father, where he led a dissolute life as a seaman, slave-trader, and virtual slave himself. The memory of his mother, and his abiding love for Mary Catlett, a young English girl he'd met when she was only thirteen (and whom he eventually married), seemed to provide his only security for several years.

His genuine conversion to the Christian faith occurred in 1754, but had roots much earlier through the influence of his reading of Thomas à Kempis's *The Imitation of Christ,* a dramatic escape from almost certain death in a storm at sea, and the Christian life-witness of a godly fellow sea captain. Returning to England he married his "angel," studied Hebrew, Greek, and the Bible, and in 1758 under the supervision of Whitefield, Wesley, and others, began to preach.[2] One of the first sermons he ever was to deliver he completely forgot and, after several "starts," he left the pulpit and ran out into the night, humiliated. But eventually he became a stirring preacher, and took Holy Orders in the Anglican Communion in 1764, being sent to the village of Olney as curate to the absentee vicar there, where he carried on an active ministry for fifteen years.

Lord Dartmouth, his patron—and by whose influence on the bishop of London enough pressure had been exerted to win Newton his ordination— gave him the use of a house, where Newton conducted weekday devotional

Glorious things are spoken of thee, O city of God. Psalm 87:3

AUSTRIAN HYMN 8. 7. 8. 7. D.

John Newton, 1779

Franz Josef Haydn, 1797

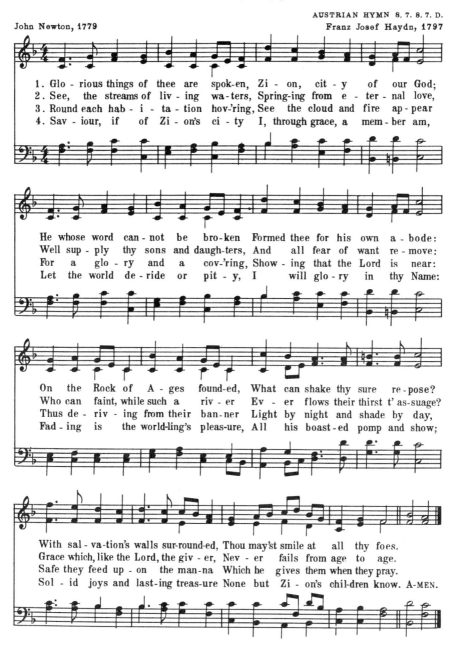

1. Glo - rious things of thee are spok-en, Zi - on, cit - y of our God;
2. See, the streams of liv - ing wa-ters, Spring-ing from e - ter - nal love,
3. Round each hab - i - ta - tion hov-'ring, See the cloud and fire ap - pear
4. Sav - iour, if of Zi - on's ci - ty I, through grace, a mem - ber am,

He whose word can - not be bro-ken Formed thee for his own a - bode:
Well sup - ply thy sons and daugh-ters, And all fear of want re - move:
For a glo - ry and a cov'-ring, Show - ing that the Lord is near:
Let the world de - ride or pit - y, I will glo - ry in thy Name:

On the Rock of A - ges found-ed, What can shake thy sure re - pose?
Who can faint, while such a riv - er Ev - er flows their thirst t' as-suage?
Thus de - riv - ing from their ban-ner Light by night and shade by day,
Fad - ing is the world-ling's pleas-ure, All his boast - ed pomp and show;

With sal - va-tion's walls sur-round-ed, Thou may'st smile at all thy foes.
Grace which, like the Lord, the giv - er, Nev - er fails from age to age.
Safe they feed up - on the man-na Which he gives them when they pray.
Sol - id joys and last-ing treas-ure None but Zi - on's chil-dren know. A-MEN.

meetings and Bible teaching-sessions for both children and adults. He used Watts's hymns and wrote additional ones himself for the congregation's edification. It was thus, in 1779, that he and his friend William Cowper, the gifted but melancholy poet, published their *Olney Hymns,* which "became the hymnbook of the Low Church party in the Established Church and was reprinted in England and America for a hundred years";[3] several of its hymns are still included in most hymnbooks. Such widespread use of this hymnbook was remarkable since up to that time Anglican Church "had rejected hymn-singing as unscriptural, schismatic, and doctrinally dangerous."[4]

Transferred to a London parish in 1780, Newton labored there for almost twenty-eight years, preaching regularly with the help of an old servant who would stand in the pulpit by his side and help him follow the headings of his sermon manuscript—a good argument, incidentally, for writing out one's sermon in full! Honored by the College of New Jersey (Princeton) with a D.D. in 1792,[5] he continued to minister humbly and faithfully until his death in 1807, the very year that Lord William Wilberforce, whose conversion Newton had aided, succeeded in getting Parliament to pass his bill to abolish slavery forever in all British domains. Shortly before his death, Newton remarked in response to being lauded: "my memory is nearly gone, but I remember two things, that I am a great Sinner, and that Jesus Christ is a great Saviour!"[6] His tombstone's epitaph, which he composed, fittingly reads:

JOHN NEWTON
Clerk
ONCE AN INFIDEL AND LIBERTINE
A SERVANT OF SLAVES IN AFRICA
was
BY THE RICH MERCY OF OUR LORD AND SAVIOUR
JESUS CHRIST
PRESERVED, RESTORED, PARDONED,
AND APPOINTED TO PREACH THE FAITH
HE HAD LONG LABORED TO DESTROY. . . .[7]

Franz Josef Haydn (1732–1809), one of Austria's most distinguished composers, the poor son of a wheelwright, once said of his own life that he was "an example that something can be made of nothing."[8] A devout man, he considered his musical talent as a trust from God, prefacing every one of his musical scores with "In the name of the Lord," and closing them with "Praise to God"; perhaps this is the key to the consistently cheerful note of his music, affirming as he did "when I think of God, my heart dances within me, and my music has to dance too."[9] This tune, "Austria," which indeed "dances," was the last tune he ever played!

After he had spent many years in poverty, Haydn's genius—of the highest order—was recognized and financially rewarded; he received a Mus. Doc. from Oxford, and was lionized, first in England, and then, upon his return, in his native Austria. It was, in fact, after he had heard Handel's oratorios at Westminster that he wrote his "The Creation" and "The Seasons," beginning their composition after his sixty-fifth birthday![10] What an inspiration!

His melodies exhibit grace and freshness; as a musician he was universally loved and honored. It is little wonder that his brother, Johann Michael, also a very fine musician who composed the tune "Lyons" for Grant's hymn "Oh Worship the King," was shy about his talent and lived constantly in his shadow!

This hymn of Newton has been fittingly called "a hymn of Christian cheerfulness," with cheerfulness meaning "a quality of the heart, a settled confidence in the ultimate certainties."[11] There is pictured here a buoyant, infectious faith in a God who is good, faithful, and able to empower those whom He sovereignly calls to fulfill their ministry.

It is, moreover, a rich tapestry of biblical passages and images, taking its title and certainly its spirit from Psalm 87. Let us examine it more closely:

Stanza One: The security of Jerusalem, capital city and religious center of Judah, formed by and founded on God—the Rock of Ages, the source of salvation Himself—is stressed. No wonder Zion may "smile at all her foes"!

Stanza Two: The image changes. Now her inhabitants crowd around streams whose source is the eternal Love, and whose refreshing flow that quenches their thirst is never-failing grace (Psalm 46, Ezekiel 47, Exodus 17, and Revelation 22 all provide biblical foundation for these ideas); as Routley reminds us, "gratitude is . . . the response to grace, and grace is the fabric of the Church, the texture of God's dealings with men."[12]

Stanza Three: Again, the author takes us back to two Old Testament incidents: when God guides His people "by a pillar of cloud by day, and a pillar of fire by night," manifesting thus His own presence with them (Numbers 9:15ff.); and when He feeds them with heavenly food, a daily-supplied manna—"white, like coriander seed, and sweet as honey" (Exodus 16:4ff.).

Stanza Four: This stanza, found in the *Trinity Hymnal,* personalizes the truth, and conveys the conviction that however much the world may derive or pity the citizen of Zion—made so by grace—he glories in God's name, and in those pleasures and provisions that are not fleeting, as are their "treasures, pomp and show," but are solid and lasting even as is Zion herself! As Routley finely comments:

> This hymn communicates the gaity and toughness of Christianity; it does [not] put a premium on vagueness, ineffectiveness, otherworldliness . . . ; [rather, it] stresses solid joys and lasting pleasures, together with living sacrifices and the royalty of being a servant—this is the Christian Manifesto.[13]

Notes

1. Haeussler, *op. cit.*, pp. 360–361.

2. *Ibid.*, p. 823.

3. Bailey, *op. cit.*, p. 128.

4. Haeussler, *op. cit.*, p. 824.

5. Stulken, *op. cit.*, p. 408.

6. Bailey, *op. cit.*, p. 127.

7. *Ibid.*

8. Moffatt and Patrick, *op. cit.*, pp. 367–368.

9. *Ibid.*

10. *Ibid.*

11. Routley, *Hymns and the Faith*, p. 222.

12. *Ibid.*, p. 225.

13. *Ibid.*, p. 227.

Title/Date	*"Guide Me, O Thou Great Jehovah"* *(1745, Welsh; 1771, English)*
Author	*William Williams*
Composer/Tune	*John Hughes "CWM RHONDDA" (1907)*
Scriptural Basis	*Psalm 48:14; Psalm 104; Psalm 105; Psalm 106*

William Williams (1717–1781), "The Sweet Singer of Wales," came from a family of prosperous farmers. He had begun the study of medicine before that fateful Sunday morning in 1738 when, out of curiosity, he went to hear the fiery Welsh evangelist Howell Harris. He thereby found his own life transformed, received a call from God to preach, and lived to become one of the greatest poets and the premier hymn-writer of Wales. Indeed, of his influence on his land and people Elvet Lewis has written:

> What Paul Gerhardt has been to Germany, what Isaac Watts has been to England, that and more has William Williams been to Wales. His hymns have both stirred and soothed a whole nation for more than one hundred years; they have helped to fashion a nation's character, and to deepen a nation's piety.[1]

Ordained a deacon in the established church and licensed to serve two small parishes as curate, after three years, his strongly Evangelical theology and inspired preaching proved an obstacle to his ordination as an Anglican priest. He thus became an itinerant evangelist in the Welsh Calvinistic Methodist Church, supervised initially by Harris and Rowland Hill. Over the next forty-five years, he traveled throughout Wales, some one hundred thousand miles, much of the time accompanied by his wife, Mary, who was a fine singer as well as a genuine, godly helpmeet.

Of his preaching—most of which was done in the open air, often interrupted by unruly mobs carrying cudgels (and using them!) and even guns to frighten him—Josiah Miller writes:

> He possessed the warm heart and glowing imagination of a true Welshman; his sermons abounded with vivid picturing, and, always radiant with

He will be our guide even unto death. Psalm 48:14

William Williams (Welsh), 1745
St. 1 tr. by Peter Williams, 1771
St. 2-3 tr. by William Williams, c. 1772

CWM RHONDDA 8. 7. 8. 7. 8. 7. with repeat
John Hughes, 1907

In moderate time

1. Guide me, O thou great Je - ho - vah, Pil - grim through this
2. O - pen now the crys - tal foun - tain, Whence the heal - ing
3. When I tread the verge of Jor - dan, Bid my anx - ious

bar - ren land; I am weak, but thou art might - y; Hold me with thy
stream doth flow; Let the fire and cloud - y pil - lar Lead me all my
fears sub - side; Death of death, and hell's De - struc - tion, Land me safe on

pow'r - ful hand; Bread of heav - en, Bread of heav - en,
jour - ney through; Strong De - liv - erer, strong De - liv - erer,
Ca - naan's side; Songs of prais - es, songs of prais - es

Feed me till I want no more, Feed me till I want no more.
Be thou still my Strength and Shield, Be thou still my Strength and Shield.
I will ev - er give to thee, I will ev - er give to thee. A-MEN.

Music copyrighted. Used by permission of Mrs. John Hughes.

the presence of his divine Master, they produced an extraordinary effect on susceptible Welshmen.[2]

But even more than his preaching, he is remembered and beloved as the author of over nine hundred hymns, eight hundred of them in Welsh, the rest in English, "characterized by simplicity, clarity of expression, and richness of imagination."[3] This hymn, first appearing in Welsh, was later translated into English, perhaps by Williams himself, to be sung at the opening of Trevecca College in South Wales, a training school for preachers supported by the devout Evangelical Anglican noblewoman, Selina, the Countess of Huntington,[4] among whose loyal partisans Williams was reckoned. It has, to date, been translated into at least seventy-five languages.

CWM RHONDDA, the splendid Welsh tune to which it has been wed most of this century, was written by a gifted hymn tune-composer, John Hughes 1783–1832); he wrote this "for the annual Baptist Cymanfaoedd Canu [singing festival] held at Pontypridd in 1905."[5] It was printed for services two years later, and over the next twenty-five years it was used in over five thousand similar hymn festivals in Great Britain alone![6] According to his widow, Hannah, Hughes wrote this tune, named after a valley in the South Wales industrial district, while worshipping (!) at Salem Chapel, a Welsh country church. But strangely enough, the tune had not been included in any Welsh hymnbook, at least not before 1952![7]

The motif of this hymn is obvious, and its imagery is drawn wholly from Scripture: the march of Israel from Egypt to Canaan, replete with the barren wilderness; the manna that El Shaddai, their Nourisher, provided; the water that gushed from the flinty rock to assuage their thirst; the guidance provided by God through "the pillar of cloud by day and the pillar of fire by night"; God as their Shield from enemy arrows and the heat of the sun and their strong Deliverer. And, finally, when they would "tread the verge of Jordon," when they would enter its icy waters to cross to the promised land—a figure of the experience of severe testing, perhaps even of death—the cry comes, "land me safe on Canaan's side," which if realized, cannot but call forth from this pilgrim everlasting songs of praise. (An interesting note of humor: the phrase "land me safe on Canaan's side" was once printed in an American hymnal as "land my safe on Canaan's side"; the discoverer of this mistranslation quipped, "No, brother, you can't take it with you!")[8]

However, we really miss the point of this stirring hymn if we fail to see that these analogies paralleling Israel's experiences with those of Christians are reflected here as entirely personal, with all first person-pronouns: "me, I, my." The pilgrims in the Sinaitic Wilderness become one pilgrim here, and thus it will ever be, in the deepest experiences of the human soul with its God. The hymn is, moreover, a description of life as so regularly experienced by its author, living as he did "in a picturesque country with rocks and mountains, valleys and brooks, dark and dangerous paths, and sunlit escarpments"—a land reflecting "wild Welsh nature in all her many moods."[9]

This love of nature, so typical of the Welsh, permeated Williams' poetry and thus his hymns. Some who could not read learned them as they heard and sang them; other illiterates learned to read so they could enjoy them; thus the hymns became the means of spiritually educating and acculturating millions of Welshmen, and assured the triumph of the eighteenth-century Welsh revival.

If Taliessin, the sixth-century Welsh bard, was accurate when he said, "No musician is skillful unless he extols the Lord, and no singer is correct unless he praises the Father,"[10] Williams was both skillful and correct. Thus a contemporary witness to his work could write:

> Many of his hymns have the property of the ode, true poetic fire, stirring imagery, glowing expressions, united with the plaintive muse of the country. Their effect on the people is astonishing; and the veneration in which they are held is little short of devotion.[11]

Notes

1. Moffatt and Patrick, *op. cit.*, pp. 545–546.
2. Haeussler, *op. cit.*, p. 985.
3. *Ibid.*, p. 986.
4. Arthur Temple, *Hymns We Love* (London: Lutterworth, 1954), p. 985.
5. Lightwood, *op. cit.*, p. 358.
6. Haeussler, *op. cit.*, p. 132.
7. *Ibid.*
8. Temple, *op. cit.*, p. 85.
9. Haeussler, *op. cit.*, p. 131.
10. Bailey, *op. cit.*, p. 106.
11. Haeussler, *op. cit.*, p. 131.

Title/Date	*"Hail to the Lord's Anointed"* (1821, 1828)
Author	*James Montgomery*
Composer/Tune	*Samuel E. Wesley "Aurelia"*
Scriptural Basis	*Psalm 72:7 et al.*

An unfortunate distinction is frequently made in some religious circles today between those who preach a social gospel and those who preach an Evangelical gospel. Properly understood, there is but one gospel, one good news for the total person, his soul and his material well-being; and proclaiming that gospel, for the whole person, was the concern of this hymnwriter. James Montgomery (1771–1854), the popularity of whose hymns ranks with those of Wesley, Watts, Cowper, and Newton, spent much of his life as a social reformer, publishing his views regarding the miserable lot and treatment of chimney-sweeps, African slaves, and oppressive factory employment practices in the *Sheffield Register,* serving jail sentences twice (where he wrote hymns as he "did time), and even forswearing the use of sugar because of his scruples of conscience. Yet the Evangelical character of his faith, and therefore of his hymns, is without question. Hymnologist John Julian declares:

> The secrets of his power as a hymnwriter were manifold: . . . poetic genius . . . ear for rhythm . . . extensive knowledge of Holy Scripture . . . broad and charitable religious views . . . a devotional spirit of the holiest type. With the faith of a strong man, he united the beauty and simplicity of a child. Richly poetic without exuberance, dogmatic without uncharitableness, tender without sentimentality, elaborate without diffusiveness, richly musical . . . he has bequeathed to the Church of Christ wealth which could only have come from a true genius and a sanctified heart.[1]

Born of Moravian missionary parents with whom he lived successively in Scotland, Ireland, and England and who both died in the West Indies when he was twelve, he was apprenticed to a baker, then a chandler. A runaway in London, "who sold one of his poems to an unusually benevolent gentleman

In his days shall the righteous flourish; and abundance
of peace so long as the moon endureth. Psalm 72:7

AURELIA 7. 6. 7. 6. D.

James Montgomery, 1821, 1828   Samuel S. Wesley, 1864

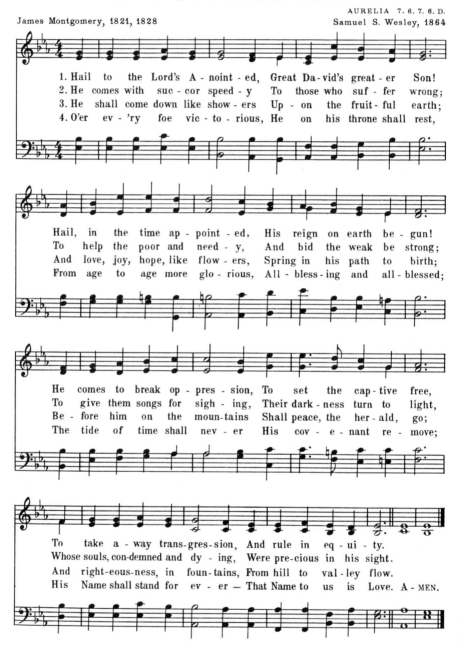

1. Hail to the Lord's A - noint - ed, Great Da - vid's great - er Son!
2. He comes with suc - cor speed - y To those who suf - fer wrong;
3. He shall come down like show - ers Up - on the fruit - ful earth;
4. O'er ev - 'ry foe vic - to - rious, He on his throne shall rest,

Hail, in the time ap - point - ed, His reign on earth be - gun!
To help the poor and need - y, And bid the weak be strong;
And love, joy, hope, like flow - ers, Spring in his path to birth;
From age to age more glo - rious, All - bless - ing and all - blessed;

He comes to break op - pres - sion, To set the cap - tive free,
To give them songs for sigh - ing, Their dark - ness turn to light,
Be - fore him on the moun - tains Shall peace, the her - ald, go;
The tide of time shall nev - er His cov - e - nant re - move;

To take a - way trans - gres - sion, And rule in eq - ui - ty.
Whose souls, con - demned and dy - ing, Were pre - cious in his sight.
And right - eous - ness, in foun - tains, From hill to val - ley flow.
His Name shall stand for ev - er — That Name to us is Love. A - MEN.

for a guinea, which staked him until he found a job,"[2] Montgomery possessed literary talents that extended far beyond his editorials. For as one of the best literary critics of his day, "he ably criticized the hymn writings of his predecessors with usually kindly criticism, made more valuable because of his insight and impartiality."[3] At one time he was considered seriously for England's Poet Laureateship.[4] Canon Ellerton declared him to be

> our first hymnologist, the first Englishman who collected and criticized hymns, and who made people who had lost all recollection of ancient models, understand something of what a hymn meant, and what it ought to be.[5]

His Christian faith, which deepened throughout his life and to which he owed the impulse for his hymn-writing, saying that "he lay in wait for his heart, to catch its highest emotions,"[6] was early nurtured during his boarding school days; there, he said,

> Whatever we did was done in the name and for the sake of Jesus Christ, whom we were taught to regard in the amiable and endearing light of a friend and brother; this attitude of informal familiarity is aptly illustrated by this prayer of one of the boys: "Oh Lord, bless us little children and make us very good. We thank Thee for what we have received. Oh, bless this good chocolate and give us more of it."[7]

"Aurelia," the tune to which this hymn is set in the *Trinity Hymnal,* was written by Samuel Sebastian Wesley (1810–1876), named after Bach, his father's idol, and considered "the greatest musical genius of the highly gifted Wesley family."[8] Like Montgomery, he was a critic of the status quo, but he aimed his fusillade at the deplorable state of music in the established English church of his day. Although the criticisms were deserved, his passionate "humors" and lack of diplomacy cost him the professorship of music at Edinburgh University, a post he was eminently qualified to fill, being "the finest extempore organist of his day"[9] as well as an excellent composer, "the first among us for talent, and diligence in improving that talent."[10]

Another, and quite unrelated interest of his deserves mention: he was an avid fisherman, and it is said that he would accept or reject new professional positions on the basis of the fishing advantages of the district. In fact, "once, while on his way to play a dedicatory recital, he stopped for a while to angle in an inviting stream not far from the church, sending his assistant on ahead to play the opening number!"[11] Wrote one of his contemporaries:

Dr. Wesley was a great Englishman. In that word lies perhaps the secret of much of his appeal. He was, above all, English. In his downrightness, his humors [using that word in its old sense], his blend of kindliness and wrongheadedness, and his love of outdoor life, no less than in his music, he bore the stamp of the country that produced him.[12]

This hymn, a metrical version of Psalm 72, was written for Christmas and first sung at the English Moravian center at Fulneck, December 25, 1821. When Adam Clarke, the famous Bible expositor, heard it at a missionary meeting he was chairing sometime thereafter, he was so impressed that he secured a copy and printed it in his *Commentary* at the end of Psalm 71;[13] he appended this note, that "while Montgomery, for his part might tremble to touch the harp of Zion, for my part, I wish he would favor the Church of God with a metrical version of the whole book"![14] Julian comments that "Of all Montgomery's rendering . . . of the psalms, this is the finest, . . . a rich and splendid Messianic hymn."[15]

Observe: This hymn plays on two themes again and again: (1) the desire and ability to free the oppressed, whether they be those in chains, the poor, the undeservedly suffering, the needy, the weak, the distressed, the "blind," the condemned and dying; (2) God's concern to establish righteousness and equity by taking away transgression and announcing peace; all of this as He, the Anointed One, the messianic David reigns on earth at God's appointed time.

Further, in the figure of gentle rainfall, refreshing and revitalizing the earth, causing flowers of love, joy, and hope to spring into birth, he adds a vivid pastoral touch. Finally, he reminds us that this Prince's rule shall increase in its gloriousness, and that the covenant He has established is eternally secure, founded as it is on *His* character, one of righteous love. True it is "that the devotion of Psalmist glows when he looks at God in the face of the reigning Messiah."[16] And Montgomery's faith has struck a fine balance between his passionate concern for fairness and justice in *this* world and his confidence in God's triumphant grace for the world and for the age to come.

Notes

1. Julian, *op. cit.,* pp. 764–765.
2. Bailey, *op. cit.,* p. 156.
3. Marks, *op. cit.,* p. 119.
4. *Ibid.*
5. Moffatt and Patrick, *op. cit.,* p. 437.
6. *Ibid.*
7. Bailey, *op. cit.,* p. 156.

8. Haeussler, *op. cit.*, p. 976.
9. *Ibid.*, p. 977.
10. Barrett, *op. cit.*, p. 171.
11. Haeussler, *op. cit.*, p. 976.
12. *Ibid.*, p. 977.
13. Stulken, *op. cit.*, p. 188.
14. Haeussler, *op. cit.*, pp. 393–394.
15. *Ibid..*, p. 393.
16. *Ibid.*

Title/Date	*"Jesus Shall Reign Where'er the Sun . . ."* *(1719)*
Author	*Isaac Watts*
Composer/Tune	*Frederick M. A. Venua "Park Street" (c. 1810)*
	John Hatton "Duke Street" (c. 1793)
Scriptural Basis	*Psalm 72:8 et al.*

The reader will note that this is the first of three of the psalms we have chosen from the hand of the illustrious Isaac Watts (1674–1748), Dissenter and beloved Congregational clergyman. Of the many causes that contributed to the sorry state of England's spiritual and moral climate in the early eighteenth century, there was one in particular that God used this brilliant young man with his spiritual concern to change: the music used in Christian worship. To Watts, "a powerful preacher, poet and scholar belongs the credit for turning England from Old Testament psalmody—much of it dreary, literalized, unlyrical, and out of harmony with the spirit of Christ—to the adoption of hymn-singing."[1]

Watts's program to improve the quality of congregational praise involved too moves. First, he believed that the psalms—while God's revealed truth, to be sure—must be, where at all possible, transmitted into truth consistent with that of the new dispensation ushered in by our Lord Jesus Christ. That not all agreed with this perspective is plain by this question asked by one of his critics: "Does Watts indeed presume to correct and instruct the Holy Ghost in writing Psalms?"[2] Second, he believed that it was perfectly legitimate for believers to compose hymns of praise to God in their own words, being careful, of course, to make such hymns of "human composure" consistent with biblical teaching and laboring prayerfully to make them as worthy as offerings made to God deserve to be.

His second goal was accomplished first when, between 1707 and 1709, he published his collection *Hymns and Spiritual Songs,* "The first true hymn-book in England,"[3] containing his first lines, written when he was but fifteen,

He shall have dominion also *from* sea to sea, and *from* the river unto the ends of the earth. Psalm 72:8

From PSALM 72
Isaac Watts, 1719

PARK STREET L. M. with repeat
Arr. from Frederick M. A. Venua, c. 1810

1. Je - sus shall reign wher - e'er the sun Does his suc - ces - sive
2. For him shall end - less prayer be made, And prais-es throng to
3. Peo - ple and realms of ev - ery tongue Dwell on his love with
4. Bless-ings a - bound wher - e'er he reigns; The pris-'ner leaps to
5. Let ev - ery crea - ture rise and bring Pe - cul - iar hon - ors

jour - neys run; His king - dom stretch from shore to shore, Till moons shall
crown his head; His Name, like sweet per - fume, shall rise With ev - ery
sweet-est song; And in - fant voic - es shall pro - claim Their ear - ly
lose his chains, The wea - ry find e - ter - nal rest, And all the
to our King, An - gels de - scend with songs a - gain, And earth re -

wax and wane no more, Till moons shall wax and wane no more.
morn - ing sac - ri - fice, With ev - ery morn-ing sac - ri - fice.
bless-ings on his Name, Their ear - ly bless-ings on his Name.
sons of want are blest, And all the sons of want are blest.
peat the loud A - men, And earth re - peat the loud A - men. A - MEN.

Behold the glories of the Lamb
   Amidst his Father's throne
Prepare new honors for His name
   And songs before unknown[4]

and including such all-time favorites as "When I Survey the Wondrous Cross" and "There Is a Land of Pure Delight." These hymns illustrate Milton's poetic ideal, in that they are "simple, sensuous and passionate."[5] To elaborate, briefly: "Simple" means that anyone with average intelligence can understand them. Watts was masterful at using short, eye-catching, one-syllable words wherever possible; he wrote: "they were . . . written to assist the Meditations and Worship of Vulgar [i.e., common/ordinary] Christians."[6] "Sensuous" meant the conjuring up through pictures—such as "wings of faith," a couch "wet with tears," "His name like sweet perfume," "time, like an ever-rolling stream"—of images, again familiar to common folk. "Passionate," or charged with emotion, meant arousing people to respond to God's mercy, grace, or judgment—in Watts, "There is nothing drab or passive; all is vivid and active."[7]

It took Watts much longer to accomplish his first goal, that of "Christian-izing the Psalms, making David speak like a Christian, a contemporary of Watts!"[8] He labored at this diligently, and finally published his *Psalms of David Imitated* in 1719, including such immortals as "Jesus Shall Reign," "Joy to the World," "Our God, Our Help," and "Before Jehovah's Awful Throne." He frankly sought to make these psalms speak truth consistent with Chris-tian revelation, and wherever possible, to relate them to his world, England, and his people's circumstances—a worthy and noble purpose that he realized with considerable success.

Our present hymn, "Jesus Shall Reign . . . ," is a case in point. When asked why he introduced Jesus into Psalm 72, "the most widely used and proba-bly the finest missionary hymn ever written,"[9] he wrote:

> Where the original runs in the form of prophecy concerning Christ and his salvation, I have given an historical turn to the sense; there is no ne-cessity that we should always sing in the obscure and doubtful style of prediction, when the things foretold are brought into open light by a full accomplishment.[10]

This hymn, which Bailey compares with that of Montgomery on this same psalm,[11] stays rather closely to its text; its original eight stanzas have been reduced to four (or five, as in the *Trinity Hymnal*). Watts's exposition, rich in pictures, follows:

Stanza One: Just as the sun circles the earth in its journeys and warms us all with its rays, so does Jesus reign as sovereign over a dominion no less ex-pansive and every bit as everlasting (Psalm 72:8, 5, 17).

Stanza Two: As Ruler, His subjects raise their voices in endless prayers; moreover, praises jostle each other vying to be His crown. And His Name, that matchless Name, Name above all Names, rises with every morning sac-rifice, its sweet fragrance mingled with those prayers (Psalm 72:15, 11).

Stanza Three: Every language and every age group are counted among those whose sweetest songs focus on the premier quality of His Being, love, for which all alike bless Him—from birthing days to dying days (Psalm 72:15, 17).

Stanza Four: The effect of His bountiful blessings is electric: prisoners lose their shackles, weary folk find a rest that is far better than any they've yet known, and the needy are fed, for that's the blessing for those who are hungry—to feed them, and clothe them, and warm them, not just to say, "God bless you brother, be ye warmed and filled" (James 2:15, 16; Psalm 72:4).

Stanza Five: Every creature, human, divine, natural—for nature has groaned and travailed, waiting for the King's redemption of her blighted state—is to bring each his own treasures,[12] "peculiar" treasures, including the gifts of songs and amens, and pile them at His worthy feet! In this spirit, a remarkable evangelistic celebration occurred close to 150 years after Watts penned these lines:

> On Whitsunday, in 1862, five thousand natives of Tonga, Fiji, and Samoa who had forsaken paganism to become Christians, gathered under the banyan trees for divine worship. Foremost among them was King George himself, surrounded by other chiefs and warriors who had shared the dangers . . . of many a battle. . . . It would be impossible to describe the deep feelings manifested as they began their service by singing this hymn. Later on, King George drew up a Constitution transforming a pagan regime into a Christian government.[13]

The tunes used with this fine biblical hymn have been several; both "Old Hundred" and "Duke Street, with its superior melody and scarcely inferior grandeur," have given these lines wings; others have preferred Handel's "Samson," since he "had no peer in the art or instinct of making a note speak a word."[14]

The *Trinity Hymnal's* choice, "Park Street," a favorite tune in our country, was introduced by the Handel and Haydn Society of Boston in 1820 and has been used regularly in Presbyterian churches. Its composer, Frederick Venua (1788–1872), was a Frenchman, an organist, and a highly esteemed member of the Royal Society of Musicians.[15]

My personal preference, however, is "Duke Street," also included in the previously mentioned hymnbook of Boston's Handel and Haydn Society in 1820, and its association with this hymn in our country goes back many years![16] Its composer, one John Hatton (d. 1793), an Englishman, apparently lived on "Duke" Street; little else is known about him other than he was killed in a stagecoach accident, and his funeral was held, fittingly, in the Presbyterian Chapel of St. Helen's in 1793.[17]

It was not until near the end of the eighteenth century that the modern missionary movement, spurred on by hymns like this, began when William Carey—undaunted by an Anglican bishop's contemptuous comment, "Young man, if God wants to save the heathen, he will do it without any help from you"—sailed for India. Since then it has been used, along with others by Watts, the Wesleys, Montgomery, and Heber, to inspire such devotion and to

72 SINGING IN WORSHIP

declare the truth of the coming reign of Jesus Christ throughout His world, from everlasting to everlasting, Amen!

Notes

1. Haeussler, *op. cit.*, p. 965.
2. Marks, *op. cit.*, p. 96.
3. Haeussler, *op. cit.*, p. 967.
4. Bailey, *op. cit.*, p. 48.
5. *Ibid.*, p. 61.
6. Benson, *op. cit.*, p. 114.
7. Bailey, *op. cit.*, p. 61.
8. Benson, *op. cit.*, p. 111.
9. Bailey, *op. cit.*, p. 53.
10. Robert G. McCutchan, *Our Hymnody* (Nashville: Abingdon, 1942), p. 465.
11. Bailey, *op. cit.*, p. 157.
12. Moffatt and Patrick, *op. cit.*, p. 129.
13. W. C. Covert and Calvin Laufer, *Handbook to the Hymnal* (Chicago: Presbyterian Board of Christian Education, 1935), p. 395.
14. Theron Brown and Hezekiah Butterworth, *The Story of the Hymns and Tunes* (New York: American Tract Society, 1906), p. 166.
15. Covert and Laufer, *op. cit.*, p. 77.
16. *Ibid.*, p. 396.
17. McCutchan, *op. cit.*, p. 41.

Title/Date	*"Joy to the World, the Lord Is Come"* *(1719)*
Author	*Isaac Watts*
Composer/Tune	*Lowell Mason "Antioch" (1836)*
Scriptural Basis	*Psalm 98:3–9; Genesis 3:17–18; Romans 5:20*

This psalm is an Old Testament doxology, an expression of an Israelite's heartfelt gratitude upon seeing some marvelous manifestations of his God's love for him and his people. Known in the *Book of Common Prayer* as the "Cantate Domino" ("O Sing to the Lord"), "it is wholly given up to praise . . . joy . . . exhilaration,"[1] for God's hard-won victory, a victory demonstrated both in the accomplished salvation of His people and in the vindication of His righteousness as revealed in all His doings.

Under Watts's hand it became a beloved Christmas hymn, with Christians responding to deliverance from the primal curse—for when sin entered our world through our parents' first act of disobedience, it brought tragic sorrows, weed-infested soils, and, ultimately, the dread specter of death itself. As Bailey says, "it is one of the most joyous Christmas hymns in existence; not in the sense of merry-making, but in the deep and solemn realization of what Christ's birth has meant to mankind."[2] Let us examine it more closely:

Stanza One: The general call to the world, the earth, heaven, and nature is balanced by the specific call to every human heart to make room, to give top priority to the King, Jehovah, who is now here, and to celebrate His coming. All creation is exhorted to sing, sing, sing! (Psalm 98:4, 7, 8).

Stanza Two: Since this reigning King is also the redeeming Savior, men have double reason to accord Him praise. Moreover, specific elements of the world of nature—fields, floods, rocks, hills, plains—all are called on again to pick up this human song and repeat it, or echo it far and wide (Psalm 98:7–8). Duffield makes an interesting point regarding the inanimate "voice" of nature, saying that

> While the whole creation uplifts its song to God, it is man alone who can truly praise. In the Esthonian legend of the origin of song . . . the god of song descended on the Domberg [hill?], where he played and sang.

Around him stood the creatures, each learning its own portion of the celestial strain . . . the tree discovering how to rustle its leaves, the brook how to murmur along its bed, and the wind, bird and beast alike caught the parts assigned to them. Man only, of them all, was able to combine everything and therefore man alone can rightly praise.[3]

Stanza Three: With the Savior reigning, His blessings flow far and wide: redemption for sins, consolation in sorrows, a land rid of all that would inhibit its productivity. Even nature has suffered from man's degraded and degrading passions, and so she, too, awaits redemption in its completest sense (Romans 8:18ff.).

Stanza Four: Watts moves from the particular to the general: the nations will themselves bear witness to His rule "with truth and grace" (Psalm 98:9). There will be no denying the "glories of His righteousness" and the "wonders of His love," for the earth will be filled with the glory of God as "the waters cover the sea"!

To this clear but simple exposition American congregations, at least, have wed a

tune that—apparently by some magic of its own—contrives to enlist the entire voice of a congregation, the bass falling in on the third beat as if by intuition. The truth is, the tune has become the habit of the hymn, and to the [tens of] thousands who know it by heart, "Antioch" is "Joy to the World," and "Joy to the World" is "Antioch."[4]

"Antioch" has a mysterious origin. Although frequent notations credit the tune to Handel and the arrangement to Lowell Mason, as Haeussler says, "those who insist on this theory, however are gaining a maximum of fiction from a minimum of fact!"[5] Hymn-tune authority James Lightwood believes the tune to be of American origin; others think that Mason may have taken it from an English collection by Clark of Canterbury,[6] since Mason himself abhorred the fugue as a tonal pattern and would not have so arranged it; McCutchan cites Prout as saying "it is very far from Handel."[7]

An interesting suggestion as to its usage is made by Haeussler, that the verses be sung antiphonally, the congregation singing the first and second lines of each verse, the choir the third and fourth lines, with all joining in the refrain, the choir thus singing the more difficult passages.[8]

While we have referred to Lowell Mason (1792–1872) earlier, he is important enough for American hymnody to deserve further treatment. In the long struggle to introduce hymnody into American worship patterns, Mason's service was invaluable; he along with Thomas Hastings and William Bradbury launched and supported singing conventions, teaching institutes,

Make a joyful noise unto the Lord, all the earth... Psalm 98:4

ANTIOCH C. M. with repeat
Lowell Mason, 1836
based on George Frederick Handel, 1742

Isaac Watts, 1719

1. Joy to the world! the Lord is come: Let earth re - ceive her
2. Joy to the earth! the Sav - iour reigns: Let men their songs em -
3. No more let sins and sor - rows grow, Nor thorns in - fest the
4. He rules the world with truth and grace, And makes the na - tions

King; Let ev - ery heart pre - pare him room,
ploy; While fields and floods, rocks, hills, and plains
ground; He comes to make his bless - ings flow
prove The glo - ries of his right - eous - ness,

And heav'n and na - ture sing, And heav'n and na - ture
Re - peat the sound - ing joy, Re - peat the sound - ing
Far as the curse is found, Far as the curse is
And won - ders of his love, And won - ders of his

And heav'n and na - ture sing

And

sing, And heav'n, and heav'n and na - ture sing.
joy, Re - peat, re - peat the sound - ing joy.
found, Far as, far as the curse is found.
love, And won - ders, won - ders of his love. A - MEN.

heav'n and na-ture sing

and children's festivals, all of which gave the reform movement much needed momentum. And the fact is that a great many of his tunes are still widely used today; McCutchan, for example, includes thirty-two of his, to twenty-seven of Dykes, with these two composers far ahead of all others.[9]

A gifted musician, Mason's early life revolved around work with choirs as a "volunteer" leader; when the manuscript for his book of choral music was finally published by the Boston Handel and Haydn Society, its success was phenomenal, going through seventeen editions in thirty years. Moving to Boston, he directed several choirs, including the one at Bowdoin Street Church where Lyman Beecher, father of Henry Ward Beecher and Harriet Beecher Stowe, was the pastor. Becoming president of the "Society," he soon introduced music into the curriculum of the Boston public schools, studied the teaching methods of Pestalozzi and Naegeli, organized singing conventions up and down the East Coast, founded the Boston Academy of Music, and received a doctorate in music from New York University, the first American to be so honored. He was a man "of keen mind, enormous energy, and a magnetic personality,"[10] dying at eighty as a well-beloved and greatly respected leader in a field whose influence on American music was incredible.

Notes

1. Derek Kidner, *Psalms* . . . (London: InterVarsity, 1973), p. 352.
2. Bailey, *op. cit.*, p. 54.
3. Duffield, *op. cit.*, p. 307.
4. Brown and Butterworth, *op. cit.*, p. 464.
5. Haeussler, *op. cit.*, p. 180.
6. Covert and Laufer, *op. cit.*, p. 141.
7. McCutchan, *Our Hymnody*, p. 123.
8. Haeussler, *op. cit.*, p. 180.
9. McCutchan, *op. cit.*, pp. 605–606.
10. Haeussler, *op. cit.*, p. 786.

Title/Date	*"O Worship the King, All Glorious Above" (1833)*
Author	*Sir Robert Grant*
Composer/Tune	*J. Michael Haydn "Lyons"*
Scriptural Basis	*Psalm 104*

Other than James Montgomery, the social activist editor of the *Sheffield Iris,* who grew up with the godly example of missionary parents strong in his memory, the other hymn-writers considered thus far have all been clergymen. Sir Robert Grant (1779–1838), whose Scottish father Charles was serving as a member of the Board of Trade in India at the time of Robert's birth, while a "man of deep Christian feelings and broad Evangelical sympathies within the Anglican Church,"[1] chose a career in law and politics— in the finest sense of the (latter) term—as his sphere of Christian witness. In this, incidentally, he was in the illustrious company of Lords Wilberforce, Dartmouth, Macauley, and Teignmouth, each of whom sought to use his resources and political influence in efforts to better the lot of oppressed peoples within the British Empire—statesmen worthy of that name!

Admitted to the English Bar after his studies at and graduation from Oxford, he served as a Member of Parliament for over twenty-five years, where he won passage for a bill emancipating the Jews in 1833;[2] later made a director of the East India Company and knighted in 1834, he became governor of Bombay, a post that he served conscientiously and well, but briefly, for he died in 1838. His genuine spirit of philanthropy, which he had "inherited" from his generous father, led to the establishment of a medical college in Bombay,[3] a living memorial to his concern, character, and influence.

The other and equally "living memorial" to this man whose life wonderfully blended Christian devotion and social conscience was his writings; says Bailey trenchantly, "though he wrote little, he wrote well."[4] Another reports that "as a man of deep feelings and poetic mind, the thoughtful beauty of his writings endeared him to a wide circle of readers."[5]

This noble hymn, a free and lyrical paraphrase of Psalm 104, regarded by many authorities as one of the finest hymns ever written[6] and assuredly "one of the six finest in the English language,"[7] has been described in these glowing terms:

All thy works shall praise thee, O Lord... Psalm 145:10

Sir Robert Grant, 1833

LYONS 10. 10. 11. 11.
Arr. from J. Michael Haydn, 1737–1806

1. O   wor-ship the King all glo-rious a-bove, O grate-ful-ly sing his
2. O   tell of his might, O sing of his grace, Whose robe is the light, whose
3. The earth with its store of won-ders un-told, Al-might-y, thy pow'r hath
4. Thy boun-ti-ful care what tongue can re-cite? It breathes in the air; it
5. Frail chil-dren of dust, and fee-ble as frail, In thee do we trust, nor
6. O   meas-ure-less Might! In-ef-fa-ble Love! While an-gels de-light to

pow'r and his love; Our Shield and De-fend-er, the An-cient of Days,
can-o-py space. His char-iots of wrath the deep thun-der-clouds form,
found-ed of old; Hath stab-lished it fast by a change-less de-cree,
shines in the light; It streams from the hills; it de-scends to the plain;
find thee to fail; Thy mer-cies how ten-der, how firm to the end,
hymn thee a-bove, The hum-bler cre-a-tion, though fee-ble their lays,

Pa-vil-ioned in splen-dor, and gird-ed with praise.
And dark is his path on the wings of the storm.
And round it hath cast, like a man-tle, the sea.
And sweet-ly dis-tils in the dew and the rain.
Our Mak-er, De-fend-er, Re-deem-er, and Friend!
With true ad-o-ra-tion shall lisp to thy praise. A-   MEN.

One finds in it magnificent imagery, flowing language, graceful measure;
. . . its double rhyme in the middle as well as at the end of the lines makes
a beautiful style; it is a combination of effortless energy, high-spirited in-
nocence, superb dignity and eloquent simplicity, with almost every word
in the common man's vocabulary.[9]

Psalm 104—of which this hymn is in part a careful paraphrase (vss. 1–3)
and in part an elaboration on the theme of God's care, love, and faithfulness
to His creatures (vss. 4–6)—is an impassioned biblical description of the Creator and His works. While the hymn's descriptions are more general, and the
psalm's nature-pictures more specific, the strong emotional content is maintained. Each of the six names given to God—King, Shield, Defender, Ancient of Days, Redeemer, Friend—arouses biblical reminiscences, with the

last two becoming intimate and personal. And it is not difficult to see here a development of thought parallel to the story of creation's six days, as recorded in Genesis 1.[10]

Stanza One: This stanza offers striking description of the King whom we are called on to worship and praise—One who is "pavilioned in splendour" (His throne is splendor) and "girded with praise" (praise encircles or envelopes Him as a glorious belt or girdle); Routley calls this "pavilioned in splendour, girded in praise" one of the hymn's two "towering lines."[11] Moreover, His power is not naked, nor His love mere sentimentality; rather they combine, each balancing the other and calling us to grateful song extolling them.

Stanza Two: Again we have the balance of two diverse characteristics: might (power) and grace are the subject of our telling; light and space, the well-nigh infinite dimensions of which we are just beginning to appreciate in our star-wars era, and the dark forebodings of His wrath, seen in the stormy heavens, complete another set of images.

Stanza Three: Here the dimension of time and of God's eternal purposes joins those of light, and space, and power as another of God's manifest wonders.

Stanza Four: Now the poet directs his focus from the infinite, eternal, changeless dimensions to the quieter but no less vivid indication of God's presence: His bountiful care that seems to pervade or permeate the atmosphere, air and light, dew and rain.

Stanza Five: As frail and feeble children—"of dust thou art, and to dust shalt thou return" (Genesis 3:19)—we trust in Him, knowing His tender mercies, another grand theological concept joining grace (vs. 2) and decrees (vs. 3). And who is this One in whom we trust, but the One who has created us and redeemed us, who is our Defender but also our Friend?

Stanza Six: "Oh measureless Might! Ineffable Love," the other of Routley's two "towering lines"[12] combining again power and love and calling us, the humbler creation (when contrasted with the angelic host), to sing, indeed to "lisp our lays," feeble though they (and we) may be!

So we may ask, Why "worship the King" (vs. 1)? And we can answer, "because of His love" (vs. 6). Thus this psalm "is a pageant, not only of God's power, but also of His love";[13] we are reminded that when He creates, He does it for the benefit of His creation!

"Lyons," the tune most often used with these inspiring lyrics, whose "vigor and spirit best fit them,"[14] was composed by the devout and warm-hearted younger brother of Franz Haydn, Johann Michael Haydn (1737–1806). A fine musician, and like his brother, also self-taught, his interests were broad: history, geography, the classics all gained his attention. Of his several hundred musical compositions written for the church during his lifetime position at Salzburg, many have served as the basis for hymn tunes; of them Franz spoke glowingly, saying that they were better than his own! Reticent about his modest attainments, Michael lived somewhat in the shadow of his older brother, publishing only a few of his works,[15] but apparently without jealousy. After visiting his grave, Franz Schubert said of him:

> The good Haydn! It almost seemed as if his calm, clear spirit were hovering over me. I may be neither calm nor clear, but no man living reverences him more than I do. My eyes filled with tears as we came away.[16]

Finally, as with others we've noted, Haydn's faith would not permit him to claim the credit for his talent, which he saw as a gift from God; he initialed all his works with "O.A.M.D.Gl." (Omnia ad Majorem Dei Gloriam— "all to God's major Glory!").[17]

Notes

1. Bailey, *op. cit.,* p. 182.
2. Moffatt and Patrick, *op. cit.,* p. 353.
3. Covert and Laufer, *op. cit.,* p. 2.
4. Bailey, *op. cit.,* p. 182.
5. Brown and Butterworth, *op. cit.,* p. 22.
6. Haeussler, *op. cit.,* p. 65.
7. Routley, *Hymns and the Faith,* p. 8.
8. Breed, *op. cit.,* p. 180.
9. Routley, *op. cit.,* p. 8.
10. Bailey, *op. cit.,* p. 182.
11. Routley, *op. cit.,* p. 8.
12. *Ibid.*
13. *Ibid.,* p. 9.
14. Brown and Butterworth, *op. cit.,* p. 23.
15. Hostetler, *op. cit.,* p. 5.
16. McCutchan, *Our Hymnody,* p. 26.
17. *Ibid.*

Title/Date	*"Our God, Our Help in Ages Past"*
Author	*Isaac Watts*
Composer/Tune	*William Croft "St. Anne" (1708)*
Scriptural Basis	*Psalm 90*

The story is told of Elizabeth Singer, a beautiful and accomplished young Englishwoman who fell in love with Isaac Watts, the gifted Dissenting hymn-writer through reading his poetry. Upon their arranged meeting, she was disillusioned, while he was smitten; when he asked for her hand in marriage, she declined as graciously as she could, and said to him with the best of intentions, "Mr. Watts, I only wish I could say that I admire the casket as much as I admire the jewel."[1] In spite of such plain talk, they remained good friends. She later married Thomas Rowe, under whose tutelage Watts had previously studied for his ordination examinations, and of whom he had written with warmth and commendation, "I love thy gentle influence, Rowe, thy gentle influence like the sun . . . dissolves the frozen snow."[2]

Watts's entire life was characterized by fragile health, which probably was prenatal in origin; a contemporary describes him in these terms:

About five feet tall, he was of slender form, with a fair but pale complexion, and small grey eyes which, when animated, became quite piercing and expressive; with a low forehead and prominent cheekbones, his countenance was, on the whole, by no means disagreeable. His voice, though weak, was pleasant . . . his glance commanded attention, even awe;[3] his rhetoric was polished, and graceful.[4]

On one occasion, Sir Thomas Abney, one of his parishioners, invited him to spend a week at his country estate; Watts accepted his invitation and stayed on for the rest of his life—some thirty-six years! It was in that beautiful, restful setting that Watts wrote most of his more than fifty works, including a textbook on logic; masterful treatises (for his day) on astronomy and geometry; books of children's poetry, including the classic *Divine and Moral Songs*; books on grammar, ethics, psychology, and theology (twenty-nine treatises on this!); and of course many of his marvelous paraphrases of the psalms.

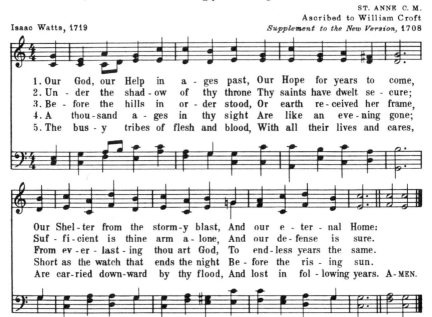

Lord, thou hast been our dwelling place in all generations. Psalm 90:1

ST. ANNE C. M.
Ascribed to William Croft
Isaac Watts, 1719
Supplement to the New Version, 1708

1. Our God, our Help in a - ges past, Our Hope for years to come,
2. Un - der the shad - ow of thy throne Thy saints have dwelt se - cure;
3. Be - fore the hills in or - der stood, Or earth re - ceived her frame,
4. A thou - sand a - ges in thy sight Are like an eve - ning gone;
5. The bus - y tribes of flesh and blood, With all their lives and cares,

Our Shel - ter from the storm - y blast, And our e - ter - nal Home:
Suf - fi - cient is thine arm a - lone, And our de - fense is sure.
From ev - er - last - ing thou art God, To end - less years the same.
Short as the watch that ends the night Be - fore the ris - ing sun.
Are car - ried down - ward by thy flood, And lost in fol - lowing years. A - MEN.

6. Time, like an ever - rolling stream,
   Bears all its sons away;
   They fly forgotten, as a dream
   Dies at the opening day.

7. Our God, our Help in ages past,
   Our Hope for years to come;
   Be thou our Guard while troubles last,
   And our eternal Home.

Samuel Johnson, though having little sympathy with Nonconformity, wrote of Watts's literary accomplishments:

he has provided instruction for all ages—from those who are lisping their first lessons, to the enlightened readers of . . . Locke; he has left neither corporeal nor spiritual nature unexamined; he has taught us the art of reasoning and the science of the stars.[5]

Moreover, he included Watts in his *Lives of the Poets*; apparently, however, although it is not clear why, he may have been less than enthusiastic about the D.D. degrees that both Aberdeen and Edinburgh Universities conferred on Watts, noting that "Academical honors would have more value if they were always bestowed with equal judgment."[6]

This hymn, "the second national anthem of England," is a grand paraphrase of Psalm 90; it has been given countless accolades: Routley refers to it as "the gravest and most universal of all English hymns";[7] Temple calls it "Watts' most stately hymn,"[8] and Haeussler adds "this magnificent hymn is, without question Watts' greatest, number one in any English poll, and in the top ten of American preferences";[9] Douglas speaks of it as "the greatest para-phrase ever written," and together with "When I Survey the Wondrous Cross" affirms these as "the very summit of English hymnody."[10] John Henry Jowett once asked a group of Oxford dons to jot down a short list of the greatest hymns; after a few moments, they each named but one, "Our God, Our Help," saying that it fulfilled "all the conditions of a perfect hymn.[11]

An indispensable hymn for the day of decision or distress, it speaks of men's hopes and fears in perils and in times of deliverance; it was sung on the *Queen Elizabeth* as she headed, with British and U.S. troops aboard, toward the Normandy beachhead prior to D-Day in World War II, and often in London churches on a hushed Sunday morning after a night of screaming bombs and devastating destruction.[12] It also gave courage to a group of eleven Norwegian civilians, who, after being tortured for being "hostile" to Germany's occupation troops, faced a firing squad; they grasped hands and sang it before they were all shot.[13]

Historically, Watts wrote this in 1714, a time of grave national danger; it appeared that the "Schism Act," designed to suppress religious dissent and forced through the British Parliament by Queen Anne's ill-advised political leaders, was about to take effect. Then, on that same day, August 1, 1714, she died; and so her successor (by a previous agreement), George I, was able to thwart the potential religious persecution. The depth of feeling about this is mirrored in this report:

> The news of the miraculous upsetting of the Catholic plans flew east, west, north and south. Men ran through town and village shouting "The Queen is dead! the Queen is dead!" That most militant and masterful London preacher Thomas Bradbury, on the following Sunday took for his text: "Go, see now this cursed woman and bury her; for she is a King's daughter."[14]

Watts later published this hymn in his *The Psalms of David, Imitated* under the heading "Man Frail and God Eternal"; one can image this being used—as hymns were very often written to be—after a sermon on this frequently experienced theme; in fact, for Watts (and other hymn-writers of consider-able talent) "Sermon and hymn emerged from the quiet of [the] study, as he was preparing for the Lord's Day."[15]

Let us examine it more closely:

Stanza One: There is the very personal focus on "our," mentioned five times, to stress that we deal not with an impersonal force or cosmic princi-ple—unfeeling, unresponsive, unknowable—but rather with One who is *our* God, a "very present help in *our* time of need!" Moreover, there is the stress on time: our help in the past, our hope in the future, our shelter in the present.

Stanza Two: As our eternal home (vs. 1), we dwell securely protected by His throne (sovereignty) and defended by His strong right arm, the symbol of His power!

Stanza Three: Time stretches out eternally in both directions; before the creation of the universe, before the ordering of the earth, God *is,* and He is *God!*

Stanza Four: Time passes; the brevity of human life compared to the ancient hills, human triviality with God's eternity—all this has its frightening aspects.

Stanza Five: Human beings, with their busy, active, care-filled lives, are swept away by the swirling waters and disappear from memory as well as sight!

Stanza Six: As streams wash the land, purifying it and carrying away debris, so time bears away its sons who fly, forgotten—much as are dreams upon awakening, however vivid they were in the night.

Stanza Seven: Again, the fivefold repetition of the plural personal pronoun, "our," with its looking to the past (our Help), to the future (our Hope), and to the present where, in the midst of our troubles, our God is our Guard and our eternal resting-place!

The tune "St. Anne," "perfectly wedded to these words, is pealed out daily from the chimes of St. Clement's Church, in the heart of London";[16] it was composed by William Croft (1678–1727), one of England's outstanding organists and composers, serving eventually at Westminster Abbey. His church music was most responsible for his significance, although he wrote much for the theater as well; three of the greatest hymn tunes came from his pen: St. Anne, Hanover, and St. Matthew. Buried in Westminster Abbey, his epitaph reads, in part:

> Near this place lies . . . William Croft, Doctor in Music. . . . In his celebrated works . . . consecrated to God, he made diligent progress. . . . By the force of ingenuity, and the sweetness of his manners, and even his countenance, he recommended them. . . . Departed to the heavenly choir on August 14, 1727, that he might add his own Hallelujah to the Concert of Angels.[17]

I wonder if they ever sing "St. Anne"?

Notes

1. Bailey, *op. cit.,* p. 44.
2. Duffield, *op. cit.,* p. 62.
3. H. A. Smith, *Lyric Religion* (New York: Century, 1931), p. 43.

4. Duffield, *op. cit.,* p. 64.

5. Smith, *op. cit.,* p. 43–44.

6. Moffatt and Patrick, *op. cit.,* p. 532.

7. Routley, *Hymns and the Faith,* p. 34.

8. Temple, *op. cit.,* p. 99.

9. Haeussler, *op. cit.,* p. 114.

10. Douglas, *op. cit.,* p. 134.

11. Moffatt and Patrick, *op. cit.,* p. 59ff.

12. Temple, *op. cit.,* p. 99.

13. Hostetler, *op. cit.,* p. 37.

14. Bailey, *op. cit.,* p. 55.

15. Reynolds, *op. cit.,* p. 50.

16. Haeussler, *op. cit.,* p. 115.

17. *Ibid.,* p. 612.

Title/Date	*"Praise, My Soul, the King of Heaven"* *(1834)*
Author	*Henry Lyte*
Composer/Tune	*Sir John Goss "Praise My Soul" (1869)*
Scriptural Basis	*Psalm 103*

Henry Francis Lyte (1793–1847), three of whose timeless hymns grace this book, was born in Scotland in 1793, orphaned when but a child, educated as a charity student in Ireland, and then at Trinity College, Dublin. While there, thrice he won a coveted prize for English poetry, thereby adding to his meager resources,[1] but even more important, encouraging him to share the deep places of his heart and spirit in his verse, even as he has done in this and other widely used hymns.

Although he originally intended to study medicine, his fragile health, worsened by his struggles with Dame Poverty, led him to pursue Holy Orders. Ordained in 1815, he served a succession of small congregations, as did scores of other Anglican clergymen. But in 1818, his life—and then his ministry—was dramatically changed; a neighboring pastor called for Lyte in his dying hours, and in that Valley of the Shadow they read from St. Paul and both found new life, light, and peace—the one to enter God's presence confidently, the other to return to his flock a different person. Lyte says of this experience's impact on him:

> I was greatly affected by the whole matter, and brought to look at life and its issue with a different eye than before; and I began to study my Bible and to preach in another manner than I had previously done.[2]

Moreover, the practical implications of his Evangelical faith were not neglected, as he also took on the support of the family of his deceased friend, a burden and financial strain that hardly made his physical stress lighter; asthma and eventually tuberculosis took their toll on his energies and led to the complete breakdown of his health and premature death in Nice, France, in 1847.

In the intervening three decades, however, he served most of his ministry in the parish of Lower Brixham, a seacoast town in Devonshire; here among

*Bless the Lord, all his works in all places of his domin-
ion: bless the Lord, O my soul.* Psalm 103:22

PRAISE, MY SOUL 8. 7. 8. 7. 8. 7.
Henry F. Lyte, 1834
Sir John Goss, 1869

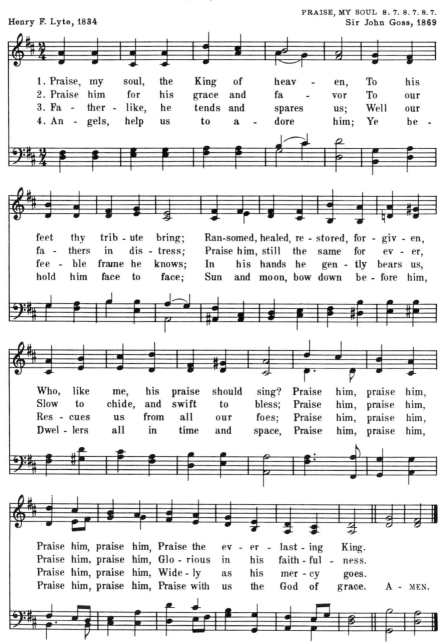

1. Praise, my soul, the King of heav - en, To his
2. Praise him for his grace and fa - vor To our
3. Fa - ther - like, he tends and spares us; Well our
4. An - gels, help us to a - dore him; Ye be -

feet thy trib - ute bring; Ran-somed, healed, re - stored, for - giv - en,
fa - thers in dis - tress; Praise him, still the same for ev - er,
fee - ble frame he knows; In his hands he gen - tly bears us,
hold him face to face; Sun and moon, bow down be - fore him,

Who, like me, his praise should sing? Praise him, praise him,
Slow to chide, and swift to bless; Praise him, praise him,
Res - cues us from all our foes; Praise him, praise him,
Dwel - lers all in time and space, Praise him, praise him,

Praise him, praise him, Praise the ev - er - last - ing King.
Praise him, praise him, Glo - rious in his faith - ful - ness.
Praise him, praise him, Wide - ly as his mer - cy goes.
Praise him, praise him, Praise with us the God of grace. A - MEN.

hearty seafaring folk who were busy and shrewd, rough, sometimes coarse and disorderly, but also warm-hearted, he gave himself sacrificially; he gathered a Sunday School of nearly eight hundred children in a day when schools were few, and trained the teachers, some seventy of them, himself![3] And it was here, far from honors, preferment, and culture in its finest sense, that he wrote all the hymns that have made him famous around the world—hymns that almost chart his spiritual biography: "Jesus, I My Cross Have Taken" (1824), with its hints of his early feeling about Brixham ("perish every fond ambition, all I've sought, or hoped, or known . . ."), "Praise My Soul, the King of Heaven" (1834), and "Abide with Me . . ." (1847).

Haeussler notes that this "lovely hymn of adoring praise, tender yet jubilant in manner and mood,"[4] was chosen by Princess Elizabeth to be sung at her wedding to Philip, Duke of Edinburgh, at Westminster Abbey in November 1947, the centenary anniversary of Lyte's death; and Routley adds that it has been used at almost every type of Christian gathering.[5] In addition to frequent use as a hymn in worship, the author has used it as a call to worship, and though less illustrious than the English sovereign, also had it sung as the processional at his wedding!

As a "free paraphrase of Psalm 103,"[6] which Routley calls "the most evangelical of the psalms, in which God looks most like Christ,"[7] it certainly does capture its spirit, which was Lyte's full intention.[8] Let us examine this objective, outward-looking hymn, speaking of God and His works, in some detail:

Stanza One: Though the psalmist calls on "angels" (vs. 20), "hosts" (vs. 21), and "all His works" (vs. 22) to bless the Lord, he begins with himself (vs. 1); here "bless" becomes "praise," and "Lord" becomes "King of heaven," with our tribute, which we lay at His feet, being our very praises themselves! And, with my/our "iniquities pardoned, diseases healed, life redeemed, being crowned with loving kindness and compassion, and (earthly) years satisfied with good things," to boot! (vss. 3–5), how could I not respond as one who is "ransomed, healed, restored, forgiven"?

Stanza Two: Here Lyte reflects on God's dealings with His people and their leader, having made known His more intimate ways to Moses, His more objective actions to Israel the nation (vss. 6–7); to "our fathers in distress" He extended His "grace and favor," was "slow to chide and swift to bless" (how often we reverse those in our dealings with the wayward!), and, even more, He was—and still is—"glorious in His faithfulness" (Lamentations 3:23). It is true that "the shape of life is determined not by what we deserve, but by God's forgiveness, and His grace."[9]

Stanza Three: The Father-like regard of God our Shepherd comes in here (vss. 13–14); Lyte focuses on God's tender care and gentle bearing of us, for He well knows how ill we can afford rough treatment, feeble-framed as we are ("from dust thou art, to dust shalt thou return," Genesis 3:19). His "infinitely resourceful mercy fashions anew our lives at each point."[10] Temple relates this to Lyte's place of service, saying,

> The Brixham fisherman are famous for their gallantry and daring in the stormy waters of the Atlantic fishing grounds, and this hymn's line "Fatherlike, He tends and spares us, for well our feeble frame He knows" has something of the tenderness of strong men in dangerous places.[11]

Stanza Four: Finally Lyte, recalling the charge of the psalmist (vss. 20–22), soars beyond the merely timebound and seeks help from another sphere; since they, the angelic host, do indeed "behold Him face to Face," see Him clearly in unclouded day, we need their help to adore Him in a fuller way. And all creation, including the natural world, comes in to add its complementary voice to praise the God of grace—first, last, and always, the God of mercy and of grace! Again Temple says, "In one grand sweep the writer brings the whole created universe into the act of praise—Angels, help us to adore Him."[12] And Bailey concludes:

> It is wonderful to see what ten years of work in little Brixham did for Lyte. Contrast the near-despair of "Jesus, I my Cross Have Taken" with the exultation of this hymn. . . . Self-pity . . . has changed to thankfulness that God in His mercy has enabled him to rise to the challenge of a great task. "Ransomed, healed, restored, forgiven"—these words have in them the ring of a man who has climbed out of despair into sunshine and selfforgetfulness. Ill-health still dogs his steps, "well our feeble frame He Knows," and every down curve somehow flattens out and then rises. No wonder his own praise seems so inadequate that he calls upon angels and heavenly bodies to join in his "Alleluia." THIS IS CHRISTIAN LIFE AT ITS BEST AND FULLEST.[13]

It remains only for us to speak of Sir John Goss (1800–1880), composer of the "soaring" tune associated with this hymn and written especially for it.[14] Goss was one of two outstanding organists to play in St. Paul's Cathedral in the nineteenth century, and after serving there for thirty-four years, he was followed by the other, John Stainer. He wrote a voluminous number of anthems, hymn settings, chants, and the like; published several musical volumes, including one that ran through thirteen editions and was used at the Royal Academy of Music, where he was professor of harmony for forty-seven years; was knighted in 1872; and was awarded a Doc. Mus. degree by Cambridge in 1876. He was a great man who served with quiet distinction; Stainer spoke of his humility, strong love of home and family ties, and genuine religious devotion.[15] Another witnesses that he always asked God's blessing on his anthems before beginning them, prefacing them with I.N.D.A. ("In Nomine Domini Amen")[16] and seeing them as sermons in music. Such a lofty view of his calling made him meticulous about just the right note or expression, sometimes delaying a work's completion for weeks until he was satisfied with the result![17] Kenneth Long's testimony concludes our study fittingly:

> As a composer . . . in an age of false values, appallingly bad taste, and shoddy workmanship he preserved high ideals and kept them untarnished. He maintained a well-ordered flow of clean worthy graceful music . . . with the best of it having proved enduring.[18]

Notes

1. Duffield, *op. cit.,* p. 282.
2. *Ibid.,* p. 283.
3. Bailey, *op. cit.,* p. 169.
4. Haeussler, *op. cit.,* pp. 56–57.
5. Routley, *Hymns and the Christian Faith,* p. 51.
6. Moffatt and Patrick, *op. cit.,* p. 10.
7. Routley, *op. cit.,* p. 52.
8. Bailey, *op. cit.,* p. 171.
9. Routley, *op. cit.,* p. 55.
10. *Ibid.*
11. Temple, *op. cit.,* p. 42.
12. *Ibid.,* p. 43.
13. Bailey, *op. cit.,* p. 171; emphasis added.
14. Moffatt and Patrick, *op. cit.,* p. 10.
15. Haeussler, *op. cit.,* pp. 679–680.
16. Stulken, *op. cit.,* pp. 548–549.
17. Barrett, *op. cit.,* p. 177.
18. Kenneth R. Long, *The Music of the English Church,* p. 352.

Title/Date	*"Praise the Lord, Ye Heavens Adore Him" (1801)*
Author	*Anonymous*
	Edward Osler (Stanza 3, 1836)
Composer/Tune	*John H. Willcox "Faben" (1849)*
	Franz Haydn "Austrian Hymn" (1797)
	Rowland H. Prichard "Hyfrydol" (1855)
Scriptural Basis	*Psalm 148*

Among the wretched social conditions of the early eighteenth century—which included gin drinking to the extent of a national curse and led to much of the crime and incredible poverty of the day, a brutal penal code (one could be hanged for 160 different offenses), debtors' prisons that make our prisons look like plush hotels, and a high infant morality rate (three out of four died before their fifth birthday)—was the "oldest profession in the world," which flourished scandalously and led to an incredible number of illegitimate births.[1] To care for these children, concerned Evangelicals established orphanages, or, as they were then termed, foundling hospitals. One such institution, founded by Captain Thomas Coram in 1738/1739 for abandoned children and after 1760 reserved for illegitimate children whose mothers were known, was known as the London Foundling Hospital.[2]

To help support this institution, various wealthy and talented people gave, either of their means or of their talents—and often of both. Handel, for example, gave a benefit concert to raise funds for it, and also supported it out of his own means; he then donated an organ for its chapel, played for its opening service in 1750, and then gave annual recitals of "The Messiah" as benefits for its support for many years thereafter.[3] Other musicians wrote both anthems and hymns to be used there; the children sang them at the morning service, led by trained voices, and could be seen dressed in their quaint costumes; many fashionable Londoners visited there, especially on Sundays. This hymn, which Routley calls "perhaps the finest of all children's hymns,"[4] was such a gift. Its author, unfortunately, remains anonymous; its third stanza, however, was written by Edward Osler, a distinguished English

All thy works shall praise thee, O Lord; and thy saints shall bless thee. Psalm 145:10

Stanzas 1-2, Anon, c. 1801   FABEN 8. 7. 8. 7. D.
Stanza 3, Edward Osler, 1836   John H. Willcox, 1849

1. Praise the Lord: ye heav'ns a - dore him; Praise him, an - gels, in the   height;
2. Praise the Lord, for he is glo-rious; Nev - er shall his prom-ise   fail:
3. Wor - ship, hon - or, glo - ry, bless-ing, Lord, we of - fer un - to   thee;

Sun and moon, re - joice be - fore him; Praise him, all ye stars and light.
God hath made his saints vic - to - rious; Sin and death shall not pre - vail.
Young and old, thy praise ex-press-ing, In glad hom - age bend the knee.

Praise the Lord, for he hath spo - ken; Worlds his might - y voice o - beyed:
Praise the God of our sal - va - tion; Hosts on high, his pow'r pro - claim;
All the saints in heav'n a - dore thee; We would bow be - fore thy throne:

Laws which nev - er shall be bro-ken For their guid-ance hath he made.
Heav'n and earth and all cre - a - tion, Laud and mag-ni - fy his Name.
As thine an-gels serve be-fore thee, So on earth thy will be done. A - MEN.

surgeon. It was first included in *Psalms, Hymns and Anthems of the Foundling Hospital,* published in 1796; however, this was one of several leaflets pasted into that earlier volume, so that it was probably not written until at least 1801.

Osler, after several years of practicing medicine, turned to religious and literary work, serving the famous Society for Promoting Christian Knowledge (S.P.C.K.) and becoming a distinguished hymnologist; he wrote over fifty hymns and fifteen psalms, all of which were published; "this doxology, which closes the hymn, is worthy of a place beside Bishop Ken's 'Praise God from Whom All Blessings Flow.'"[5]

"Faben," the tune chosen for use in the *Trinity Hymnal,* was composed by John Willcox (1827–1875), an American who was born a Southerner but died a Yankee, in Boston, where he'd been a talented organist and organ builder for many years; much of his music was written for Roman Catholic liturgies. This tune, among those most popular in the late nineteenth century, has simple patterns of rhythm and melody that are consistently developed, making them easy to sing; however, it should not be sung too fast or the short notes become too choppy and the effect of the whole is spoiled.[6]

Routley claims that this hymn was written to carry the tune "Austria";[7] another weds it with Wesley's "Alleluia";[8] McCutchan favors the tune "Hyfrydol," saying that it is "a very happy tune and an appropriate setting for such an exhilarating hymn, with its marked characteristic the simplicity of its melody, which, except for one note, is confined to the limits of a fifth–from 'do' to 'sol.'"[9] "Hyfrydol" was composed by Rowland Pritchard (1811–1887), the great Welsh revival preacher, while he was still in his teens! Music was his love, and his fine voice led many a congregation of singing Welshmen in song; included in his ministry was his compilation of songs for children as well as *The Singer's Friend,* a hymnbook for adults.

Let us examine this marvelous hymn of praise, based on Psalm 148, said to be "the most primitive and universal of the praise psalms, calling on all nature as it does, to join in praising and enjoying God";[10] all things, living and inanimate, have their ways of giving glory to God—in sound or in visible grandeur! Bernard of Clairvaux (1090–1153), writing of his brother's death, refers to some of the lines of this psalm:

God grant, Gerard, that I may not have lost thee, but that thou hast only gone before me; for, of a surety, thou hast joined those whom in thy last night below, thou didst invite to praise God, when suddenly, to the surprise of all, thou, with a serene countenance and cheerful voice didst commence chanting that psalm "Praise ye the Lord from the heavens: praise him in the heights. Praise ye him, all his angels; praise ye him all his hosts." At that moment, oh my brother, the day dawned on thee, though it was night to us; the night to Thee was all brightness.[11]

Stanza One: This is a paraphrase of parts of Psalm 148:1–12; there are mentioned a wide variety of creatures, weather conditions, and human beings. The hymn focuses not so much on the creation as on the Creator, and not so much on what He did as on what He said; it reminds me of Psalm 19! Moreover, while inanimate nature "praises" God involuntarily, man chooses to do so, being free in that respect. Routley says with a note of wistfulness:

> How wonderful would it be were our human praise as enduring as the hills and as inexhaustible as the waterfalls, and as innocent as the birds and as effortless as the wind.[12]

Stanza Two: As marvelous as God's creation is, His redemption is even more glorious, just as His power over a willful, rebellious man whose life is changed is far greater than creating winds, or waves, or even tornados! We are victorious as we are in Him, and all the powers of deepest darkness—sin, death, hell itself—cannot wrest us away from the security of His love! Now that Christ has come, bringing salvation, we see with new clarity; we are in contact as persons with our Maker, and we know, indeed, that "heaven and earth, and all creation laud and magnify His Name."[13]

Stanza Three: Osler's addition serves to call every believer—saints on earth as well as those who've gone on to their reward, young as well as old, human as well as angelic—to bring to our Lord worship, honor, glory, and blessing as our offerings, in a spirit of glad humility, on bended knee. And, to demonstrate that we are not just paying Him lip service, which is ever so easy to do, we are to *do* His will. We recall our Lord's solemn question, "Why call ye me Lord, Lord, and do not the things which I say"? and we call for him to search our hearts in the spirit of the psalmist:

> Search me oh God and know my heart;
> Try me and know my anxious thoughts;
> And see if there be any wicked [hurtful] way in me,
> And lead me in the way everlasting. (139:23–24, NASB)

A fitting prayer to close a hymn of praise!

Notes

1. Bailey, *op. cit.,* p. 73–75.
2. *Ibid.,* p. 140.
3. McCutchan, *Our Hymnody,* p. 35.
4. Routley, *Hymns and the Faith,* p. 4.
5. Covert and Laufer, *op. cit.,* p. 14.

6. *Ibid.*, p. 15.

7. Routley, *op. cit.*, p. 4.

8. Covert and Laufer, *op. cit.*, p. 15.

9. McCutchan, *op. cit.*, p. 35.

10. Routley, *op. cit.*, p. 4.

11. Covert and Laufer, *op. cit.*, pp. 14–15.

12. Routley, *op. cit.*, p. 5.

13. *Ibid.*

Title/Date	*"Praise to the Lord, the Almighty, the King . . ." (1680)*
Author	*Joachim Neander*
	Catherine Winkworth, trans. (1863)
Composer/Tune	*Stralsund Gesangbuch "Lobe den Herren" (1665)*
Scriptural Basis	*Psalm 103:1–6; Psalm 150*

Joachim Neander (1650–1680), the author of this "magnificent song of praise, perhaps the finest there is, when we consider the tune"[1] was born and died in the German city of Bremen. Though he tutored at the universities in both Heidelberg and Frankfort for several years, and then served as headmaster of the Reformed Church grammar school at Dusseldorf and as the assistant pastor of the Reformed Church there until his pietistic tendencies got him into trouble with the ecclesiastical authorities, he finally returned to Bremen in 1679, where he served as the assistant pastor of St. Martin's parish, from which he had begun his spiritual pilgrimage more than a dozen years earlier.

As we have seen before, terms originally used in derision often become "badges" of honor for their adherents: thus German Protestants began as "Protest-ants," rejecting the unfair terms of the Diet at Speier (Speyer) in 1529; English "Methodists" were called that because of Wesley's "methodical" small group emphasis and organization, which he found necessary to nurture new converts in their faith; and German pietists were so-named after the "collegia pietatis"—cottage prayer-meetings that Lutheran Pastor Spener held for Christian nurturing, Bible study, and hymn-singing. These became, in the eyes of the state church establishment, unauthorized and therefore suspect, if not downright dangerous religious gatherings. It was through the powerful Evangelical preaching of Undereyke, one of the young pastors influenced by Spener—whom Neander and several of his student friends had gone to hear, not to listen, but to "sit in the seat of the scoffers"—that Neander's own heart was stirred and his life changed.

Later, as the schoolmaster at Dusseldorf, his concern for the spiritual needs of the community led him to begin prayer-meetings, alter some practices in the school, and in general operate independently of the controlling

Bless the Lord, O my soul, and forget not all his benefits. Psalm 103: 2

Joachim Neander, 1680
Tr. by Catherine Winkworth, 1863

LOBE DEN HERREN 14. 14. 4. 7. 8.
Stralsund *Gesangbuch,* 1665
Arr. in *Praxis Pietatis Melica,* 1668

1. Praise to the Lord, the Al-might-y, the King of cre - a - tion!
2. Praise to the Lord, who o'er all things so won-drous-ly reign - eth,
3. Praise to the Lord, who doth pros - per thy work and de - fend thee!
4. Praise thou the Lord, who with mar - vel - ous wis-dom hath made thee,
5. Praise to the Lord! O let all that is in me a - dore him!

O my soul, praise him, for he is thy health and sal - va - tion!
Shel - ters thee un - der his wings, yea, so gen - tly sus - tain - eth!
Sure - ly his good-ness and mer - cy here dai - ly at - tend thee;
Decked thee with health, and with lov - ing hand guid - ed and stayed thee.
All that hath life and breath, come now with prais - es be - fore him!

All ye who hear, Now to his tem - ple draw near,
Hast thou not seen How thy de - sires e'er have been
Pon - der a - new What the Al - might - y will do,
How oft in grief Hath not he brought thee re - lief,
Let the A - men Sound from his peo - ple a - gain;

Join me in glad ad - o - ra - tion.
Grant - ed in what he or - dain - eth?
If with his love he be - friend thee!
Spread - ing his wings to o'er - shade thee!
Glad - ly for aye we a - dore him. A - MEN.

Reformed Church's Consistory (Board of Elders). This led to his suspension, and when later reinstated (on his promise that he would not persist in such activities) his role as assistant pastor had been taken away from him, thus creating not only some financial hardship but also much humiliation as he saw it as a demotion, over which he brooded. Tuberculosis eventually ended his life. The question is frequently repeated in church history: What is the proper balance between necessary ecclesiastical control, "doing things decently and in order," and the freedom of the Christian man to serve his Lord in a creative and unrestricted fashion? And the answer has yet to be determined, if indeed there is one answer for all times, people, and places!

Neander was an accomplished scholar, poet, musician, and theologian whose heart was warm toward God. He is generally accepted as the first poet of the Reformed Church in Germany[2] and as "the greatest of the Reformed hymn-writers,"[3] having written some sixty hymns, with nineteen of them set to his own chorale tunes.[4] Neander's

> love of nature was deep. No doubt his familiarity with the lovely Heidelberg region, the Rhine, the hills and valleys and streams of the Neanderthal region around Dusseldorf, turned his thoughts toward beauty as a revelation of God.[5]

Of his best hymns, those that have found their way into Lutheran and other hymnbooks, Julian writes:

> their glow and sweetness . . . their firm faith, originality, Scripturalness, variety and mastery of rhythmical forms, and genuine lyric character fully entitle them to the high place they hold.[6] [And of this hymn he says,] A magnificent hymn of praise to God, perhaps the finest production of its author, and of the first rank in its class.[7]

In its English translation, by Catherine Winkworth (1829–1878), it has become well known and widely used, with but few changes for well over a century. Winkworth, whom many count to be the foremost translator of German hymns (understanding as she did both the language and the people), was a devout Anglican with a warm pietism that expressed itself not in sentimentality but in genuine Christian concern, especially for the higher education of the young women of her day, which she ardently supported.[8] On the wall of Bristol Cathedral a tablet in her honor affirms that she "opened a new source of light, consolation, and strength in many thousand homes"[9] through her selfless labors. Her *Lyra Germanica* is a devotional classic.

The tune "Lobe den Herren," selected by Neander himself and universally wed to this hymn ever since, first appeared in 1665; its composer is unknown, although one authority credits it to Johann Flitner;[10] in its present form it comes from Cruger's *Praxis Pietatis Melica,* published in 1668.[11] It is greatly beloved as a German hymn, sung on many occasions of national celebration.

Let us examine this, "one of the most widely sung hymns of praise in the Church universal."[12]

Stanza One: One of the striking features that we observe immediately is the way Neander exhorts everyone to respond to his call to praise, including himself. Moreover, the Lord whom we are called upon to adore is not only the Almighty, the Creator, and the Ruler of creation—terms that suggest power and strength—but He is also our Healer and our Redeemer. These are concerns that Neander would sense personally, relating them to his own physical illnesses and to his spiritual empathy with those with whom he yearned to share the deep realities of Christ.

Stanza Two: Here there is a moving testimony both to God's sovereignty in human life ("oer all things so wondrously reigneth" and "granted in what he ordaineth") and to the fact of God's sheltering care in all its gentleness. His will thus becomes what I desire to do, as I find it to be "good, acceptable, and perfect" (Romans 12:1–2). Does Neander here also intend to comfort himself, believing that his desires have in fact been granted in so far as they were within God's will, even though that might have meant his dismissal from his beloved pastoral duties at Dusseldorf?

Stanza Three: As "a friend of God," a name often attached to pietists, he reminds himself that Almighty God will indeed "prosper his work and defend him" (from unwarranted criticism?), and will *daily* encompass his life with His goodness and mercy. Thank God, he doesn't have to depend on human agents who are cruel and insensitive, who may deal him crippling blows, for he rests on God's mercy!

Stanza Four: Again the figure of an eagle or a mother hen is used to express God's overarching care or succor, as it was earlier (vs. 2). God's wisdom, which had fashioned him and had given him health (which by now, 1679, was well-nigh gone), had guided his steps and relieved him in his many and prolonged grieving seasons. That unerring wisdom is another reason to praise the Lord!

Stanza Five: Here is a final summons for all to praise God, to adore Him gladly and forever. Not only does Neander exhort himself to such praise with everything he is and has, but he then calls every living thing—which would include all animate creation—to similar acts of devotion; and from His people, the redeemed community, will the final Amen resound. This indeed is a hymn of praise, from first to last, with thought that is simple, powerful, and straightforward! The author frequently sings it in the morning in order to "get into the day" with a joyful spirit!

Notes

1. Haeussler, *op. cit.*, p. 61.
2. Covert and Laufer, *op. cit.*, p. 9.
3. Haeussler, *op. cit.*, p. 814.
4. Bailey, *op. cit.*, p. 331.
5. *Ibid.*
6. Julian, *op. cit.*, p. 791.
7. *Ibid.*, p. 683.
8. Covert and Laufer, *op. cit.*, p. 9.
9. *Ibid.*
10. Haeussler, *op. cit.*, p. 62.
11. McCutchan, *op. cit.*, p. 90.
12. Haeussler, *op. cit.*, p. 61.

Title/Date	*"Sun of My Soul, Thou Savior Dear"* *(1820)*
Author	*John Keble*
Composer/Tune	*From Katholisches Gesangbuch "Hursley"* *(c. 1774)*
Scriptural Basis	*Psalm 139:12; Luke 24:29*

For more than a quarter century I benefited from the faithful daily prayers of an elderly Presbyterian minister Edwin Baker, and his wife, Fannie, who only recently went to be with our Lord Jesus, whom they served, first as missionaries with the China Inland Mission for fifteen years in northwest China; then as pastor and helpmeet of the Onondaga Hills Presbyterian Church in upstate New York for thirty-three years; then finally in a ministry of intercessory prayer and encouragement of young pastors, until in their nineties, they "lost themselves in the ocean of God's great love, in heaven above." This hymn, written by the shy, saintly John Keble (1792–1866), was Edwin Baker's favorite hymn, and it was he who first introduced me to it in our weekly prayer-meeting, back in 1958! Moreover, the Bakers' quiet but earnest faith, faith "as of a little child," certainly reflected the simple heart-cries of these lines. Apparently, there were two stanzas (which no longer appear in our hymnals) before the one with which the hymn now begins; they were:

'Tis gone! That bright and orbe'd blaze
Fast fading from our wistful gaze;
Yon mantling cloud has hid from sight
The last faint pulse of quivering light.[1]

In darkness and in weariness
The traveler on his way must press
No gleam to watch on tree or tower
whiling away the lonesome hour.[2]

This hymn was taken from Keble's monumental work, *The Christian Year*, published in 1827, a devotional manual whose

Yea, the darkness hideth not from thee; but the night shineth as the day: the darkness and the light are both alike to thee.   Psalm 139:12

HURSLEY L. M.

John Keble, 1820   Alt. from *Katholisches Gesangbuch*, Vienna, c. 1774

1. Sun of my soul, thou Sav - iour dear, It is not night if thou be near; O may no earth - born cloud a - rise To hide thee from thy serv - ant's eyes.
2. When the soft dews of kind - ly sleep My wea - ry eye - lids gen - tly steep, Be my last thought, how sweet to rest For ev - er on my Sav - iour's breast.
3. A - bide with me from morn till eve, For with - out thee I can - not live; A - bide with me when night is nigh, For with - out thee I dare not die.
4. If some poor wan - d'ring child of thine Have spurned to - day the voice Di - vine, Now, Lord, the gra - cious work be - gin; Let him no more lie down in sin.
5. Watch by the sick; en - rich the poor With bless - ings from thy bound - less store; Be ev - ery mourn - er's sleep to - night, Like in - fant's slum - bers, pure and light.
6. Come near and bless us when we wake, Ere through the world our way we take, Till in the o - cean of thy love We lose our - selves in heav'n a - bove. A - MEN.

purity, delicate poetic feeling, and apostolic spirituality . . . won the hearts of the educated and refined English people as no other book of sacred poetry has ever done.[3]

It went through ninety-six editions in Keble's own lifetime, selling in excess of three hundred thousand copies, and of it Thomas Arnold said, "There is nothing equal to it in the English language."[4]

There is herein expressed an obvious love of the natural world and delight in God's care; the lone traveler, pressing on his journey after dark, indeed entrusts himself to God's protection and guidance, but his thoughts move beyond concern for himself alone to concern for others: the sick, the poor, and the bereaved. And he moves from the natural or physical world to the spiritual.

Stanza One: Just as the sun on a cloudless day dispels physical darkness, so does our Savior dispel our spiritual darkness; clouds (of gloom or despair?) are not able to hide Him from our eyes. Tennyson, incidentally, also likened Christ to the sun; looking at a flower in his garden, he said, "What the Sun is to that flower, Jesus Christ is to my soul. He is the Sun of my soul!"[5]

Stanza Two: Just as the dew, falling on the grass in the evening, refreshes it, so sleep refreshes me, as my head is pillowed on His breast—but forever, not just for a few hours.

Stanza Three: Just as we cannot live without the sun (it brings warmth, light, sustenance), so we cannot live without His light, and we dare not die apart from Him who is Life and Light itself!

Stanza Four: Here Keble's pastoral heart shines through. In his close to thirty years of service as the vicar of the parish at Hursley he, no doubt, had occasion to work with many who had "spurned the Divine voice" and who were wandering from the fold; and his request that God's gracious work begin—or continue, as the case may be—so that such a one "no more lie down in sin" is a prayer breathed both by vicars and by parents times without number, and increasingly moreso in the treacherous world into which we send our "children"!

Stanza Five: Keble continues in his pastoral tone, seeking God's boundless blessings on the sick, the poor, and the bereaved—whose sleep, he asks, be as pure and undisturbed as that of a little infant. Keble himself knew of these afflictions firsthand: he and his wife Charlotte had cared for his invalid sister until she died; he had mourned the earlier loss of another sister and his father; and his life was lived within quite limited means, since he'd rejected several opportunities to take "larger livings" (i.e., parishes where the salaries were much larger than his £200), preferring to remain closer to his large family. The considerable royalties from *The Christian Year,* incidentally, were placed in a special fund for the restoration of the church at Hursley,[6] long before he became its vicar!

Stanza Six: A final prayer for God's daily blessing as we make our way through life, fulfilling our chosen responsibilities, "ready to give thanks and live, on the least that heaven may give,"[7] confident in the thought that the day will come when, in God's unveiled presence, we will experience His abundance—the ocean of His love, forever.

The tune "Hursley" apparently first appeared in a Vienna choral book, published around 1774; the arrangement for this hymn with which it is universally associated was made by William Henry Monk (1823–1889), the musical editor of *Hymns Ancient and Modern.* It is "a choice example of polyphonal sweetness in uniform long notes of perfect chord";[8] another advises:

This tune should not be sung slowly, but at a moderately quick tempo. . . .
Rising to a climax on the note D at the beginning of the last line; much of

its charm lies in the three repeated notes at the beginning of the first, second, and last lines, and in the fact that the rhythmic pattern in the first line is carried out with only slight modifications in all the other lines.[9]

John Keble has been characterized as quiet and shy, conscientious and unaffected, content to serve in an obscure little parish with a very modest living, a most lovable man who was one of the most influential Englishmen of his century. He graduated from Oxford with double first-class honors, a rare feat, at nineteen; had been selected to a fellowship at Oriel the year before, received his M.A. at twenty-one, and was ordained two years later, to serve for over a half century in Anglican parishes. Loyal to his communion and desirous of deepening the spiritual lives of his fellow Anglicans he prepared his literary masterpiece, *The Christian Year,* as a devotional manual to be used, daily, with the *Book of Common Prayer;* "marked by simplicity of expression, a genuine piety, and a quiet faith,"[10] it became a prized, much used, and deeply loved aid to the devotional life of the hundreds of thousands who came under its sturdy influence. Writes Prescott:

> I know of no body of uninspired poetry, where purity and power, where knowledge of Holy Scripture and knowledge of the human heart, where the love of nature and the love of Christ are so wonderfully combined. [And adds Canon Barry] It is a book which leads the soul up to God, not through one, but through all of the various faculties which he has implanted in it.[11]

And it was originally published anonymously! That fact itself says something about Keble's character; however, this humility was balanced by a sense of meekness of the Mosaic variety; if he believed he was right about an issue, "he was inflexible, and would take the toughest road necessary to accomplish what he believed to be the right course of action."[12] An indomitable spirit, when coupled with his brilliant mind and simple eloquence, made him hard, if not impossible, to best in controversy. He has been memorialized through the founding, in 1869, of Keble College at Oxford, a school erected on land he had donated for "a poor man's college"—though if its students were anything like Keble they would be poor in worldly goods alone, and could be a delight to teach!

Notes

1. Breed, *op. cit.,* p. 196.
2. Moffatt and Patrick, *op. cit.,* p. 35.

3. *Ibid.*, p. 390.

4. Haeussler, *op. cit.*, p. 739.

5. Hostetler, *op. cit.*, p. 19.

6. Haeussler, *op. cit.*, p. 740.

7. Bailey, *op. cit.*, p. 162.

8. Brown and Butterworth, *op. cit.*, p. 160.

9. Covert and Laufer, *op. cit.*, p. 162.

10. Haeussler, *op. cit.*, p. 739.

11. Duffield, *op. cit.*, p. 501.

12. Moffatt and Patrick, *op. cit.*, p. 115.

Title/Date	*"The Day Thou Gavest, Lord, Has Ended" (1870)*
Author	*John Ellerton*
Composer/Tune	*Clement C. Scholefield "St. Clement" (1874)*
Scriptural Basis	*Psalm 113:3*

The English Anglican Church has long taken pride in its ability to include a broad spectrum of theological beliefs and ecclesiastical practices within itself as a "Communion of the Saints"; in jest, one prominent Anglican characterized the three schools of thought in his church as "Low and lazy, Broad and hazy, High and crazy."[1] If Henry Lyte, with his warm Evangelical piety represented the Low Church ideal, and John Keble, with his strong commitment to ecclesiastical authority and the church year represented the High Church, John Ellerton, author of our present hymn, might be considered to represent the Broad Church, in that he did develop a strong interest in the working class and gave attention to issues we would consider to be social issues; however, it was true of him, as it has been of many others, that he combined in himself the best characteristics of all three, "the subjective piety of the Evangelical, the objective adoration of the High, and the intellectual freedom of the Broad"[2]—a truly unbeatable combination!

Ellerton (1826–1893), an honors graduate of Cambridge University, served over forty years as an Anglican clergyman in a series of mostly small country parishes. His work was characterized, in turn, by three concerns: first, serving Crewe Green, an industrial area southeast of Liverpool, he gave much attention to the needs of the poor, and became especially involved in their educational institution, the Mechanics Institute (roughly equivalent to our vocational high school) where he taught both English and scriptural history and served as its chief reorganizer administratively;[3] second, recognizing as he did the crucial role of singing in parish churches, he organized one of the first choral societies in the Midlands, The Choral Society of Nantwich;[4] third, and without question, his greatest contribution to his beloved church was his work as a hymnologist. He wrote or translated eighty-six hymns, several of which are still widely sung (ten are found in the *Trinity Hymnal*) and none of which he ever copywrited, saying that "if they were counted worthy

From the rising of the sun unto the going down of the
same the Lord's name is to be praised. Psalm 113 : 3

ST. CLEMENT 9. 8. 9. 8.

John Ellerton, 1870

Clement C. Scholefield, 1874

1. The day thou ga - vest, Lord, is end - ed, The dark - ness
2. We thank thee that thy church, un - sleep - ing While earth rolls
3. As o'er each con - ti - nent and is - land The dawn leads
4. The sun, that bids us rest, is wak - ing Our breth - ren
5. So be it, Lord; thy Throne shall nev - er, Like earth's proud

falls at thy be - hest; To thee our morn - ing hymns as -
on - ward in - to light, Through all the world her watch is
on an - oth - er day, The voice of prayer is nev - er
'neath the west - ern sky, And hour by hour fresh lips are
em - pires, pass a - way: But stand, and rule, and grow for

cend - ed, Thy praise shall hal - low now our rest.
keep - ing, And rests not now by day or night.
si - lent, Nor dies the strain of praise a - way.
mak - ing Thy won - drous do - ings heard on high.
ev - er, Till all thy crea - tures own thy sway. A - MEN.

to contribute to Christ's praise in the congregation, one ought to feel very thankful and humble."[5] Moreover, he served as editor for several important hymnals, including the final edition of *Hymns Ancient and Modern,* which above all others

> is dearest to the heart of the English Church; [in fact, it is] no exaggeration
> to say that his hand may be traced and his voice heard in every hymnbook
> of importance during the last thirty years before his death.[6]

Of his interest in hymns, which Bailey[7] refers to as a "consuming passion," evidence is abundant; on his deathbed, for example, though he was only half-conscious, hymn lyrics flowed from his lips almost unceasingly.

Now let us examine this hymn, which John Julian speaks of as "elevated in tone, devotional in spirit, elegant in diction,"[8] a hymn originally written as a missionary hymn, stressing the worldwide outreach of the church universal. In Ellerton's day it was boasted that "the sun never sets on the Union Jack." Daniel Webster, whose speeches were widely read in England, has this famous passage:

> A power which has dotted over the surface of the whole globe with her possessions and military posts, whose morning drumbeat following the sun, and keeping company with the hours, circles the earth with one continuous and unbroken strain of the martial airs of England.[9]

And it is surmised that this may have been the source of Ellerton's inspiration for all or at least part of this hymn. For in a much greater sense it is true that the sun never sets on the church of Jesus Christ! Whether it be a small rural chapel, an inner-city mission, a thatched-roofed hut, a suburban church replete with gymnasium, or a stately cathedral, all are part of that church universal. For as the Christian faith is neither provincial nor nationalistic, its church is a worldwide fellowship as no other organization can ever hope to be. So it is little wonder that Queen Victoria chose this hymn to be sung at the Diamond Jubilee Service in 1897[10]—and sung it was in tens of thousands of churches throughout the world.

Based on Psalm 113, Ellerton's hymn celebrates this universal praise of God by His people: it begins at daybreak, as the hymns, extolling God and His wondrous works on our behalf, rise from the lips of countless believers one after another; prayers likewise continue to be lifted throughout the day to God's throne, a throne which—unlike the time-bound thrones of earth's proud empires—will "not only not pass away" but will be ever-growing, until all are under its rule. Moreover, this constant watchfulness of the church is made possible as the earth "rolls onward into light," day succeeding night and night following day in a natural pattern.

There is, of course, "a marked difference between earthly empires and God's kingdom, the difference between the transitory and the abiding, the temporal and the eternal";[11] therefore, in considering this as a missionary hymn, P. T. Forsyth, in 1899, reminded us that reaching the world for Christ would inevitably involve suffering, not just "glory"; he wrote:

> You cannot separate the mission and the Passion in Universal Christianity. There is no world Crown without the Cross. Let us go back to the holy, tender sacrifices of the Father's Cross, and the contagious obedience of the beloved Son. [Referring to the suffering, and premature deaths of over half of all the missionaries who went abroad, he then said,] I think my

life a piece of disheartening self-indulgence when I read missionary biography and track its quavering red line of apostolic succession from the beginning until now.[12] [So,] let this hymn be sung always at the foot of the Cross . . . which is *the* mission from God to man, and all will be well.[13]

As indicated earlier, Ellerton had a real heart for people, and sought to do his "missionary" work in an industrial city, then in obscure rural parishes, where for all of his brilliance and gifts he would receive little earthly recognition and even lesser financial rewards. In this missionary hymn is reflected something of the vision and passion of his heart; Temple affirms that "if a singer sings what he believes, a sharp test of hymn writing, [then] Ellerton passes with high credit."[14]

The tune "St. Clement" was written expressly for these words by Clement Cotterill Schoefield (1839–1904), a self-taught musician, hymn tune-composer, and clergyman, who served for a decade as chaplain of Eton College. It was possibly named in honor of Clement Marot, the French psalm-writer whose metrical version of the Ten Commandments appeared in the French psalter of 1549.[15] It first appeared in a collection of *Church Hymns and Tunes,* published by Sir Arthur Sullivan in 1874;[16] he is the Sullivan whose fame was secured in the Gilbert and Sullivan light operas; he also wrote the tune for "Onward Christian Soldiers."

As one contemplates the simple truth of this hymn, with its series of vivid pictures and its obvious love of nature, as Julian points out,

> Unlike many writers who set forth their illustrations in detail, and then tie to them the moral which they are to teach, Ellerton weaves his moral into his metaphor, pleasing the imagination and refreshing the spirit together.[17]

And so it is—a delightfully refreshing hymn to sing, and to ponder, and then to translate into genuine personal action!

Notes

1. Haeussler, *op. cit.,* p. 643.
2. Moffatt and Patrick, *op. cit.,* p. 328.
3. *Ibid.*
4. Haeussler, *op. cit.,* p. 644.
5. Moffatt and Patrick, *op. cit.,* p. 329.
6. Smith, *op. cit.,* p. 132.
7. Bailey, *op. cit.,* p. 426.
8. Julian, *op. cit.,* p. 328.
9. Haeussler, *op. cit.,* p. 103.

10. Bailey, *op. cit.*, p. 427.
11. Haeussler, *op. cit.*, p. 104.
12. Routley, *Hymns and the Faith*, p. 260.
13. *Ibid.*, p. 261.
14. Temple, *op. cit.*, p. 103.
15. McCutchan, *Our Hymnody*, p. 83.
16. Covert and Laufer, *op. cit.*, p. 59.
17. Haeussler, *op. cit.*, p. 644.

Title/Date	*"The King of Love My Shepherd Is"* *(1868)*
Author	*Sir Henry W. Baker*
Composer/Tune	*John B. Dykes "Dominus Regit Me"* *(1868)*
Scriptural Basis	*Psalm 23*

In this hymn Sir Henry Baker (1821–1877) has exhibited "the grace of a modern Romantic poet, in transforming a Hebrew Psalm—the most beloved of all those psalms—into a Christian rhapsody";[1] moreover, while the paraphrased version found in the Scottish psalter of 1650 and possibly written by Francis Rous (*Trinity Hymnal,* p. 77), is the most widely used version,[2] this one would certainly not be far behind in usage or popularity, owing at least in part to Baker's ability to fuse "the old and the new, metaphor with parable, the physical with the spiritual, the Judaic with the ecclesiastical, well-nigh a work of genius."[3] The author remembers, with considerable pleasure, having sung this in its anthem form, written by Harry Rowe Shelley,[4] as a high school student in the Presbyterian church choir; his friend Nancy Murchie, possessor of a fine alto voice, sang the opening alto solo—for the first time in practice—and sang it so well that the choir broke into spontaneous applause, much to her embarrassment!

Baker, ordained to the Anglican ministry in 1844, became vicar of the parish of Monkland in 1851, a parish so named because it had originally been the site of a twelfth-century Norman monastery, with its priory church, which he had restored in 1866. His entire ministry there lasted over a quarter century; the quiet parish, in its lovely rural setting, provided him with the peaceful serenity and seclusion necessary for him to realize his greatest ambition, the publication in 1861 of *Hymns Ancient and Modern,* which he served as

Editor Supreme, captain of men under him, ruthless hymn-mender and adjuster, a man of tremendous power, and yet of tremendous tenderness;[5] [one contributer, chagrined and dismayed by Baker's editing of work he'd submitted, commented that] H. A. and M. meant hymns asked for and mutilated, [but time has vindicated Baker's judgment!].[6]

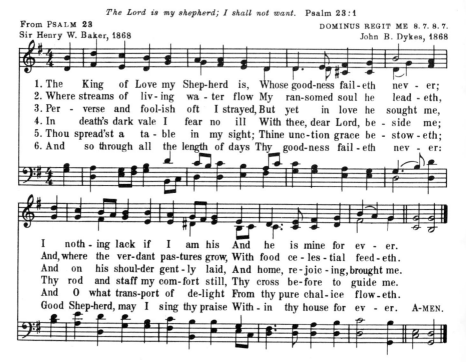

The Lord is my shepherd; I shall not want. Psalm 23:1

From PSALM 23   DOMINUS REGIT ME 8. 7. 8. 7.
Sir Henry W. Baker, 1868   John B. Dykes, 1868

1. The King of Love my Shep-herd is, Whose good-ness fail-eth nev-er;
2. Where streams of liv-ing wa-ter flow My ran-somed soul he lead-eth,
3. Per-verse and fool-ish oft I strayed, But yet in love he sought me,
4. In death's dark vale I fear no ill With thee, dear Lord, be-side me;
5. Thou spread'st a ta-ble in my sight; Thine unc-tion grace be-stow-eth;
6. And so through all the length of days Thy good-ness fail-eth nev-er:

I noth-ing lack if I am his And he is mine for ev-er.
And, where the ver-dant pas-tures grow, With food ce-les-tial feed-eth.
And on his shoul-der gent-ly laid, And home, re-joic-ing, brought me.
Thy rod and staff my com-fort still, Thy cross be-fore to guide me.
And O what trans-port of de-light From thy pure chal-ice flow-eth.
Good Shep-herd, may I sing thy praise With-in thy house for ev-er. A-MEN.

The immense popularity of this hymnbook, used at its peak by over 15,000 churches and chapels in England and Wales, the official hymnal of their Army and Navy, having sold over 60 million copies,[7] has been widely attributed to Baker's ability to "accurately diagnose the needs of the Anglican Church and with the skill of a master, to provide for them."[8] An interesting note: this book had on its spine "Hymns A M"; one indignant editor demanded, for his library, the "other volume," Hymns N–Z![9]

But Baker was not just a hymnologist; he was also a beloved pastor caring for his flock even as the Shepherd, of whom he wrote; as a High Churchman, he was a convinced celibate, but his tender care for his people can be seen in the book of prayers he wrote and published for them, *Family Prayers for the Use of Those Who Have to Work Hard!*[10]

Of all his hymns—many of which are still found in various hymnals and two others still widely sung ("Lord, Thy Word Abideth" and "Of the Father's Love Begotten")—this is his finest; as he lay dying, Ellerton says that he was repeating its lines "perverse and foolish oft I strayed, but yet in love He sought me, and on His shoulder gently laid, and home rejoicing, brought me";[11] and Julian adds "This tender sadness, brightened by a soft, calm peace, was an epitome of his poetical life."[12]

John Bacchus Dykes (1823–1876), eminent hymn tune-composer—fifty-five of his appeared in *Hymns Ancient and Modern*—wrote this tune especially for this hymn, which was included in the 1868 Appendix to *Hymns Ancient and Modern,* and it was later sung at his own funeral in 1876. Dykes, a superb musician, was also a clergyman; awarded a Doc. Mus. in 1861 by Durham University, he spent himself, serving his parish, writing, and composing over three hundred tunes. Benson writes that he, along with several others,

> crystallized the musical tendencies of the time into a definite form of Anglican hymn tune, with restrained melodies and close harmonies wonderfully adapted to liturgical worship and yet appealing to the taste of the people.[13]

Of this tune, a "beautiful and vivid interpretation of the fearless Shepherd, ready to dare any peril for his sheep," H. Augustine Smith says:

> The melody is pronounced, giving opportunity to bring out clearly and strongly the emphatic words or syllables, such as "King," "Shepherd," "goodness," "never," "nothing," "he," "forever" in the first stanza. It has a descending note, suggesting the genuine restfulness of this great hymn of trust. Its rhythm is even and steady, fitting the syllables in a remarkable manner, while its harmony is rich, with unusual strength of movement in the inner voices.[14]

And another adds,

> the music . . . fits the thought of each stanza. The melody is scalewise and flows along evenly with just enough rhythmic variety to avoid monotony and still maintain the quiet thought of spiritual confidence. . . . It is also interesting to note that each of the four harmonic parts has motion and vitality and, except in the last line where the bass has one full measure on the dominant, there is no monotonous repetition.[15]

Now let us examine this hymn, which Ellerton once described as "perhaps the most beautiful of all the countless versions of Psalm 23,"[16] and which Erik Routley claims is still "the favorite version of Psalm 23 among the English people, a source of endless inspiration, and the cream of Baker's work."[17]

Psalm 23 is probably the best known and best loved poem ever written. Where is there any other work of art—painting, sculpture, music, or architecture—that has entered into the hearts and minds of such diverse people, and lingers so long in our human memories? As H. Augustine Smith observes,

As a precious treasure its beauty has glowed in tent and tabernacle, cottage, camp, palace and Temple these three thousand years and more. It blossoms perennially in all earth's languages, translated or paraphrased more than any other piece of literature. It comes down through English history rendered variously by such leaders as Alfred the Great, Milton, King James I, Lord Byron, and by innumerable peasants, clerks and courtiers, changing as the language has changed, yet bearing always the same sure and joyful faith in the Good Shepherd.[18]

As we examine Baker's hymn we note, immediately, that he has transformed this Hebrew psalm into a thoroughly Christian hymn; there are references to, or traces of the parable of the Good Shepherd (vs. 6; John 10), the River of the Water of Life and Food Celestial (vs. 2; Revelation 22), the Parable of the Lost Sheep (vs. 3; Luke 15); the Shepherd's rod becomes the cross (vs. 4), the unction grace is the anointing of the Spirit and with oil (vs. 5; James 5); the pure chalice is the cup of Holy Communion (vs. 5); finally, "thy house forever" is the church, redeemed believers saved by His grace, provided for and secure forever (vss. 6, 1).

Adjectives are used throughout with striking effect: "living" water, "ransomed" soul, "verdant" pastures, "celestial" food (vs. 2); "gently" laid—no rough treatment for even the perverse, the rebellious, let alone for the foolish (vs. 3); "dark" vale (vs. 4); "pure" chalice (vs. 5); "Good" Shepherd (vs. 6). Moreover, affirmation of the singer's well-being is strong, so "never" faileth, "nothing" lack (vs. 1); "no" ill (vs. 4); "never," "forever" (vs. 6).

Just as David saw and knew the Lord as his Shepherd in his work as a shepherd, amid dangers, cold, heat, and monotony, so we are to similarly find our confidence in our Shepherd in our labors as undershepherds! Routley sees the message of this hymn as a judgment on the modern church. Just as the shepherd was a host, providing food and drink, and a refuge, providing shelter, safety, and security, so he sees the church as

the host par excellence; there you most fully enjoy the shepherd's care and the Lord's hospitality; that's what the Lord meant the Church to be—a place of hospitality where the stranger would feel welcome, where he'd find warmth, friendship, grace, power, redemption, comfort, sustenance.[19]

Notes

1. Bailey, *op. cit.,* p. 364.
2. *Ibid.,* p. 16.
3. *Ibid.,* p. 364.
4. Wienandt and Young, *op. cit.,* pp. 339–340.

5. Smith, *op. cit.,* p. 36.

6. McCutchan, *op. cit.,* p. 373.

7. Benson, *op. cit.,* pp. 510–511.

8. Moffatt and Patrick, *op. cit.,* p. 258ff.

9. Temple, *op. cit.,* p. 104.

10. Moffatt and Patrick, *op. cit.,* p. 258ff.

11. Duffield, *op. cit.,* p. 525.

12. Julian, *op. cit.,* p. 107.

13. Benson, *op. cit.,* p. 521.

14. Smith, *op. cit.,* p. 395.

15. Covert and Laufer, *op. cit.,* p. 114.

16. Stulken, *op. cit.,* p. 484.

17. Routley, *Hymns and the Faith,* pp. 63–68.

18. Smith, *op. cit.,* p. 393.

19. Routley, *op. cit.,* p. 68.

4

Singing in Worship:
"As You Sing Hymns . . ."

Hymns comprise the second of Paul's three categories of music that he urges believers to sing, both to glorify God and to edify one another. We have previously indicated that these are understood to have been either scriptural passages, such as the "Magnificat" and the "Benedictus" from Luke, or specifically written "hymns of praise to Christ." St. Augustine, in his commentary on the second book of Psalms (Psalms 42–72), wrote:

> Hymns are praises of God with singing. If there be praise, and not praise of God, it is not a hymn. If there be praise, and praise of God, and it is not sung, it is not a hymn. It is necessary, therefore, if it be a hymn, that it have these three things: both praise, and praise of God, and that it be sung.[1]

Another, more comprehensive definition of a hymn is this one, adopted some years ago by the Hymn Society of America:

> A Christian hymn is a lyric poem, reverently and devotionally conceived, which is designed to be sung and which expresses the worshipper's attitude toward God, or God's purposes in human life. It should be simple and metrical in form, genuinely emotional, poetic and literary in style, spiritual in quality, and in its ideas so direct and so immediately apparent as to unify a congregation while singing it.[2]

Erik Routley, in his characteristically casual way, says that a "hymn, basically, is an opportunity for a congregation to declare its experience and to rejoice in Christian doctrine, corporately."[3]

A study of these three statements yields several important criteria by which a hymn is to be defined. First, hymns focus the attention of the worshipper on God, in a spirit of reverence, adoration, and praise; second, hymns are poetic and literary in style—at least the truly great ones, those worthy of being sung, are. As Benson writes,

After all, beliefs of the first rate in influence receive, and I have the impression, always have received their best and final embodiment in poetry, and especially in lyric poetry.[4]

Third, hymns are to express genuine emotion; they belong "with the things of the spirit, in the sphere of religious experience and communion with God."[5] And while some authorities have scorned the individualistic emphasis in even the greatest hymns, like Wesley's "Jesus, Lover of My Soul," Lyte's "Abide with Me," and Keble's "Sun of My Soul," Patrick points out to the contrary:

> Many hymns that are individualistic in expression utter universal feelings, and doubtless do it better because their sentiments are intensely personalized.[6]

Fourth, hymns are to be *sung,* and they are to be sung by a congregation together; this of course does not preclude singing the parts in harmony, but rather emphasizes the common voice of the people being lifted to God. It is indeed this characteristic, as Benson points out, that makes the "Congregational Hymn . . . thus distinctively, the child of the Reformation."[7]

Breed contributes a helpful list of qualities both for a true hymn and for a good hymn tune. Among the qualities of a true hymn he lists the following:[8]

(1) "It is Scriptural both in sentiment and in expression," that is, it expresses both the truth and the spirit of its scriptural basis.

(2) It is devotional; there is within it a "God-ward motion, expressing profound reverence"; it "brings God to mind," and thus is worshipful.

(3) It is lyrical; it must be sung; it must be better when set to music than if merely read!

McCutchan[9] notes that great hymns, while expressing profound truths, use primarily monosyllabic or disyllabic words. For example, in Wesley's "Jesus, Lover of My Soul," of the 188 words in the 4 most commonly used stanzas, 157 are one syllable, and most of the others, 2 syllables; in Watts's "Our God, Our Help in Ages Past" there are 113 words in the 5 stanzas, of which 91 are one syllable and 17 are 2 syllables; and in Lyte's "Praise, My Soul, the King of Heaven," the 4 stanzas contain 152 words, of which 129 are one syllable and 17 are 2 syllables. As McCutchan observes, "not always are simple things great, but great things are always simple."[10]

Breed's criteria for a good hymn tune are the following:[11]

(1) It must be singable, that is, it cannot have too great a range so that most voices can easily reach the notes.

(2) It must be adapted to the words, that is, it must prove to be a good "fit," like a hand in a glove; one of the clearest illustrations of this would be Heber's immortal hymn, "Holy, Holy, Holy," wedded to Dyke's tune, "Nicea," which was written by him expressly for it.

(3) It must be sung at the rate it is written; it "should be neither dragged, nor raced."

(4) It should "avoid florid counterpoint, and difficult melodic intervals"; since the music is the vehicle of the words, it should complement and reinforce the message, not strive to overshadow it nor even to compete with it. It is instructive that Edmond Sears, who has been called "the representative of orthodoxy in Unitarianism" and who once wrote to Bishop Bickersteth "I believe and preach the divinity of Christ" and who consistently maintained this christological position in his scholarly writings, had very high regard for the role of the hymn in worship. He wrote:

> In our church service, the sermon consumates in the hymn . . . which makes the heart lyrical with the truth it sets forth. . . . The hymn should be a summing up of the sermon, helping us to take home its truth, and so carry it with us to fill our daily life with its melodies.[12]

I close with an interesting anecdote that shows a far different attitude toward hymns. Dr. Dearmer quotes a learned lawyer, speaking of an eminent judge, and showing his contempt for this recent musical invention, by saying of him

> 'Ere 'e comes, the 'oly 'umbug, 'umming 'is 'ymn!
> 'Ow I 'ate 'im![13]

Notes

1. McCutchan, *Hymns in the Lives of Men*, p. 23.

2. Haeussler, *op. cit.*, p. 1.

3. Donald Hustad, *Jubilate: Church Music in the Evangelical Tradition* (Carol Stream: Hope, 1980), p. 244.

4. Benson, *op. cit.*, p. vi.

5. *Ibid.*, p. viii.

6. Moffatt and Patrick, *op. cit.*, p. xvii.

7. Benson, *op. cit.*, p. 20.

8. Breed, *op. cit.*, p. 89–92.

9. McCutchan, *op. cit.*, p. 36.

10. *Ibid.*

11. Breed, *op. cit.*, p. 322ff.

12. Haeussler, *op. cit.*, p. 901–902.

13. Percy Dearmer, *Songs of Praise Discussed* (London: Oxford University Press, 1933), p. 123.

Title/Date	*"Abide with Me, Fast Falls . . ." (1820; 1847)*
Author	*Henry Francis Lyte*
Composer/Tune	*William H. Monk "Eventide" (1861)*
Scriptural Basis	*I John 3:24; Luke 24:29*

Considerable attention has already been given elsewhere in this book to the life and ministry of Henry Lyte, scholar, poet, musician, and hard-working curate, a man "of frail physique, with a face of almost feminine beauty, and a spirit as pure and gentle as a little child's";[1] but he had not always been such a saintly man, a fact to which he himself alludes in an omitted verse of this hymn before us now:

> Thou on my head in early youth didst smile;
>   And though rebellious and perverse meanwhile,
> Thou hast not left me, oft as I left Thee:
>   On to the close, O Lord, abide with me.[2]

When this hymn was "made public," he knew that the close of his earthly life was probably not far off. There is a question as to when this hymn was first composed, and the best solution to the puzzle seems to be as follows: In 1820, Lyte was visiting his old friend, William A. LeHunte, who was dying and who kept saying to Lyte, "Abide with me"; after leaving his bedside, Lyte wrote these verses and gave a copy of them to William's brother, and they were among his papers passed on to his nephew at his death. Years later, feeling that his own end was near, Lyte's mind reverted to these lines, and he apparently wrote them out again, giving them to his family on the evening of the balmy September Sunday in 1847, on which he had preached his farewell sermon and served his beloved Brixham congregation Communion for the last time as their pastor. As Haeussler comments finely of this hymn,

> It looks westward to a greater glory than that of the setting sun. It spans the present and the future and is radiant with anticipation and with trust.[3]

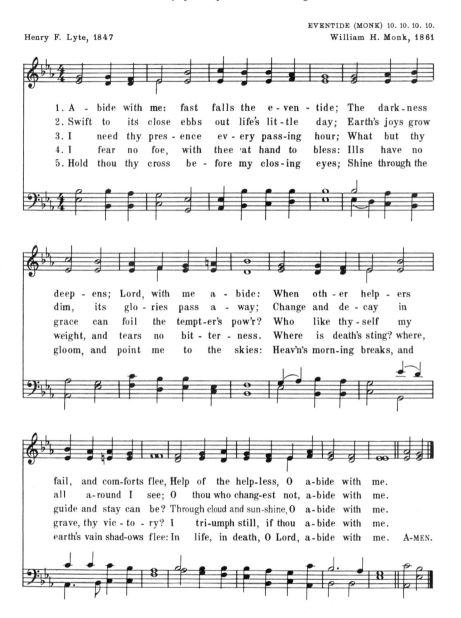

We know that he abideth in us, by the Spirit which he hath given us. I John 3:24

EVENTIDE (MONK) 10. 10. 10. 10.

Henry F. Lyte, 1847

William H. Monk, 1861

1. A - bide with me: fast falls the e - ven - tide; The dark-ness
2. Swift to its close ebbs out life's lit - tle day; Earth's joys grow
3. I need thy pres - ence ev - ery pass-ing hour; What but thy
4. I fear no foe, with thee 'at hand to bless: Ills have no
5. Hold thou thy cross be - fore my clos-ing eyes; Shine through the

deep - ens; Lord, with me a - bide: When oth - er help - ers
dim, its glo - ries pass a - way; Change and de - cay in
grace can foil the tempt-er's pow'r? Who like thy - self my
weight, and tears no bit - ter - ness. Where is death's sting? where,
gloom, and point me to the skies: Heav'n's morn-ing breaks, and

fail, and com-forts flee, Help of the help-less, O a-bide with me.
all a-round I see; O thou who chang-est not, a-bide with me.
guide and stay can be? Through cloud and sun-shine, O a-bide with me.
grave, thy vic - to - ry? I tri-umph still, if thou a-bide with me.
earth's vain shad-ows flee: In life, in death, O Lord, a-bide with me. A-MEN.

That entire month had been difficult for him; at his doctor's advice, urg-ing him to leave his charge and seek a more healthful climate, for whatever years were left to him, he cringed inwardly, saying,

I know no divorce I should deprecate more than leaving [my ocean]. From childhood it has been my friend and playmate, and I have never been weary of gazing on its glorious face. [But, forced to see the wisdom of that advice, he continues:] The swallows are preparing for flight, and inviting me to accompany them; and yet, alas! while I talk of flying, I am just able to crawl, and I ask myself whether I shall be able to leave England at all.[4]

But prepare to leave he did, and not without much personal suffering; reflected in his last sermon to his rough fisherfolk is his concern for their—not his—ongoing and eternal well-being. He said,

Oh, brethren, I can speak feelingly, experimentally on this point; and I stand before you seasonably today, as alive from the dead, if I may hope to impress upon you, and to induce you to prepare for that solemn hour which must come to all, by a timely acquaintance with, appreciation of, and dependence on the death of Christ.[5]

Lyte made his way south, hoping to reach Italy, but died shortly after he reached Nice, France; ministered to in his last hours by Henry Edward Manning, Lyte died pointing upward, smiling and whispering, "Peace, joy."[6] When George Baker, a clergyman from Philadelphia, went to see Lyte's grave in the English cemetery at Nice, he met a young man, weeping at the graveside, who told him that his own faith in Jesus Christ had been kindled through the words of "Abide with Me";[7] certainly Lyte's own desire which he had earlier expressed in these lines

O Thou, whose touch can lend
  Life to the dead, Thy quickening grace supply,
And grant me, swanlike, my last breath to spend
  In song that may not die.[8]

had been realized in this immortal hymn.
    While Lyte himself wrote a tune for this hymn, it was little used, because "it contained several very awkward intervals which made it difficult for inexperienced singers."[9] Lightwood tells us that the tune "St. Agnes" was originally composed for this hymn by J. Langran (1835–1909), a young composer who had been taught by the Frenchman, J. Baptiste Calkin (1827–1905); of Calkin he writes,

a painstaking and thoroughly conscientious teacher, and a polished performer, Calkin exerted a strong moral influence over the students who studied under him.[10]

The tune, however, that has made this hymn immortal, "too well-known and too-beloved to even need description, a tune that has brought consolation to countless hearts in their darkest hours,"[11] is "Eventide," written by William Henry Monk.

Monk (1823–1889), an eminent organist, composer, and professor of vocal music in King's College, London with a Doc. Mus. from Durham, who "taught many to praise God, who had never praised Him before, and others to praise Him more worthily than hitherto,"[12] was the first musical editor of what came to be the most widely used hymnbook in history, *Hymns Ancient and Modern,* first published in 1861 for the Anglican Communion. He wanted to include this hymn, but had no suitable tune for it, so he wrote this one! Some have said[13] he sat down and composed it in a few minutes. It seems to this writer far more likely that it emerged as his widow wrote:

> The tune was written in a time of great personal sorrow, when together we watched . . . the glories of the setting sun. As the last golden ray faded, my husband took up some paper and pencilled that tune which has gone all over the world.[14]

Monk's authority as music editor of *Hymns Ancient and Modern* was absolute, as was Sir Henry Baker's; one unhappy author, whose efforts were apparently either rejected or modified drastically, said that its popular initials "H.A.M." stood for "Hymns asked for and mutilated!"[15] But others write of Monk:

> being a man of deep religious conviction and devout feeling, he devoted his powers entirely to the enrichment and elevation of congregational worship music. The first thing in his mind in all church music was its value for worship. And the organ was to him an instrument, not for the display of skill [of which, incidentally he possessed considerable], but for touching the souls of men.[16]

Of this tune H. Augustine Smith has written:

> Eventide, almost a perfect hymn tune, has adaptation to the text, singable melody and parts, sound musical writing, and a haunting unforgettable quality. . . . It has much elasticity, bending to the softest and slowest breathings of "Hold thou thy cross before my closing eyes"; stretching and square-timbering to such challenges as "I fear no foe with thee at hand to bless," and "Where is death's sting, where, grave, thy victory!" It is all accomplished within the range of six tones and through a total of forty black and white notes.[17]

In other words, it is easily singable, a concern that Monk had for congregational singing of the highest order, and he saw to it that churches where he
directed music were hymn-loving and hymn-singing congregations. Temple
tells us that this hymn, with its contemplation on the transitoriness of life, the
soul's need for God, and the assured hope of a life to come, with its haunt-
ingly beautiful tune,

> solaced the explorer Lord Shackleton, as he lay dying in the antarctic
> snows; was played and sung as the *Titanic* sank, in 1912; was sung, regularly,
> by prisoners of war in a WWII Polish prison camp, with moving re-
> sponses; [and, that its] secret is its great simplicity, easily grasped and un-
> derstood by the ordinary man, regardless of his religious creed.[18]

Let us turn to an examination of it, relating it as we may, to Lyte's own
personal odyssey:

Stanza One: Beginning here, and carrying throughout the entire hymn,
the emphasis is singular and personal—each request or plea is for *my* Lord
to abide with *me*. Moreover, His companionship, desired all the time, is especially needed in the night seasons, when loneliness is most present. Routley says what many of us have experienced that "it is in the evening . . . that
the recluse is most haunted and the solitary most open to temptation."[19] And
if Lyte was using eventide here in a metaphorical sense, meaning the approach of death, as he well may have been, God's presence certainly is
needed as the tide of one's life is ebbing.

Stanza Two: Here there is the obvious contrast between this transitory
human life and God's eternality: life's day is indeed brief, and the joys and
glories of it are quickly fading; and even when it's just nostalgia for the "good
old days, and better ways of the past," there is still something unsettling about
change. So thanks be to God, for He is the stable, unchanging Reality,
whose Name is Faithful! As Hodson says, "we should sink into despair were
not our hope and peace rooted in the depths of His unchanging love; we
have comfort, for His arm is strong, and His heart is very wide."[20]

Stanza Three: Here is Lyte's heart-cry: "I *need* thy presence every passing
hour." Time does not stand still, though for the ill it may move ever so
slowly, and the great need of the invalid is for a reassuring Presence. The battle is more against the weakened believer, whose only resource is God's
never-failing grace—"Grace, 'tis a charming sound"; as Rendel Harris cried,
"Man's weakness leaning on God, its end can never miss."[21]

Stanza Four: Here Lyte deals with death, "the last decisive engagement in
the battle of life."[22] This is life's difficult side in that there are enemies, and
ills, and tears, and even the last great enemy, death; but the ills have no
weight, the tears are not bitter tears, and the enemies—even death—can be

viewed with sorrow and solemnity, but not with despair, loathing, and resentment: for He has conquered death, and He, "at hand to bless," still abides with me! As he lay dying Baxter cried, "I have pain . . . but I have peace, I have peace"; and A. J. Gordon's last word was "VICTORY."[23]

Stanza Five: With death conquered through our Lord's victory on the cross, the promise of eternal life in endless day shines brighter than any current gloom or shadows; the vision of the empty cross thus brings peace to every weary, troubled, burdened soul! Again, as Routley says,

> each time he closes his eyes at the end of a day, he can think, without fear, of the day when he will close them for the last time, and he need not fear![24]

We close this study with a pre-eighth-century prayer, a prayer which, had Lyte known it, could have been on his lips as he entered that land of eternal day:

> Jesus, our Master, do Thou meet us while we walk in the way, and long to reach Thy country; so that following Thy light we may keep the way of Righteousness, and never wander away into the darkness of this world's night, while Thou, who art the Way, the Truth, and the Life, art shining within us; for Thine Own Name's sake. Amen.[25]

Notes

1. Brown and Butterworth, *op. cit.,* p. 217.
2. Haeussler, *op. cit.,* p. 101.
3. *Ibid.*
4. Duffield, *op. cit.,* p. 8.
5. *Ibid.,* p. 9.
6. Haeussler, *op. cit.,* p. 778.
7. Duffield, *op. cit.,* p. 10.
8. H. A. Smith, *Lyric Religion,* p. 7.
9. Covert and Laufer, *op. cit.,* p. 46.
10. Lightwood, *op. cit.,* p. 195.
11. Covert and Laufer, *op. cit.,* p. 46.
12. Hostetler, *op. cit.,* pp. 25–26.
13. Brown and Butterworth, *op. cit.,* p. 219.
14. Lightwood, *op. cit.,* p. 496.
15. Moffatt and Patrick, *op. cit.,* p. 258.
16. *Ibid.,* p. 435.
17. Smith *op. cit.,* pp. 7–8.
18. Temple, *op. cit.,* pp. 54–55.

19. Routley, *Hymns and the Faith,* p. 171.

20. J. H. Hodson, *Hymn Studies* (London: H. R. Allenson, n.d.), p. 225.

21. *Ibid.,* p. 229.

22. Routley, *op. cit.,* p. 172.

23. Hodson, *op. cit.,* p. 229.

24. Routley, *op. cit.,* p. 173.

25. Hodson, *op. cit.,* p. 231.

Title/Date	*"All Glory, Laud and Honor"* (c. 820)
Author	*Theodulph of Orleans*
	John Mason Neale, trans. (1854)
Composer/Tune	*Melchior Teschner "St. Theodulph"*
	(c. 1615)
Scriptural Basis	*John 12:12–19; Mark 11:1–10; Psalm*
	24:7–10; Psalm 118:25–26

If it is argued, as I believe it can be, that the greatest hymns frequently cross ecclesiastical boundaries, this hymn is a case in point. Its words came from the mind and hand of a Roman Catholic bishop, its tune from the heart of a Lutheran choirmaster, composer, and clergyman, and its translation from Latin into beautiful English poetry from the skill of an Anglican High Church rector "whose memory is kept green by such hymn translations as this."[1]

Theodulph of Orleans (c. 760–821) lived in the age of Charlemagne, who was crowned Holy Roman Emperor in A.D. 800, and who sought to bring together the best elements of Roman civilization—literature, education, art, and law, with the Christian faith—and to offer these to the barbarous peoples over whom he ruled. Recognizing Theodulph, at the time abbott of a monastery in Florence,[2] to be an outstanding leader, a warm-hearted pastor, and a gifted poet, Charlemagne brought him to his court (c. 781), thereafter making him bishop of Orleans (in 785). Theodulph carried out extensive reforms, established schools, including free ones for poor children in his diocese, authored an important work on the Holy Ghost,[3] and wrote many beautiful hymns. Unfortunately, after Charlemagne's death (814), his son Louis the Pious faced a threat to his throne in the form of a plot by distant relatives; believing—though probably falsely—that Theodulph supported the plotters, Louis had him imprisoned in Angers (in 818), where he apparently died of poisoning in 821.[4]

It was while he was in prison that he wrote much beautiful devotional poetry, which formed the basis for this and other hymns. Originally a poem of thirty-nine couplets, Neale translated this hymn from a cento of twenty-four lines,[5] further reduced in our hymnal to three stanzas. There is a pious legend that on Palm Sunday, as the king and his retinue were on their way to Mass,

Blessed is the King of Israel that cometh in the name of the Lord. John 12:13

Theodulph of Orleans, c. 820
Tr. by John Mason Neale, 1854   ST. THEODULPH 7. 6. 7. 6. D.
St. 1, line 1; st. 2, alt. in *Hymns Ancient and Modern*   Melchior Teschner, c. 1615

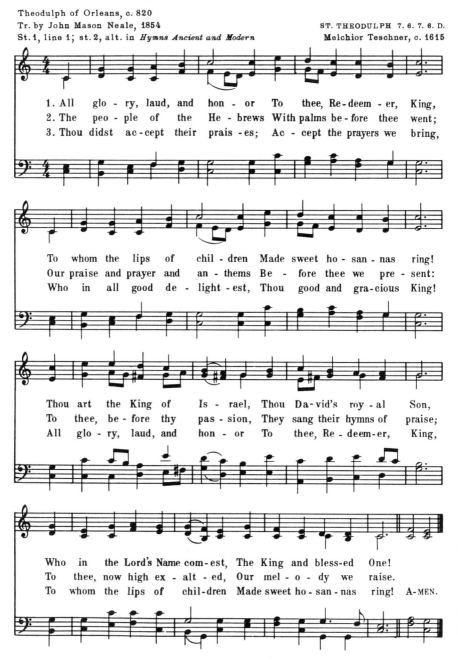

1. All glo - ry, laud, and hon - or To thee, Re - deem - er, King,
2. The peo - ple of the He - brews With palms be - fore thee went;
3. Thou didst ac - cept their prais - es; Ac - cept the prayers we bring,

To whom the lips of chil - dren Made sweet ho - san - nas ring!
Our praise and prayer and an - thems Be - fore thee we pre - sent:
Who in all good de - light - est, Thou good and gra - cious King!

Thou art the King of Is - rael, Thou Da - vid's roy - al Son,
To thee, be - fore thy pas - sion, They sang their hymns of praise;
All glo - ry, laud, and hon - or To thee, Re - deem - er, King,

Who in the Lord's Name com - est, The King and bless - ed One!
To thee, now high ex - alt - ed, Our mel - o - dy we raise.
To whom the lips of chil - dren Made sweet ho - san - nas ring! A - MEN.

they passed under the window of the cell in the monastery where Theodulph was imprisoned, heard him singing this hymn, and were so taken by it that the king had Theodulph released from prison and restored to his old bishopric; but that is only pious legend![6]

The chorale tune "St. Theodulph," now generally used with this hymn, was written by Melchior Teschner (1584–1635), a musician of considerable ability who was interested in enriching public worship through congregational singing. He composed it, originally, for a "hymn for the dying"[7] written during a time of pestilence by Valerius Herberger;[8] it was later used by Bach in his "St. John's Passion"[9] and with another hymn by Paul Gerhardt; Teschner, who was a Lutheran pastor and choirmaster as well as composer, is remembered chiefly for this tune.[10]

John Mason Neale (1818–1866), the "Prince of Translators," was himself an Anglican clergyman whose labors included serving as warden of Sackville College, a home for elderly men and women; by his day the buildings were dilapidated, so he sought to have them restored. He also introduced liturgical changes that reflected his High Church views, but for this he was maligned as a "Papist" and barred for thirteen years from holding services in his own chapel. Yet he gave himself unstintingly to his pastoral duties and to the work he loved best: translating the great Latin and Greek hymns, thereby making their treasures accessible to Christians in his day and ever since, a "contribution to hymnody which is unsurpassed."[11]

This hymn, "one of imperishable vitality,"[12] is a hymn for use, particularly—although not exclusively—on Palm Sunday, and especially as a processional hymn with its moving 7.6.7.6.D. meter. One of its verses, although part of Neale's original translation, is no longer sung, since some believe that a worshipping Palm Sunday congregation really deserves a better description than

> Be Thou, O Lord, the rider, And we the little ass,
> That to God's holy city together we may pass.[13]

Raby has reconstructed the great Palm Sunday celebration at Orleans, in the days of Theodulph; he writes:

> At the head of the procession were bourne the Gospels, . . . the Cross and the banners; then followed . . . Jesus seated on an ass, followed by a throng of people carrying branches and singing the Hosannas. When the gates of the city were reached, they were closed, the procession halted while the Gospel [lesson] was sung and a prayer was said for the city and its inhabitants. Then a choir of children sang, from the city walls, the "Gloria, laud

et honor"; the refrain was taken up by the crowd, the gates were opened, and the ceremony ended at the cathedral.[14]

Let us examine this hymn more closely:

Stanza One: As Jesus approached Jerusalem on Palm Sunday, announcing Himself as Israel's promised Messiah, he anticipated the cross on which He would accomplish the redemption of His people. As the Lion of the tribe of Judah, He was both David's son and anointed King; to this witnesses the hosannas "Lord, save us now!" of little children—either literally or a reference to His disciples, whose joyous testimony the Pharisees tried to stifle but to no avail (Luke 19:39–40).

Stanza Two: Just as the disciples had preceded Him with their palm branches and their praises, so we, as His current followers, raise our voices in concerted song. And we with far more reason than they, for we stand this side not only of the dark night of crucifixion, but also of the glorious morning of resurrection!

Stanza Three: Our King and our Redeemer, who is good and gracious, continues to receive "glory, laud, and honor"; but He also is One who delights in *all* that concerns us, even in the prayers we bring—even prayers for the mundane needs of life—and accepts these offerings as readily, we trust, as our praises. Thus, while Stanzas One and Two are declarations of fact, Stanza Three focuses on a simple request; for the sovereign God, who calls forth our praise also responds to our heartfelt cries for help!

Notes

1. Covert and Laufer, *op. cit.,* p. 57.
2. Haeussler, *op. cit.,* p. 940.
3. Bailey, *op. cit.,* p. 236.
4. Stulken, *op. cit.,* p. 207.
5. Haeussler, *op. cit.,* p. 189.
6. Moffatt and Patrick, *op. cit.,* p. 518.
7. Stulken, *op. cit.,* pp. 207–208.
8. Moffatt and Patrick, *op. cit.,* p. 518.
9. Smith, *op. cit.,* p. 16.
10. McCutchan, *Our Hymnody,* p. 163.
11. Bailey, *op. cit.,* p. 201.
12. Smith, *op. cit.,* p. 15.
13. Haeussler, *op. cit.,* p. 190.
14. Bailey, *op. cit.,* p. 238.

Title/Date	*"Brightest and Best of the Sons of the Morning" (1811)*
Author	*Reginald Heber*
Composer/Date	*James P. Harding "Morning Star" (1892)*
	Lowell Mason "Wesley" (1830)
Scriptural Basis	*Matthew 2:1–12*

Just two years before writing this hymn, Reginald Heber (1783–1826), the young pastor of the parish church in Hodnet, concerned to improve the hymn-singing of his staid Anglican congregation, wrote to a London publishing house:

> My psalm-singing continues bad. Can you tell me where I can purchase Cowper's *Olney Hymns* with the music, and in a smaller size, without music, to put into the seats? Some I greatly admire, and any novelty is likely to become a favorite, and draw more people to join in the singing.[1]

Unable, however, to solve his dilemma in this way, he resolved to prepare his own hymnal, so that he could wed the liturgy from the *Book of Common Prayer,* his sermon text, and his hymns for each Sunday of the ecclesiastical year. The fruits of these labors, which he carried on during the sixteen years of his ministry, were published, some in the *Christian Observer* (1811–1816) and the remainder, posthumously, in *Hymns Written and Adapted to the Weekly Service of the Year* (1827).[2] Of his many beautiful and stirring hymns—several of which are still widely sung (*Trinity Hymnal* contains seven of them)— Heber wrote:

> in these lyrics no fulsome or indecorous language has been knowingly adopted; no erotic addresses to Him whom no unclean lips can approach; no allegory, ill-understood and worse applied.[3]

As a poet, having won two major prizes for his Latin verse at Oxford; as a brilliant author, writing for *The Quarterly Review;* and, as an admirable lecturer, giving the Bampton Lectures on the Holy Spirit in 1815,[4] he

For we have seen his star in the east, and are come to worship him. Matt. 2:2

MORNING STAR 11. 10. 11. 10.

Reginald Heber, 1811   James P. Harding, 1892

1. Bright-est and best of the sons of the morn-ing,
2. Cold on his cra-dle the dew-drops are shin-ing;
3. Say, shall we yield him, in cost-ly de-vo-tion,
4. Vain-ly we of-fer each am-ple ob-la-tion,
5. Bright-est and best of the sons of the morn-ing,

Dawn on our dark-ness, and lend us thine aid;
Low lies his head with the beasts of the stall;
O-dours of E-dom, and off-'rings di-vine,
Vain-ly with gifts would his fa-vor se-cure;
Dawn on our dark-ness, and lend us thine aid;

Star of the East, the hor-i-zon a-dorn-ing,
An-gels a-dore him in slum-ber re-clin-ing,
Gems of the moun-tain and pearls of the o-cean,
Rich-er by far is the heart's ad-o-ra-tion;
Star of the East, the hor-i-zon a-dorn-ing,

Guide where our in-fant Re-deem-er is laid.
Mak-er and Mon-arch, and Lord o-ver all.
Myrrh from the for-est or gold from the mine?
Dear-er to God are the prayers of the poor.
Guide where our in-fant Re-deem-er is laid. A-MEN.

St. 2, line 4, alt.

demonstrated his keen intellectual prowess; and, as a parish pastor, he gave himself unstintingly, prompting Thackeray to pay him this tribute:

> the charming poet, possessor of all sorts of gifts and accomplishments . . . he was the beloved priest in his own home of Hodnet, counselling the people in their troubles, advising them in their difficulties, kneeling often at their sick beds at the hazard of his own life; where there was strife, the peace-maker, where there was want, the free giver.[5]

Of this last-named characteristic, his generosity, Bailey notes that

> his parents found it necessary to sew into the lining of his pockets the bank-notes given him for his half-year's spending money when he went away to boarding school, so that he might not give them away in charity on the road![6]

Twice he was offered the bishopric of Calcutta, a diocese that included all of India, Ceylon, and Australia! Both times he refused, preferring to stay where he was; but after being urged to reconsider, he accepted it as a call from God and responded. From his missionary heart came not only the enormous energy required to administer such a vast field of service, but also a keen and genuine interest in the spiritual nurturing of his wider flock, including as it did both many missionary-priests and thousands of native Indian Christians; and it was in this unstinting service that he met his untimely death, after only three years in India, leaving behind his widow and two young daughters.

His death occurred while he was in southern India,[7] in Trichinopoly, a center of Dravidic Brahmanism, near both the vile pagoda of Vishnu and the still viler shrine of Shiva, two of the three gods of the Hindu "trinity." That Sunday, April 2, 1826, he preached to an overflow congregation at St. John's Church, and baptized and confirmed forty-two native Christians—a thrilling experience for all to witness. After worship, he continued to minister, visiting the sick, writing letters, conducting evening prayers—all in the intense heat which sapped his energy even more. Arising early, and continuing administrative labors, he decided to take a bath in the large, cold pool; when his servant, alarmed, sought him out he found his body in the pool, probably the victim of a stroke; he was buried in the English churchyard there, where a memorial window commemorates his selfless life.[8]

It is fitting that "Morning Star," the tune to which this hymn is often sung, was composed by James P. Harding (1850–1911), a lover of children and a fine organist who wrote this especially for a children's festival at Gifford Hall Mission in 1892; this mission, located in one of the worst slum districts in

London, was one of the special concerns of both he and his brother Edmund; as benefactors of the unfortunate, one has written:

> These two men were magnificent specimens of the true gentleman, gifted
> . . . each in his particular way above the ordinary, possessing a charm of
> character unique, with wit and wisdom wonderfully united. They lived
> glorious lives, seeking ever the material and spiritual well-being of the
> poor.[9]

Of the tune itself, carol-like in its structure, with a well-curved melodic line, one writes:

> the absence of dotted notes makes it possible to sing it with flowing
> smoothness. The rhythm of each line of the music is the same, yet in this
> tune this does not produce monotony. It should not be sung too rapidly.[10]

Haeussler also discusses this hymn tune, indicating that music critics objected to the meter, which to them

> was too suggestive of a dance, appealing more powerfully to the feet than
> to the heart. [But he goes on to say, sardonically,] Just why God, who apparently accepted the praise of Israel when accompanied by cymbals and
> dance, should take special offense at a stately dactylic 11.10.11.10. meter
> was not made clear. [At any rate, since nothing inherently good can be indefinitely suppressed, this hymn] finally gained merited recognition.[11]

Let us examine this hymn, written originally for use on Epiphany Sunday, which celebrates the adoration of the Magi; the Gospel lesson for that day, from Matthew's Gospel, tells the story of their coming—guided by the star in the East—to adore the newborn King of the Jews.

Stanza One: Our attention is focused on the "Star of the East," which is "the brightest and best of the sons of the morning," an expression that comes from Job 38:7, where stars are personified as sons. This star functions as none other ever has, for it not only scatters darkness, brings beauty to the horizon, and gives guidance; it also leads us to our Redeemer.

Stanza Two: Here the poet's imagination adds some details not mentioned in the biblical account, but certainly consistent with it: dew drops sparkling on his cradle, beasts circled around Him (to provide warmth?), angels adoringly watching Him as He sleeps, recognizing that He is indeed Lord over all—the supernatural, as well as the natural world!

Stanza Three: Here, added to the biblical treasures of gold ("from the mine"), frankincense ("odours of Edom"), and myrrh ("from the forest"),

Heber offers gems dug out of the mountains (was he thinking of South Africa's diamond deposits?), and even pearls, harvested from the oceans around England's colonies!

Stanza Four: But, valuable as these gifts are, none of them will win us our Monarch's favor; indeed, they are vain or empty offerings compared to the one thing He really wants and deserves from us: the adoration of our hearts and the sincere prayers of those who are poor. Perhaps by this final phrase he is suggesting that, since apart from Him we are all poor, we have nothing of worth to bring Him except our devotion, our prayers? A beautiful adorning, with nature's images, of the straightforward Gospel story.[12]

Notes

1. Bailey, *op. cit.,* p. 144.
2. Smith, *op. cit.,* p. 145.
3. Duffield, *op. cit.,* p. 79.
4. Covert and Laufer, *op. cit.,* p. 53.
5. Smith, *op. cit.,* p. 145.
6. Bailey, *op. cit.,* p. 143.
7. Smith, *op. cit.,* p. 146.
8. Bailey, *op. cit.,* p. 146.
9. McCutchan, *Our Hymnody,* p. 153.
10. Covert and Laufer, *op. cit.,* p. 153.
11. Haeussler, *op. cit.,* p. 181.
12. Bailey, *op. cit.,* p. 146.

Title/Date	*"Christ the Lord Is Risen Today"* (1739)
Author	*Charles Wesley*
Composer/Tune	*Robert Williams "Llanfair"* (1817)
	From Lyra Davidica "Easter Hymn" *(1708)*
Scriptural Basis	*I Corinthians 15:55–57*

John Julian (1839–1913), the greatest authority on English hymns and hymn-writers, has declared that Charles Wesley was the greatest hymn-writer of all the ages, especially when one considers both quantity (well in excess of 6,500) and quality (many "rise to the highest degree of excellence");[1] he continues:

> Wesley's feelings on every important occasion, whether private or public, found their best expression in a hymn. His own conversion, his own marriage, the earthquake panic, the rumors of a French invasion, Prince Edward's defeat at Culloden, the Gordon riots, every Festival of the Christian Church, every doctrine of the Christian Faith, striking scenes in Scripture history, striking scenes (which he saw), the deaths of friends . . . all furnished occasions for the exercise of his divine gift. It would be impossible . . . even to enumerate those of his hymns which have become really classical, and his death alone stopped the course of the perennial stream from his pen![2]

High words of praise, indeed; but consider that even in the *Trinity Hymnal,* which represents a theological perspective considerably different from Wesley's in several important areas, the only writer who has more of his hymns included is Isaac Watts, something of a staunch Calvinist himself! Watts, Wesley's chief rival for the number one position among hymn-writers, has forty-one, and Wesley nineteen, even eclipsing that eminent Scottish Calvinist Horatius Bonar, who has seventeen! However, statistics aside, it is well to observe that all three of these godly men were men of deep faith and strong biblical convictions who, like the Apostle Paul, rejoiced in the mystery of Christian revelation; and of them it could be said that they "used almost entirely the language of the English Bible [which] gave them at once bounds

Thanks be to God, which giveth us the victory through our Lord Jesus Christ. I Cor. 15:57

Charles Wesley, 1739

LLANFAIR 7. 7. 7. 7. with alleluias
Robert Williams, 1817

1. "Christ the Lord is risen to - day," Al - - le - lu - ia!
2. Vain the stone, the watch, the seal; Al - - le - lu - ia!
3. Lives a - gain our glo - rious King; Al - - le - lu - ia!
4. Soar we now where Christ has led, Al - - le - lu - ia!
5. Hail, the Lord of earth and heav'n! Al - - le - lu - ia!

Sons of men and an - gels say; Al - - le - lu - ia!
Christ has burst the gates of hell: Al - - le - lu - ia!
Where, O death, is now thy sting? Al - - le - lu - ia!
Fol - lowing our ex - alt - ed Head; Al - - le - lu - ia!
Praise to thee by both be giv'n; Al - - le - lu - ia!

Raise your joys and tri - umphs high; Al - le - lu - ia!
Death in vain for - bids his rise; Al - le - lu - ia!
Once he died, our souls to save; Al - le - lu - ia!
Made like him, like him we rise; Al - le - lu - ia!
Thee we greet tri - um - phant now; Al - le - lu - ia!

In unison

Sing, ye heav'ns, and earth, re - ply; Al - le - lu - ia!
Christ hath o - pened Par - a - dise. Al - le - lu - ia!
Where thy vic - to - ry, O grave? Al - le - lu - ia!
Ours the cross, the grave, the skies. Al - le - lu - ia!
Hail, the Res - ur - rec - tion Thou! Al - le - lu - ia! A - MEN.

Harmony from *The Revised Church Hymnary* by permission of the Oxford University Press, London.

and freedom—the only freedom really worth having!"[3] Moreover, this source of truth, on which they constantly drew for their inspiration, provided them with inexhaustible treasures.

Charles Wesley (1707–1788), younger brother of John, with whom his name, ministry, and destiny were inevitably linked, was born in the Epworth rectory, the eighteenth child of Samuel, an Anglican clergyman, and Susannah, his remarkably gifted wife and daughter of a Nonconformist Divine; well-disciplined herself, she trained her children with all diligence. For example,

> they did not eat between meals; they were in bed by eight o'clock and expected to go to sleep, without any fuss; they learned the Lord's Prayer and used it regularly; said "brother," or "sister" to their siblings—i.e., Brother John, Sister Susannah; they read by their fifth year, and studied, with their parents as their teachers, six hours daily; Bible-reading and prayer were regularly and punctually attended to, and discipline was carried out, lovingly but firmly.[4]

As Duffield comments, "certainly the results are not discouraging to any who reflects on the process."[5] Where are the homes preparing the John and Charles Wesleys for the world today?

Their father, something of a poet himself, worked hard as a parish pastor, and added to his very meager income through writing devotional literature, but still had to spend several months in a debtor's prison because of debts incurred providing the bare necessities for his family.[6] This poetic gift he passed along to his sons, so that when their mother died, having asked them "Children, as soon as I am released, sing a Psalm of praise to God," they sang "Blessing, honor, thanks and praise," a hymn Charles had written previously for this very purpose.[7]

Another anecdote about Charles' early life in the near poverty-stricken Epworth rectory involves the offer of a wealthy Irish namesake to adopt him. But Charles, given the option, declined the honor; the lad taken in his stead became an Earl and grandfather to the Duke of Wellington,[8] while Charles, providentially, was spared material wealth so that his life could be used, so marvelously, to enrich the lives of countless millions!

Charles, who had accompanied his brother John to Georgia where he was to serve as Governor Oglethorpe's private secretary, while John was to serve the English (Anglican) colony at Savannah as their chaplain, apparently got into trouble through some adventurous but deceitful ladies, and had to return to England. Of this he wrote:

> I could not be more trampled on were I a fallen minister of state. The people have found out that I am in disgrace. . . . The servants that used to wash

my linen sent it back unwashed. . . . Today Mr. Oglethorpe gave away my bedstead from under me and refused to spare one of the carpenters to mend me up another![9]

However, God does move in mysterious ways! For it was not long after Charles' return that he made his way to a meeting-place of a small group of devout Christians, called Moravians—the famous Aldersgate site—where he "found peace with God and rejoiced in the hope of a living Christ"[10] on May 21, 1738. It was on the first anniversary of this conversion experience that he wrote one of his better-known hymns, "Oh, for a Thousand Tongues," as a personal testimony to the matchless grace and mercy of God.

The hymn before us, "Christ the Lord Is Risen Today," was also written within this first year of his conversion, and that may well account for the "note of joy and gladness, of confident trust and assurance of victory"[11] that runs throughout it! Apparently Wesley had seen the Latin-based hymn, "Jesus Christ Is Risen Today," with something of a composite authorship; that, it is believed,[12] inspired him to write this, which has become one of the greatest and certainly most popular of all the Easter hymns! Having reduced it from its original eleven verses to the five in our hymnal, Martin Madan (or someone else) also added the "Alleluias" at the end of each stanza; of this ascription of praise, very common in Methodist singing, H. Augustine Smith writes:

> Jerome said that "Christian ploughmen shouted 'Alleluia' while at their work"; Apollinaris said that "sailors used it as their shout of encouragement while plying their oars"; St. Germanus' victory was known as the "Alleluia" victory, the Britons shouting the word as their battle cry. And from earliest times Christians saluted each other on Easter morning with "Alleluia, the Lord is risen. He is risen indeed!"[13]

The tune "Llanfair" was named, as hymn tunes frequently were, after the name of the small Welsh village where the composer Robert Williams (1781–1821) was born; actually, the village's name is one of the longest words that exists in any language: Llanfairpwllgwyngyllgogerychwyrndrobwllllantysiliogogogoch; it means "Church of St. Mary in the hollow of white hazel near the rapid whirlpool of the Church of St. Trysillio by the red cave"![14]

Williams, born blind, was trained to earn his living as a basketmaker.[15] He had an excellent ear for music and a beautiful voice; "hearing a tune once, he could write it out without a single mistake."[16] Of this tune, which appeared in his manuscript book as "Bethel," dated July 14, 1817, one has written:

> In its simplicity, smoothness, and the ease with which it attains its climax, it is ideal for congregational singing. It provides, incidentally, an interesting effect to give the alleluias to an antiphonal choir.[17]

Let us examine this hymn, which calls to mind the various incidents related to Jesus' crucifixion and resurrection, more closely:

Stanza One: After declaring the fact of the resurrection, he calls upon everyone, human and angelic, animate and inanimate, to raise their voices in a common paen of praise, which is to echo and re-echo throughout the universe.

Stanza Two: From the depths of hell to the lofty regions of Paradise, Christ's resurrection triumph is in full force; death, the last great enemy, has been conquered, and nothing that puny human authority could order—neither the stone rolled against the opening of the burial vault, nor the seal of the mighty Roman emperor (which meant death for its violator), nor even the proud Roman guards who prided themselves on their faithfulness to duty—*nothing* could stop Him!

Stanza Three: Our Redeemer, Jesus ("for He shall save His people from their sins"), lives again, but no longer as a carpenter in Nazareth, fashioning furniture to earn His bread; no, now He lives as our glorious King, *victor* over death and the grave!

Stanza Four: Having opened and emptied the graves, He leads the way into Paradise, and "where He leads us, we will follow"! Indeed, having become like Him, we soar into His skies—but only after we have "died with Him"; and, only after we have "taken up our own crosses, daily, and followed Him" will we actually realize wings like eagles! What a prospect!

Stanza Five: As the subject bows in the presence of his earthly sovereign—and Wesley surely had done this, or watched it done in his day—a sign of submission and an act of adoring humility, so all of earth and heaven, including we as mortal subjects, bow in His presence, greeting our triumphant Lord who "is the Resurrection and the Life"! Alleluia, again and again, is the only appropriate response!

It is no surprise to learn that Thomas Lacy, an earnest Methodist, who lay dying one Easter Sunday, repeated these lines to his sister, though in a faltering voice; told that his end was near he said, "Then I have a pleasant prospect ahead of me"; and he entered God's presence in peace.[18]

Notes

1. Julian, *op. cit.,* pp. 1257–1258.
2. *Ibid.,* p. 1258.
3. Haeussler, *op. cit.,* p. 974.
4. Duffield, *op. cit.,* p. 348.
5. *Ibid.*
6. Bailey, *op. cit.,* p. 74.
7. Duffield, *op. cit.,* p. 349.

8. *Ibid.,* p. 350.

9. Bailey, *op. cit.,* p. 82.

10. Haeussler, *op. cit.,* p. 973.

11. Smith, *op. cit.,* p. 59.

12. Covert and Laufer, *op. cit.,* p. 182.

13. Smith, *op. cit.,* p. 60.

14. Stulken, *op. cit.,* p. 227.

15. Moffatt and Patrick, *op. cit.,* pp. 544–545.

16. McCutchan, *Our Hymnody,* p. 193.

17. Covert and Laufer, *op. cit.,* p. 18.

18. Duffield, *op. cit.,* p. 91.

Title/Date	*"Christ, Whose Glory Fills the Skies"* *(1740)*
Author	*Charles Wesley*
Composer/Tune	*Charles F. Gounod "Lux Prima" (1872)*
Scriptural Basis	*Luke 1:78–79; Malachi 4:2*

While it was certainly true that John and Charles Wesley, together with the rest of their large family, worked hard to have even the barest of the material necessities of life, they were not lacking in culture, good breeding, and scholarship. Charles received his education from Westminster School and both he and John from Christ Church College, Oxford, from which John graduated in 1725 and Charles in 1729.[1] Both were members of the Oxford "Holy Club," a name derisively used to describe a number of young men who were especially concerned about spiritual matters—a most uncommon interest in their day, even among those studying for Holy Orders. John, ordained in 1725, had returned to Oxford after serving as his father's curate for about two years and had assumed spiritual leadership of the small band of earnest Christian disciples who at times floundered for want of mature spiritual guidance.

While his profound Christian conversion came several years later, the seeds sown in their Epworth rectory certainly were germinating during these college experiences; moreover, Charles, a fine and diligent scholar, was enabled to use both his training received at Oxford and his poetic gifts when he began to make what was to be, not his only, but certainly his greatest contribution to the development of his brother's "Methodism." As one writer observes:

> Like Schubert with his melodic instinct, every thought that came to the mind of Charles Wesley seemed to shape itself in poetic form. Not only was he . . . the "sweet singer" of Methodism, but more than any other, he was successful in presenting religion and religious experiences in lyrical form.[2]

It has been said that he could write hymns anywhere—on the streets, on horseback, in the fields, in church (even during the service!)—and was ap-

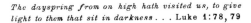

*The dayspring from on high hath visited us, to give
light to them that sit in darkness . . . Luke 1:78, 79*

LUX PRIMA 7. 7. 7. 7. 7. 7.

Charles Wesley, 1740

Charles F. Gounod, 1872

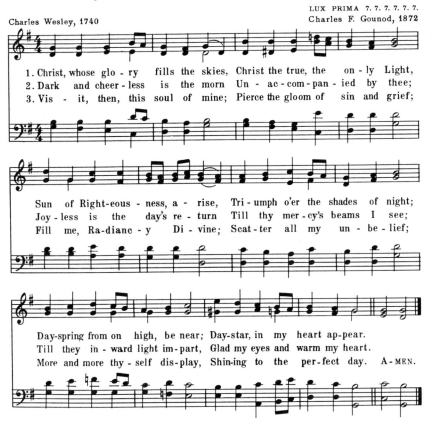

1. Christ, whose glo - ry fills the skies, Christ the true, the on - ly Light,
2. Dark and cheer - less is the morn Un - ac - com - pan - ied by thee;
3. Vis - it, then, this soul of mine; Pierce the gloom of sin and grief;

Sun of Right-eous - ness, a - rise, Tri - umph o'er the shades of night;
Joy - less is the day's re - turn Till thy mer - cy's beams I see;
Fill me, Ra-dianc - y Di - vine; Scat - ter all my un - be - lief;

Day-spring from on high, be near; Day-star, in my heart ap-pear.
Till they in - ward light im-part, Glad my eyes and warm my heart.
More and more thy - self dis-play, Shin-ing to the per-fect day. A - MEN.

parently rarely distracted from the task at hand! Some years ago, a modern
American poet witnessed to Charles' ability in this poem—published, incidentally, on the author's birthday, May 13, 1942, in the *Christian Century,* a
theologically liberal Protestant journal:

Charles Wesley sang his songs to God.
　　With the clop-clop-clop of the horse's feet
In the slushy mud of country roads,
　　And the saddlebags slapped out the beat.

Charles Wesley's heart was broader than night.
　　His spirit went high through the nights and the days.
"Oh, for a thousand tongues to sing"—
　　To sing "my great Redeemer's praise."

Across the moors, and from town to town,
   He thought out his hymns alone—alone;
The weary way, the lonely road
   He sang, "Come, O Thou Traveler unknown."

They gave him a robe and a pulpit square,
   A church that reached up to the skies.
Now a thousand voices sing his songs—
   A song that lives and never dies.

Charles Wesley sang his songs for men
   With the clop-clop-clop of the horse's feet,
For men who know no temple or church
   But the long and dusty city street.[3]

The allusion here to "men who know no temple or church, but the long and dusty city street" is of course a reference to the fact that early on, both John and Charles, though remaining in the church of their childhood until they died, were denied access to any Anglican pulpits; therefore they preached the unsearchable riches of Christ wherever they could gather a crowd, and those crowds were often at best a "mixed multitude," with many among them who delighted in disruptive tactics. But in their mission to take the gospel to the poor and outcast—including the felons at notorious Newgate Prison and those heading for the gallows at Tyburn—they were partners; of them Jones writes:

> John was the calm general who directed operations, Charles was the brilliant cavalry leader who plunged into the thickest of the fray. . . . Later, Charles began a fifteen year period of itinerant evangelism in which he showed extraordinary energy, courage, self-sacrifice, and a power in preaching that even surpassed John's![4]

But Charles was ever, and preeminently, the hymn-writer, and of this hymn, which James Montgomery calls "one of (his) loveliest progeny,"[5] MacMillan writes:

> it is one of the greatest morning hymns in our language, but it is more. It is a glorious hymn to Christ, the Sun of Righteousness, the Light of the World.[6]

It is interesting to note Bailey's commendation of this hymn for its *lack* of "dogma which one is obliged to accept in order to be saved";[7] while dogma or doctrine doesn't save anyone, by itself—for "the devils believe and tremble"—all of our grounds for assurance as redeemed children of God are rooted in the great doctrinal truths regarding who Jesus of Nazareth was and what He came to do and did ultimately accomplish! Any heroic figure may inspire me, but only God the Son can redeem me; He can illumine me in the deep places of my inner life precisely because He is the Light who overcomes my darkness; and that is the thrust of this "true lyric, as poetry superior to most, this prayer for spiritual illumination."[8] Let us examine it further:

Stanza One: Wesley uses a series of figures of speech—Light, Sun, Dayspring, Day-star—all of which are bearers or heralds of light, each intended to add to the stature of the Lord Jesus Christ and to make Him more than simply an enlightened and enlightening human being!

Stanza Two: In the light of Who Christ is, when His presence is unknown or unsensed, the day—the life—is dark, cheerless, joyless, cold, and foreboding; certainly since "it is of His mercies that we are not consumed," we plead those mercies as the basis for His coming to us again in light, joy, and warmth.

Stanza Three: The prayer of the Christian is therefore simple: "visit me again in the depths of my heart, where I struggle with sin and unbelief which cause me untold sorrow; pierce, and scatter these evils, and display Yourself—in all Your Radiance and Glory, and above all, fill me with that light!" Routley's comments are instructive here:

> While the sun's glory fills the skies, bringing both light and heat to our universe, it is "naked and capricious power"; Christ's power is not irresponsible and capricious, because His is "power limited by love"; so He is the "Sun in whose rays all good things flourish and all mean things wither, dissipating the gross darkness of this world." Moreover the prayer "Dayspring in my heart appear" seeks His entrance into my life—that He may live in my will and affections as He lived in Nazareth; the context is joy, the color is golden, in this richly happy hymn.[9]

The tune, "Lux Prima," which maintains its interest by building the melody up toward the climax occurring at the word "Day-Star,"[10] was written by a godly French composer, Charles Gounod (1818–1893), who began his studies in theology, intending to take Holy Orders. But after two years, he decided he could serve God best by his music. All of his first compositions were of a sacred character, and, with the exception of his well-known opera "Faust," most of his later great work, including "The Redemption," maintained this basically religious emphasis. This latter work begins with the creation, fall, and promise of a Redeemer; moves to Christ's passion and crucifixion, His glorious earthly life from the resurrection to His ascension; and finishes with the spread of Christianity through the apostolic missionary labors.[11] While composing this oratorio, Gounod spent hours in Notre Dame Cathedral in prayer and meditation.[12]

Notes

1. Julian, *op. cit.*, pp. 1257–1258.
2. Haeussler, *op. cit.*, p. 974.
3. *Ibid.*
4. Bailey, *op. cit.*, pp. 82–83.
5. McCutchan, *Our Hymnody*, p. 58.
6. *Ibid.*
7. Bailey, *op. cit.*, p. 102.
8. *Ibid.*
9. Routley, *Hymns and the Faith*, pp. 141–144.
10. Covert and Laufer, *op. cit.*, p. 38.
11. *Ibid.*, pp. 37–38.
12. Hostetler, *op. cit.*, p. 16.

Title/Date	*"Crown Him with Many Crowns"* *(1851)*
Author	*Matthew Bridges*
Composer/Tune	*Sir George Elvey "Diademata" (1868)*
Scriptural Basis	*Revelation 19:12; 22:1; 5:11–14*

While the authorship of this hymn has been the occasion for some debate among musicologists, the consensus seems to be in favor of Matthew Bridges (1800–1894), English poet and scholar,[1] whose interests included both ancient and modern history. Brought up in the Church of England, he published in 1828 *The Roman Empire under Constantine the Great,* which

> examined the real origin of certain papal superstitions, whose antiquity has been so often urged against Protestants, with no little triumph and presumption.[2]

Apparently, however, his attempt to disprove the historicity of those claims backfired, for he became, some twenty years later, one of that small but influential group of Anglicans to follow Cardinal John Henry Newman into the Roman Catholic fold.

Among his several books of poetry, some of which were the basis for his "spiritual and beautiful" hymns,[3] was a volume called *Hymns of the Heart* in which this hymn first appeared. A fine hymn of praise, it was later included in the 1868 edition of *Hymns Ancient and Modern.*[4] At the centenary Thanksgiving celebration of the London Bible Society, held in 1905, the Marquis of Northampton read congratulatory messages from all of the Protestant rulers of Christendom; then he said,

> Now that we have read these messages from earthly rulers, let us turn our minds to the King of Kings; we will sing "Crown Him with Many Crowns."[5]

As we have seen before, a great hymn is a blend of lyrics and music; the right tune, one that reinforces the message, is therefore crucial. When Sir Henry Baker, editor of *Hymns Ancient and Modern,* chose to include this

On his head were many crowns . . . Rev. 19:12

DIADEMATA S. M. D.

Matthew Bridges, 1851   Sir George J. Elvey, 1868

1. Crown him with man - y crowns, The Lamb up - on his throne;
2. Crown him the Lord of love; Be - hold his hands and side,
3. Crown him the Lord of peace; Whose pow'r a scep - ter sways
4. Crown him the Lord of years, The Po - ten - tate of time;

Hark! how the heav'n - ly an - them drowns All mu - sic but its own:
Rich wounds, yet vis - i - ble a - bove, In beau - ty glo - ri - fied:
From pole to pole, that wars may cease, Ab - sorbed in prayer and praise:
Cre - a - tor of the roll - ing spheres, In - ef - fa - bly sub - lime:

A - wake, my soul, and sing Of him who died for thee,
No an - gel in the sky Can ful - ly bear that sight,
His reign shall know no end; And round his pierc - ed feet
All hail, Re - deem - er, hail! For thou hast died for me:

And hail him as thy match-less King Through all e - ter - ni - ty.
But down-ward bends his burn-ing eye At mys-ter - ies so bright.
Fair flowers of Par - a - dise ex - tend Their fra-grance ev - er sweet.
Thy praise shall nev - er, nev - er fail Through-out e - ter - ni - ty. A-MEN.

hymn, his choice was based, at least in part, upon this fine tune written for it by Sir George Elvey. As Covert states with some forcefulness:

If the primary function of a hymn tune is to reinforce and to convey the feeling of the text, then in "Diademata" and "Crown Him with Many

Crowns" we behold a perfect union. The tune fully conveys the triumphant and ecstatic joy of the text, and yet its great dignity and solidity are preserved. It is a tune which organists like to play, and which choirs and congregations enjoy singing.[6]

Sir George Elvey (1816–1893) was an outstanding English organist and composer whose early musical interests were shaped at Canterbury Cathedral, where he was a choirboy. A student at London's Royal Academy of Music, at nineteen he became organist of St. George's Chapel, Windsor, a post he held for forty-seven years. A graduate of Oxford (Bac., 1838, Mus. Doc., 1840), he composed much of the music for important events of State, including a festival march for Princess Louise's wedding, which led to his being knighted in 1877![7] While he did write much church music, he did not compose many hymn tunes; yet those he did compose are models of what a good one should be. As an earnest and faithful man, one wrote of him:

No one could be long in his presence without being struck by his devout, religious spirit, and it was this spirit that went into all of his work.[8]

And of his philosophy, or, if you will theology, of church music, another writes:

Elvey believed that mighty Cathedrals and profound music should go together; that the music should suggest worship just as much as soaring nave, springing arch, and beautiful window. He desired to make his compositions so genuinely worshipful that a stranger, listening at a distance and unable to catch the words, would be compelled to say "That is sacred music."[9]

Let us examine this "song of the seraphs"; in its original version, incidentally, there were six stanzas, with Bridge's second stanza ("Crown Him the Virgin's Son") and his third stanza ("Crown Him the Son of God") being omitted from most hymnals, including the *Trinity Hymnal*. A seventh stanza ("Crown Him the Lord of Life"), written by Geoffrey Thring (1823–1903), was often included with Bridges' hymn; Thring may have felt that this was appropriate in that seven was the sacred Jewish number, the number of perfection;[10] in any event, that stanza also—though it has, I believe, considerable merit—is usually omitted (I will cite it later). Here then is the hymn as we have it:

Stanza One: The scene is the court of heaven, where the anthem is being sung by all of its inhabitants to praise the Lamb of God, who is worthy "to receive glory, and honor, and blessing," worthy to be crowned. For, as my Savior, dying in my place, He reigns also as my King—my matchless King, incomparably worthy of my awakened soul's song! (Revelation 22:1; 5:11–14).[11]

Stanza Two: The mystery of the suffering Savior, "wounded for me, wounded for me," a mystery that even—or perhaps, especially—the angels cannot bear to look upon; and it was *love* that took Him to that cross! "Behold, what manner of love that is," when Almighty God is willing to give Himself, in the Person of His dearly beloved Son that I might be forgiven and redeemed. Crown Him! Crown Him, indeed, the LORD of Love! (John 3:16; 15:13).[12]

Stanza Three: Peace, the gift of the Prince of peace, can only come to men when their rebellious hearts are conquered by His love and their energies are "absorbed in prayer and praise." Another beautiful image is that of the Lord of Peace upon His throne, flowers encircling His pierced feet, an ever-present reminder of the road He took to win for me the right to be in His Kingdom (Isaiah 9:6–7; 52:7; 26:3; Psalm 72:7–8; Revelation 1:8; 22:13).[13]

Stanza Four: This crown, making Him "Lord of the years, Ruler of time" itself, adds the dimension of power to His other attributes; however, it is not capricious power but creative power, resulting in a work that is "ineffably sublime"—beyond imagination's description! But again, Bridges calls us back to the fact of our redemption, and uses this most vulnerable experience our Lord had to remind us of the reason for our praise; "I'll live for Him who died for me" sings another—and yes, I'll praise Him too, the One who wears the crowns! (Colossians 1:16–17).[14]

Such a stirring theme requires "a forward moving tune, . . . strong as a march in its rhythm, which does indeed summon us as singers to step in line and march"![15] So we will

Crown Him the Lord of Life
Who triumphed o'er the grave
And rose victorious in the strife
For those He came to save.

His glories now we sing
Who died and rose on high
Who died, eternal life to bring
And lives, that death may die.[16]

Notes

1. Haeussler, *op. cit.,* p. 228.
2. Moffatt and Patrick, *op. cit.,* p. 278.
3. Duffield, *op. cit.,* p. 126.

4. Haeussler, *op. cit.*, p. 228.

5. McCutchan, *Our Hymnody*, p. 217.

6. Covert and Laufer, *op. cit.*, p. 206.

7. McCutchan, *op. cit.*, p. 218.

8. *Ibid.*

9. Smith, *op. cit.*, pp. 73–74.

10. Bailey, *op. cit.*, pp. 206–207.

11. *Ibid.*, p. 206.

12. *Ibid.*

13. *Ibid.*

14. *Ibid.*

15. Haeussler, *op. cit.*, p. 228.

16. Bailey, *op. cit.*, p. 207.

Title/Date	*"For All the Saints, Who from Their Labors . . ." (1864, 1875)*
Author	*William Walsham How*
Composer/Tune	*Sir Joseph Barnby "Sarum" (1868)*
Scriptural Basis	*Revelation 14:13; Hebrews 11*

Imagine yourself in a slum section of the city of London about a century ago. Down the street comes a tall man, striding along with steady gait and curious appearance; he wears a flat hat, cloak, apron, and gaiters,[1] and carries a pastoral staff—for all the world resembling one of the bishops you've seen elsewhere, except that they usually ride in carriages and have a servant or two attending them. But this man is alone, and he seems to mingle easily with everyone he meets on his way—and well he should, for he *is* the bishop of this parish, East London. And his people, young and old alike, love and respect him as one of them—the "poor man's bishop," the "people's bishop," the "omnibus bishop," for he rode the buses with them, declining to use the episcopal carriage that smacked of privilege and wealth.[2]

By this stage in his ecclesiastical career, William How (1823–1897) was known for his broad sympathies, genial humanity, and apostolic zeal; a master of the art of pastoral care—reflected even in the lines carved on his pastoral staff ("Feed with the Word, feed with the life")—he attracted all classes.[3] Like his early prototype, St. Barnabas, he was a "good man, full of faith and the Holy Ghost," a hard worker, well-organized, concerned to redeem the time, as he ministered, selflessly, to all in his parish.

Earlier, he had rejected several offers of ecclesiastical preferment: the bishopric of Manchester—without even mentioning it to his good wife, and later that of Durham, a prestigious and wealthy "call."[4] Totally without worldly ambition, his only concern was where he could best serve the Lord who had called him; thus he was long remembered as a shepherd of souls, a most unselfish, lovable man, with a tender fondness for children. Of him, Francis Pigou, the dean of Bristol Cathedral, wrote:

Walsham How . . . was a man of great personal piety which shone transparently in him. His well-known hymns are fragrant with it. All brought

That they may rest from their labours; and their works do follow them. Rev. 14:13

SARUM 10. 10. 10. 4. 4.

William Walsham How, 1864; text of 1875

Sir Joseph Barnby, 1868

1. For all the saints who from their la - bors rest, Who thee by
2. Thou wast their Rock, their For - tress, and their Might; Thou, Lord, their
3. O may thy sol - diers, faith - ful, true, and bold, Fight as the
4. The gold - en eve - ning bright - ens in the west; Soon, soon to
5. But lo! there breaks a yet more glo - rious day; The saints tri -
6. From earth's wide bounds, from o - cean's far - thest coast, Through gates of

faith be - fore the world con - fessed, Thy Name, O Je - sus,
Cap - tain in the well - fought fight; Thou, in the dark - ness
saints who no - bly fought of old, And win with them the
faith - ful war - riors comes their rest; Sweet is the calm of
umph - ant rise in bright ar - ray; The King of Glo - ry
pearl streams in the count - less host, Sing - ing to Fa - ther,

be for ev - er blest. Al - le - lu - ia! Al - le - lu - ia!
drear, their one true Light. Al - le - lu - ia! Al - le - lu - ia!
vic - tor's crown of gold. Al - le - lu - ia! Al - le - lu - ia!
Par - a - dise the blest. Al - le - lu - ia! Al - le - lu - ia!
pass - es on his way. Al - le - lu - ia! Al - le - lu - ia!
Son, and Ho - ly Ghost, Al - le - lu - ia! Al - le - lu - ia! A - MEN.

into contact with him were conscious of it. . . . Not a man of great intellectual power . . . yet his ministry was singularly owned and blessed of God. It is true that more men are won to God by holiness than by cleverness.[5]

In addition to these personal and pastoral gifts, How was a fine musician, whose sixty hymns—several of which are still widely used—had to measure up to his own ideal: "a good hymn should be like a good prayer—simple, real, earnest, and reverent."[6] Moreover, consistent with the rest of his way of living, his hymn-writing was undertaken not to make him famous, but to be helpful; therefore he gave free use of his hymns to everyone, at all times, with his only reward the knowledge that they had ministered to the souls of men. Carpenter wrote of him:

The writer dies; the hymn remains; the song goes on; tired men [and women] listen and find rest. The struggling are encouraged to struggle on again; statesmen, philanthropists, the broken-hearted, and the despairing, are helped. Sing on: you know not [whom] you comfort; such a reward is indeed better than fame. It is, as if even after the life is ended, the power to give a cup of cold water to a fainting soul in the name of Christ was not denied to the singer of the Church.[7]

One further fact of significance for his musical contributions: he served as joint editor of *Church Hymns,* published in 1871, "the most formidable rival of *Hymns Ancient and Modern,* its appeal being its lesser sacramentalism and less assertive high churchmanship."[8] Most of his hymns, "including many for children—who knew him, loved him, and ran out to greet him as he made his pastoral rounds,"[9] were written during his twenty-eight years as pastor at Whittington, a pleasant farming village on the Welsh border. While serving there he, a man of some means, had both the ancient church and the rectory rebuilt at his own expense. He is buried in the churchyard, with a monument commemorating his life of devoted service to God, the church, and the people. Perhaps the crowning tribute to his ability as a poet came in the final year of his life, when he was honored by Queen Victoria, who asked him to write a national hymn for the British Empire's observance of her Jubilee; in part, he wrote:

O royal heart, with wide embrace
For all her happy children yearning;
O happy realm, such mother-grace
With loyal love returning.
Where England's flag flies wide unfurled,
All tyrant wrongs repelling,
God made the world a better world
For man's brief earthly dwelling.[10]

Sir Joseph Barnby (1838–1896), composer of the tune "Sarum," mated to these words in the *Trinity Hymnal,* was a well-known organist and composer—indeed, one of the most prolific in late-nineteenth-century England, with his collection of almost 250 being published, posthumously, in 1897. He edited five hymnbooks, and set high standards of performance as conductor of London's Royal Choral Society, which did both Dvorak's "Stabat Mater" and Wagner's "Parsifal" for the first time in England[11] under his baton. Knighted in 1892, he was one of that "group of English musicians whose work, though often secular, was reverent in spirit";[12] in fact, one of his best-known tunes, "Laudes Domini," sung to Caswell's "When Morning

Gilds the Skies," is a good illustration of the melodic, vigorous, and uplifting music he was capable of writing.

The tune, "Sarum," composed for this hymn, appeared initially in a collection of hymns and tunes for use in the diocese of Salisbury—hence the
name.[13] One caution is made: This hymn cannot be sung too slowly, else the
congregation will not be able to sing each alleluia easily in one breath.

Let us examine this hymn, written for All Saints' Day and expressing
"basic truth in simple, forceful diction, with vivid detail, and bold, broad
strokes."[14]

Saints, from the New Testament perspective, are simply Christians —a
term Paul uses in this general sense frequently. However, throughout the ages
particularly devout persons, often allegedly possessing miraculous powers,
have been set aside and called "saints"; on November 1, the many saints, not
"honored" with their own specific day, are honored as a group—thus All
Saints' Day. Moreover, the Apostles' Creed contains the clause "I believe in
. . . the communion of saints," an affirmation of the solidarity of Christians of
all ages, times, and races—the Church Militant here on earth and the
Church Triumphant in heaven. It is with this latter emphasis that we of the
Reformed tradition can most heartily agree, and in this spirit that we can
enter into singing this fine hymn, which

> has the long time sense; singing it, we seem to be living in history. The past
> merges with the present and the future. We are, for a moment, living
> members of a vast fellowship that extends beyond the borders of earth and
> time into the eternal heavens, a fellowship that knows both the agony of
> mortal strife and the joy of victory. Singing, our voices become part of the
> Church's unending song.[15]

Stanza One: We bless and thank our Lord Jesus for all those believers who
confessed His Name before a world that was at times indifferent and at
other times hostile to the point of making them martyrs; and they did it by
faith—*the* quality essential to sainthood. And what is faith? Faith Routley
describes it as

> the act of mental and spiritual submission by which each one (in Hebrews
> 11) allowed himself to be built into the plan which God had for the world;
> . . . each put that before his own desires, his own reputation. . . . They were
> at God's disposal . . . because they lived with the assumption that God is
> honest.[16]

Stanza Two: Here Bishop How ascribes a series of epithets to our Lord,
military in character, to reinforce the battle image; in the dreary darkness, He

provides security, strength, safety, and light that is true—that shows the picture as it really is, an important factor if one is not to be ambushed in battle!

Stanza Three: A prayer that we, His soldiers today, may "quit ourselves strong as men," fight as did our fathers and mothers of old, and like them also win the victor's golden crown. Faithfulness, courage, and nobility are the virtues of such a true contemporary soldier.

Here are two additional stanzas coming before our fourth:

O blest communion! fellowship divine!
We feebly struggle, they in glory shine;
Yet all are one in Thee, for all are Thine.

And when the strife is fierce, the warfare long
Steals on the ear the distant triumph song;
And hearts are brave again, and arms are strong.[17]

Stanza Four: As evening falls, both literally and figuratively, faithful warriors receive their reward, the restful peace of blessed Paradise—a welcome change for these who have borne the heat of the day and the stress of battle.

Stanza Five: But the more glorious day is coming—the day of resurrection when, clothed in the white raiment of martyrs, the Church Triumphant meets its coming King! To the Christian, "who confessed Christ in his life, in his speech, in his thought, it is given to see the King of Glory passing on His way."[18]

Stanza Six: A procession the magnificence of which dwarfs that of the Olympic athletes, when people of every tongue, clime, age, and station in life shall stream through those magnificent gates of pearl, singing exultantly the thrice holy to the Triune God! From war to peace, from death to life, from suffering to glory; "exalted language, and sustained emotion."[19] Indeed!

Notes

1. Marks, *op. cit.,* p. 160.
2. Bailey, *op. cit.,* p. 421.
3. Moffatt and Patrick, *op. cit.,* p. 379.
4. Bailey, *op. cit.,* p. 421.
5. McCutchan, *op. cit.,* p. 244.
6. Bailey, *op. cit.,* p. 421.
7. McCutchan, *op. cit.,* p. 244.
8. Moffatt and Patrick, *op. cit.,* p. 379.
9. McCutchan, *op. cit.,* p. 244.
10. Smith, *op. cit.,* p. 313.

11. Covert and Laufer, *op. cit.*, p. 5.
12. *Ibid.*
13. *Ibid.*, p. 443.
14. Smith, *op. cit.*, p. 313.
15. Covert and Laufer, *op. cit.*, p. 443.
16. Routley, *Hymns and the Faith*, p. 303.
17. *Ibid.*, p. 301.
18. *Ibid.*, p. 306.
19. Bailey, *op. cit.*, p. 422.

Title/Date	*"Hark, the Herald Angels Sing"* (1739)
Author	*Charles Wesley*
Composer/Tune	*William H. Cummings "Mendelssohn" (1856)*
	(arranged from Mendelssohn's "Fest-gesang . . . " [1840])
Scriptural Basis	*Luke 2:14; Isaiah 9:6*

Since we have already illumined our readers through considerable biographical material related to Charles (and John) Wesley, we focus our attention here on biographical data regarding both the composer and the arranger of the hymn's tune—a tune that is used, universally, with this greatest of Christmas hymns,[1] the only hymn by Charles Wesley to be included in the Church of England's *Book of Common Prayer!*[2] There is, incidentally, some mystery surrounding this fact; Haeussler details at least some of the possible explanations:

> One wonders how this hymn got into the *Book of Common Prayer,* since the Wesleys were under a cloud with reactionary Anglicans. Was it because public pressure for its inclusion was so great that it could not well be ignored? Was it slipped in as a "filler" by a printer who did not wish to waste any blank space in the rear of the book? Or was it "bootlegged" into it by him while the ecclesiastical "brass hats" weren't looking because the printer, like most of England's ordinary people, greatly admired the Wesleys? No one knows; but once the hymn was printed in that book, no one dared to remove it from later issues.[3]

And, of course, we are reminded that for all of his lifetime of ministering outside the "proper" bounds of Anglicanism, Charles never left that Church, insisting even as he lay dying (though John remonstrated with him),

> I have lived, and I die, in the Communion of the Church of England, and I will be buried in the yard of my parish Church [Marylebone churchyard].[4]

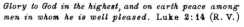

Glory to God in the highest, and on earth peace among
men in whom he is well pleased. Luke 2:14 (R. V.)

MENDELSSOHN 7. 7. 7. 7. D. with refrain
Arr. from Mendelssohn
by William H. Cummings, 1856

Charles Wesley, 1739, alt.

1. Hark! the her - ald an - gels sing, "Glo - ry to the new - born King;
2. Christ, by high - est heav'n a - dored, Christ, the Ev - er - last - ing Lord!
3. Hail, the heav'n-born Prince of Peace! Hail, the Sun of Right-eous - ness!

Peace on earth, and mer - cy mild, God and sin - ners rec - on - ciled!"
Late in time be - hold him come, Off - spring of the Vir - gin's womb.
Light and life to all he brings, Ris'n with heal - ing in his wings.

Joy - ful, all ye na - tions, rise, Join the tri - umph of the skies;
Veiled in flesh the God - head see; Hail th' In - car - nate De - i - ty,
Mild he lays his glo - ry by, Born that man no more may die,

With th' an - gel - ic host pro - claim, "Christ is born in Beth - le - hem!"
Pleased as man with men to dwell, Je - sus, our Em - man - u - el.
Born to raise the sons of earth, Born to give them sec - ond birth.

REFRAIN

Hark! the her - ald an - gels sing, "Glo - ry to the new-born King." A - MEN.

The composer of the music, from which the tune for this hymn was later taken, was the renowned Felix Mendelssohn-Bartholdy (1809–1847), brilliant pianist/organist and composer of several oratorios, who had been baptized and raised a Lutheran, but whose grandfather was Moses Mendelssohn, the famous Jewish philosopher. Extraordinarily gifted as a musician, he was profoundly influenced by Johann Sebastian Bach,[5] reviving the study and performance of his works, including his "St. Matthew's Passion," in 1829 in Berlin. Lionized on several tours of England and inspired by Bach, he performed his own oratorios there: "Elijah" (1847), "St. Paul" (1836), and "Hymn of Praise" (1840). As an organist he excelled, and was received with signal honor by Queen Victoria and Prince Albert.[6] Unfortunately, a frail constitution, coupled with considerable overwork and the news of his beloved sister's death, combined to hasten his own end; everyone mourned this man of

> sunny, enthusiastic, generous, lovable nature,[7] [who was] unselfish and pure in his private life, unspoiled by wealth and applause. As a humble and earnest Christian he consecrated his genius to the highest ends.[8]

This tune was originally written for a male chorus and sung in a festival in Leipzig in 1840, commemorating the invention of printing![9] When William Hayman Cummings (1831–1915), the famous organist, composer, conductor, writer, lecturer, musicologist, and tenor soloist who sang in the chorus when Mendelssohn conducted his "Elijah" in 1847 at Exeter Hall, was going through some of Mendelssohn's music, it occurred to him that this chorus could be easily adapted for Wesley's hymn. This task he accordingly undertook, and ever since he published it in 1856 it has been the recognized tune. Had Mendelssohn still been living, he might have objected since he once said of this chorus: "I am sure that piece will be liked very much by singers and hearers, but it will *never* do to sacred words."[10] Cummings, who possessed one of the finest private musical libraries of his day, and who, as a founder of the Purcell Society served as editor for several volumes of its publications (including the biography of Purcell himself), traveled extensively, singing in this country in several cities, including Boston. An author, he also wrote a widely used text, *The Rudiments of Music;* he was elected as the principal of the Guildhall School of Music in 1896[11] and was also a marvelously gifted musician.

This hymn, "perhaps the most popular English hymn in the world,"[12] was also written within a year after Charles had "consciously believed"; with the exception of a few minor revisions, it is sung today as he wrote it. The *Trinity Hymnal* has included the best of his lines, although there are several of lesser quality, which it omits. Of these lines Covert says:

This hymn can best be appreciated if one hears it sung as a carol in the darkness of the night under the open sky, when the hard lines of daylight are obscured and sensible objects are lost to sight, when the mystery of the night stirs the imagination, and when we can take our place with the humble Shepherds . . . to whom the wondrous news was first revealed. . . . When we gather the wealth of the meaning of Jesus to men into the simplicity of the Christmas story, its sacred beauty can be celebrated only by the song of the angels.[13]

Let us examine it more closely, noting several of its distinctive features:

First, there is the summons to join the angelic hosts in ascribing glory to the Infant who is also King; that initial summons is thrice repeated, focusing our attention on Messiah King. Moreover, not only the angels, but all the nations and we as individuals are also summoned, for He is *our* Emmanuel.

Second, we note the benefits of His coming among us. As the Prince of Peace, He brings peace on earth; as the merciful Redeemer He reconciles the Holy God and sinful human beings; as "the . . . Life, and the Light of men" He brings life—with its beneficial healing and light, for guidance; as God Incarnate, He gives hope for newness of life.

Third, we stand sobered in His presence when we contemplate who He is: King; Everlasting Lord; Incarnate God; Emmanuel, God actually with us in human form, flesh and blood, without question the ultimate miracle and mystery; Prince of Peace; Sun of Righteousness, risen, with healing in His wings (Malachi 4:2). Epithets are piled one on another, with the cumulative effect of overwhelming the thoughtful. What could we then possibly do, other than join in "giving Him the glory due His Name"? And how could we adore Him any less, knowing that He is the Adored of His Father?

It is encouraging to remember, in this day of widely advancing secularism, that this marvelously theological hymn is one of the all-time favorites for the extended Advent and Christmas season. Let us sing it at other times, too, loved as it is!

Notes

1. Covert and Laufer, *op. cit.,* p. 135.
2. Marks, *op. cit.,* p. 102.
3. Haeussler, *op. cit.,* p. 151.
4. Julian, *op. cit.,* p. 1258.
5. Moffatt and Patrick, *op. cit.,* p. 427.
6. Covert and Laufer, *op. cit.,* p. 17.
7. Moffatt and Patrick, *op. cit.,* p. 428.
8. Covert and Laufer, *op. cit.,* p. 17.

9. *Ibid.*

10. Haeussler, *op. cit.,* p. 152.

11. *Ibid.,* p. 616.

12. McCutchan, *Our Hymnody,* p. 118.

13. Covert and Laufer, *op. cit.,* p. 135.

Title/Date	*"Holy, Holy, Holy" (1826, 1827)*
Author	*Reginald Heber*
Composer/Tune	*John B. Dykes "Nicaea" (1861)*
Scriptural Basis	*Revelation 4:6–11; John 3:1–15*

From one of the greatest Christmas hymns ever written, we turn our attention to "Holy, Holy, Holy," called by Alfred Lord Tennyson, the late Poet Laureate of England,

> the finest hymn ever written, taking into consideration its purity of language, its devotion, its spirituality, and the difficulty of treating such an abstract theme, poetically.[1]

Of this marvelous hymn written for Trinity Sunday, surely Heber's finest, Bailey writes:

> No hymn has greater dignity and uplifting power; none is more thoroughly liturgical, fit to be sung by vast multitudes in grand cathedrals, while the organ rolls its thrilling thunders through "long-drawn aisle and fretted vault" . . . That this hymn . . . satisfies the needs of the Church Universal is proved by its presence in nearly all the hymnals [currently published].[2]

And Julian, easily the greatest hymnologist to publish his work, adds his accolades when he writes of this hymn as

> that majestic anthem, founded on the rhythm of the English Bible "Holy, Holy, Holy, Lord God Almighty," a splendid metrical paraphrase . . . pure and graceful devotional poetry, . . . true and reverent, an unfailing pleasure, evidence of Heber's refined taste.[3]

To this estimate of Reginald Heber (1783–1826)—poet, author, lecturer, pastor, bishop for an all-too-brief ministry of the whole of the British Indian Empire—others have added their witness, including his servants in his boarding school days, who affirmed "Master Reginald: chivalrous, unselfish, gentle, is never in a passion";[4] and his schoolmates, who reminisced in later

They rest not day and night, saying, Holy, holy, holy, Lord God Almighty...Rev. 4:8

NICAEA 11. 12. 12. 10.

Reginald Heber, 1783-1826   John B. Dykes, 1861

1. Ho-ly, Ho-ly, Ho - ly, Lord God Al-might-y! Ear-ly in the
2. Ho-ly, Ho-ly, Ho - ly! All the saints a - dore thee, Cast-ing down their
3. Ho-ly, Ho-ly, Ho - ly! Though the dark-ness hide thee, Though the eye of
4. Ho-ly, Ho-ly, Ho - ly! Lord God Al-might-y! All thy works shall

morn - ing our song shall rise to thee; Ho - ly, Ho - ly, Ho - ly!
gold - en crowns a - round the glass-y sea; Cher-u-bim and ser-a-phim
sin - ful man thy glo - ry may not see, On - ly thou art ho - ly;
praise thy Name, in earth and sky and sea; Ho - ly, Ho - ly, Ho - ly!

Mer - ci - ful and Might-y! God in three Per-sons, bless-ed Trin-i - ty!
fall-ing down be-fore thee, Who wert. and art, and ev - er-more shalt be.
there is none be-side thee Per-fect in pow'r, in love, and pur-i - ty.
Mer - ci - ful and Might-y! God in three Per-sons, bless-ed Trin-i - ty! A-MEN.

years: "If his heart had no other covering than a glass, its thoughts were so pure, no one need fear to read them."[5] These comments are all the more significant when considered in their historical context, for vice, and vices, were as prevalent in his day as they are today, and there were not a few cynics then even as there are now, persons eager to search out and make public the chinks in everyone's armor!

A final note regarding Heber: the poet Southey wrote this inscription for the monument erected in his honor in India:

He performed his humblest as well as his highest duties carefully, with all his heart, with all his soul, with all his strength![6]

Let us examine this hymn "of pure adoration," of which Reeves has written: "the lines suggest cathedral heights and spaces . . . the spirit of the Hebrew prophets approaching the Sovereign God."[7] We note that the context of this hymn is the court of heaven, where the four beasts and the twenty-four elders are pictured (Revelation 4:6–11) as worshipping "the Lord God, Almighty," who as the Eternal One is "worthy to receive glory, and honor, and power" from His creation, the work of His hands, designed to give Him pleasure.

The refrain "Holy, Holy, Holy," which pours forth from their lips, unceasingly, is repeated six times in the four stanzas of the hymn, riveting our attention on this characteristic of God. Holiness, from the Hebrew root that means to cut or separate, actually means "to be separated: to God, and from evil"; in the Old Testament, God withheld the sight of His countenance from His people "not so much in protection of His own dignity as because the sight of His perfection would shrivel up their enfeebled souls!"[8]

But Heber has wed to this concept of awesome holiness the equally important quality of mercifulness (vs. 1), for without this we could never stand before Him, even to praise! In fact, the very darkness that hides Him from the eyes of sinful mortals does so to give us a measure of protection—for our God is a consuming fire!

Another feature is that this universal call to praise involves everyone and everything God has created: we who are still here on earth (vs. 1), all the saints (i.e., believers now in heaven) (vs. 2), all His works, which include the animals (on earth), the birds, stars, and other heavenly bodies (in the sky), and the fish, the denizens of the deep (in the sea); and, of course, those mysterious angelic beings, the cherubim and the seraphim, whose nature is unclear but whose task is praise (vs. 2).

Finally, it is the Triune God, "God in three Persons," the blessed Trinity whose perfection combines power, love, and purity that we are incessantly urged to adore—lost in wonder, love, and praise. As Routley finely says of this hymn, which praises rather than explains the Trinity, "it presents theology in its completeness, as you find it in doctrine rather than in its more glorious incompleteness, as we find it in Scripture."[9]

While Bailey calls the uniquely Christian doctrine of the Trinity

> a stumbling-block, divisive, deadly; an attempt to raise a figure of speech that expresses the functions of God as creator, redeemer and inspirer, into a metaphysical dogma the acceptance of which is essential to salvation,[10]

which we'd be better off to discard, others do not agree! Routley, for example, says that our doctrine must be thoughtful, a credit to our God-given minds, but also humble, recognizing "both intellectual achievement and intellectual renunciation."[11] Moreover, God, even in His "mystery," is still personal, more "personal even than we are, and is to be treated as a friend"![12]

For He seeks a community to which and within which He can communi-
cate Himself. Finally, quoting Newman, he writes:

> Our image of God is . . . broken into numberless partial aspects. . . . We
> know one truth about Him, and another truth, but we cannot imagine
> both of them together. Attempt to combine them into one and you gain
> nothing but Mystery. Be reverent and expectant before Mystery. Accent
> wonder . . . , for what we think God is, is of less importance than what
> God turns out to be.[13]

Some suggestions about singing this magnificent hymn are offered by H.
Augustine Smith, who points out that the long verse line of the poetry, with
its double rhyme, is peculiarly suited to the expression of quietness, reverence, and adoration. He writes:

> Sing the hymn at a moderately slow pace, pronouncing the initial words
> carefully—not ho-lay, ho-lay, ho-lay! Observe the commas, pausing
> slightly after each; one beat in the middle, and one at the end of each long
> line should be reserved for breathing, so that one can attack the note fol-
> lowing with firmness. Begin each line with soft tones increasing in power
> as the notes rise, decreasing as they go lower on the scale. A quiet third
> stanza, with the fourth opening majestically, and rising to a veritable shout
> in the second line "all thy works shall praise thy name . . . ," gives a won-
> derful contrast and affords a brilliant ending for the hymn. And of course,
> SING ALL THE STANZAS![14]

Grand as this hymn is, however, it really came into its own when John
Dykes (1823–1876) wrote this immortal tune expressly for it, calling it
"Nicaea" after the fourth-century council that met in that city. In A.D. 325,
Christendom's bishops met there to discuss and settle a number of controversial issues; among them, one related to the nature of Christ and His relationship to God the Father and God the Holy Spirit. Arius, bishop of Egypt,
maintained that while Christ was higher than man, He was lesser than God,
being of similar but not the same "substance" as the Father. Athanasius, a
brilliant young layman who later was to become one of the leading bishops
of his day, defended the Trinitarian view (i.e., that Jesus Christ was God the
Son) and his argument carried the day, with only five dissenting votes out of
some three hundred.[15] The Nicene Creed was formulated, making explicit
what the Scriptures teach implicitly. Since Heber's hymn exalts the Trinitarian nature of God—Father, Son, and Holy Spirit, three in one yet one in
three—Dykes' choice of name reflects his awareness of the importance of
historical perspective for the Christian faith!

Dykes, himself an Anglican clergyman, wrote over three hundred hymn tunes, including some nineteen used in the *Trinity Hymnal* (only Lowell Mason is better represented, with some twenty-eight included). This is easily one of his best! It is interesting, incidentally, to see critics—even of such a gifted and versatile writer—attempting to find fault with his work. Thus Kenneth Long complains that

> Often one of his tunes begins with a really arresting first line, powerful and uplifting, sweeping onwards with irresistible drive. Then, quite unexpectedly, it collapses in a heap. The rest of the tune limps feebly home, slipping and sliding over treacherous chromatics.[16]

And Long cites "Melita," the tune sung with "Eternal Father, Strong to Save . . . ," as an illustration. It is my opinion that long after Long's opinion is laid to rest in the grave of facile iconoclasticism, Dykes, never a man who could be accused, justly, of being a prima donna, will be enjoying the knowledge that his marvelous hymn tunes continue to lift the spirits and bless the hearts of all who hear and sing them!

Notes

1. McCutchan, *Our Hymnody,* p. 17.
2. Bailey, *op. cit.,* p. 151.
3. Julian, *op. cit.,* pp. 503, 530.
4. Smith, *op. cit.,* p. 145.
5. *Ibid.*
6. McCutchan, *op. cit.,* p. 18.
7. Haeussler, *op. cit.,* p. 53.
8. Routley, *Hymns and the Faith,* p. 72.
9. *Ibid.,* p. 70.
10. Bailey, *op. cit.,* p. 152.
11. Routley, *op. cit.,* p. 76.
12. *Ibid.,* p. 77.
13. *Ibid.*
14. Smith, *op. cit.,* pp. 147–148; emphasis added.
15. Haeussler, *op. cit.,* p. 54.
16. Long, *The Music of the English Church,* p. 361.

Title/Date	*"How Sweet the Name of Jesus Sounds"*
	(1779)
Author	*John Newton*
Composer/Tune	*Alexander R. Reinagle "St. Peter"*
	(1836)
Scriptural Basis	*Song of Solomon 1:3*

In the final years of his lengthy ministry at St. Mary's Woolworth in London, John Newton (1725–1807) was compelled by failing eyesight to have his old servant assist him in his pulpit. One morning Newton read the words "Jesus Christ is precious," paused, and then repeated them. Thinking Newton had become confused, the servant whispered, "Go on, go on, you said that before." Newton turned and said,

"John, I said that twice, and I'm going to say it again." And his voice took on a different quality as he repeated more firmly than before, "Jesus Christ *is* precious!"[1]

And for John Newton, profligate, vagabond, deserter from the Royal Navy, libertine, slave-trader (indeed, captain of a ship engaged in that nefarious traffic for some six years in Sierra Leone), who had been gloriously redeemed by the amazing grace of God—grace greater than all the enormity of his sin—Jesus Christ *was* precious indeed!

It is sobering to note again the immense impact that one's mother can have on a child's life. For although Newton's mother died of tuberculosis when he was only seven, she had "constantly prayed and earnestly hoped for his salvation," intending him from his birth for the ministry; as Julian says, "she stored his childish mind with Scripture,"[2] taught him the *Westminster Catechism* with its texts, and had him learn, by heart, both the *Child's Catechism* and the many hymns for children Isaac Watts had written. And, of course, it is easy to see the bearing of all this training and teaching—hidden in his heart—on his own eventual calling as a servant of God.[3]

Newton's experiences are regularly reflected in his verses, which is one reason why they were and continue to be so widely used by persons of almost every theological persuasion. Many of them, intended for use at the

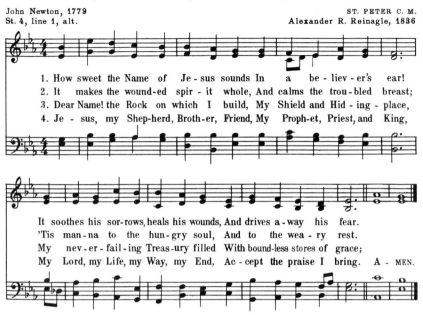

Thy name is as ointment poured forth . . . Song of Solomon 1 : 3

John Newton, 1779
St. 4, line 1, alt.

ST. PETER C. M.
Alexander R. Reinagle, 1836

1. How sweet the Name of Je - sus sounds In a be - liev - er's ear!
2. It makes the wound-ed spir - it whole, And calms the trou-bled breast;
3. Dear Name! the Rock on which I build, My Shield and Hid - ing - place,
4. Je - sus, my Shep-herd, Broth-er, Friend, My Proph-et, Priest, and King,

It soothes his sor-rows, heals his wounds, And drives a - way his fear.
'Tis man - na to the hun-gry soul, And to the wea - ry rest.
My nev - er - fail - ing Treas-ury filled With bound-less stores of grace;
My Lord, my Life, my Way, my End, Ac - cept the praise I bring. A - MEN.

5. Weak is the effort of my heart,
And cold my warmest thought;
But when I see thee as thou art,
I'll praise thee as I ought.

6. Till then I would thy love proclaim
With every fleeting breath;
And may the music of thy Name
Refresh my soul in death.

end of a sermon to drive the truth proclaimed home to the hearts of those assembled in worship, were not of a high poetic order; but then, that was not his purpose. In his preface to *Olney Hymns,* which became a treasured "body of experimental divinity," he wrote:

> There is a style and manner suited to the composition of hymns, which may be more successfully . . . attained by a versifier than by a poet. They should be *Hymns,* not *Odes,* if designed for public worship, and for the use of plain people. Perspicuity, simplicity and ease, should be chiefly attended to; and the imagery and colouring of poetry, if admitted at all, should be indulged very sparingly, and with great judgment.[4]

Yet, at the same time, we should not judge Newton's work as careless, shoddy, or unworthy; for as eminent an authority on hymns as John Julian highly appraises the character and the work of this gifted but most humble servant of Jesus Christ, who never completely got over the humiliating experiences of his unregenerate days and even of his first years as a Christian. In fact, he was often criticized for having continued his slaving for several years after his conversion! But as one points out, as a fact, not as an excuse, "the hymn doesn't say 'how sweet the name of *Newton* sounds";[5] and William Jay, who saw Newton at the end of his life, quotes perhaps his most well-known statement: "My memory is nearly gone, but I remember two things, that I am a great sinner, and that Jesus Christ is a great Saviour."[6] So, as Julian writes,

> The story of his sins and his conversion, published by himself, and the subject of lifelong allusion, was the base of his influence; but it would have been little except for the vigor of his mind, . . . his warm heart, candour, tolerance and piety; . . . his renown as a guide in experimental religion made him the center of a host of inquirers, with whom he maintained patient, loving, and generally judicious correspondence. . . . As a hymn-writer . . . Lord Selbourne's contrast of Newton's "manliness" and Cowper's "tenderness" is . . . just. . . . His rich acquaintance with Scripture, knowledge of the heart, directness and force, and a certain sailor's imagination tell strongly. [His hymn] "One there is above all others" has a depth of realizing love, sustained excellence of expression, and ease of development. . . . His most characteristic hymns are those which depict, in the language of intense humiliation, his mourning for the abiding sins of his regenerate life, and the sense of the withdrawal of God's face, coincident with the never-failing conviction of acceptance in the BELOVED.[7]

The tune "St. Peter" was composed by Alexander R. Reinagle (1799–1877), whose grandfather, Joseph, was a trumpeter to the king of Scotland and whose father, Joseph Jr., was an eminent violoncellist who led the orchestra in the Edinburgh Theatre.[8] Alexander served as organist at a church in Oxford for thirty-one years; both he and his gifted wife, a fine pianist, taught music, and he edited several books, publishing one of his own in 1830, which included this and other hymn tunes.[9] It was named for the church he served; hence "St. Peters, Oxford" was its full designation.[10] Of it, as an unusual tune, one author writes:

> Few Western tunes are pleasant to oriental ears, but [this one] is an exception. [I] have seldom been so thrilled by mass singing as when [I] was leading a congregation of nearly one thousand Hainanese as they sang it in unison with stately rhythm. This is one of our majestic hymns, to be sung in moderate time and with strong rhythmic accent.[11]

Let us now turn to an examination of this hymn, of which Julian says: "it is in Scriptural richness superior to, and in structure, cadence, and, . . . tenderness, the equal of Cowper's 'Oh! For a Closer Walk with God.'"[12] Inspired as it may have been by an earlier Latin hymn written by the devout and intense mystic St. Bernard of Clairvaux, it is indeed characterized "by directness, simplicity, virility, and evangelistic urgency."[13]

This hymn focuses first on the Name of Jesus Christ and what it means to the writer, and then on the ministry of that same Jesus in His multifaceted relationships to him. A person's name is a precious possession, and it is not to be smeared, forged, ridiculed, or treated with false diffidence in order to gain personal rewards. For a name discloses one's person, especially when it is purposefully given, as was His: "you shall call His name 'Jesus,' for He shall save His people from their sins" (Matthew 1:21).

Stanza One: For the believer, whose sins have led to heartache, fear (perhaps of judgment), and even sickness, Jesus, the provider of redemption, can both heal and give solace.

Stanza Two: Wholeness of spirit and quietness of heart, food for the hungry soul (and who could ever deny that deepest hunger, having experienced it long years apart from the God of his mother's prayers), and rest for the weary body are also found in Jesus.

Stanza Three: Here Newton piles up epithets, principally from the psalms, reflecting both the security and the boundless provision he finds in that dear Name. He continues to build as he has for over three decades on that foundation, his conversion, which he dated March 21, 1748.[14]

Stanza Four: Relationships—person to person, subject to Ruler, human to Divine—are mentioned here; they range from the most tender, husband (brother, in the *Trinity Hymnal*) and friend, to the most exalted, Lord and Life—for each and all of which he offers praise.

Stanza Five: Newton knew his heart and was aware of the depth of its possibilities for sin and corruption. Weak, when he should be strong, and cold when he should be warm with conviction and zeal, he did not despair; for he believed that the day would come when his sanctification would be complete—when he would be standing in the unclouded presence of his Jesus—and then his stammering praises would be as they should be.

Stanza Six: In Newton's eightieth year, as mentioned previously, his failing eyesight threatened to still his voice, for he could no longer read his sermon manuscripts; when one suggested he stop preaching he responded, "What, shall the old African blasphemer stop while he can still speak?"[15] Here is expressed that same ardent resolve, to give himself unceasingly to the preaching of the gospel—proclaiming "God so loved the world" to anyone who would listen. And with that as the habit of his life, his last breath would be drawn with "Jesus" on his lips, and death would be "but his entrance into glory!"

In a profound sense, John Newton's life demonstrates the truth of a comment made by philosopher Will Durant, who said, "a good man who is not great is a hundred times more precious than a great man who is not good,"[16] for Newton was a *good* man!

Notes

1. McCutchan, *Our Hymnody*, p. 52.
2. Julian, *op. cit.*, p. 803.
3. Duffield, *op. cit.*, p. 248.
4. McCutchan, *op. cit.*, p. 51.
5. Moffatt and Patrick, *op. cit.*, p. 143.
6. *Ibid.*
7. Julian, *op. cit.*, pp. 803–804.
8. Moffatt and Patrick, *op. cit.*, p. 474.
9. McCutchan, *op. cit.*, p. 428.
10. Smith, *op. cit.*, p. 173.
11. Covert and Laufer, *op. cit.*, p. 96.
12. Julian, *op. cit.*, p. 803.
13. Covert and Laufer, *op. cit.*, p. 332.
14. Duffield, *op. cit.*, p. 253.
15. Julian, *op. cit.*, p. 803.
16. Bailey, *op. cit.*, p. 127.

Title/Date	*"Jesus, I My Cross Have Taken"* *(1824)*
Author	*Henry Francis Lyte*
Composer/Tune	*Henry Smart "Crucifier" (1867)*
	W. A. Mozart "Discipline" (1831)
Scriptural Basis	*Mark 10:28–30*

Theological controversy began in the Garden of Eden when God's character was apparently the subject of a debate between Satan, the master of deceit, and Eve, his easily bested opponent. But while it began there, it certainly didn't end there or then, continuing as it has to create strife and division among God's people down to our present day. Moreover, it has occurred not only in idyllic garden settings, but also in noisy, busy little fishing villages like Lower Brixham was during the early nineteenth century. In spite of the desire and earnest labors of its godly pastor, Henry Lyte, to maintain a harmonious congregation and to focus his people's energies on "the things which make for peace" and spiritual growth, there were the ever-present agitators, spoiling for debate; one in particular, an old man of Arminian persuasion,

> was seen, of a Sunday morning just outside the door of the Calvinistic chapel, stirring a very filthy pool with a stick. Notorious as a controversialist, his opponents gathered around him and asked what he was looking after. Still probing in the mud he said "I am searching for the eternal decrees."[1]

It was such people with whom Lyte's sensitive nature and less-than-robust health had to deal almost daily; here in Brixham he relinquished every scholarly, cultural, and social ambition he may have had, and took up his own cross, daily, following his Lord Jesus Christ. As a true mystic he sought his refuge in Christ Himself and walked his own Via Dolorosa—Brixham, in Devonshire—behind his Lord![2] And, in spite of their rough, coarse ways, Lyte won their hearts so completely that his church was crowded every Sunday. Moreover, he went to them, visiting them on their boats, making certain each one had a Bible on board before they left port, and expressing his practical concern for their wives and children. He also gave of his energies

There is no man that hath left house, or brethren . . . for my sake, and the gospel's, but he shall receive an hundredfold now . . . with persecutions; and in the world to come eternal life. Mark 10:29-30

CRUCIFER 8. 7. 8. 7. D.

Henry F. Lyte, 1824; text of 1833   Henry Smart, 1867

1. Je - sus, I my cross have tak-en, All to leave, and fol - low thee;
2. Man may trou-ble and dis-tress me, 'Twill but drive me to thy breast;
3. Take, my soul, thy full sal-va-tion, Rise o'er sin and fear and care;
4. Haste then on from grace to glo-ry, Armed by faith, and winged by prayer;

Des - ti-tute, de-spised, for - sa-ken, Thou from hence my all shalt be:
Life with tri - als hard may press me, Heav'n will bring me sweet-er rest:
Joy to find in ev - 'ry sta-tion Some-thing still to do or bear;
Heav'n's e - ter - nal day's be - fore thee, God's own hand shall guide thee there.

Per - ish ev - 'ry fond am - bi - tion, All I've sought, or hoped, or known;
O 'tis not in grief to harm me While thy love is left to me;
Think what Spir - it dwells with - in thee, What a Fa - ther's smile is thine,
Soon shall close thy earth - ly mis-sion; Swift shall pass thy pil-grim days;

Yet how rich is my con-di-tion, God and heav'n are still my own.
O 'twere not in joy to charm me, Were that joy un-mixed with thee.
What a Sav-iour died to win thee: Child of heav'n, shouldst thou re-pine?
Hope soon change to glad fru - i - tion, Faith to sight, and prayer to praise. A - MEN.

in support of larger issues, especially Lord Wilberforce's attempts to get a bill passed in Parliament securing the abolition of slavery in all British domains.

While Lyte has been characterized as a gloomy poet, that, I believe is not true, and would remind the reader of his magnificent "Praise My Soul, the King of Heaven," studied earlier. At the same time, it is true that life has its low places for every Christian, and it was his desire to minister, through his verse, to people in the valley of despair or despondency. He wrote:

> Might verse of mine inspire
>   One virtuous aim, one high resolve impart-
> Light in one drooping soul a hallowed fire,
>   Or bind one broken heart,
> Death would be sweeter then,
>   More calm my slumber 'neath the silent sod
> Might I thus live to bless my fellow men,
>   Or glorify my God.[3]

Beautiful, stirring lines, I believe; and bless his fellow men he has in the hymn we are considering, written apparently during these first months of his ministry in Brixham, where controversy and division in his church added to the weight on his spirit.[4]

Let us examine this hymn that Bodine reports[5] had appeared in 103 of 107 hymnals in England, making it in his day Lyte's most popular hymn, underscoring the fact that many Christians can identify with Lyte in their "down" times!

Stanza One: At first reading, one would certainly think that either Lyte was overreacting to his limiting situation, or that it was much more wretched than we can imagine. But, while "destitute, despised, forsaken" may appear to be an overreaction, "perish every fond ambition, all I've sought, or hoped or known" may be realistic since he probably felt he'd have few in his parish who would have a taste for the more refined touch he was capable of bringing to them. However, since the Lord had placed him in Brixham, his focus would be on Jesus, "from hence his all," and recognizing who that Jesus is—from his earlier conversion experience—well could he affirm his "rich condition," owning, in a personal, experiential sense, both God and heaven.

Stanza Two: Again, reflecting on his current circumstances he takes them—stressful troubles, hard-pressing trials, harmful grieving—to his Lord in a very intimate series of affirmations. Life here may mean hard labors, but heaven will bring rest; God's love is constant, and true joy is also His gift!

Stanza Three: As he ponders his daily sources of challenge—sin, fear, care, each of which would be characteristic of the folk in any seacoast town, especially in a fishing village—he compares challenges and the regular round of duties that at times lay heavy upon his fragile constitution. Yet, aware of the Triune God—the indwelling Spirit, the smiling Father, the redemptive Son—he asks the rhetorical question, probably with a slightly-ever-so-chiding smile on his face, "Child of heaven, shouldst thou repine?"

Stanza Four: While the author is not an expert in literary criticism, it is his judgment that this stanza, as poetic exhortation, is of the highest order, with every phrase beautifully turned and each word carefully chosen. Say it aloud, with his situation in mind:

> Haste then on from grace to glory,
>   Armed by faith and winged by prayer;
> Heaven's eternal day's before thee,
>   God's own hand shall guide thee there.
> Soon shall close thy earthly mission;
>   swift shall pass thy pilgrim days;
> Hope soon change to glad fruition,
>   faith to sight, and prayer to praise.

The first sentence and the last sentence are parallel, with the movement from now to the future, from promise (grace, hope) to fulfillment (glory, glad fruition); faith as one's weapon and prayer as one's "wings" become sight, which leads to praise, for the prayer has been answered. The second and third sentences convey that sense of being in transition here in this world, for one's present task (mission) will be completed, one's being a pilgrim will be ended, and God's guiding hand will see us safely to our ultimate and glorious destination. How much more exquisite is his poetry than my clumsy prose! If it was true, as Lyte said of his preconversion ministry, that "he had been breaking for others the Bread of Life on which he himself had not fed," [6] it certainly was true no longer, for his experience of God's grace now was rich indeed!

"Crucifer," the tune that the *Trinity Hymnal* has chosen for this hymn, was written by Henry Smart (1812–1879), a lawyer turned (largely self-taught) organist and composer, some of whose organ compositions "have been considered worthy of Beethoven." [7] When he was only fifty-two, he became blind, but he continued his work of composing, playing, and even supervising the construction of fine organs for many years thereafter. He favored the use of the slower, more dignified style of the old psalm tunes for congregational singing, rather than the quicker measures of many of his contemporaries; [8] however, his were anything but dull and ponderous, when one thinks of (and hums) "Regent Square," his tune recognized as "Angels, From the Realms of Glory" (*Trinity Hymnal,* p. 164).

My choice of tune for this hymn, having sung it scores of times, is one known by many names, especially "Ellesdie," and in the *Trinity Hymnal,* "Disciple" (see hymn 691). This tune "presents another of the hymn-tune puzzles which . . . defy solution," [9] for while it has been widely attributed to Mozart, students of that famous composer cannot find it, clearly, in his works. Louis

Benson dates its first appearance in the *Christian Lyre* in 1831, where it is called "Disciple";[10] various musicians have arranged it, including Hubert P. Main, a prolific hymn tune-composer who worked with and later for William Bradbury.

One final note about Lyte, and the mood he has set in this immortal hymn. Elsewhere he similarly writes of his trustful obedience in words that almost could form another stanza of this hymn:

> Let good or ill befall, it must be good for me;
> Secure of having Thee in all, of having all in Thee.[11]

A marvelous affirmation of trust!

Notes

1. Duffield, *op. cit.,* p. 489.
2. Bailey, *op. cit.,* p. 170.
3. Covert and Laufer, *op. cit.,* p. 18.
4. Brown and Butterworth, *op. cit.,* p. 221.
5. Haeussler, *op. cit.,* p. 282.
6. Breed, *op. cit.,* p. 199.
7. Covert and Laufer, *op. cit.,* p. 74.
8. *Ibid.*
9. McCutchan, *op. cit.,* p. 297.
10. Haeussler, *op. cit.,* p. 283.
11. Duffield, *op. cit.,* p. 380.

Title/Date	*"Jesus, Lover of My Soul"* (1740)
Author	*Charles Wesley*
Composer/Tune	*Joseph Parry "Aberystwyth"* (1879)
	Simeon B. Marsh "Martyn" (1834)
Scriptural Basis	*Romans 8:35; Isaiah 25:4; Wisdom of Solomon 11:26*

This, the most famous of Wesley's hymns, has been called "the greatest hymn of all time, which, together with the Twenty-third Psalm . . . voice the creed, the hope, and the prayer of Christendom";[1] Breed states, without hesitation, that the entire church is unanimous in assigning the first-place rank to this hymn,[2] and Reeves, concurring, says,

> This, one of the supreme hymns of the world, has gone to the corners of the earth . . . translated into virtually every language there is . . . a treasury of spiritual wealth. . . . Countless . . . men and women have found in it deep refreshment of spirit as from a cool spring and shade by the road when tired and thirsty; and uncounted multitudes have passed out of this life with its words on their lips.[3]

As "the finest heart-hymn in the English language,"[4] the stories of it being used by God to bless, encourage, comfort, and provide solace to persons of all ages, stations, and circumstances in life are legion, McCutchan and others claiming that "it would require a good-sized book to print all the (verified) incidents told in connection with its use."[5]

To cite but a few:

1. Spurgeon tells of a man who, after hearing it sung, asked, "Does Christ love even me?" and upon being assured he was converted, declaring, "Why should I live (any longer) in enmity to Him?"[6]

2. During the Civil War a Presbyterian chaplain asked a dying soldier if he had any last request, and when he said, "Yes, Sir, sing 'Jesus, Lover of My Soul,' he responded; though normally a psalm-singer only, he sang the hymn, and the young man died, but his face was beautifully lighted up; the chaplain left him saying, "If this hymn is good to die by, it is good to live by."[7]

*For thou hast been a strength . . . to the needy in his distress,
a refuge from the storm, a shadow from the heat.* Isa. 25:4

MARTYN 7. 7. 7. 7. D.
Simeon B. Marsh, 1834

Charles Wesley, 1740

Harmonized by Rhys Thomas, 1916

3. A New York City pastor visiting Bellevue Hospital, urged to bring comfort to a dying sailor, spoke these words to his upturned ear; but he was apparently too far gone, for he made no response. Then, several hours later, he sat up on his cot, spoke the words of the entire hymn and added lines

from others, then sank back and died. How great a bridge had those familiar words made across the gulf of memory, and what comfort did they bring
him in his dying hour![8]

George Duffield, author of "Stand Up, Stand Up for Jesus," bears his
witness:

> One of the most blessed days of my life was when I found, after my harp
> had long hung on the willows, that I could *sing* again; that a "new song was
> put into my mouth"; and when I was aware, I was singing "Jesus, lover of
> my soul"; if there is anything in Christian experience of joy and sorrow, of
> affliction and prosperity, of life and death—that hymn is *the* hymn of the
> ages![9]

And Henry Ward Beecher, whose clergyman father loved this hymn
dearly, affirmed that

> I would rather have written that hymn of Charles Wesley's than to have the
> fame of all the kings that ever sat on earth; it is more glorious, it has more
> power in it. I would rather be the author of that hymn than to hold the
> wealth of the richest man in New York. He will die, and pass out of men's
> thoughts, and what will there be to speak of him? . . . But that hymn will
> go on singing until the last trump brings forth the angel band; and then I
> think it will mount upon some lips to the very presence of God.[10]

While we cannot be certain of the circumstances out of which this magnificent hymn of strengthening in time of temptation and struggle was born,
some worthy suggestions have been made. Wesley had had three dramatic
experiences in the years prior to 1739, the year this hymn was written.

First, returning from America to England in 1736, the ship he was on was
caught in a terrible storm—probably a hurricane—which washed away
much of the ship's cargo, strained her seams so that even the hardest pump-
ing could barely keep pace with the inrushing water, and terrified everyone
on board, including Wesley. After much prayer, he was encouraged to believe
that he did "abide under the shadow of the Almighty," and so was able to be
of spiritual strength to crewmen and fellow passengers alike; he never forgot
that much-too-close brush with death, and later penned these lines:

> O Thou who didst prepare
> 　　The Ocean's caverned cell,
> And teach the gathering waters there
> 　　to meet and dwell;
> Tossed in our reeling bark

Upon this briney sea,
Thy wondrous ways, O Lord, we mark
And sing to Thee.

Borne on the dark'ning wave,
In measured sweep we go,
Nor dread th' unfathomable grave,
Which yawns below;
For He is nigh who trod
Amid the foaming spray,
Whose billows own'd th' Incarnate God,
And died away.[11]

Second, for some weeks before his conversion in May 1738, Wesley had been ill with a fever, pleurisy, and dysentery. Alone in his rooms he had a "vision"—or, as Bailey thinks, an hallucination[12]—in which a Mrs. Musgrove entered his room and said, "In the name of Jesus of Nazareth, arise and believe, and thou shalt be healed of all thy infirmities"; calling for her, he learned she had not been in the house at all. Opening his Bible, he found comfort and recorded in his *Journal:*

I arose and looked into the Scripture, reading "And now Lord, what is my hope? Truly my hope is in Thee" . . . then Isaiah 40:1 "Comfort ye, comfort ye my people . . . that her iniquity is pardoned." . . . I found myself at peace with God. . . . At midnight I gave myself to Christ: assured I was safe, waking or sleeping . . . (knowing) that He was able to do exceedingly abundantly for me. [And from this hour his bodily strength returned.][13]

The third experience of Wesley that sunk deeply into his soul was his ministry with the felons at Newgate. On one occasion ten were condemned to death on the gallows at Tyburn Hill, and he spent much time during the preceding week (not long after his own conversion) seeking to help them prepare to meet their Maker. The gruesome details do not need to be repeated, but the sense of spiritual joy several experienced was genuine, and as he gave them Communion, for their last—and for several, their first—time, it was a moving scene. He says:

We had prayed that our Lord would show that there was a power superior to the fear of death. They were all cheerful, full of comfort, peace and triumph, persuaded that Christ had indeed died for them, and waited to receive them into Paradise. . . . None showed any natural terror of death; no

fear, no crying or tears; I never saw such calm triumph, such incredible indifference to dying.[14]

It was experiences such as these that turned Wesley

from a self-distrustful and over-anxious clergyman with uncertain aim
[into] a flaming evangelist, a veritable voice of God, moving vast out-of-
doors audiences all over England, Wales and Ireland; he pleaded with the
lowest of men, society's outcasts to accept the free salvation of Christ and
lead lives of holiness, thereafter.[15]

Let us examine this hymn, keeping these experiences he had in mind, for
they had proven to be catalysts.

Stanza One: The storms of life could certainly include the storm he survived on the Atlantic, but it could also refer to the waves of the world—
temptations, troubles, sorrow, losses. The "nearer waters" are described by
Julian:

In life, as in nature, storms are local; one ship may be dashed to pieces by
the fury of the nearer waters—i.e., the waves surrounding it, while other
ships may be, some distance off, completely becalmed. So it is that men
cry for help, not against dangers that are both distant and undefined, but
out of the depths of their immediate troubles. Their life is amid the "nearer
waters" of local surroundings, passions and temptations, and to them the
Lover of souls is indispensable.[16]

For safety is always in the same haven; Bickersteth has it:

Peace, perfect peace, with sorrows surging round,
on Jesus' bosom naught but calm is found.[17]

And Rutherford says well, "many heads are lying in Christ's bosom, but there
is room for yours"![18]

Stanza Two: Again, one could see his experience of the storm and the terrible debilitating illness he suffered behind these lines. When we are despairing and defenseless, we put all our trust in Him, a secure and complete
refuge, and we get all the help we need. A young soldier wrote home: "Many
a time as we went to the trenches I sang it to myself; nobody realizes the
meaning of 'cover my defenseless head' like a soldier with bullets pinging
over his head."[19]

Stanza Three: Some enemies can be bested by personal courage and even
on occasion by a defiant attitude (i.e., one can "stare them down"). But,

when dealing with self, those weapons are unreliable.[20] When we realize, by the grace of God, that we are "false and full of sin," that we are "all unrighteousness," we need help to effectively deal with it. One saint of God was described:

> To his children daily he grew more like the Lord, and yet daily his sense of sin and the depth of the wickedness of his own heart became more vivid to him.[21]

Note, also, the contrasts here: I am false, Christ is true; I am full of sin, He is full of grace; I am unrighteous, He is just and holy, thoroughly righteous; He is everything I'm not, and can therefore supply my every need. As Rutherford said: "How little of the sea can a child carry in his hand? As little do I take away from my great Sea, my boundless and running over Christ-Jesus."[22]

Stanza Four: Rather than being in bondage to our past, our fears, our guilty consciences, we must draw on these inexhaustible stores of grace to cover my sins—all of them; to heal, to purify, and to quicken me both now and in eternity. As Faber says, "They wash the wound until the poison is all gone."[23] It is grace that conquers; not strength, not instruction, not wisdom, not gentleness, but grace. "My Grace is sufficient for thee"; and that grace is plenteous, leading beyond all else to a joyous, multidimensional life! Meditate on this prayer by Thomas à Kempis:

> Ah, Lord God, Thou holy Lover of my soul, when Thou comest into my soul all that is within me shall rejoice. Thou art my glory and the exultation of my heart. Thou art my hope and refuge in the day of my trouble. Set me free from all evil passions, heal my heart of all inordinate affections, that being inwardly cured and thoroughly cleansed I may be made fit to love, courageous to suffer, steady to perservere. Nothing is sweeter than love, nothing more courageous, nothing fuller nor better in heaven and earth; because love is born of God, and cannot rest but in God.[24]

The tune "Aberystwyth," one of the two most often associated with this hymn, was written by Joseph Parry (1841–1903), born of poor parents in Wales' southeast iron district. At ten he quit school to work in the iron furnaces as a puddler, and enjoyed singing "on the job" with his co-workers, demonstrating a remarkable musical talent and the training his gifted mother had given him. Emigrating to America in the 1850s, they later returned to Wales. There he submitted a harmonized hymn tune at the Swansea Eisteddfod in 1865;[25] this so impressed Brinley Richards, an adjudicator for the competition, that he raised the money for Parry to attend the Royal

Academy of Music at Cambridge. Parry, making the most of his opportunity, worked hard, earning both his Mus. Bac. degree and, seven years later, his Mus. Doc.! He served as professor of music at two Welsh colleges, and exercised enormous influence on Welsh music. By far the most popular Welsh composer—with his music being sung in virtually every hamlet—he was given renown nationally and a six hundred pound prize for his services to Welsh music. This tune, as most hymn tunes, was named after one of his teaching posts, the college town of Aberystwyth.[26]

"Martyn," the other tune frequently used with this hymn, was written by an American, Simeon B. Marsh (1798–1875), from childhood a gifted singer, and later, a teacher of singing and conductor of singing schools for more than thirty years in upstate New York. His love for music and children led him to instruct them without being paid, both in schools and in churches; he was, in fact, instrumental in introducing music to the public school curriculum.[27] This tune was written in the fall of 1834; en route to one of his singing schools, he dismounted from his horse and wrote out the melody. Early associations of it with a hymn by Newton have been replaced by its use with this hymn, especially after Hastings discovered how well these words and this melody fit together[28]—a wedding that has indeed lasted and a marriage that has worn well!

A third tune, "Hollingside," by the eminent John Dykes, which he wrote while living in his charming home with his new bride, was used with it in the first edition of *Hymns Ancient and Modern;* this tune, however, is not heard as often as are those previously mentioned.

Ponder the truth of this marvelous "hymn for a time of crisis"—yes, but also for any time in life when one needs the quiet, peaceful place of refuge from whatever storms are brewing!

Notes

1. McCutchan, *Our Hymnody,* p. 357.
2. *Ibid.*
3. *Ibid.*
4. Marks, *op. cit.,* p. 103.
5. McCutchan, *op. cit.,* p. 358.
6. *Ibid.,* p. 359.
7. Brown and Butterworth, *op. cit.,* pp. 362–363.
8. Duffield, *op. cit.,* pp. 290–291.
9. *Ibid.,* p. 291.
10. Hostetler, *op. cit.,* pp. 98–99.
11. Brown and Butterworth, *op. cit.,* p. 361.
12. Bailey, *op. cit.,* p. 91.

13. *Ibid.*, pp. 91–92.

14. *Ibid.*, pp. 93–94.

15. *Ibid.*, p. 91.

16. Julian, *op. cit.*, p. 591.

17. *Trinity Hymnal*, p. 590.

18. Hodson, *op. cit.*, p. 26.

19. *Ibid.*, p. 27.

20. Routley, *Hymns and the Faith*, p. 177.

21. Hodson, *op. cit.*, p. 29.

22. *Ibid.*, p. 30.

23. *Ibid.*, p. 31.

24. *Ibid.*, p. 32.

25. Moffatt and Patrick, *op. cit.*, pp. 455–456.

26. Lightwood, *op. cit.*, p. 406.

27. Covert and Laufer, *op. cit.*, p. 252.

28. McCutchan, *op. cit.*, p. 361.

Title/Date	*"Jesus, the Very Thought of Thee . . ."* *(11th century)*
Author	*Bernard of Clairvaux*
	Edward Caswell, trans. (1849)
Composer/Tune	*John Dykes "St. Agnes" (1866)*
Scriptural Basis	*Ephesians 3:19; Song of Solomon*

It has frequently been claimed that words such as Newton's "How SWEET the name of Jesus sounds," Wesley's "Jesus, LOVER of my soul," and Bernard's "Jesus, the very thought of Thee with SWEETNESS fills my breast" are somehow inappropriate in hymns—at least, in such hymns as men are supposed to sing; for since such terms of endearment have been labeled "unmanly," various attempts have been made to substitute other words for these, such as Cotterill's "blest" for Newton's "sweet"—an attempt, incidentally, which failed.[1]

It is the author's conviction that these and similar words, while not common in our usual discourse, are nevertheless legitimate, for they express the deeply felt concerns of the heart that faithful believers of both sexes can—and frequently do—experience. These are among those tender expressions of feeling which, moreover, should not be labeled "feminine," as though men should not or could not experience them; and if men can experience them, men should be encouraged to speak of them—forthrightly!

All of this relates, of course, to the hymn we are about to consider, "Jesu dulcis memoria," a hymn that apparently has been taken (along with another in these studies) from a much longer poem, best known as the "Joyful (or Jubilee) Rhythm of St. Bernard, on the Name of Jesus."[2] Julian, noted hymnologist of nineteenth-century England, informs us that

> the earliest form of the text now known (and, it may be added, the best and most probably the original) is contained in a MSS. of the end of the 12*th* century, now in the Bodleian, Oxford "Laud Misc." 668f 101, in 42 st. of 41.[3]

I cite this somewhat technical data because while some authorities question Bernard of Clairvaux's authorship, several others affirm Julian's judgment as

186

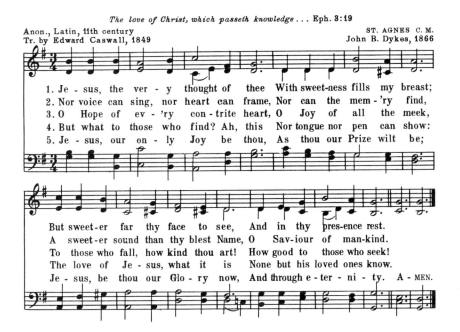

The love of Christ, which passeth knowledge . . . Eph. 3:19

Anon., Latin, 11th century
Tr. by Edward Caswall, 1849

ST. AGNES C. M.
John B. Dykes, 1866

1. Je - sus, the ver - y thought of thee With sweet-ness fills my breast;
2. Nor voice can sing, nor heart can frame, Nor can the mem - 'ry find,
3. O Hope of ev - 'ry con - trite heart, O Joy of all the meek,
4. But what to those who find? Ah, this Nor tongue nor pen can show:
5. Je - sus, our on - ly Joy be thou, As thou our Prize wilt be;

But sweet-er far thy face to see, And in thy pres-ence rest.
A sweet-er sound than thy blest Name, O Sav-iour of man-kind.
To those who fall, how kind thou art! How good to those who seek!
The love of Je - sus, what it is None but his loved ones know.
Je - sus, be thou our Glo - ry now, And through e - ter - ni - ty. A - MEN.

correct. For example, Archbishop Trench favors Bernard, as do Moffatt and
Patrick, who cite evidence that this poem was attributed to Bernard within
a century of his death;[4] Bailey cites *The Catholic Encyclopedia* as pronounc-
ing against Bernard, but then mentions an eleventh-century manuscript as
"containing most of the hymn."[5] Alfred Edersheim cites it, in part, in his *The
Jubilee Rhythm of St. Bernard of Clairvaux* (1867),[6] and Philip Schaff in his
Christ in Song strongly defends its Bernardian authorship, justly styling the
hymn as

> the sweetest and most evangelical . . . hymn of the Middle Ages . . . the
> finest and most characteristic specimen of St. Bernard's "subjective loveli-
> ness," and in its honied sweetness vindicates his title of doctor mellifluus.[7]

Finally, after listing, in fine print, eight columns of translations—in several
languages—which have been made of this 192-line poem, Julian says,

> This elaborate and extensive use of St. Bernard's "Rhythm" is almost if not
> entirely unique in hymnody. A few hymns exceed it in the number of
> their translations into English, such as "Adeste fideles" and "Ein feste
> Burg" but no other poem in any language has furnished to English and
> American hymnbooks so many hymns of sterling worth and well-deserved
> popularity.[8]

Bernard of Clairvaux (1091–1153) was born of a noble French family near Dijon; his father was a knight, and his mother a woman of radiant goodness, who encouraged his bent for piety and learning. A handsome youth, elegant of speech and gracious in manner, he distinguished himself in his studies at the University of Paris. After his mother's death, which he deeply mourned, he was intending a political or military career, when a vision of his mother, disapproving of his choice, stopped him in his tracks and changed the course of his life—note again the power of a mother's prayers!

Becoming a Brother in the reform-minded monastery at Citeaux, which stressed the features that had originally characterized the (by then) lax Benedictine Order—strict discipline, manual labor, farming, and concern for the material as well as the spiritual needs of the peasants—he threw himself into this work with such passion that he drew to his side his father, his uncle, most of his brothers, and several other young noblemen—all becoming Cistercian monks.

Within three years Bernard, a natural leader, was delegated to found a branch house farther north, in the area known as the Valley of Wormwood; it was aptly so named, for it was a most unhospitable site—wild and desolate. After their first terrible winter, which they barely survived, they built a strong work there, and renamed it "Clara Vallis," or in French "Clairvaux." Bernard, an intense man with severe self-discipline, never relaxed his pattern of daily living. Work, reading, prayer, preaching followed each other inexorably; eventually, by the end of his lifetime, and largely through his inspired leadership, Citeaux had "mothered" 162 similar monasteries, and scores more followed until there were over five hundred; they remained the chief religious power in Western Europe for three centuries, before they declined as the mendicant orders of the Franciscans and the Dominicans arose.[9]

Bernard also exercised great influence in the wider political affairs of Europe, intimately related as they often were to religious concerns; as one writes,

> For more than thirty years he was the personal power that directed belief, quieted turbulence, and arbitrated disputes, with kings and even popes seeking his counsel. Moreover, it was his eloquent preaching that inspired the second crusade.[10]

Unfortunately for Bernard, and for the tens of thousands involved, that Crusade turned out to be a nightmare, and in fact, he wrote a moving letter of apology for his advocacy of such a disaster. Actually, while it was he who almost single-handedly aroused Europe to undertake it as a great spiritual enterprise—to drive the Saracens out of God's city of Jerusalem—he did so at the pope's insistence; then when the incompetence and sinfulness of its leaders made it a total loss, he was almost solely blamed, which was obviously unfair.[11]

Bernard was, preeminently, a devout mystic, spending long hours in Bible reading, prayer, and contemplation. Given to allegorical imagery to clothe the spiritual truths he found in Scripture, he composed eighty-six sermons on Song of Solomon 1–2;[12] moreover, he utilized it much in this long poem, "The Joyful Rhythm," from which our present hymn, "which breathes the deepest love to Christ as the fountain of all peace and comfort,"[13] is taken.

Edward Caswell (1814–1878), one of the many who have translated portions of this poem, has given us this hymn, the most widely used version of all. Caswell, active in the Tractarian Movement, was one of that small number of Anglican priests who eventually became Roman Catholics. After his wife Louisa's sudden death from cholera in 1849, and deeply mourning the loss of this devout and scholarly woman, he entered the Oratory at Edgbaston, which was directed by his close friend, John Henry Newman. There he gave the rest of his life, some twenty-eight years, to hymn-writing and semi-monastic duties, "works of piety and charity."[14] Of him a contemporary wrote, "He was a humble man; every good deed others did was wonderful to him; what he himself did was nothing."[15] And it was fitting that he and Newman, close friends to the end, were buried side by side in a country graveyard at Rednal.[16]

Let us examine this, his "almost unapproachably" fine, poetic translation, "familiar and dear as it is to all English-speaking believers."[17]

Stanza One: Here, and in each succeeding stanza (except for the fourth) Jesus is directly addressed, making this, incidentally, a hymn in the strictest sense. Moreover, there is a progression of intimacy here: sweet it is to think of Him, sweeter yet to see Him, and best of all, to rest in His presence! Simple ideas, bringing to mind our common experience when apart from one whom we love; we relive in our memory the times we were together, the way he or she looked, and looked at us; and most tender, the emotions we felt in the very presence of our beloved. All of this is raised to the highest plane as we contemplate our Lord.

Stanza Two: Jesus is my Savior, yes; but even more, He is the Savior of all of my human brothers and sisters, a fact that exalts His Name as blessed; there are no worthy rivals of Jesus, for His is the matchless Name, the only Name "given among men whereby we must be saved" (Acts 4:12).

Stanza Three: Here are listed several categories of those persons to whom He makes the difference in daily life: the contrite, who is truly repentant for his sin, has hope through Jesus; the meek, who is prepared to respond, directly, at the sound of His voice, has joy through Jesus; the fallen, painfully aware of his lapse, is treated kindly by Jesus—though he certainly isn't often by the world; and the seeker finds what he is looking for in Jesus—and it is good, indeed!

Stanza Four: And what is it that the seeker sought and found but the timeless love of Jesus, a love "that will not let him go," a love that must be experienced, firsthand, if its reality is to be known! In its depths it cannot be spoken, it cannot be written—words do not do it justice, it must be felt; but once felt, it can never be denied.

Stanza Five: Both now, in the present, and then, in the future, both in this world and in the next, our one lasting sense of true joy, our greatest of all prizes, and the One in whom we dare ever glory, is Jesus. "Jesus, Jesus, Jesus, there is something about that Name"—to an eleventh-century monk, a nineteenth-century translator, or a twentieth-century reader—that is indeed "like the fragrance after the rain." Thus does this medieval hymn still "shine with a constant glow."[18]

John Dykes' (1823–1876) tune, "St. Agnes," is well adapted to the sentiment of this hymn with its accent on devotion to our Lord. Composed by him in 1866 expressly for this hymn, its "pensive tone, bordering on pathos,"[19] and the exquisite way in which it blends with the words, makes it a most acceptable interpreter of this poem; clearly one of Dykes' finest efforts, it is to be sung quietly and in a spirit of genuine reverence.

Notes

1. Julian, *op. cit.,* p. 539.
2. *Ibid.,* p. 585.
3. *Ibid.*
4. Moffatt and Patrick, *op. cit.,* pp. 43–44 (supplementary notes).
5. Bailey, *op. cit.,* p. 248.
6. Julian, *op. cit.,* p. 587.
7. *Ibid.,* p. 585.
8. *Ibid.,* p. 588.
9. Bailey, *op. cit.,* p. 250.
10. Brown and Butterworth, *op. cit.,* p. 100.
11. Bailey, *op. cit.,* p. 251.
12. *Ibid.,* p. 252.
13. Hostetler, *op. cit.,* p. 95.
14. Haeussler, *op. cit.,* p. 588.
15. Moffatt and Patrick, *op. cit.,* p. 293.
16. *Ibid.*
17. Brown and Butterworth, *op. cit.,* p. 101.
18. Covert and Laufer, *op. cit.,* p. 331.
19. *Ibid.*

Title/Date	*"Jesus, Thou Joy of Loving Hearts"*
	(11th century)
Author	*Bernard of Clairvaux*
	Ray Palmer, trans. (1858)
Composer/Tune	*Henry Baker "Quebec" (1862)*
Scriptural Basis	*John 15:11*

This, the second of the hymns in our study to be taken from Bernard's "Jubilee Rhythm," is actually something of "a free paraphrase," and while it is on all counts the most popular version of this hymn, Haeussler feels that Palmer has "really created another hymn."[1] Whatever we choose to label it technically, it was a great inspiration to the noted missionary David Livingstone, who said of it:

> That hymn of St. Bernard's, although in what might be termed dog-Latin, pleases me; it rings in my ears as I wander across the wide, wide wilderness.[2]

For those interested, the author cites further evidence supporting Bernard's authorship of this lengthy poem, the basis for several refreshingly devotional hymns, including both of those in our studies and Caswell's "Jesus, King Most Wonderful"; Duffield, in his fine study *Latin Hymns,* states:

> Of the Latin poetry ascribed to him the "Jesu dulcis Memoria" is certainly Bernard's, for Morel discovered it in an Einsiedeln MS., "older than 1288."[3]

Moreover, since the Bodleian Library, Oxford, has a manuscript from the twelfth century and since the hymn is usually dated to about 1140, the idea that it was the work of an eleventh-century Benedictine abbess can be laid to rest![4] Without hesitation it can be said that the majority of those who have made an intensive study of the hymn are in agreement that it was the work of St. Bernard.

Bernard, of whom we have written previously, was called "the greatest monk who ever lived"[5] by another great monk, Martin Luther! Studious and

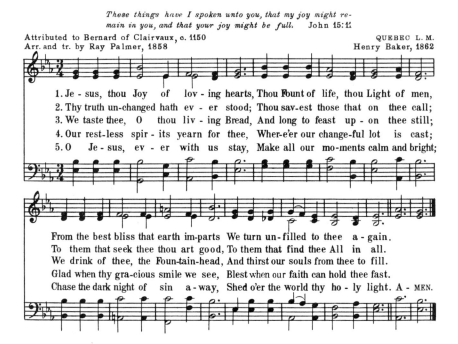

These things have I spoken unto you, that my joy might remain in you, and that your joy might be full.   John 15:11

Attributed to Bernard of Clairvaux, c. 1150
Arr. and tr. by Ray Palmer, 1858

QUEBEC L. M.
Henry Baker, 1862

1. Je - sus, thou Joy   of   lov - ing hearts, Thou Fount of life, thou Light of men,
2. Thy truth un-changed hath ev - er   stood; Thou sav-est those that on   thee call;
3. We taste thee,   O   thou liv - ing Bread, And long to feast up - on   thee still;
4. Our rest-less spir - its yearn for thee,   Wher-e'er our change-ful lot   is   cast;
5. O   Je - sus, ev - er   with us   stay, Make all our mo-ments calm and bright;

From the best bliss that earth im-parts We turn un-filled to thee   a - gain.
To   them that seek thee thou art good, To them that find thee All   in   all.
We drink of thee, the Foun-tain-head, And thirst our souls from thee to fill.
Glad when thy gra-cious smile we see, Blest when our faith can hold thee fast.
Chase the dark night of   sin   a - way, Shed o'er the world thy ho - ly light. A - MEN.

naturally reclusive, he had to renounce his own inclinations and make himself available to counsel kings and popes as well as his fellow monks; while he by nature sought peaceable solutions to the various problems he and his Order faced, he was at the same time willing to enter into the most strenuous debates when the truth of the Scriptures and its expression in the Church's creeds was at stake. Thus he was willing to enter the lists against the Schoolmen in general, and the brilliant, but heretical Abelard in particular; demonstrating that their views were in error and their concerns were largely irrelevant to the needs of the people, Bernard's eloquence won the day, stressing that God champions a "life of holiness: simplicity, devotion, prayer, preaching, and ministering to the physical and spiritual needs of people."[6] But for us, his greatest legacy lies in his hymns; of these Richard Storrs has written:

> I do not overestimate these hymns; they show his profound evangelical spirit, how the meek and sovereign majesty of the Lord continually attuned and governed his thoughts, and how the same hand which wrote letters, treaties, notes of sermons, exhortations to pontiffs, reproofs of kings, could turn itself at pleasure to the praises of Him in whose grace was his hope, in whose love was his life. If these hymns had not remained after he was gone, we should have missed, I think, a lovely luster of his work and his fame.[7]

This hymn's most often used translation was made by Ray Palmer (1808–1887), who "enshrines here both the spirit of its author, and his own, regarded as he is, one of God's noblemen,"[8] and considered by many to be America's greatest hymn-writer. Of his many hymns Julian writes:

> The best of them, by their combination of thought, poetry and devotion, are superior to almost all others of American origin. [And those he translated from the Latin] rank among the best that America has produced.[9]

Of the man himself, another writes, in conjunction with this hymn:

> a man of sterling character, strong of conviction yet gentle of soul, his love for Christ, his fellowship with Christ, his satisfaction in Christ, and his devotion to Christ are all suggested by the words of this lovely translation. Perhaps the key to the verses is in the lines:[10]

> > "From the best bliss that earth imparts
> > We turn, unfilled, to Thee again."

Palmer began life in a rather inauspicious fashion, first being taught at home by his father and then set to work in a dry goods store when he was but thirteen. Providentially, he joined Boston's Park Street Congregational Church, and its pastor, seeing that he was a bright, gifted lad, helped him to attend Phillips Andover Academy, his first formal education. From there he went to Yale College, graduating in 1830; he then taught in a girls' school while he studied a theological course, from which he gained his moderate Calvinistic theology.[11] This training led to his ordination in 1835.

He served two lengthy pastorates, in Bath, Maine, and in Albany, New York; but it is for his hymns that he is remembered. He wrote them, he said, "as the Spirit moved him"; he would never allow any changes to be made in them, nor would he accept any remuneration for them—a refreshing, although potentially impoverishing principle! The first one he ever wrote, "My Faith Looks Up to Thee," would, of itself, "have immortalized his name in sacred song."[12]

The tune "Quebec," less commonly known as "Hesperus," was composed by Henry Baker (1835–1910). He received his early education at Winchester, then studied civil engineering; he became involved as an engineer, constructing railways in India for many years. With a marked gift for music—though he never considered himself more than an amateur in the field—he finally was persuaded by the eminent composer John Dykes to formally pursue its study; he did, and graduated from Oxford (Bac. Mus.) in 1867.[13] He originally wrote this tune in 1854; some years later, when the London *Penny*

Post called for tunes suitable for Keble's "Sun of My Soul," he sent it in, anonymously; after it appeared in 1871 in a hymnal published by Bishop Edward Bickersteth, he claimed it as its rightful composer.[14]

Let us examine this hymn, noting several of its striking features.

First, contrasts abound: thus, earthly bliss versus spiritual emptiness, or at least, lacking (vs. 1); unchanged truth (vs. 2) versus our changing circumstances (vs. 4); we eat, but are not satisfied; we drink, but are still thirsty (vs. 3); and finally, the night of sin versus the day bright with God's holy light (vs. 5).

Second, adjectives also abound: so, "loving" hearts, "best" bliss (vs. 1); "unchanged" truth (vs. 2); "living" Bread (vs. 3); "restless" spirits, "changeful" lot, "gracious" smile (vs. 4); and finally, "dark" night, and "holy" light (vs. 5).

Third, as in Bernard's earlier hymn, Jesus is addressed directly throughout this one, making this also a hymn by strictest definition; moreover, this direct address makes the singer a participant in the realities he or she is expressing, with the "singer becoming the song," the messenger incarnating the message!

Fourth, the fact that this has been noted, frequently, as a Communion hymn is quite understandable; much of its language certainly would qualify it for such usage, and Stanza Three comes right out of our liturgy, in essence and in spirit if not almost literally.

Fifth, while much of what we say here is objective affirmation of facts about Jesus' character and ministry to and among His people, there is also the subjective element, whereby I express my longings, my restlessness, my needs, my unfulfilled desires. I am reassured that He, knowing all this about me, will hold me steady to my course, when I walk by faith and not by sight—when I cannot see His smile. "For I would rather walk in the darkness with God than walk in the light alone."[15]

Finally, there is in the closing stanza a prayer, spoken directly to Jesus—He who has been recognized as our Light (vs. 1)—that He will shed that Light over our sin-darkened world; just as when we enter a darkened room, and snap on the lights, the disquieting effect of the darkness is taken away, we lose our fears and can see again.

Notes

1. Haeussler, *op. cit.,* p. 371.
2. *Ibid.*
3. *Ibid.,* p. 370.
4. Covert and Laufer, *op. cit.,* p. 374.
5. McCutchan, *op. cit.,* p. 236.
6. Bailey, *op. cit.,* pp. 251–252.
7. McCutchan, *op. cit.,* p. 236.

8. Covert and Laufer, *op. cit.,* p. 374.

9. Julian, *op. cit.,* p. 877.

10. Covert and Laufer, *op. cit.,* pp. 374–375.

11. Duffield, *op. cit.,* p. 363.

12. *Ibid.*

13. McCutchan, *op. cit.,* p. 311.

14. *Ibid.*

15. Cowman, *Streams in the Desert,* p. 100.

Title/Date	*"Just as I Am, without One Plea . . ."* *(1836)*
Author	*Charlotte Elliott*
Composer/Tune	*William Batchelder Bradbury "Wood-worth" (1849)*
Scriptural Basis	*John 6:37; Revelation 22:17*

Few Christian hymns have been more widely used or as frequently translated into other languages as this simple, powerful penitential hymn, which "ranks with the finest hymns in the English language"[1] and which Breed calls "the greatest evangelistic hymn in English."[2] Certainly for most Americans this hymn with its familiar tune has become well known through its regular usage in the Billy Graham Crusades; prior to these it had also been used frequently in other evangelistic or revival meetings. And as an "invitation hymn," used to encourage people to respond to the gospel of God's grace, it is most appropriate, for "it includes all the elements of justification: welcome, pardon, cleansing, relief"[3]—the breaking down of every barrier, imagined or real, that would keep the unworthy person from experiencing God's amazing grace and mercy, forgiveness and love.

This hymn was written by Charlotte Elliott (1789–1871), whom Duffield cites as illustrating the adage "grace runs in the blood,"[4] for she had a noble spiritual heritage indeed. Her devout grandfather was Henry Venn, beloved evangelical leader, co-laborer with the Wesleys and George Whitefield, and a chaplain of Lady Huntington. Her uncle, the Rev. John Venn, had presided at the meeting when the Church Missionary Society was formed in 1799; as curate of the Clapham parish he ministered to many noted evangelical Anglicans, including Lord William Wilberforce and other members of the so-called Clapham Sect, whose efforts led to the abolishing of slavery in the British Empire in 1831.[5]

Elliott, though an invalid much of her life, did not allow her physical weakness and periodic bouts of depression to stymie her usefulness; in fact, she made her afflictions her servant, not her master—for Jesus Christ was her Master; of her physical condition she wrote:

My Heavenly Father alone knows what it is, day after day . . . to fight against bodily feelings of almost overpowering weakness, languor and ex-

Him that cometh to me I will in no wise cast out.   John 6:37

WOODWORTH 8. 8. 8. 6.

Charlotte Elliott, 1836   William B. Bradbury, 1849

1. Just as I am, with-out one plea But that thy blood was shed for me,
2. Just as I am, and wait-ing not To rid my soul of one dark blot,
3. Just as I am, though tossed a-bout With ma-ny a con-flict, ma-ny a doubt,
4. Just as I am, poor, wretch-ed, blind; Sight, rich-es, heal-ing of the mind,
5. Just as I am! thou wilt re-ceive, Wilt wel-come, par-don, cleanse, re-lieve;
6. Just as I am! thy love un-known Has bro-ken ev-'ry bar-rier down;

And that thou bidd'st me come to thee, O Lamb of God, I come, I come.
To thee, whose blood can cleanse each spot, O Lamb of God, I come, I come.
Fight-ings and fears with-in, with-out, O Lamb of God, I come, I come.
Yea, all I need, in thee to find, O Lamb of God, I come, I come.
Be-cause thy prom-ise I be-lieve, O Lamb of God, I come, I come.
Now, to be thine, yea, thine a-lone, O Lamb of God, I come, I come. A-MEN.

haustion, and to resolve as He enables me, not to yield to the slothfulness, depression, and irritability such a body causes me to long to indulge; but rather, to rise every morning determined on taking this for my motto "If any man will come after Me, let him deny himself, take up his cross daily, and follow Me.[6]

So, as she wrote her hymns, devotional poetry, and many personal letters to other sufferers, using "her splendid intellect, fine imaginative powers, and deep love for music,"[7] it was always with the concern that she might minister encouragement through them. As Duffield notes:

An appreciation of the fact that bruise and wrench and pain [underlie] the noblest of [her] hymns will do much to make us devout in our use of them, and reverent in their handling. . . . Abundantly charitable, patient and devout . . . the length of [her] days taught wisdom to all who beheld her.[8]

While there is some question regarding the precise circumstances surrounding the writing of this hymn, the facts appear to be these. When Elliott was in her early thirties and living at home, the family received a visit in May

1822 from the honored French Reformed pastor and leader, Henri Cesar Malan, noted both for his hymns, "expressing as they did bright assurance, peace and gladness,"[9] and for his special concern to share the gospel wherever he was with people on an individual basis; whether it was

> on the steamboat, the mountain trail, or in the hotel, no opportunity was lost. On one occasion, an old man whom he visited drew from under his pillow a copy of [Malan's] hymn-book, *Chants de Sion,* and told him how he had prayed to see the author of it before he died.[10]

During his visit, in talking with Charlotte he discovered that she was still trying to work out her own salvation, but without trusting fully in Christ; he said to her,

> Dear Charlotte, cut the cable; it will take too long to unloose it; cut it, it is a small loss; the wind blows, and the ocean is before you—the Spirit of God and Eternity.[11]

Upon his repeated urging of her to come to Christ, she asked "How do I come? I don't know how to come," and he responded "Come, just as you are."[12] Apparently she did, for she counted the experience of his visit and their talk as the spiritual turning-point in her life, "the birthday of her soul," and maintained through correspondence a friendship with him over the next forty years, until he died in 1864.[13]

Some twelve years later, invalided and living with her brother in Brighton, she was despondent over the fact that she was unable to assist the family in their preparations for an upcoming bazaar, "intended to raise money for a new college where the daughters of poor clergymen might receive their education at low expense."[14] She lay in her bed, "tossed about with many a conflict, many a doubt" as to her usefulness; the following day, while the others were gone, she wrote this hymn; as Bailey writes:

> She gathered up in her soul the great certainties, not of her emotions but of her salvation—her Lord, his power, his promise—and deliberately set down for her own comfort the formula of her faith, restating to herself the gospel of pardon, peace and heaven.[15]

Not only has it become one of the most helpful ever penned, used more than any other "in the raising up of those that are bowed down"[16] and blessing millions of lives, but it also earned considerably more money for the girls' college than the bazaar ever had; published first in 1836 in *Hymns of the Week,* the title page always bore the note "sold for the benefit of St. Margaret's Hall, Brighton."[17]

Moreover, over a thousand letters were found among her personal papers after she died; they were from people from all over, thanking her for this hymn and telling her how it had ministered to them personally.[18] And her brother, an evangelical Anglican clergyman, wrote in later years:

> In the course of a long ministry I hope I have been permitted to see some fruits of my labors; but I feel far more has been done by a single hymn of my sister's.[19]

"Woolworth," the tune most often associated with this hymn, at least during this century, is one of those American hymn tunes that "mark the transition from Lowell Mason's more churchly tunes to the livelier gospel songs that followed;"[20] at the same time, many editors and music critics have sanctioned its use, and its hold on American Christians has been strong. Of it one editor writes:

> It should be sung in very moderate time, reflectively and with deep feeling. It is especially important that due regard be given to the phrasing, which will help to prevent a too frequent overemphasis of the strongly rhythmic character of the tune.[21]

It was composed by William Bradbury (1816–1868), born into a musical family, with his father a choir director and his mother a singer. Moving to Boston at age fourteen, he saw his first piano and organ, and learned to play them while living at the home of musician Sumner Hill. Later he took formal studies at the Boston Academy of Music and sang in Lowell Mason's church choir; his organ-playing abilities secured a job for him, playing in a small church at an annual stipend of twenty-five dollars! Eventually he took a position in New York City at the Baptist Tabernacle, taught singing schools, and led a variety of children's choirs; "he also organized the Juvenile Music Festivals, which were ultimately responsible for introducing music into the public schools there."[22] (Isn't it ironic that the use of most religious music is no longer allowed in those same schools today?)

After a period of study in Europe—where he practiced, arduously—under some of its greatest Masters, he returned to the United States and gave himself largely to editing and compiling songbooks, many for children's voices. He published fifty-nine in the years 1841–1867; they sold in excess of two million copies, arousing much envy, and therefore, considerable criticism,[23] most of which was unmerited. His compositions are represented in the *Trinity Hymnal* by thirteen tunes, including ones for "'Tis Midnight, and on Olive's Brow," "He Leadeth Me," "Sweet Hour of Prayer," "Jesus Loves Me," and "Saviour, Like a Shepherd Lead Us"; tuberculosis ended his productive, useful life when he was only fifty-two years old.

Let us examine this hymn, a "simple, candid expression of trust and personal confession."[24] Among its features we note these, as distinctive:

First, there are no requirements one has to fulfill in order to be counted worthy of being saved by God's unmerited grace; regardless of my condition—besmirched soul, confused and doubtful, inner conflicts, fearful, poor, wretched, blind (physically or spiritually)—whatever my state, I can come!

Second, it is "*I* who come to *Thee,*" with the accent on the personal, the one-to-One relationship throughout this hymn; it is not an exhortation to others, but rather a plea to oneself, a plea to respond. As Routley says so well:

> The most familiar and persuasive of the Gospel imperatives is the word COME! Secular life drives us in two other directions (1) if we are satisfied we will never come, thinking we are good enough as we are; (2) if life does us in, we become cynical and suspect "come to Me" is a hoax, thinking we are not good enough to come. But both are wrong! The arrogant man says "I'm good enough and don't have to come"; the falsely humble says "I'm not good enough, so won't come"; the former must learn to give, the latter to receive. Therefore every verse contains the conviction that once we come we must expect to be changed.[25]

Third, in every verse (but the first), there is the expectation of change; "He will receive us just as we are, but He will not leave us just as we are"![26] Here is the crucial theological marriage of justification and sanctification; for I am ever redeemed by grace, *as I am,* but that begins a process by which I am made over into the image of my Lord Jesus. So: the dark blots do not remain; they are cleansed, everyone of them (vs. 2); my conflicts without, my doubts within are resolved (vs. 3); riches for my poverty, sight for my blindness, emotional health replaces my sense of wretchedness (vs. 4); God's promise is welcome, pardon, cleansing—I believe He will receive me, for He is a Person of His Word, He cannot lie! (vs. 5). And, of course, all of these—and every other unnamed barrier ever erected—comes crashing down under the weight of His incredible love, a love that in its fullness is as yet unknown to me until I respond—O, Lamb of God, I come!

Finally, the figure of the sacrificial Lamb, who shed His blood for our redemption, blood that can cleanse each spot, is repeatedly emphasized. Bailey is correct when he says:

> It is easy to recognize beneath this hymn the Calvinistic [I'd say, better, biblical] doctrine of the saving power of the blood of Christ, which constituted the orthodox Evangelical belief.[27]

And Haeussler writes, sympathetic to the Scriptures,

> Sometimes modern folk have experienced a deep revulsion to what are called "blood and gore" theories. But John, Peter, Paul and the others could not and would not circumvent His death on Calvary, with all of its stark and bloody realism any more than our American reporters would minimize the great price paid by our soldiers to capture a little atoll called Tarawa. No wonder the Apostles exclaimed "The blood of Jesus Christ, His Son, cleanses us from all sin . . . We have redemption through His Blood. . . ." Miss Elliott and others . . . have seen, like the Apostles of old, in the death of Christ more than the sufferings of a martyr. . . . However we explain it, He died, and gave up His life for us. No one can deny that. . . . [So this] hymn, while recognizing "many a conflict, many a doubt" insists nevertheless that everyone who comes in humility and faith to the Crucified One will find himself "welcomed, pardoned, cleansed, relieved."[28]

Finally, we cite one incident, verified as to its accuracy by Amos Wells in his work, *A Treasury of Hymns:*

> John Gough was once seated in a pew with a man so repulsive in appearance that he moved to the other end of the seat. The congregation began to sing "Just as I am . . ." and the man joined in so heartily that Gough decided that he could not be so disagreeable, so moved close, though the man's singing "was positively awful." At the end of the third stanza . . . the man leaned toward Gough and whispered "won't you please read me the first line of the next verse?" Gough read "Just as I am, poor, wretched, blind" and the man replied "that's it; and I am blind—God help me; and I'm a paralytic." Then as he tried with his poor twitching lips to sing the glorious words, Mr. Gough said that never in his life had he heard music so beautiful as the blundering singing of that hymn by the paralytic.[29]

Notes

1. Julian, *op. cit.,* p. 609.
2. Breed, *op. cit.,* p. 187.
3. *Ibid.,* p. 190.
4. Duffield, *op. cit.,* p. 368.
5. Covert and Laufer, *op. cit.,* p. 247.
6. Haeussler, *op. cit.,* p. 645.
7. Covert and Laufer, *op. cit.,* p. 247.

8. Duffield, *op. cit.*, p. 369.
9. Julian, *op. cit.*, p. 712.
10. *Ibid.*
11. Duffield, *op. cit.*, p. 307.
12. Moffatt and Patrick, *op. cit.*, p. 330.
13. Haeussler, *op. cit.*, p. 645.
14. McCutchan, *Our Hymnody,* p. 246.
15. Bailey, *op. cit.*, p. 183.
16. McCutchan, *op. cit.*, p. 246.
17. Bailey, *op. cit.*, p. 183.
18. Moffatt and Patrick, *op. cit.*, p. 42 (supplement).
19. Covert and Laufer, *op. cit.*, p. 248.
20. *Ibid.*
21. *Ibid.*, p. 249.
22. McCutchan, *op. cit.*, p. 168.
23. Haeussler, *op. cit.*, p. 564.
24. *Ibid.*, p. 255.
25. Routley, *Hymns and the Faith,* pp. 181–184.
26. *Ibid.*, p. 184.
27. Bailey, *op. cit.*, p. 183.
28. Haeussler, *op. cit.*, p. 255.
29. Smith, *op. cit.*, p. 216.

Title/Date	*"Love Divine, All Loves Excelling"* *(1747)*
Author	*Charles Wesley*
Composer/Tune	*John Zundel "Beecher" (1870)*
	George Le Jeune "Love Divine" (1887)
Scriptural Basis	*John 14:21; I John 4:16–19; et al.*

This "evergreen song-wreath to the Crucified"[1] joins Wesley's earlier "Jesus, Lover of my Soul" in its emphasis on the infinite love and grace of God, though here the focus is on the somewhat uncommon thought that God *is* love; not merely that He is loving, but that His essence is love, "giving the human soul immediate, or direct access to the Infinite"[2] in some mystical or existential way. And this should not startle us, for Wesley was

> The poet of the soul, and knew its every mood. . . . There is no article of belief . . . ; no moral sentiment peculiarly characteristic of the gospel that does not find itself . . . pointedly and clearly conveyed . . . in his poetry . . . as the most gifted minstrel of the modern Church.[3]

Moreover, Charles Wesley (1707–1788) was no stranger to human love, for he—unlike his brother John, whose marriage to a widow of some means was a wretched experience, creating perhaps some reason for his itinerant ministry of a quarter of a million miles on horseback(!)—had a happy marriage. When he was past forty he met Sarah Gwynne, a young Welsh woman whom he married April 8, 1749, and by whom he had eight children, two of whom became eminent as musicians. But this union, happy though it was, did not occur until after Charles had pondered, and consulted, and written many hymns! Let him tell us himself:

> Not a cloud was to be seen from morning till night. I rose at four; spent three hours and a half in prayer, or singing, with my brother, with Sally, with Beck. At eight, I led MY SALLY to the Church. Her father, sisters, Lady Rudd, Grace, Betty, and I think Billy Tucker and Mr. James were all who were present. At the church-door I thought of the prophecy of a jealous friend "that if we were even at the church-door to be married, she was

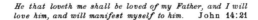

sure, by revelation, that we could get no farther." We both smiled at the re-
membrance. We got farther. Mr. Gwynne gave her to me (under God); my
brother joined our hands. It was a most solemn season of love! Never had
I more of the Divine Presence at the sacrament. My brother gave out the
following hymn "Come, Thou everlasting Lord." He then prayed over us

in strong faith. We walked back to the house, and joined again in prayer.
Prayer and thanksgiving was our whole employment. We were cheerful
without mirth, serious without sadness. . . . My brother John seemed the
happiest person among us.[4]

This blending of human love and divine love, as well as of human purity
and compassion with divine purity and compassion, characterized their ministry as well as their lives. For nothing short of God's grace and mercy, God's
power and compassion could have changed the England of their day. Smith
reminds us that

> it was unbelievably wicked; the clergy were idle, remiss in their labors, cor-
> rupt in practice. Among men of fashion, drunkenness and vile talk were
> marks of distinction. Plays depicted vulgar morals and manners. . . .
> Among working people there was brutality and torture of animals. On
> holidays, for twopence, one could go through Bethlehem Hospital and
> amuse oneself at the expense of the lunatics. London's gin shops invited
> passers-by to get "drunk for a penny, or dead drunk for twopence"—and
> straw, to sleep it off, was free! Penal laws were cruel, with hanging meted
> out for robbing a hen-roost, or the writing of a threatening letter.[5]

And in this context they labored, diligently, to change men's hearts,
knowing that thereby they could ultimately change their nation—and they
did! Their revival brought in its wake a new concern for suffering humanity: with hospitals, a concern for criminals, the abolishing of slavery, reaching
out to orphans, widows, and the illegitimate, and a host of other similar ministries of compassion being established—all by the transforming love of God.
Let us then examine this hymn, whose "tapestry is woven with threads from
the Bible."[6]

Stanza One: Wesley begins with this prayer to the Lord Jesus who, as
God's Incarnate Love and who excells all human loves, has come to earth
from His dwelling in heaven, where He was the supreme object of the adoration of all its residents, human and divine—its *joy.* He is asked to dwell in
us, to "visit us" with His salvation, to enter into each of our hearts, hearts unworthy, and therefore "trembling" with anticipation. Moreover, as the Divine
is thus "humbled," His mercies are crowned, that is, completed and glorified,
and His compassionate nature demonstrated. Routley writes that this verb,
"visit," means

> come and inspect us, admonish us, correct us—even punish us, a strong
> word. When the Bishop visits, "we better be prepared"; the Latin means
> "I am coming to see you and you won't forget it." So we are asking Christ

to come, again and again, driving His salvation deep into our hearts and minds, for we need daily receiving and renewing.[7]

This stanza recalls all these verses: I John 4:8; Colossians 2:9; Revelation 5:11–14; John 14:16–17; II Timothy 1:14; Revelation 21:3; Matthew 9:36; Psalm 86:15; and Psalm 106:4.[8]

Stanza Two: Here the prayer is continued, that Christ will breathe His Holy Spirit into every one of us, whether we be still "troubled," wearied, or continuing to "love sin." This last phrase was originally "our power of sinning," and it was questioned by Wesley's friend John Fletcher, who asked him,

> Is not this expression too strong? Would it not be better to soften it by saying "Take away the love of sinning"? (or the bent of the mind toward sin). Can God take away from us our *power* of sinning without taking away our power of free obedience?[9]

Moreover "the promised rest" was originally "that second rest," thought by some to be a reference to the doctrine of moral perfection attainable in this life, sometimes known as the "second blessing," an idea softened in our modern hymnals. "Alpha and Omega" are, of course, the first and last letters of the Greek alphabet; the prayer is that Christ will be both the One who begins and who completes or matures our faith, thus relieving our apprehension—so that we can be free, knowing that "He who has begun a good work in us will bring it to completion" (Philippians 2:10–11). The Scripture verses recalled here are John 14:1; 20:22; Matthew 19:29; Hebrews 4:3, 8–11; Isaiah 59:7; Proverbs 21:10; Revelation 1:8, 11; Colossians 3:11; Galatians 5:1.[10]

Stanza Three: The prayer continues, with both a request and a promise. A request that He as the Almighty abide in these, our earthly temples, never leaving us—the plea sounds strangely like one for the eternal security of the believer. And a promise, that we will continuously bless and serve, pray to and praise Him as do the angelic hosts in heaven—in a sense, a tall order! Smith asks:

> does Wesley pray for the life beyond, or for this present life of here and now? And when "would we be always blessing"—after death, amid the glories of heaven, or now, in the midst of toil, and testing, and trouble?[11]

Again, the Scriptures recalled include: Psalm 109:21; II Peter 2:9; James 4:6; Malachi 3:1; I Corinthians 6:19; Hebrews 13:5; Romans 1:9; Revelation 7:15; Psalm 138:2; Psalm 145:2; Psalm 146:2.[12]

Stanza Four: Here is a fuller expression of the doctrine of perfection as possible to obtain in this life, which created much heartache for the Wesleyan movement and divided its ranks. Actually, the *desire* to be pure and spotless, to be holy, is not unscriptural, for we are called to holiness; the fact is, however, that when we are honest regarding our spiritual attainments, we recognize with Paul that we are, or at least have the potential for being, the "chief of sinners"—false and full of sin! Yet we should ever desire "the sincere milk [and meat] of the Word, that we may grow thereby" (I Peter 2:2) and should "seek holiness, without which no man shall see the Lord (Hebrews 12:14). As Routley points out,

> As we go along the road, and the vision gets brighter, "changed from glory into glory," we don't need to veil our eyes because we get stronger; we also become a cleaner and truer mirror for reflecting that brightness." Humility is in evidence here, for we cast down our crowns at His feet, "lost in wonder, love and praise." This is indeed sanctification, the increasing of the power to absorb for oneself and to reflect for the world the glory and brightness of the character of Christ. And of course, it is, all of it, His work![13]

The Scriptures recalled here are John 3:3; II Corinthians 5:17; Galatians 6:15; II Peter 3:14; Jude 24; II Corinthians 3:18; Revelation 4:10.[14]

It remains for us to consider the tunes cited in the *Trinity Hymnal*. The one most widely used in American churches is "Beecher," composed for this hymn in 1870 by John Zundel (1815–1882), who at the time was the organist at Plymouth Church in Brooklyn, pastored by Henry Ward Beecher, a close friend of President Abraham Lincoln and a fiery abolitionist leader. Zundel, a superb musician, was born and eventually died in Germany, but over thirty years of his service as an organist, composer, and editor was spent with Beecher. Thousands thronged to their church "to hear Beecher and Zundel";[15] working in tandem with Darius Jones, their choral director, they published two hymnals, the second of which, *The Plymouth Collection* (1855), drew material from a wide variety of sources, including both Moravian and Roman Catholic—a truly bold venture. Although criticized, it sold widely and was even published in a special Baptist edition![16] This tune, named in honor of Beecher, reflects the influence of both Thomas Hastings and Lowell Mason, written as it is in a popular strain; congregations sing it joyfully—as he intended!

The second tune, "Love Divine," a favorite one for carillon players, is heard often on Sunday evenings in large cities.[17] It was composed by George LeJeune (1871–1904), a gifted English organist and composer who studied organ in Canada and later served great churches in Hartford, Philadelphia, and New York. There, as an organist and composer, he "popularized sacred music, and his musical services, and skill as an organ recitalist, attracted wide attention."[18] This tune, appearing in a published collection of twenty-four of his in 1887, was dedicated to one of his students, also an organist. His active ministry in music was cut short, tragically, when he died at thirty-three; "Love Divine" became an experienced reality to him then.

Notes

1. Brown and Butterworth, *op. cit.,* p. 111.
2. Covert and Laufer, *op. cit.,* p. 329.
3. Brown and Butterworth, *op. cit.,* p. 46.
4. Duffield, *op. cit.,* p. 115.
5. Smith, *op. cit.,* p. 245.
6. Bailey, *op. cit.,* p. 95.
7. Routley, *Hymns and the Faith,* pp. 137–138.
8. Bailey, *op. cit.,* p. 96.
9. McCutchan, *op. cit.,* p. 387.
10. Bailey, *op. cit.,* p. 96.
11. Smith, *op. cit.,* p. 246.
12. Bailey, *op. cit.,* p. 96.
13. Routley, *op. cit.,* pp. 138–140.
14. Bailey, *op. cit.,* p. 96.
15. Haeussler, *op. cit.,* p. 1003.
16. *Ibid.,* p. 1004.
17. Covert and Laufer, *op. cit.,* p. 330.
18. *Ibid.*

Title/Date	*"My Faith Looks Up to Thee" (1830)*
Author	*Ray Palmer*
Composer/Tune	*Lowell Mason "Olivet" (1832)*
Scriptural Basis	*Hebrews 12:1–2*

Ray Palmer (1808–1887), an American Congregationalist pastor and hymn-writer, has already been the subject of one of our earlier studies ("Jesus, Thou Joy of Loving Hearts"). Palmer, earning his way as a clerk in a Boston dry goods store by the time he was in his early teens, is a good illustration of Duffield's observation:

> The lives of the English hymn-writers, as a rule, show the presence of wealth and culture; those of Americans—equally as a rule—show the presence and pressure of poverty and hard surroundings.[1]

However, while his beginnings may have been humble, they were not without opportunities, for his early education, received at home and supervised by his father, Judge Thomas Palmer—an inauspicious but nevertheless substantial preparation—undergirded his studious inclinations, and eventually he received his degree from Yale College!

Thence begins the tale of the writing of this hymn. Palmer, who never enjoyed robust health and lonely for more familiar surroundings, was experiencing a certain amount of religious uncertainty as he sought to establish himself in New York City shortly after his graduation from Yale. Teaching in a select school for young ladies, he was residing in the home of the woman who supervised it, and it was there that the hymn was written. Smith tells us:

> He had been translating . . . a German poem . . . about a suppliant at the Cross. With these . . . verses freshly in mind, there came to him a vision of Christ "an hour," as he himself describes it "when Christ in the riches of His grace and love, was so vividly apprehended as to fill the soul with deep emotion." In the quietness of his room he penned some six stanzas, in rough form, on sheets of paper, and later copied them into a small

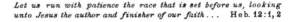

OLIVET 6. 6. 4. 6. 6. 6. 4.

Ray Palmer, 1830

Lowell Mason, 1832

1. My faith looks up to thee, Thou Lamb of Cal - va - ry,
2. May thy rich grace im-part Strength to my faint - ing heart,
3. While life's dark maze I tread, And griefs a - round me spread,
4. When ends life's tran-sient dream, When death's cold, sul - len stream

Sav - iour Di - vine: Now hear me while I pray, Take all my
My zeal in - spire; As thou hast died for me, O may my
Be thou my guide; Bid dark-ness turn to day, Wipe sor - row's
Shall o'er me roll, Blest Sav-iour, then, in love, Fear and dis -

guilt a - way, O let me from this day Be whol - ly thine.
love to thee Pure, warm, and change-less be, A liv - ing fire.
tears a - way, Nor let me ev - er stray From thee a - side.
trust re-move; O bear me safe a - bove, A ran-somed soul. A - MEN.

morocco-covered book he kept in his pocket, for just such "moments of
inspiration." Moreover, he had no intention that these be seen by other
eyes, "least of all . . . of writing a hymn for Christian worship. I recall that
the stanzas came with little effort, and I wrote them with very tender
emotion, writing the last one in tears."[2]

While Palmer wrote close to forty hymns in all, "more that were widely
known and prized by all English-speaking churches than any other American,"[3] this, his very first, is by far his finest and most famous. And it has been
translated into scores of languages, including Arabic and Chinese![4] Moreover,
he also excelled as a hymn-translator, "matching the best of the (English)
High Churchmen in the beauty, and inspirational power of his translations";[5]
he has been described as

a wise teacher, and simple-minded and devout Christian, a healthy, cheerful and buoyant man, loved by everyone who knew him.[6]

The tune "Olivet," written expressly for these lyrics, also has an interesting origin. About two years after he had written these lines he and Lowell Mason (1792–1872) met on a busy Boston street and Mason asked him to furnish some hymns for a hymnal that he was going to publish; Palmer himself writes:

> I showed him my hymn, and he asked for a copy (which I had made and gave to him). He put it in his pocket. . . . Later at home he took an interest in it, and wrote for it the tune "Olivet" to which it has almost universally been sung. A few days later we met again, and he earnestly exclaimed "Mr. Palmer, you may live many years and do many good things, but I think you will be best known to posterity as the author of 'My Faith Looks up to Thee.'"[7]

And of course, Mason—a fine musician in his own right—was correct, although, as Ninde suggests, "had it been intended for the public eye, it could never have been written,"[8] as intensely personal as it is!

Lowell Mason, composer and influential music educator, has been discussed earlier. The estimate of his importance is amply attested; Reynolds tells us that

> Mason, the outstanding musician of his day, was a pioneer in the work of training music teachers, . . . providing [this country] for more than a generation with most of its trained public school music teachers, as well as a large proportion of its trained church musicians and other professional musicians.[9]

And McCutchan testifies:

> Universally esteemed, of sterling character, kind and generous . . . through his musical conventions, through his publications of much material for their use, as well as for public and Sunday Schools, he did more for music in America than anyone else this country has produced. And, excelling in the writing of hymn-tunes, he is one of the few Americans whose tunes have been [used widely] abroad.[10]

And even Ellinwood, who was critical of what he considered to be the low standards of some of Mason's work, wrote, grudgingly,

> For sixty years he was a dominating factor in Church . . . music, and in the philosophy and pedagogy of music education, . . . doing much to stimulate interest in singing.[11]

Another writes that this hymn and its tune

> present a simple, potent, worshipful sermon on faith in God. The echos
> linger long with the worshiper. From the first measure "Olivet" springs to
> the realms of faith, giving natural voice to the spirit that looks to Him
> who bore the cross on Calvary.[12]

It is without question that it has immortalized these two men in sacred song.

Let us examine this hymn, whose "theology shows a deep undercurrent of
Calvinism, emphasizing the inevitability of human guilt, [and] the sacrificial
role of Jesus in salvation,"[13] more closely:

Stanza One: The emphasis here and throughout this hymn is on the first
person; Palmer is expressing his own feelings and concerns directly to his
Savior, Jesus the Lamb of God "who taketh away the sins of the world."
Moreover, while this expresses an objective fact, it must be made personal,
it must be subjectified, so that I can enter into and appropriate its truth for
myself. Furthermore, this stanza is a supplication, not a demand—a prayer
that I might be heard, cleansed of *all* my guilt, and completely consecrated to
God, the focus of, as well as the source of, my faith.

Stanza Two: Here again what happened on the cross ("as Thou hast died
for me") comes into view; and my prayer is that my fainting heart may be
strengthened and my zeal inspired by His rich grace. Moreover, as a response
to the incredible love demonstrated on the cross for me, personally, may my
love never waver, never grow cold, never be compromised; may it be fire
which—fed with divine fuel, that same grace—continues to burn brightly in
spite of whatever life may bring to me!

Stanza Three: Here he enumerates some of those potentially "fire-quench-
ing" experiences: despair, grief, darkness, sorrow, each of which interlocks
with the others in our normal human lives. When my own way is uncertain,
and heart-wrenching experiences threaten to take me off course, "be Thou
my guide." A guide knows the way, and accompanies me on the journey. And
then, when daybreak comes, my sorrows can be set aside, my tears turned
into triumphs, and I am ever safe in Your presence.

Stanza Four: The final enemy to be faced in this vale of mortal tears is
death—and apart from the Lord's prior return, it will come to us all, and it
will come to me! Just as Pilgrim steps into its cold, foreboding waters, which
threatened but were unable to sweep him away, so must I; but again, I know
by faith that He can and will take away my fears, and bring me safely across
even as He brought Israel safely through the Red Sea and across the Jordan
River. Here is a picture of realistic faith: acknowledging the heartaches and
tragedies of life as real, but not Reality; and affirming in a thousand ways,
"greater is He who is in me than he who is in the world"—therefore,

though I tremble, I still trust, "for when I am weak, then am I strong" indeed!

Notes

1. Duffield, *op. cit.*, p. 362.
2. Smith, *Lyric Religion*, p. 259.
3. Moffatt and Patrick, *op. cit.*, p. 454.
4. Haeussler, *op. cit.*, p. 262.
5. Bailey, *op. cit.*, p. 488.
6. Moffatt and Patrick, *op. cit.*, p. 454.
7. McCutchan, *Our Hymnody*, p. 260.
8. *Ibid.*
9. Reynolds, *op. cit.*, p. 94.
10. McCutchan, *op. cit.*, p. 44.
11. Ellinwood, *op. cit.*, p. 109.
12. Covert and Laufer, *op. cit.*, p. 308.
13. Bailey, *op. cit.*, p. 488.

Title/Date	*"O Come, O Come, Emmanuel . . ."* *(1851)*
Author	*Anonymous 12th-century Latin antiphon* *John Mason Neale, trans. (1851)*
Composer/Tune	*Ancient Plainsong "Veni Emmanuel" (13th century)* *Adapted by Thomas Helmore (1856)*
Scriptural Basis	*Isaiah 59:20; 7:14; 11:1; Matthew 1:23; Luke 1:78; Revelation 3:7–8; Exodus 19:16; Zechariah 9:9*

This well-known Advent hymn is one of two ancient plainsongs that are still widely sung in spite of their rather unusual melody patterns. It has an interesting and somewhat complex history, the details of which are not entirely agreed upon, but fit within this general historical framework. At least as early as the ninth century, patterns for worship instituted by Pope Gregory were widely used; among these were Seven Greater Antiphons, described by Bailey as

> short verses, sung at the beginning or close of the Psalm, or of the Magnificat, at Vespers during Advent . . . ; the lines were sung alternately by two choirs sitting opposite each other in the chancel.[1]

At some point in the twelfth or thirteenth century, someone took these seven separate sentences—each of which was based on a Scripture passage—revised their order, discarded two, wove them into a hymn, and added the refrain, "Rejoice! Rejoice! Emmanuel shall come to thee, O Israel." While several Latin medievalists have translated this material, the most widely used translation today, and the one in our *Trinity Hymnal,* comes from the pen of the eminent and gifted English Anglican clergyman, John Mason Neale (1818–1866), whose life we have considered in connection with an earlier study, "All Glory, Laud, and Honor."

While he missed taking honors in his classical course due to his dislike for mathematics, his degree from Cambridge included many literary honors and

And the Redeemer shall come to Zion... Isa. 59:20

Latin antiphons, 12th century. Latin hymn, 1710
Tr. by John Mason Neale, 1851

VENI EMMANUEL 8.8.8.8. with refrain
Ancient plain song, 13th century
Adapted by Thomas Helmore, 1856

1. O come, O come, Em - man - u - el, And ran - som cap - tive
2. O come, O come, thou Lord of might, Who to thy tribes, on
3. O come, thou Rod of Jes - se, free Thine own from Sa - tan's
4. O come, thou Day-spring from on high And cheer us by thy
5. O come, thou Key of Da - vid, come And o - pen wide our

Is - ra - el, That mourns in lone - ly ex - ile here,
Si - nai's height, In an - cient times didst give the law
tyr - an - ny; From depths of hell thy peo - ple save,
draw - ing nigh; Dis - perse the gloom-y clouds of night,
heav'n - ly home; Make safe the way that leads on high,

REFRAIN

Un - til the Son of God ap - pear.
In cloud and maj - es - ty and awe.
And give them vic - t'ry o'er the grave. Re - joice! Re - joice! Em -
And death's dark shad-ows put to flight.
And close the path to mis - er - y.

man - u - el Shall come to thee, O Is - ra - el. A - MEN.

prizes, including the Seatonian Prize for Poetry eleven times, a remarkable accomplishment.[2]

Partly because of fragile health and partly because of his High Church views, Neale did not have any significant parish opportunities, but he was appointed warden of Sackville College, an asylum for old men and old women; apparently he had some independent means, since his yearly stipend was £28; however, Duffield makes the point that his children's stories were written as a means of securing additional needed income[3]—and both facts could be true. In addition to his literary work, during his ministry of some twenty years there, he established the Sisterhood of St. Margaret, a superb nursing order; of this Bailey writes:

> Neale's idea for this was inspired by the wretched living conditions of the peasantry in that district, fanned by Charles Kingsley's denunciations in his novels of the virtue-throttling slums in city and country, and organized after the pattern set by St. Francis of Assisi and others. The Order grew from humble beginnings till at present it has houses all over the world . . . ; the outstanding, if not the only social result of the Oxford Movement . . . , a work which occupied most of Neale's time during the last decade of his life.[4]

But it is, of course, Neale's marvelous hymn translations that have immortalized this quiet, compassionate scholarly pastoral figure; of these translations Julian writes,

> his exquisite ear for melody prevented him from spoiling the rhythm by too servile an imitation of the original, while the spiritedness which is a marked feature of all his poetry preserved that spring and dash which is so often lacking in a translation.[5]

And John Brownlie says of him and his style:

> His work was that of a discoverer and a scientist . . . mapping the territory through which he passed; he took the height of its mountains, traced its rivers, and sounded its lakes. [He] stands as the interpreter, par excellence, of the praise literature of the early and medieval Church. [His] patient study of the past, uniting a monk's love for an old missal, to a scholar's evaluation of the treasures of antiquity, . . . unearthed and discovered jewels of great price—the crown jewels of the Church.[6]

Moreover, Neale had an engaging sense of humor. On one occasion, while visiting John Keble, author of the famed *Christian Year,* Keble left the sitting room where they had been visiting; returning a few minutes later, Neale said, "Why, Keble, I thought you told me the *Christian Year* was entirely original." Keble said "Yes, it certainly is"; "then," Neale asked "how come this"? and placed before him the Latin of one of Keble's hymns! Keble, dumbfounded, professed that he had never seen "that Latin original" before.

After a few minutes, Neale relieved his mind, owning up to the fact that he had just translated it from English into Latin while Keble had been out of the room![7]

Finally, Neale was a man of sterling character, a happy mixture of gentleness and firmness; he held to the courage of his remarkably strong convictions, but at the same time maintained the greatest charity toward, and forbearance with, those who disagreed with him. He not only lived his opposition down, but he also ended his life loved and widely respected by nearly everyone within the area of his "parish." His charity was unbounded, and his liberality was extended to friend and "foe" alike—winning over most, if not all, the latter.[8] While "worldly success" passed him by, he lives on in his music, a rich memory indeed.

The tune "Veni, Emmanuel" is an adaptation of an ancient plainsong kyrie of the thirteenth century, which "does not follow the pretty curves of modern melodies, but what it lacks in grace, it makes up in freedom and vigor,"[9] and is suited for congregational use, especially when sung in unison. It may well, in fact, have been specifically adapted for this hymn, as McCutchan notes, by Thomas Helmore, "editor of *The Hymnal Noted* and one of the pioneers in the revival of the use of the Gregorian Tones in the Anglican service."[10] Of it, one hymnologist and editor writes:

> it has a melody which flows blithely in the joyfully expectant mood of the words. [Its] harmony is largely in the normal minor mode, which gives it a quaint and distinctive flavor. . . . It is effective with men's voices singing in unison, the refrain being sung by all voices in harmony; it also lends itself to interesting effects when sung antiphonally.[11]

Let us examine this hymn, which uses the Babylonian exile of Old Testament Israel, the people of God, as a symbol of the estrangement of believers from their God; for

> sin and sorrow, failure and suffering, have put great distance between God and His people, and their cry is for a Redeemer who will ransom His captive people and restore them to the status of beloved children.[12]

Stanza One: As are each of the other stanzas, so is this a prayer; here, addressing the Lord directly as Emmanuel—"God with us" (Matthew 1:23, quoting Isaiah 7:14), the Son of God—the writer pleads for release from their painful captivity, exiled in a strange and foreign land, a land in which the singing of the song of Zion is unthinkable! (See Psalm 137.)

Stanza Two: Here the appeal is made to God as the mighty Lawgiver, and the context is the giving of the Decalogue on Mount Sinai (Exodus

20:1–17); the singer can almost visualize the sight: the clouds covering the mountain, and later standing at the door of the tabernacle, where Moses met and talked with God; and the awesomeness of God's majesty causing the Israelites to say to Moses, "You speak with us, but let not God speak to us, lest we die (Exodus 20:18–20).

Stanza Three: Here the image is of the Branch of Jesse (Isaiah 11:1ff.)—David's father and a son of Judah—the rightful King of God's heritage, Israel, who is asked to free His people from the usurper's tyranny and ultimate condemnation in hell! "Death, and the curse were in His cup," but love drained that cup to its last bitter drop—hallelujah, what a Savior!

Stanza Four: Scripture relates the Dayspring (Luke 1:78) and the daystar to the sons of God, angelic beings, who are the bearers of light; ultimately, of course, Christ is the Light whose power alone can truly illumine the darkness—whether it be physical or spiritual—and remove the sting of death by destroying death itself.

Stanza Five: The final prayer is that the "Key of David" (Revelation 3:7–8)—the Christ who alone can open doors no one can ever again close, doors that lead to life eternal—will do precisely that. The adverb "wide" is appropriate—"open thy mouth *wide* and I will fill it"—as is the request that the path to misery be closed off; the picture that comes to mind here is of a dangerous open cave sealed up with concrete and then barricaded with huge, immovable rocks.

The hymn is indeed "a stately song of gladness because the Promised One is coming";[13] as Bailey comments, "if you begin humming the tune you will have difficulty in stopping."[14]

Notes

1. Bailey, *op. cit.,* p. 272.
2. Duffield, *op. cit.,* p. 272.
3. *Ibid.*
4. Bailey, *op. cit.,* p. 200.
5. Julian, *op. cit.,* p. 787.
6. Smith, *op. cit.,* pp. 282–283.
7. Julian, *op. cit.,* p. 787.
8. *Ibid.,* p. 786.
9. Smith, *op. cit.,* p. 283.
10. McCutchan, *Our Hymnody,* p. 116.
11. Covert and Laufer, *op. cit.,* pp. 124–125.
12. *Ibid.,* p. 124.
13. *Ibid.*
14. Bailey, *op. cit.,* p. 273.

Title/Date	*"O Little Town of Bethlehem" (1868)*
Author	*Phillips Brooks*
Composer/Tune	*Lewis H. Redner "St. Louis" (1868)*
Scriptural Basis	*Micah 5:2; Isaiah 9:2; Matthew 1:23*

It has been said that Phillips Brooks (1835–1893), one of the princes among American preachers, has left three memorials, each significant in its own way. Two of them are found in the city of Boston, where he served for over twenty-two years as the pastor of Trinity Church and where he became "the dominant pulpit force of all New England . . . daring to preach Jesus Christ"[1] in that Unitarian stronghold. Trinity Church, which the author visited in 1981, has long had an active and far-reaching ministry, and its magnificent sanctuary—well-filled during Brooks' days there—serves as the first of these memorials, since it was built within the first few years of his ministry, the earlier edifice having burned down during the fire of 1871.

The second memorial, equally impressive to the eye, is the famous statue of Brooks executed by the eminent sculptor, Augustus St. Gaudens;[2] it stands in a small garden next to the church. Behind the stalwart figure of Brooks stands Jesus Christ, ever his inspiration, with His hand on Brooks' shoulder. I recall standing there several minutes, admiring the artistic impression, but also reflecting on some of the inscriptions about his life that I had read, from bronze plaques, inside the various rooms and corridors of the church.

The third of these enduring memorials is found all over the world; wherever the gospel of Jesus Christ has been taken, and wherever the tale of His birth has been sung, people—young and old alike—have translated, and learned, and sung this beloved Christian hymn, one of the "finest tributes of praise to God for His wonderful gift so silently given,"[3] Brooks' deathless words enshrined as "O Little Town of Bethlehem."

Brooks' life and ministry centered in Jesus Christ. Born in Boston, he grew up in a home where the children were encouraged to learn hymns by heart; he sang them in the mornings when he awoke, a practice he apparently continued throughout his life, and filled his sermons with their lines, often unconsciously. Graduating from Harvard, and later, from Virginia's Episcopal Theological Seminary—after a brief, ill-fated attempt to teach Latin in the Boston Latin School—he was ordained in 1859. His first charges

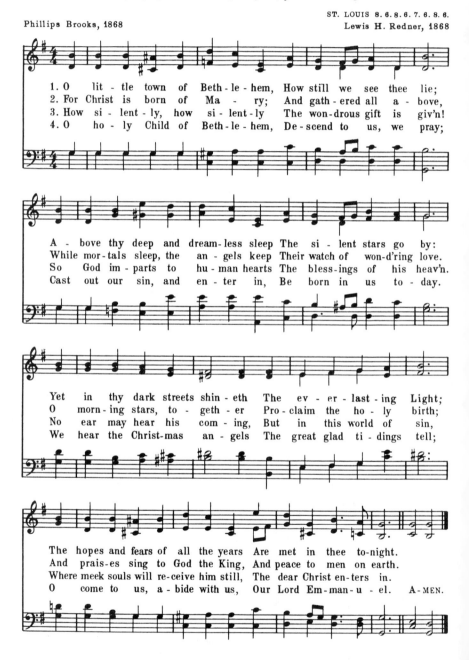

But thou, Bethlehem Ephratah, though thou be little... yet out of thee shall he come... whose goings forth have been from of old, from everlasting. Micah 5:2

Phillips Brooks, 1868

ST. LOUIS 8.6.8.6.7.6.8.6.
Lewis H. Redner, 1868

1. O lit - tle town of Beth - le - hem, How still we see thee lie;
2. For Christ is born of Ma - ry; And gath - ered all a - bove,
3. How si - lent - ly, how si - lent - ly The won - drous gift is giv'n!
4. O ho - ly Child of Beth - le - hem, De - scend to us, we pray;

A - bove thy deep and dream - less sleep The si - lent stars go by:
While mor - tals sleep, the an - gels keep Their watch of won - d'ring love.
So God im - parts to hu - man hearts The bless - ings of his heav'n.
Cast out our sin, and en - ter in, Be born in us to - day.

Yet in thy dark streets shin - eth The ev - er - last - ing Light;
O morn - ing stars, to - geth - er Pro - claim the ho - ly birth;
No ear may hear his com - ing, But in this world of sin,
We hear the Christ - mas an - gels The great glad ti - dings tell;

The hopes and fears of all the years Are met in thee to - night.
And prais - es sing to God the King, And peace to men on earth.
Where meek souls will re - ceive him still, The dear Christ en - ters in.
O come to us, a - bide with us, Our Lord Em - man - u - el. A - MEN.

were in Philadelphia: at Holy Trinity he worked with his Sunday School superintendent, Lewis Redner, to build up membership; when Brooks left there to go to Boston in 1869, the Sunday School enrollment had multiplied many times from the original thirty-six, and continued growing until it exceeded a thousand students, regularly in attendance![4] This love for children, incidentally, was one of Brooks' hallmarks; a bachelor, he kept several dolls at his rectory for nieces, nephews, and other children who visited him, and he could frequently be seen out romping—all six-foot-four inches of him—with the children.

Moreover, he had a good sense of humor, witnessed to by these anecdotes Bailey cites:

> One April Fool's day, as he was out walking, he saw a little boy trying in vain to reach a doorbell. Brooks mounted the steps, saying "let me help you," and rang the bell; the little boy scampered away, saying "now run like the devil!"
>
> His customary remark, when visiting a mother with a new baby, was "Well, well, this *is* a baby."
>
> One Saturday, busy finishing his sermon, he told his maid not to admit any visitors, "not even St. Peter himself." By chance Robert Ingersoll, the famous lecturer and atheist, stopped to see him. Ignoring the maid's protest, Ingersoll said "Oh, he will see me all right" and pushed into Brooks' study, where he was warmly greeted. "Come now, you told your maid you wouldn't even see St. Peter this morning"; "never mind," said Brooks, "I'll have plenty of time to see him in the next world. You sit down!"[5]

Phillips Brooks was a phenomenal person; his

> great heart, keen mind, sunny disposition, magnetic personality, ready command of language richly laden with metaphor, and profoundly earnest spirit attracted people of all walks and stations in life to hear him preach.[6]

One contemporary, who worshipped there, wrote to a friend:

> I have never heard preaching like it, and you know how slow I am to praise preachers. So much thought and so much life combined; so much reach of mind and such depth of insight and soul: I was electrified; I could have gotten up and shouted![7]

And the crowds who came to hear him preach, winsomely, about "Christ and Him crucified" included them all: from intellectuals like Oliver Wendell

Holmes and scores of Harvard students, to well-known handicapped figures like Helen Keller, to whom "he radiated sunshine and hope";[8] children crowded around him without hesitation, in spite of his towering figure; "by special request he preached to Queen Victoria, filling Westminster Abbey and St. Paul's Cathedral with eager hearers."[9] Of him, British Lord Bryce wrote:

> Few other men have possessed in equal measure the power of touching what is best in men and lifting them suddenly by sympathetic words to the elevation of high-strung feeling and purpose which they cannot reach of themselves, save under some wave of emotion due to some personal crisis in life.[10]

His life constantly maintained a glow that was divine in origin, yet he was an authentic man; after declining the office of preacher for the Harvard Chapel, several professorships, and other ecclesiastical preferments, he was finally prevailed upon to become the bishop of Massachusetts, but served only two years before his untimely and greatly lamented death. When hearing that he had gone to live with God, a five-year-old girl exclaimed, "Oh mama, how happy the angels will be."[11]

One of the finest tributes to this great, but humble American preacher, pastor, poet, and, preeminently lover of those in his care, was penned by the bishop of Westminster. Dedicating a volume of his sermons to Brooks, he wrote, movingly,

To the Memory of
PHILLIPS BROOKS
Bishop of Massachusetts
Strong, Fearless, Tender, Eloquent
Incapable of Meanness
Blazing with Indignation at All Kinds of Wrong
His Heart and Mind Deep and Wide as
the Ocean at His Door
Simple and Transparent as a Child
Keen with All the Keenness of his Race
This Volume is Inscribed
by a Brother Across the Water
Who Cherishes His Friendship as a
Treasure Laid up in Heaven
at the Resurrection of the Just[12]

During his ministry in Philadelphia he was given a leave of absence to travel abroad; writing home—and addressing his letter to the children of his Sunday School—he shared his Christmas week experience with them:

After an early dinner we took our horses and rode to Bethlehem . . . about two hours away. . . . The town, situated on an Eastern ridge of a range of hills is surrounded by terraced gardens. Before dark we rode out of town to the field where they say the shepherds saw the Star. . . . As we passed, the shepherds we saw were still "keeping watch over their flocks," or leading them home to their folds.[13]

Later that evening, he attended the Christmas service in the Church of the Nativity, which lasted some five hours in all! And it was just two years later, when Brooks was back in Philadelphia that, recalling this experience, he wrote this now familiar and beloved carol for his Sunday School's Christmas service in 1868; however, it was relatively unknown until it was published in the *Hymnal of the Episcopal Church* in 1892.[14]

The tune "St. Louis," with which this hymn is well-nigh universally linked, was written for it by Lewis Redner (1831–1908), Brooks' organist and Sunday School superintendent in his Philadelphia church. It was written, Redner tells us, the night before the Christmas service in which it was to be sung! Redner, who waited in vain for an inspiration, went to bed that evening with "his brain in a whirl," and later was awakened with the strains of this melody running through his mind;[15] he wrote it down, filled in the harmony the next morning,[16] and it was sung that day in the Sunday School service—though neither man ever dreamed that it would prove useful beyond their own limited services![17]

Redner, its composer, was a native Philadelphian who, at sixteen, was employed by a real estate firm. Showing great promise, he became a member of the firm at twenty-one, and eventually operated his own business with considerable financial success.[18] A bachelor, he gave himself unstintingly to church work, serving as organist in four churches during his lifetime and developing the Sunday School as a vital ministry. Of him, a fellow church member wrote:

He held to the old paths, not in any blind conservatism which forbade growth, but with the firm conviction that the religion of our fathers is still needed to bring men to God. . . . That such a man has lived and done his work is but another proof of the undying presence of Christ with His Church.[19]

Let us now examine this hymn, which "unnumbered multitudes, who will never hear the matchless voice of the great preacher, or even read one of his fine sermons, are singing with grateful joy."[20] It is still true that the Christ who came to Bethlehem in the silent night watches centuries ago can come today, and be born in the hearts of all who will receive Him!

Stanza One: For those readers who have been to Bethlehem in the recent past this description might not appear to be too accurate; but for Brooks, in his visit there over a century ago, it was; as Bailey points out,

> There were no street lights, no night clubs, no students burning the midnight oil; people worked outdoors from sunrise to sunset, went to bed at dark and slept till dawn.[21]

Moreover, for Brooks the everlasting Light was a reference, not only to the star that guided the Magi, but even more to Jesus, born there that night, but born to be the "Light of the world," an appellation He expressly gives to Himself (John 8:12). The "hopes" were those centered in the promised Messiah, while the "fears" were those numberless experiences they had wherein things "just didn't turn out right"—similar to our own times and lives. But there, tonight—with the reality of His having come—we all can and should have hope!

Stanza Two: Here Brooks focuses on various aspects of the ministry of the angels, or angelic host, in some places paralleled with the "morning stars" (Job 38:7). While the Holy Family sleeps, the angels serve as their protection or security—awed by what they are seeing in the incarnation and the expression of God's love, which calls forth from them an answering response. Their task also includes bearing witness to this unique event, extolling the God who has brought it to pass and extending—in their song—peace to the human family.

Stanza Three: Silence has always played a major role in spiritual life—witness the number of biblical characters who met God in the vast silence of the desert (Abraham, Jacob, Moses, etc.) or the wilderness (Elijah, Jesus, Paul, etc.). Here God, from out of the eternal silence, the heavenly silence, imparts Himself, when the incarnate Christ enters into the fabric of human life, and, more personally yet, human lives—yours, and mine, and anyone's who has the requisite meekness to be receptive. Moreover, living in this sinful world where raucous noise is all-too-prevalent, we can even more appreciate God's coming in wondrous silence!

Stanza Four: From the declaration of facts in the first three stanzas to a prayer in this, from the objective to the subjective, Brooks moves; and the prayer is the "sinner's prayer," whereby we personally seek the new birth (John 3:1–17). Not only do we live in a world of sin, but we are personally involved in it, and so we ask that *our* sin be cast out, and that its presence be replaced with His presence within us. Those herald angels who brought the good tidings on that night, in that place so long ago, still in this place, on this night, continue to bring those glad tidings. Finally, we want God, Emmanuel, "God with us," to abide with us, to settle down and make Himself at home in our hearts, to become a permanent resident, not an infrequent visitor, or even an honored guest—but one who lives within us for ever! As Bailey says, "Thank God, Christmas comes every year, for we need to be reminded!"[22]

Notes

1. McCutchan, *Our Hymnody*, p. 135.
2. Haeussler, *op. cit.*, p. 568.
3. Smith, *op. cit.*, p. 296.
4. Haeussler, *op. cit.*, p. 870.
5. Bailey, *op. cit.*, p. 546.
6. Haeussler, *op. cit.*, pp. 567–568.
7. Smith, *op. cit.*, p. 297.
8. Haeussler, *op. cit.*, p. 568.
9. *Ibid.*
10. Marks, *op. cit.*, p. 198.
11. McCutchan, *op. cit.*, p. 135.
12. Haeussler, *op. cit.*, p. 569.
13. Smith, *op. cit.*, pp. 298–299.
14. Covert and Laufer, *op. cit.*, p. 140.
15. Brown and Butterworth, *op. cit.*, p. 470.
16. Covert and Laufer, *op. cit.*, p. 140.
17. *Ibid.*, p. 139.
18. McCutchan, *op. cit.*, p. 136.
19. *Ibid.*
20. McCutchan, *op. cit.*, p. 135.
21. Bailey, *op. cit.*, p. 548.
22. *Ibid.*

Title/Date	*"O Sacred Head Now Wounded" (1830)*
Author	*Bernard of Clairvaux*
	Paul Gerhardt, trans. (1656)
	James W. Alexander, trans. (1830)
Composer/Tune	*Hans Leo Hassler (1601)*
	Harmonized by J. S. Bach "Passion Chorale" (1729)
Scriptural Basis	*Isaiah 53:5; Mark 15:17–20*

The hymn before us is an English translation (by James Waddell Alexander) of a German translation (by Paul Gerhardt) of a Latin hymn/poem by the famous medieval churchman, scholar, mystic, and monastic leader, St. Bernard of Clairvaux (1091–1153), about whom we have written in two earlier studies.

From his abbey in the French valley they had renamed Clairvaux, he stood out as the man of destiny, with kings, bishops, cardinals, and even popes seeking his wisdom, counsel, support, and common sense at a critical time for the medieval church; in fact,

> The Church tried to win him to its highest honors, with Milan vehemently declaring him to be the only fit successor to the illustrious Ambrose, and Rheims, noblest city in France, equally eager to place him on its arch-episcopal throne. But he chose to continue as Abbott of Clairvaux, and influenced the Christian world through his visits and his writings.[1]

Bernard, however, was more than "a terror to evil doers and heretics"; he was an earnest believer, whose faith bordered on the mystical and whose personal knowledge of and trust in Jesus Christ was fervent, one who would be called an Evangelical today. One has called him "a doctor whose lips distilled honey"; hear his own words to that effect from one of his sermons:

> Jesus is honey to the lips, in the ear melody, in the heart joy. Medicine also is that Name. Is any sad? Let Jesus come into his heart, and thence leap to his tongue.[2]

He was wounded for our transgressions, he was bruised for our iniquities . . . Isa. 53 : 5

Ascribed to Bernard of Clairvaux, 1091-1153
Tr. by Paul Gerhardt, 1656
Tr. by James Waddell Alexander, 1830

PASSION CHORALE 7. 6. 7. 6. D.
Hans Leo Hassler, 1601
har. by Johann Sebastian Bach, 1729

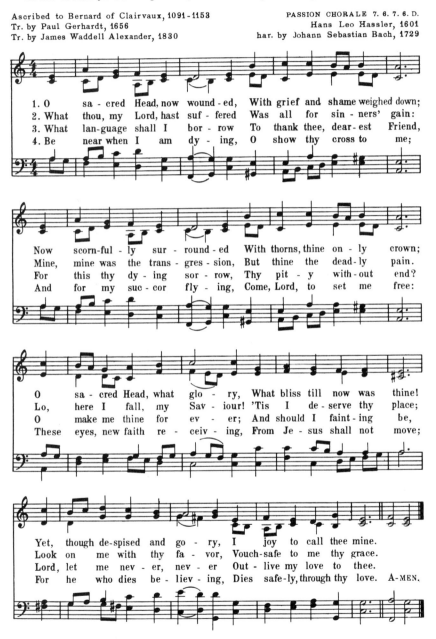

1. O sa-cred Head, now wound-ed, With grief and shame weighed down;
2. What thou, my Lord, hast suf-fered Was all for sin-ners' gain:
3. What lan-guage shall I bor-row To thank thee, dear-est Friend,
4. Be near when I am dy-ing, O show thy cross to me;

Now scorn-ful-ly sur-round-ed With thorns, thine on-ly crown;
Mine, mine was the trans-gres-sion, But thine the dead-ly pain.
For this thy dy-ing sor-row, Thy pit-y with-out end?
And for my suc-cor fly-ing, Come, Lord, to set me free:

O sa-cred Head, what glo-ry, What bliss till now was thine!
Lo, here I fall, my Sav-iour! 'Tis I de-serve thy place;
O make me thine for ev-er; And should I faint-ing be,
These eyes, new faith re-ceiv-ing, From Je-sus shall not move;

Yet, though de-spised and go-ry, I joy to call thee mine.
Look on me with thy fa-vor, Vouch-safe to me thy grace.
Lord, let me nev-er, nev-er Out-live my love to thee.
For he who dies be-liev-ing, Dies safe-ly, through thy love. A-MEN.

As one would expect, he loved music and encouraged its use in his monastery; he regulated the chanting at Citeaux, giving this practical counsel:

> It is necessary that men sing in a virile manner and not with voices shrill and artificial like the voices of women, or in a manner lascivious and nimble like actors, [adding cautions that] singers should manage their respiration, and not sing through their noses![3]

While agreement as to the source of this hymn is not unanimous, the consensus of scholarly opinion among hymnologists is that it was taken by Paul Gerhardt in the mid-seventeenth century from the long poem, the "Rhythmica Oratio" composed by Bernard,[4] and it was translated by Gerhardt into German from that section of the poem that focuses on our Lord's head as the object of contemplation, thus "Salve Caput Cruentatum."[5] Of Gerhardt's hymn, headed "To the suffering face of Christ," Lauxman says:

> Bernard's original is powerful and searching but Gerhardt's hymn is still more powerful and more profound, as redrawn from the deeper spring of evangelical Lutheran piety, Scriptural knowledge, and fervency of faith.[6]

And of James Alexander's fine translation of Gerhardt's German version, a specialist in German hymnody, Philip Schaff, has written this confirmation:

> This classical hymn has shown an imperishable vitality in passing from the Latin into the German, and from the German into the English, and proclaiming in three tongues, and in the name of three Confessions—the Catholic, the Lutheran, and the Reformed—with equal effect, the dying love of our Saviour and our boundless indebtedness to Him.[7]

Paul Gerhardt (1607–1676), next to Luther the most gifted and popular hymn-writer Germany has ever produced, whose hymns, in marking the transition from an objective to a subjective emphasis, are the "pure and spontaneous utterance of a fervent and beautiful faith,"[8] has been described as a "divine sifted in satan's sieve,"[9] for his career as a pastor was fraught with heartache and frustration, mostly through no fault of his own. After completing his studies for the Lutheran ministry at Wittenburg in 1642, he settled in Berlin, where he served as a tutor for several years, awaiting a pastoral call, without which he could not be ordained. In love with his employer's daughter, but without a call, they could not marry, and the future looked bleak. Eventually a country parish, Mittlewalde, extended him a call in 1651; he was ordained, and, in 1655, at forty-eight years of age, he married Anna Maria Berthold.

The ten years that followed were his happiest ones, for his published hymns, adopted widely for use by Lutheran communities, gave him a well-deserved reputation and led to a call, in 1657, to the great Church of St. Nicholas in Berlin, where he served, effectively and faithfully, for almost a decade. As a pastor, hymn-writer, and preacher, he was loved, respected, and admired. Catherine Winkworth, the eminent translator of German hymns, tells us:

> Of quiet but firm and cheerful bearing . . . crowds flocked to hear him; his preaching is said to have been very earnest and persuasive, full of Christian love and charity, which he practiced as well as preached by never turning a beggar from his doors, and receiving widows and orphans who needed help and shelter into his own house. His religion and his temperament alike made him cheerful, and not all the many disappointments of his life seem ever to have embittered his mood.[10]

These disappointments were many: much of his early life and ministry came during the terrible times of the Thirty Years' War (1618–1648), which could not help but weigh heavily on his mind, gentle and peace-loving as he was; four of their five children had died in infancy; and another tragic blow struck him in 1665.[11]

In that year, Elector Frederick Wilhelm I required all ministers to obey his edict designed to forbid discussion of the differences between the Lutheran and Reformed theological perspectives, since he wanted to make peace between these two elements. But, in good conscience, Gerhardt refused to comply; he was deposed from his office and not allowed to perform any of his clerical functions.[12] Then, he lost his beloved Anna Marie; eventually, he retired to the small parish in Lubben, where he labored as an archdeacon,[13] living there with his one remaining son in a very uncongenial atmosphere until he died. Thus it is quite appropriate to say, as one has, that he wrote many of his hymns "under circumstances which would have made most men cry rather than sing!"[14] Of his hymns Haeussler writes:

> He went back to Luther's most genuine type of hymn in such a manner as no one else had done . . . his joyful confidence inspired [by his] belief in the Love of God . . . [and his belief that] the merciful Righteous One is a gentle, loving Man. Like the old poets of the people he is sincerely . . . pious . . . and hearty, the blissfulness of his faith [making] him benign and amiable.[15]

While many have undertaken to translate this hymn into English, we are indebted to James W. Alexander (1804–1859), son of the eminent Princeton theologian Archibald Alexander,[16] whose scholarship and poetic gifts are combined in this hymn translation. His career was varied, and his positions influential, ranging from several pastorates—the last, of New York City's famed Fifth Avenue Presbyterian Church, where he was serving at the time of his untimely death—to professorships at both the College of New Jersey (Princeton) and at the Princeton Theological Seminary. One writes:

> Brilliant, scholarly, beloved and revered, he was one of the most influential ministers of his generation. Author of many volumes, pastor, teacher, poet, it is probable that upon his version of this hymn his abiding fame in no small measure will depend.[17]

The tune "Passion Chorale," which first appeared in a work by Hans Leo Von Hassler (1564–1612), was one of Bach's favorites, using it as he did five times in his "St. Matthew Passion" and frequently in other works as well.[18] Hassler was one of three sons of Isaac Hassler, the eminent Nuremberg organist, each of whom distinguished himself as a musician. At twenty Hans went to study music in Italy, the first of many German musicians to do so, and was greatly influenced by that brief but significant experience. He served as organist in a succession of important posts, his final one at the court of the elector of Saxony. As one of the most significant composers of his epoch, he is numbered among the five men considered to be the founders of German music, with his own style strongly influenced by Italy's Gabrielis.[19]

This originally "secular" tune, adapted for "sacred" usage by Bach, is in itself a "melody of beauty and simplicity," and it has become "one of the most profoundly reverent musical expressions in all hymnody,"[20] a tune that should be sung with great dignity and smoothness. It was played by an orchestra at the funeral of Frederick William I, as ordered in his will; and as Christian Schwartz, the noted missionary in India lay on his deathbed in 1798, his pupils sang this hymn in their own Malabar language, he himself joining in their singing until he died.[21]

Let us examine this hymn which Ritschl, the infamous critical scholar and liberal, criticized for its "undue stress on Jesus' physical sufferings," but then on his deathbed[22] asked for its closing verse to be repeated to him!

Stanza One: Here is the most vivid picture of Jesus as He hung on the cross; crowned with the thorns that wound His flesh, causing His head to be "gory"; weighted down by the sins of the world, the occasion of His "grief and shame"; scorned by His enemies, who had had the "crown" plaited, or at least, had allowed it, and had done nothing to remove this cynical mockery of His position as King of the Jews—in spite of all this, I not only still own Thee, "I *joy* to call Thee mine"! An intensely personal response of the believer who "trusts where he cannot understand"!

Stanza Two: Here is the doctrine of the vicarious atonement: the suffering and death of Jesus Christ in my place, the innocent for the guilty; the author stressed both the universal "*sinners*' gain" and the particular, or individual "*mine* was the transgression"; I recognize that I deserve to be there in the place of judgment because of that sin, but I plead with Him for His favor and His grace—"grace greater than all my sin," from *my* Lord, *my* Savior.

Stanza Three: Here again there is intimacy in the words "dearest Friend," and in the request "make me thine forever," so that I shall "never, never outlive my love to Thee." And the author is right, for what language, what human words could ever really adequately convey what we feel, or should feel, of gratitude to our Lord for what He was willing to endure for us?

Stanza Four: In my hour of death, the reality of the cross—or, what *happened* on the cross—should certainly be for my encouragement, as it is "rehearsed" either verbally or pictorially; and knowing that I have been forgiven and can therefore face my Maker unafraid should certainly make me free. It is a glorious truth—and I can sympathize with Ritschl for wanting to be reminded of it as he was preparing to enter Jordan's icy waters—that "he who dies believing" in Jesus Christ and Him crucified, does indeed "die safely through His love." And he will awaken on that farther shore, secure in the arms of His loving and waiting Father.

Notes

1. Smith, *Lyric Religion,* p. 309.
2. *Ibid.,* p. 310.
3. *Ibid.*
4. Haeussler, *op. cit.,* p. 194.
5. Smith, *op. cit.,* p. 310.
6. McCutchan, *Our Hymnody,* p. 176.
7. *Ibid.*
8. Moffatt and Patrick, *op. cit.,* p. 347.
9. *Ibid.*
10. McCutchan, *op. cit.,* p. 126.
11. Haeussler, *op. cit.,* p. 670.
12. Bailey, *op. cit.,* p. 326.
13. Brown and Butterworth, *op. cit.,* p. 86.
14. McCutchan, *op. cit.,* p. 126.
15. Haeussler, *op. cit.,* p. 671.
16. *Ibid.,* p. 524.
17. Covert and Laufer, *op. cit.,* p. 165.
18. McCutchan, *op. cit.,* p. 177.
19. Covert and Laufer, *op. cit.,* p. 166.
20. *Ibid.,* pp. 166–167.
21. Haeussler, *op. cit.,* p. 196.
22. Moffatt and Patrick, *op. cit.,* p. 41.

Title/Date	*"Ride On, Ride On in Majesty . . ."*
	(1827)
Author	*Henry Hart Milman*
Composer/Tune	*John B. Dykes "St. Drostane" (1862)*
Scriptural Basis	*Matthew 21:1–11; Zechariah 9:9*

Henry Hart Milman (1791–1868), the distinguished poet and author of some thirteen superb hymns, including this one, judged the "most popular Palm Sunday hymn in the English language,"[1] was born into wealth, culture, and privilege, the youngest son of Sir Francis Milman, knighted as an eminent court physician. He was educated at Eton, and then at Brasenose College, Oxford, where he took first-class honors in classics and won the Newdigate Prize with what Dean Stanley called "the most perfect of Oxford prize poems,"[2] described by another in these lines:

> His lines on Apollo
> Beat all the rest hollow
> And gained him the Newdigate prize.[3]

In addition, he also won three other literary prizes, demonstrating his future potential as a writer. Ordained into the Anglican Church in 1816, he continued writing his poetry and dramatic works, which brought him fame and considerable income and which led to his being appointed Poetry Professor at Oxford in 1821; it was also during this period that he wrote his hymns in response to a request by his close friend, Bishop Reginald Heber, who was proposing the publication of a new hymnbook. After reviewing this hymn, Heber wrote to Milman:

> You have indeed sent me a most powerful reinforcement to my projected hymnbook. A few more such and I shall neither need nor wait for the aid of Scott and Southey[4] [from whom he had also solicited new hymns].

In 1827, Milman gave the Bampton Lectures, thus marking his transition to theological studies, and two years later he published his epoch-making

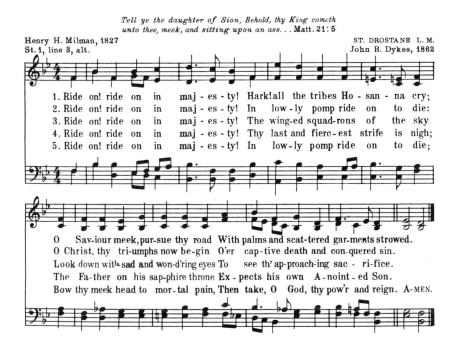

Tell ye the daughter of Sion, Behold, thy King cometh
unto thee, meek, and sitting upon an ass. . . Matt. 21: 5

Henry H. Milman, 1827
St. 1, line 3, alt.

ST. DROSTANE L. M.
John B. Dykes, 1862

1. Ride on! ride on in maj - es - ty! Hark! all the tribes Ho - san - na cry;
2. Ride on! ride on in maj - es - ty! In low - ly pomp ride on to die:
3. Ride on! ride on in maj - es - ty! The wing-ed squad-rons of the sky
4. Ride on! ride on in maj - es - ty! Thy last and fierc - est strife is nigh;
5. Ride on! ride on in maj - es - ty! In low - ly pomp ride on to die;

O Sav-iour meek, pur-sue thy road With palms and scat-tered gar-ments strowed.
O Christ, thy tri-umphs now be-gin O'er cap-tive death and con-quered sin.
Look down with sad and won-d'ring eyes To see th' ap-proach-ing sac - ri-fice.
The Fa-ther on his sap-phire throne Ex - pects his own A - noint - ed Son.
Bow thy meek head to mor-tal pain, Then take, O God, thy pow'r and reign. A-MEN.

History of the Jews—which he later revised considerably—which was both at-
tacked and denounced from the university pulpit, and not without reason;
for, as Dean Stanley points out,

> It was the first decisive inroad of German theology into England, the first
> palpable indication that the Bible could be studied like another book, that
> the characters and events of the sacred history could be treated at once
> critically and reverently.[5]

As a historian, his greatest work, *Latin Christianity*, published in 1854, was
thus reviewed:

> for vast and varied learning, indefatigable industry, calm impartiality, and
> subtle and acute criticism [it is] among the most memorable works in our
> language; [compared to Gibbon, the famous historian, favorably,] his nar-
> rative [has] rapidity of movement . . . his complex paragraphs [have] a
> splendour of imagination as well as wealth of thought.[6]

Critical thinker though he was, however, he did not sympathize with the ex-
treme speculation of some of the German rationalist scholars; he commented
that

he should like an Ewald to criticize Ewald, [and believed that] Christianity would survive the criticism of Dr. Strauss, [and the] bright, flashing artillery of Renan.[7]

And of course, it has!

Made dean of St. Paul's Cathedral in 1849, he served there with distinction for almost two decades, overseeing such a mundane matter as the redecoration of its interior, but also beginning its famous Sunday evening services. He was known for his brilliant scholarship, his earnest Christian faith,[8] his social charm, and as "the last of the great conversationalists."[9] But he also was one who had to prove himself early in his career, for his first parish had looked askance at any clergyman who was a successful playwright, as he had been—his first drama having proved a success in both England and America![10] One final personal note about this remarkably gifted man, who gave himself so unstintingly to his varied labors. He is one more illustration of the truth of the text from Proverbs, "He who finds a wife finds a good [thing], and obtains blessing from the Lord" (18:22); he was happily married to Mary Ann Cockell for close to forty-five years; she bore him six children, and was indeed a precious and worthy helpmeet, whose price was "far above rubies, for she did him good . . . all the days of her life" (31:10–12).

John Dykes, of whose compositions and life we have previously written, was both a superb musician and a dedicated clergyman. As vicar of St. Oswald's in Durham, he became embroiled in a controversy with his bishop, a Low Churchman; since he disagreed with Dykes' High Church views about certain liturgical matters, regarding them as "popish," he placed severe restrictions on any curate serving under Dykes. In fact, as Dykes argued, these restrictions were unwarranted and the bishop's action was illegal; however, even though Dykes was probably correct, the Court of the Queen's Bench in London upheld the bishop, ruling that he had sole jurisdiction in such matters.[11] Dykes, thoroughly shocked by their decision and continuingly overburdened by his heavy pastoral and administrative duties, died just two years later, when he was only fifty-three—a sad and tragic commentary on the injustice of man to man, so often seen in ecclesiastical, as well as other, disputes.

Dykes' tune, "St. Drostane," was written specifically for this hymn, and eventually appeared with it in *Hymns Ancient and Modern* (the 1875 edition). Smith lauds the tune, saying that "it carries [these words] with peculiar appropriateness, through awe and grief to the high rapture of redemption";[12] but McCutchan apparently does not share his estimate, saying,

There is no finer poetry in our hymnals, and it is a pity that we have not had written for it a tune strong enough to carry the climax in the last stanza,[13] [a judgment with which Haeussler concurs].[14]

Let us now examine this objective, robust hymn, possessing as it does "that peculiar combination of tragedy and victory which draws the singer into the very center of the Palm Sunday drama,"[15] as it describes the Palm Sunday events in "a city that lost its chance."[16]

Stanza One: Here the author speaks directly to Jesus as He rides His donkey into Jerusalem: in Milman's original, the text reads "Thine humble beast pursues his road"[17] for the altered "O Saviour meek, pursue thy road," and I prefer that original reading; moreover, he characterized the welcoming throng as representative of all the twelve tribes of Israel, whose cry of "Hosanna—Lord, save us, now!" lends a poignancy to the scene, as the hopes expressed by captive peoples always do!

Stanza Two: The contrast between Jesus' approach to Jerusalem "in majesty," and the number of terms that express humility, begins here, with "lowly pomp," and includes "meek" (vs. 1, altered version), "lowly pomp," and "meek" (vs. 5); somehow, "lowly pomp" almost seems to be inherently contradictory! Moreover, the triumphs of the Christ begin now, as He is riding on. Death will be destroyed, and sin defeated.

Stanza Three: Thus, His sacrifice is observed by the angels, "the winged squadrons of the sky," whose reaction is both sad and amazed, in that they are witnessing "Christ, the mighty maker (dying) for man, the creature's, sin"— which is an incredible plan, another dimension of redemption that staggers the mind, realizing that all of this is God's great provision for humanity, and not a hastily conceived afterthought.

Stanza Four: Here death is singled out as the "last and fiercest strife" with which the Man on the beast will have to contend; and when we consider that hell unleashed all of its terrors against Christ—"death and the curse were in its cup; Oh Christ, t'was full for Thee, but Thou didst drain the last dark drop"—we get something of the magnitude of this act! And then the encouragement, that the Father, who reigns from His throne, awaits His Son—His Anointed, sent-to-be-the-Messian-Son!

Stanza Five: Again, the Man on the beast rides into Jerusalem, majestic yet humble, accepting death, but assured that having given up His life, willingly, as God He will take the power that is rightfully His, and reign, thus establishing "the cosmic significance of the vast plan of redemption."[18]

This magnificent hymn, triumphant in both its tone and its teaching, demonstrates Milman's "lyric grace . . . free use of refrains . . . excellent structure, and sometimes burning style"[19]—the work of an artist with words.

Notes

1. Covert and Laufer, *op. cit.,* p. 164.
2. Julian, *op. cit.,* p. 736.

3. Smith, *Lyric Religion,* p. 343.

4. Haeussler, *op. cit.,* p. 188.

5. Julian, *op. cit.,* p. 736.

6. *Ibid.*

7. Haeussler, *op. cit.,* p. 800.

8. Marks, *op. cit.,* p. 130.

9. Julian, *op. cit.,* p. 737.

10. Marks, *op. cit.,* p. 130.

11. McCutchan, *Our Hymnody,* pp. 18–19.

12. Smith, *op. cit.,* p. 345.

13. McCutchan, *op. cit.,* pp. 159–160.

14. Haeussler, *op. cit.,* p. 188.

15. Stulken, *op. cit.,* p. 219.

16. Smith, *op. cit.,* p. 344.

17. McCutchan, *op. cit.,* p. 159.

18. Bailey, *op. cit.,* p. 168.

19. Julian, *op. cit.,* p. 737.

Title/Date	*"Rock of Ages" (1776)*
Author	*Augustus M. Toplady "Toplady" (1830)*
Composer/Tune	*Richard Redhead "Ajalon" (1853)*
Scriptural Basis	*I Corinthians 10:4; Exodus 33:22; Isaiah 26:4; 33:2; 48:21*

Someone has made the observation that there are "lies, damned lies, and statistics," making the last the most nefarious kind of deceptive tactic. While there may be some truth to this estimate of the reliability of statistics, they can serve at least to confirm objectively what one may have believed on more subjective grounds. Thus we note that this hymn, called by Robinson "the supreme hymn of the English language"[1] and estimated by Haeussler as "one of its finest . . . expressions of evangelical faith and worship,"[2] has ranked near or at the top in several studies conducted by eminent hymnologists. For example, in King's study of fifty-two hymnals, "Rock of Ages" was one of four at the top;[3] and in Benson's study, involving 107 hymnals, it was number one;[4] moreover, fifty years ago Doving cited its translation into 130 languages, that number exceeded only by 171 for Luther's "A Mighty Fortress Is Our God."[5] Thus Julian is accurate when he writes that "no other English hymn can be named which has laid so broad and firm a grasp on the English-speaking world,"[6] probably because it has served men and women well in the hours of their greatest need—when facing the reality of their sin, or perhaps pondering their destiny and how they might find assurance of the grace of God for themselves.

We know, for example, that

- General J. E. B. Stuart, the famous Confederate Cavalry leader, mortally wounded . . . and in a Richmond hospital, called for his minister and requested that it be sung to him.
- The last sounds heard by the few saved from the wreck of the steamer *London* in the Bay of Biscay, in 1866, were the voices of the helpless passengers singing it as the ship went down.
- A company of Armenian Christians sang it in their native tongue while they were being massacred in Constantinople.[7]

And that Rock was Christ. I Cor. 10:4

- When Prince Albert, Queen Victoria's consort, was on his death bed, in 1861, he frequently repeated portions of it, and said "If in this hour I had only my worldly goods and dignities to depend upon, I should be poor indeed"[8]
- As it echoed through Westminster Abbey at the funeral of Prime Minister William Gladstone—who once had translated it into Latin verse as he sat in the House of Commons[9]—an observer present wrote "To have written words which should come home to people in moments of high, deep and passionate emotions, consecrating, consoling, uplifting: . . . There can hardly be anything better worth doing than that."[10]

The author of this hymn was Augustus Montague Toplady (1740–1778), the son of an English major killed at the siege of Carthegena in 1741. His mother, a devout woman with strength of character, may have overindulged him as a child, since he was apparently rather sickly. His tempestuous nature, which later showed itself in his eager willingness to enter into polemics against any and all comers, was early evident; as a schoolboy, he attempted to check this fighting spirit by composing and using a daily prayer that he might be kept from quarreling with his fellows; but his attitude toward his aunt was less kindly, for he wrote of her in his diary: "Aunt Betty is so vastly quarrelsome . . . fractious . . . captious, and insolent that she is unfit for human society."[11] And, apparently, Aunt Betty felt equally kindly toward him!

When circumstances led them to move to Ireland, he continued his schooling at Trinity College, Dublin, whence he graduated, taking Holy Orders in the Church of England in 1762. Meanwhile, he was sixteen when he experienced a profound Evangelical conversion; let him give his account of it:

> Strange that I who had so long sat under the means of grace in England should be brought right unto God in an obscure part of Ireland, midst a handful of people met together in a barn, and by the ministry of one who could hardly spell his own name. Surely it was the Lord's doing and is marvelous. The excellency of such power must be of God, and cannot be of man. The regenerating spirit breathes not only on whom but likewise when and where and as He listeth.[12]

A. B. Grosart, author of Julian's article on Toplady, makes the interesting comment that this should be taken "cum grano salis" (with a grain of salt), since he knew the lay preacher, Wesleyan Methodist James Morris; he states not only that Morris was not illiterate, but that "he had far more brain power than his convert, and was a born orator, though reticent and lowly-minded!"[13]

In any event, Toplady served the parish of Broadhembury for most of his active ministry, and it was probably there that he wrote this hymn, or at least the initial draft of it. Actually, it appeared in *The Gospel Magazine,* March 1776, as "A Living and Dying Prayer for the Holiest Believer in the World"; it was appended to a curious article in which Toplady first discussed the enormous national debt of England, a debt he believed could never be repaid (what would he have done with *our* present national debt) and then he calculated the enormous number of sins the average person commits in his lifetime; his figures show that, committing one sin per second, a fifty-year-old would be guilty of over 1,576 million transgressions.[14] However, the good news is that while we could never even come close to paying such a debt, Christ—"who has redeemed us from the curse of the Law"—will through His merit "infinitely overbalance *all* the sins of the *whole* believing world."[15]

He later served, briefly, as a pastor in London to the French Calvinist community there, but his frail health failed him, and he died of tuberculosis before his fortieth birthday. Saying to a friend who sought to pray for his recovery, "No, no, I shall die. For no mortal could endure such manifestations of God's glory as I have, and live,"[16] he died, singing one of his hymns.

While the estimate of Toplady's character and work varies widely according to whether the writer is Calvinistic or Arminian, this judgment of Lord Earl Selbourne appears to be a balanced one:

Few writers of hymns had higher gifts than Toplady, . . . a man of ardent temperament, enthusiastic zeal, strong convictions, and great energy of character. He had "the courage of a lion, but a frame as brittle as glass." Between him and John Wesley there was a violent opposition of opinion, and much acrimonious controversy; but the same fervor and zeal which made him an intemperate theologian gave warmth, richness and spirituality to his poems . . . his art never inconsistent with a genuine flow of real feeling.[17]

And the judgment of another regarding the theological disputes he had with John Wesley is equally gracious:

The controversies between this fervent, powerful preacher (who was heard by crowds as immense as Wesley's) and that esteemed Divine, show neither disputant at his best. It is charitable to suppose that much of Toplady's bitterness may have been due to his ill-health.[18]

There are two tunes that have found widespread usage with this hymn, one in England and the other in the United States. Thomas Hastings (1784–1872), the composer of "Toplady," was born on the New England frontier and migrated with his family by sleigh and ox sledge (!) to Clinton, New York, home of Hamilton College (the present author's alma mater!). Gifted with talent and a passionate love for music, at eighteen he was directing the village choir. After several years on the family farm—his father was a doctor and farmer—he moved to nearby Utica, where he edited a religious weekly *The Western Recorder*.[19] Believing that church music needed reforming, he lectured and wrote, and established singing classes for congregations and schools for young musicians. Moving to New York City, he continued, with unbounded energy for over forty years,

teaching, training choirs, composing (over one thousand hymn tunes!), compiling and publishing (some fifty works), writing hymns (over six hundred), some alone but much in collaboration with Lowell Mason; [he did] valuable service in his day in stemming the tide of deteriorating influences in American hymnody, and maintaining the ideal of devoutness in church praise.[20]

In 1858, New York University honored him with the Doctor of Music degree, one well-earned in every sense.

"Ajalon" the second tune, loved and used in England, was composed by Richard Redhead (1820–1901), known as "an accompanist of devotional spirit, whose extemporizing seemed inspired by his faith."[21] Early influenced by Frederick Oakeley (translator of "Oh Come, All Ye Faithful"), he became, at Oakeley's invitation, organist at one of the churches prominent in the Oxford Movement; working with Oakeley "his musical collections exercised a leading influence on the musical side of the Roman Catholic revival."[22] His tune "Ajalon" is as popular in England as is Hastings' "Toplady" in this country, both apparently wed to those immortal words for life. Let us examine this beloved hymn.

Stanza One: Routley informs us that hymns which are so meritorious that no good hymnal omits them have three properties: familiar teaching, vivid language, and an arresting opening phrase.[23] Certainly this hymn meets all those criteria, and especially the last. Whence the phrase "Rock of Ages"? The translation of Isaiah 26:4 reads "Trust in the Lord forever, for in God the Lord we have an everlasting Rock" (NASB); the marginal readings are "The Rock of Ages"[24] and of course, this image of God as our strength, refuge, and place of security abounds in the Old Testament. Moreover, just as God made the water flow out of the rock (Isaiah 48:21), so Toplady uses this image to represent the "life giving stream" that flowed from Christ's side (in pictorial language). Again, the image is of Moses, hiding himself in the "cleft" of the rock as God "passed by," a place of safety and deliverance from possible death—for no one sees God's face and lives. Finally not only is the Rock of Ages, Jesus Christ, a shelter and a place of shade, but His shed blood is a double cure for sin, cleansing me from its guilt (atonement) and enabling me to overcome it (sanctification).

Stanza Two: Here again he focuses on my total inability to do anything to deal with my past sin; it catches up with me; it is a disease that needs to be cured and cleansed away; as Routley says with some dramatic flair,

> Sin involves shyness, secretiveness, laborious deceptions, hysterical self-defense, caution, coverup of defects, and keeping up a reputation; I've tried zeal, cried tears; fretted and worried—but nothing will do it, it's no use; "All for sin could not atone; Thou must save, and Thou alone." And it's never too late, for His mercy is timeless—even in death and beyond it, He is there, and He is ALL we need.[25]

And Thomas Chambers adds:

> On the basis of "this do and live" no peace, and even no true and worthy
> obedience can ever be attained. It is "believe on the Lord Jesus Christ and
> you shall be saved." When this belief enters the heart, joy and confidence
> come along with it, . . . and with a new principle and a new power we be-
> come new creatures in Christ.[26]

Stanza Three: Moreover, this hiding-place of Christ's cross and fountain is
freely accessible; there are no waiting periods, no barriers to be climbed over;
I do not need fancy clothes; I do not have to try to "clean up my act" first;
if I tried to come with my hands full, how could I cling to Christ? The allusion to "nakedness" is probably related to being clothed with the "filthy
rags" of my own righteousness, which will never gain me any standing with
God. Look, moreover, at these terms—empty-handed, clinging, naked,
helpless, foul—none of which bespeak of self-confidence, success, or "having it all together," terms that are the buzz words in all too many Evangelical circles today! How do we regain God's estimate of the enormity of our
human sin, rebellion, corruption?

Stanza Four: But Jesus is not just for this world's concerns; He is an eternal place of security. Every day I need Him; as I am dying—and each day
we are!—and after I die and am confronted by Him in His awesome majesty,
I also need Him.

So this hymn touches the believer at every stage, inspiring the new-born,
comforting and sustaining the mature, and smoothing the final way of the
lonely pilgrim as he approaches his end. As Hodson has written:

> "Rock of Ages, cleft for me" sung above the coffin lid
> Underneath, all restfully, all life's joys and sorrows hid;
> Nevermore, O storm-tossed soul, nevermore from wind and tide
> Nevermore from billows' roll wilt Thou need thyself to hide.
> Could the sightless, sunken eyes closed beneath the soft grey hair
> Could the mute and stiffened lips move again in pleading prayer,
> Still, aye still the words would be "Let me hide myself in Thee."[27]

And Christina Rossetti prayed:

> Oh Lord, who art as the shadow of a great Rock in a weary land, Who be-
> holds Thy weak creatures weary of labor, weary of pleasure, weary of hope
> deferred, weary of self, in Thine abundant compassion and unutterable
> tenderness, bring us, we pray Thee, unto Thy rest. Amen.[28]

Finally, Percy Dearmer writes, somewhat wistfully:

> . . . the intensity of religious passion has surely endued Toplady with a
> power beyond his normal gifts: here is much vigor of unconscious art—
> the violence of the opening cry, the sweeping negatives (verses 2, 3), the
> growing exultation of the last, and the quiet return at the end in a changed
> tone of gentle confidence. . . . It remains a notable monument of the re-
> ligion which gripped our fathers.[29]

Certainly true, but no less the kind of religion which we too need in
these critical days!

Notes

1. Haeussler, *op. cit.*, p. 259.
2. *Ibid.*, p. 258.
3. Marks, *op. cit.*, p. 39.
4. *Ibid.*, p. 40.
5. *Ibid.*, p. 44.
6. Julian, *op. cit.*, p. 972.
7. Brown and Butterworth, *op. cit.*, p. 139.
8. McCutchan, *Our Hymnody*, p. 251.
9. Brown and Butterworth, *op. cit.*, p. 140.
10. McCutchan, *op. cit.*, p. 251.
11. Bailey, *op. cit.*, p. 118.
12. Julian *op. cit.*, p. 1182.
13. *Ibid.*
14. Covert and Laufer, *op. cit.*, p. 258.
15. *Ibid.*
16. *Ibid.*, p. 257.
17. McCutchan, *op. cit.*, p. 252.
18. Moffatt and Patrick, *op. cit.*, p. 522.
19. Smith, *op. cit.*, p. 352.
20. Moffatt and Patrick, *op. cit.*, p. 363.
21. Lightwood, *op. cit.*, p. 17.
22. Moffatt and Patrick, *op. cit.*, p. 473.
23. Routley, *Hymns and the Faith*, pp. 145–146.
24. Guthrie and Motyer, *The New Bible Commentary, Revised*, p. 605.
25. Routley, *op. cit.*, p. 148ff.
26. Hodson, *op. cit.*, p. 14.
27. *Ibid.*, p. 19.
28. *Ibid.*
29. Dearmer, *op. cit.*, p. 337.

Title/Date	*"When I Survey the Wondrous Cross . . ."*
	(1707, 1709)
Author	*Isaac Watts*
Composer/Tune	*Lowell Mason "Hamburg" (1824)*
	(arranged, or adapted, from a
	Gregorian Chant)
Scriptural Basis	*Galatians 6:14; 2:20; Philippians 3:7-8*

Among the many splendid hymns written by Isaac Watts, whose "learning and piety, gentleness and largeness of heart earned for him the title of the Melanchthon of his day,"[1] two stand out clearly above all the others—masterpieces, each designated as his greatest. Since we have already considered his superb paraphrase of Psalm 90, "Our God, Our Help in Ages Past," we turn to the other, "When I Survey the Wondrous Cross," in Matthew Arnold's considered judgment, the greatest of all English hymns, barring none.[2] On the last Sunday of his life Arnold had worshipped at Liverpool's Sefton Park Presbyterian Church, where he heard John Watson (Ian Mclaren), one of the finest preachers of his day; Arnold was, however, even more impressed by this hymn as that great congregation sang it. Later that day he was fatally stricken, and in his dying moments he was heard singing those lines;[3] as they brought him comfort, they were fulfilling Watts's design, for his desire was to ever be "a servant to the churches and a helper to the joy of the . . . Christian."[4]

What is it about this hymn that makes it "the royal jewel of all his lyric work"?[5] Certainly "its imaginative quality, its absolute self-surrender,"[6] as Breed suggests, contributes to its worth; so does its "simplicity, its splendid phrase and melody, its deep solemnity, its passion of pure religion,"[7] as H. Augustine Smith describes it.

Watts originally wrote this hymn to illuminate his sermon text, Galatians 6:14,

But far be it from me to glory, save in the cross of our Lord Jesus Christ, through which the world hath been crucified unto me, and I unto the world,

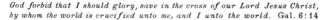

*God forbid that I should glory, save in the cross of our Lord Jesus Christ,
by whom the world is crucified unto me, and I unto the world.* Gal. 6:14

Isaac Watts, 1707, text of 1709

HAMBURG L.M.
Arr. from a Gregorian chant by Lowell Mason, 1824

1. When I sur-vey the won-drous cross On which the Prince of glo-ry died, My rich-est gain I count but loss, And pour con-tempt on all my pride.

2. For-bid it, Lord, that I should boast, Save in the death of Christ my God: All the vain things that charm me most, I sac-ri-fice them to his blood.

3. See, from his head, his hands, his feet, Sor-row and love flow min-gled down: Did e'er such love and sor-row meet, Or thorns com-pose so rich a crown?

4. Were the whole realm of na-ture mine, That were a pres-ent far too small; Love so a-maz-ing, so di-vine, De-mands my soul, my life, my all. A-MEN.

the sermon being preached at the Communion service. As we examine it, keep in mind its strong, clear, and simple lines, as well as its restrained language.[8]

Stanza One: Immediately one is struck by the incongruities here: the throne of the Prince of Glory is a cross, He reigns through suffering, and I gain by losing—my pride is humbled, my losses extolled. Hodson writes: "Had God been merciful without the satisfaction of His justice, He would have lost the throne of His righteousness."[9] Moreover, note some of these words: "survey," which describes pondering, not just seeing, an intentional consideration, trying to realize what it all really means: "wondrous," when you consider that the Romans had devised the cross as a method of torturing the condemned as they died—yet in God's purpose, it becomes the way of victory; and Christ as the Prince of Glory "seated on the Father's right hand," deigned to become a Man that He might be God's Messiah.

Stanza Two: Here the biblical text comes into use directly: God forbid that we should find any occasion for glorying in ourselves—no pride, no pomp, no show; and just as we are to count what could be looked at as our richest gains, losses, so we are to sacrifice all those "little charmers," the empty vanities of life. Paul, with his Pharisaic training and his heritage as a full-blooded son of Abraham, was naturally in an enviable position, but he deliberately set all that aside, counting it as dung, that he might have Christ—not earning his salvation thereby, but coming into the fulness of life in Christ by His grace alone. Hear also the testimony of another: "nothing in my hand I bring, simply to Thy cross I cling."

Stanza Three: This stanza, which has been said to "surpass every other stanza in the range of hymnody for solemn beauty and intense sorrow,"[10] focuses on the "rich crown" that the Prince of Glory wore as He hung on the cross, a crown composed of two precious human experiences, sorrow and love; here they are mingled together with the blood He shed, and the pain of the braided thorns in an incredibly vivid pictorial experience! Add to this the derelict cry "my God, my God, why hast Thou forsaken Me?" and the picture is completed. Well does James Denney say, "In Gethsemane Christ shrank from His death in deadly agony; as it came near, the prospect appalled Him,"[11] and Browning adds,

> It went up from the Holy's lips amid His lost creation,
> That of the lost, no son should use
> those words of desolation.[12]

Stanza Four: Seen with the eye of faith, surveying its length and breadth, its depth and height, the amazing love of this Prince of Glory calls forth from me far more than the material universe, even were I able to give it in its entirety to God—for it is not mine, it is His already! But "what can I give Him? I'll give Him my heart"! So, as Routley urges, I will yield everything freely, and change "the burden of possession for the burden of praise."[13] St. Ambrose prayed,

> Oh Lord, how worthy art Thou of love, who doest so much for love of us.
> Wherefore I will love Thee, O Lord, my Strength, my Refuge, and my
> Deliverer.[14]

Thus this hymn is a song of the offering and sanctification of human life, since the Prince of Glory, who reigns from the cross, reigns over our common life!

Two interesting anecdotes regarding its use:

(1) After it was sung at St. Edmund's Church, in London, Father Ignatius repeated to his congregation these lines in a very impressive manner:

Love so amazing, so divine
  Demands my soul, my life, my all.

Then, after a brief silence he commented:

Well, I'm surprised to hear you sing that. Do you know that altogether you put only fifteen shillings in the collection bag this morning?[15]

(2) John Hall tells of a Scotchman, who, while singing the words

Were the whole realm of nature mine
That were a present far too small

was fumbling in his pocket to find his smallest silver coin for the collection box![16]

The tune, "Hamburg," is an arrangement by Lowell Mason (1792–1872), a man of keen intellect and boundless enthusiasm, a keen teacher and reformer of church music who rendered a service of enormous value in his era; his singing conventions "did much to extend interest in music, and to raise its standards in nineteenth-century America."[17]

This music originally was a Gregorian chant, a musical style developed by Gregory the Great (540–604), designated by some as the first pope. He "arranged the Ambrosian and Greek scales into eight tones, or scales, establishing a system of chanting" that has prevailed for centuries throughout the Roman Catholic Church; he also encouraged congregational singing, and trained the monks in the use of music in liturgical worship at his Schola Cantorum that he founded at Rome.[18]

Gregory was born of illustrious parents, and as a youth experienced all the advantages of wealth and culture. After he became the Bishop of the leading Church in Rome, he was looked to for more and more leadership from the people as well as from the "faithful," his pastoral charge. On one occasion the city suffered under a terrible plague, with scores dying and cries for help increasing daily. He formed musical processions, including choirs singing litanies, in the streets; this had the desired effect of calming the people's fears, giving them hope, and increasing their responsiveness to the Faith.[19] A remarkable blend of piety, earnestness, musical ability, and administrative leadership characterized this medieval church leader.

Thus Watts's hymn is enhanced by this simple tune, employing only five tones yet reinforcing the hushed reverence and solemnity of the text.[20]

Notes

1. Julian, *op. cit.*, p. 1236.
2. Haeussler, *op. cit.*, p. 213.
3. *Ibid.*
4. Smith, *op. cit.*, p. 448.
5. Brown and Butterworth, *op. cit.*, p. 42.
6. Breed, *op. cit.*, p. 103.
7. Smith, *op. cit.*, p. 448.
8. Routley, *Hymns and the Faith*, pp. 111–112.
9. Hodson, *op. cit.*, p. 39.
10. Smith, *op. cit.*, p. 448.
11. Hodson, *op. cit.*, p. 40.
12. *Ibid.*
13. Routley, *op. cit.*, pp. 115–117.
14. Hodson, *op. cit.*, p. 43.
15. Haeussler, *op. cit.*, p. 213.
16. Duffield, *op. cit.*, p. 595.
17. Moffatt and Patrick, *op. cit.*, p. 423.
18. Covert and Laufer, *op. cit.*, pp. 168–169.
19. Smith, *op. cit.*, p. 449.
20. Covert and Laufer, *op. cit.*, p. 169.

Title/Date	*"When Morning Gilds the Skies..."* *(1853, 1858)*
Author	*Edward Caswell*
Composer/Tune	*Sir Joseph Barnby "Laudes Domini"* *(1868)*
Scriptural Basis	*Psalm 30:4–5; Psalm 34:1; I Thessalonians 5:18*

This delightful hymn, whose tune is so joyful that it sometimes is played or sung without an appropriate measure of dignity or genuine devotion, is another of those whose authorship is unknown. The consensus of scholarly hymnological opinion is that it came originally from German sources, first appearing in 1828 in the *Katholisches Gesangbuch*.[1] Duffield considers it a good possibility that the unknown German "original" was based on a Latin hymn, perhaps by Gregory the Great, whom we have just discussed; in summary, Duffield writes:

> Such, then, in its affiliation with English, Latin, and German hymnody; in its connection of ancient and modern thought; in its deep relations to literature, and in the wide catholicity of its religious faith, is the story of "When morning gilds the skies"—the opening hymn of *Laudes Domini,* and a true strain from the "Lord's Praises," whence it takes its name.[2]

Edward Caswell (1814–1878) who, along with John Mason Neale and Catherine Winkworth, have provided us with a rich store of hymns in translation from their original Latin, Greek, and German sources has been discussed earlier. He began his life of ministry as a clergyman in the Church of England and ended it as a priest, serving in the Roman Catholic Oratory of Edgbaston, near Birmingham, where

> his life was spent, marked by earnest devotion to his clerical duties and a loving interest in the poor, the sick and afflicted, and little children—a man who "loved God and little children."[3]

Julian, writing of his capability as a translator, speaks of his

His praise shall continually be in my mouth. Psalm 34:1

Anon., German, c. 1800
Tr. by Edward Caswall, 1853, 1858

LAUDES DOMINI 6.6.6.D.
Sir Joseph Barnby, 1868

... general faithfulness to the originals, and the purity of his rhythm, the latter feature specially adapting his hymns to music, and for congregational purposes. [Unfortunately, while] his original compositions are marked by considerable poetical ability their strong Roman Catholic doctrinal emphasis has precluded their widespread adoption outside of that Communion.[4]

"Laudes Domini," the joyous tune sung to this "fine outburst of praise,"[5] was composed especially for it by Sir Joseph Barnby (1838–1896), and it first appeared in *Hymns Ancient and Modern* in 1868. Barnby, whom we have discussed earlier, was one of the most prolific of all nineteenth-century hymn tune-writers, with many of his compositions still being widely used. Barnby became increasingly impatient with the general attitude in his day that all tunes should be written in the style of the seventeenth century. He argued that, just as those earlier composers had been free to develop their own style, so should he and his peers be similarly free, and not have to slavishly imitate the old Masters; he said, "For my part, I have elected to imitate the old writers in their independent method of working rather than their works!"[6]

Among other honors, Barnby was chosen to conduct outstanding music events, such as the Leeds Festival in 1892 and the Cardiff Festivals in 1892 and 1895; he was a fellow of the Royal Academy of Musicians, a member of the Philharmonic Society, and was honored by being knighted by Queen Victoria in 1892,[7] just a few years before his untimely death, at only fifty-eight. Of him one has commented:

> He had outstanding gifts as a choirmaster, and did a great work in popularizing music, but he was primarily a church musician, before and beyond everything [else] a servant of those solemn rites in which, faithfully carried out, there is more than enough to satisfy the craving soul.[8]

Our present hymn, which first appeared with the title "A Christian Greeting,"[9] originally had fourteen verses, now reduced to six in the *Trinity Hymnal*. Long a favorite with worshippers at Saint Paul's Cathedral in London, it was—like other old German hymns—to be sung on all possible occasions—washing, enjoying the fire, beginning work, undressing (where getting into bed is compared with getting into the grave), at a house warming. Incidentally, of another hymn, one for a merchant, the accompanying note read:

> By the use of this hymn, merchants may be kept heedful to the snares and temptations which they become liable unto by their negotiations; and what peace and profit will ensue if they be just and merciful in their dealings.[10]

As one reads through this hymn, it is obvious that its original author was probably a lover of the natural world and possessed an infectious faith. If he lived in Franconia (as is conjectured), his poetic soul found much to inspire it in this region:

> of small mountain ranges, forests full of fairies—the birthplace of Jacob Grimm, author of Fairy Tales—little towns with castles, ancient Romanesque churches and monasteries scattered here and there, with valleys

and rivers.[11] [Where Luther did some of his work in translating the biblical prophets and psalms.]

Let us examine its distinctive features:

First, its regularly repeated refrain, "May Jesus Christ be praised," stands out boldly as a call to everyone to worship—to get and keep life in proper perspective by focusing one's heart on Jesus Christ Himself. While this begins at dawn, as I struggle to be aroused from my sleep, it does not end there, but rather carries with me throughout each activity of the day, so that "whatever I do, in word [prayer] or in deed [work], I do all in the name of the Lord Jesus, giving thanks through Him to God the Father" (Colossians 3:17, NASB).

Second, it runs the gamut of life's various situations and conditions in which the child of God—and me, the singer, in particular—is found: sleepless nights become occasions for praising Jesus, as do times of temptation, when the evil one would attack me through my thoughts (vs. 2); when I am sad, I find solace, and when I lose some precious earthly person (or thing), I find comfort, again, in praising Jesus (vs. 3). Moreover, even in the midst of heaven's bliss, praising Him is still my premier joy, driving fear into all the wicked powers of darkness who, like the demons in Jesus' day, know that the day of their ultimate demise is near, and it will be accomplished by Jesus— even the "wrath of man (and demonic spirit too!) will praise Him" (vs. 4). Next, he calls upon all of the natural world, from earth to the heavens— length and breadth, depth and height—to join its joyful "voice" in praising Jesus (vs. 5). Finally, both now as I live day by day, and then as I live, eternally, my divine song will continue to be in praise of Jesus! (vs. 6).

Third, as I have thought about this hymn—the favorite of the great pulpiteer, Canon Liddon, who had requested that it be sung at his funeral[12]— I have been impressed by the simplicity of its very clear ideas; the verbs are arresting (e.g., "gilds," "repair," "shield," and "resound"), and, some of the other words almost paint pictures: "my heart cries," "silent spirit sighs," "shield my breast," "faded bliss," "sweet chant."

As H. Augustine Smith points out, Barnby's tune has an "upward lift and quick pace, which admirably interprets these exultant words";[13] he goes on to give some good suggestions as to how it should be sung. He advises:

> The spirited refrain "May Jesus Christ be praised" may well be sung in unison, with full voice. The stanza-lines may be sung by choir or congregation in harmony. The pace should be fairly quick and strictly in time to the end. The closing refrain of half notes makes an admirable Doxology or Gloria, particularly when following a praise-hymn in same key. Try it, for example with "All Glory, Laud, and Honor," to the tune "St. Theodulph."[14]

One final suggestion: as it is sung, using brass (cornets, trumpets, trombones), especially on the refrain, elevates the sense of praise, and can be a very moving experience—an offering of praise to God "with the sound of trumpets."

Notes

1. Covert and Laufer, *op. cit.,* p. 4.
2. Duffield, *op. cit.,* p. 599.
3. McCutchan, *Our Hymnody,* p. 57.
4. Julian, *op. cit.,* p. 215.
5. McCutchan, *op. cit.,* p. 57.
6. Metcalf, *op. cit.,* p. 106.
7. Haeussler, *op. cit.,* p. 543.
8. Moffatt and Patrick, *op. cit.,* p. 260.
9. McCutchan, *op. cit.,* p. 57.
10. Smith, *op. cit.,* p. 453.
11. Bailey, *op. cit.,* p. 340.
12. Covert and Laufer, *op. cit.,* p. 4.
13. Smith, *op. cit.,* p. 453.
14. *Ibid.*

5

Singing in Worship:
"As You Sing Spiritual Songs . . ."

"Spiritual songs" is the third category of song mentioned by the Apostle Paul in his exhortation to Christians both in Colosse and in the churches centering, perhaps, in Ephesus. As we have noted previously, this was the general term for a song; and while Paul may have had in mind a type of musical utterance that apparently was common at least in the Corinthian church, "unpremeditated words sung in the Spirit, voicing holy aspirations," as Bruce suggests,[1] we certainly cannot be dogmatic about this. So, while the lines that distinguish psalms from hymns may be fairly well drawn—although overlap certainly is not uncommon—no such clear distinctions can easily be made between hymns and spiritual songs, at least not strictly on the basis of scriptural terminology.

For our purposes in this study I am defining "spiritual songs" as those in which the primary focus of the lyrics is manward rather than Godward; in these "spiritual songs" the message is thus addressed to others. It may be in a didactic fashion, as in Stone's "The Church's One Foundation," or in Alexander's "There Is a Green Hill Far Away"; it may be in an exhortative mood, as in Monsell's "Fight the Good Fight with All Thy Might," or as in the anonymous writer's "Oh Come, All Ye Faithful"; or it may be as a type of personal testimony—in the finest sense of that sometimes hackneyed expression—as in Bonar's marvelous dialogue "I Heard the Voice of Jesus Say," or as in Cowper's almost biographical gem "God Moves in a Mysterious Way." In any event, these "spiritual songs" are certainly not to be equated with that type of offering which sometimes goes by the name "gospel song," a label that has, alas, in these times come to include almost any kind of poor poetry, weak sentiment, and bad, if not heretical theology, coupled with the kinds of tunes that are certainly more fit for the dance floor than for the worshipping congregation. Of this type of music, Routley says,

> It, as a style . . . ministers to immaturity, and when over-used (as I believe
> it is in far too many of even our Presbyterian Churches!) keeps people im-

mature; it is too strong in calories and too short in protein to make a good diet for those who hope to grow.[2]

And elsewhere he makes this same point by contrast:

> The finest [church] music is hallowed by tradition, inspired by spiritual ex-
> perience and capable of satisfying our deepest spiritual needs when there
> is an understanding and sympathetic mind ready to receive it. Between the
> kind of emotion stimulated by the [gospel] crooner, and the emotion stim-
> ulated by good church music . . . there is a gulf fixed as wide as that be-
> tween Lazarus in Abram's bosom and the souls in torment.[3]

And finally Routley avows, "hymns as entertainment are a very dubious self-indulgence."[4]

This is of particular concern to the writer because of the fact that he lives in Branson, the self-styled "Country Music Capital of the World." Here "gospel music" is a drawing card, sometimes being performed by those who seem to have little understanding of the truth of what they are singing, and perhaps lesser conviction as to its practical implications for daily life! With Luther—and countless others since—he believes that Christians should both sing God's truth, and also make a faithful, serious effort to *do* what is taught by God's truth.

Let us now consider a number of the very finest of the spiritual songs in much the same fashion as we have done for both psalms and hymns, recognizing among the authors and composers to be considered some of the most earnest and devout believers ever to grace our communities of faith.

Notes

1. Simpson and Bruce, *The Epistle to the . . . Colossians,* p. 285.
2. Routley, *A Short History of English Church Music,* p. 75.
3. Erik Routley, *Church Music and Theology* (Philadelphia: Muhlenburg, 1959), p. 62.
4. Routley, *Christian Hymns Observed,* p. 66.

Title/Date	*"All Hail the Power of Jesus' Name"*
	(1779/1780)
Author	*Edward Perronet*
Composer/Tune	*Oliver Holden "Coronation" (1793)*
	William Shrubsole "Miles Lane" (1779)
	James Eller "Diadem"
Scriptural Basis	*Philippians 2:9–10; Isaiah 62:3;*
	Revelation 5:11–13; 19:16

The author well remembers the first time he ever sang this magnificent hymn extolling the matchless Name of Jesus Christ to the tune "Diadem" by James Eller; it was at the InterVarsity Urbana Missionary Conference in 1951. I and my friend, Walt, another recent convert through the ministry of an InterVarsity chapter, had hitch-hiked together through a raging blizzard for some forty-eight hours, from Oswego, New York, to Urbana, Illinois. Arriving weary, and with bad colds, after we enjoyed a hot shower and an ample meal, we even managed to stay awake throughout the lengthy evening meeting! And this was the hymn that rolled throughout the great meeting hall, where some eight or nine thousand had gathered—the "Crown Him, crown Him, crown Him, crown Him" building in volume to the final "crown Him Lord of all"! And I still remember whispering to Walt, "I think I've died and gone to heaven," for it had really lifted my spirits, and I'm sure, everyone else's too!

That tune "Diadem," which (thankfully) the *Trinity Hymnal* includes, was composed by James Eller (1819–1899), a nineteen-year-old hatmaker and self-taught musician, especially for his home church—an English Methodist congregation—which was having a Sunday School anniversary celebration.[1] Bringing it to work with him, he sang it for and then with his fellow hatters, who received it enthusiastically, sang it at the following Lord's Day services, and made it so popular that it was widely circulated and used frequently on anniversary occasions.

Leaving his hatter's trade some years later, he took a position working on railroad construction near Manchester, England, and then in 1843 emigrated to America, where he resumed his original hatmaking trade; little else is known of his life other than that he died nearly blind.[2]

Wherefore God also hath highly exalted him, and given him a name which is above every name: that at the name of Jesus every knee should bow . . . Phil. 2:9-10

Edward Perronet, 1779, 1780
St.1, line 4, alt.; st.5 recast;
St.6 added by John Rippon, 1787

CORONATION C. M. with refrain
Oliver Holden, 1793

"Coronation," to which this hymn is most commonly sung in this country, was composed by Oliver Holden (1765–1844) in 1792, the very year that Perronet, the author, died. Holden, who was trained as a carpenter, later successfully sold real estate and ran a general store for a time; but his real love was music, which he taught to children in singing schools that he established.[3] He also edited several collections of music, and was honored by being asked to write a hymn commemorating the visit of General Washington to Boston's Old State House in 1789; he did, trained a choir, and had it sung for that auspicious event![4] This deeply devout man, for whom music was an avocation, evidenced creativity to the end of his life; on his deathbed he whispered,

I have some beautiful airs running through my head, if I only had strength to note them down.[5]

Such beautiful themes! Such beautiful themes! But I can write no more.[6]

This tune, named obviously for the phrase "And crown Him Lord of all," was written shortly after the birth of his first child, a little daughter, an occasion of unalloyed joy, as demonstrated in the tune's melodic pattern.[7] It was one of the favorite tunes of Timothy Dwight, Yale's great president and a devout Christian gentleman, "who would sing it, ardently, with the choir of his college whenever he was present."[8]

The third tune named above, and the one most frequently used in England, is "Miles Lane," written especially for this hymn by William Shrubsole (1760–1806), a young friend of Perronet and a superb musician whose formal training included participation in the Canterbury Cathedral Choir for seven years and extensive organ instruction. Dismissed from his post as organist at Bangor Cathedral because of his too close association with Dissenters, he went to London, taught music, and eventually became organist for one of Lady Huntington's chapels. In spite of Perronet's hot temper, Shrubsole managed to genuinely befriend him at a most difficult period in his life, and in consequence, he was made one of the executors of Perronet's will! Perronet, who also left him some property, said that his action was

in consideration of that fine disinterested affection he has ever shone me from our first acquaintance, even when I was a proverb of reproach, cast off by all my relatives, disinherited unjustly, and left to sink or swim as afflictions and God's providence should appoint.[9]

Of this tune, first printed anonymously in Toplady's *The Gospel Magazine* in 1779, one has stated:

more difficult to perform than "Coronation" because of its wide melodic range, sustained notes, and interrupted pace, it does, however, achieve true majesty in its stately movement, and a thrilling climax in the fourfold repetition of "Crown Him."[10]

And the story is told of Henry Smart, who was criticized for refusing to play musical interludes between hymn stanzas; he said nothing, but waited for his opportunity. When this hymn was announced, Smart was ready:

All went well with the first stanza and everyone was making a joyful noise. But in the interlude between verses one and two, the organist modulated ever so cleverly and imperceptably, into the key of B; between stanzas two and three into the key of C; and between stanzas three and four into the key of D flat, and so on until the high notes on "Crown Him" must have joined the company of the "Last Chord." Thus he silenced his critics![11]

Edward Perronet (1726–1792), whose authorship of this majestic hymn, sometimes likened to the "Te Deum," was not finally proven until established, conclusively, by Louis Benson well over a century after it was first published,[12] was the son of Vincent Perronet, a saintly and gracious French Hugenot pastor, whose long-term relationship with John and Charles Wesley was warm and supportive—indeed, he was sometimes called the "Archbishop of Methodism."[13] Unfortunately, Edward did not inherit his father's disposition, though he was equally earnest about his Christian faith and convictions, and for a time threw himself enthusiastically into the Wesleyan Movement. On one occasion Wesley writes of Perronet's venturing outdoors to confront a mob, who

immediately closed in, threw him down and rolled him in the mire; so that when he managed to scramble from them and got into the house again, one could scarce tell what or who he was![14]

Moreover, Wesley admired Perronet, and knowing of his preaching abilities, wanted to hear him; since Perronet refused, perhaps from a genuine sense of humility, Wesley seeing him in his congregation one day announced—but without asking his permission—that he would preach at the 5:00 A.M. service the next morning! Out of his respect for Wesley, Perronet appeared at the appointed time and place, but announced that he was there contrary to his own wishes and that he felt ill at ease and poorly prepared. However, he told them he would preach them the best sermon ever delivered, and opened to the Sermon on the Mount, which he read in its entirety without any comment. He closed the service with singing and prayer, and all averred that the effect of his deed was without equal—it was remarkable.[15]

Perronet, however, became more and more violent in his opposition to the Church of England, even though he'd been baptized and brought up in her bosom. In 1757, he published *The Mitre,* a biting satirical criticism of her; Julian says of it:

it is priceless as a reflex of contemporary ecclesiastical opinion and sentiment. It is pungent, salted with wit, gleams with humor, hits off vividly the well-known celebrities in Church and State, and is well wrought in picked and packed words.[16]

But it angered Wesley, and he insisted on suppressing its sale and distribution, which was done; more and more Perronet found his views at odds with Wesley's, and eventually, when he defied Wesley's ban, that none of his preachers were to celebrate Communion but were to commune within an Anglican parish church, they parted company and Perronet became for a time one of Lady Huntington's Connection. However, while he always "lived close to His Master, his passionate, compulsive and strong-willed nature"[17] led to a rupture in that relationship also, and he ended his ministry pastoring an Independent congregation in Canterbury, an evangelist to the end, full of fire and enthusiasm, but all too often volatile!

As indicated earlier, this hymn has had a long history of anonymity and has suffered from several revisions. Generally—while *Trinity Hymnal* has six—of its original eight stanzas, only three are used, with the fourth, and final one, the stanza written by John Rippon (1751–1836), a Baptist minister who served one congregation in London for over sixty years! Awarded a D.D. by the Baptist College in Providence, Rhode Island, in 1792, Rippon was a leading Dissenting clergyman in his day.[18] His hymnbook, *Selection,* first appeared in 1787 and went through many editions, revisions, and enlargements, with the 1844 *Comprehensive Rippon* containing almost twelve hundred hymns,[19] some few of which he wrote himself, including these great lines attached to Perronet's hymn,

> Oh that with yonder sacred throng we at His feet may fall,
> We'll join the everlasting song and crown Him Lord of all.

which have gone far to make him also famous! And, unlike so many hymnwriters who never profited, financially, from their work, he did, gaining a considerable estate through the sales of the many editions of his *Selections.*[20]

Let us examine this hymn, which Breed extols for its "vast comprehensiveness . . . faultless rhythm . . . effective rhyme, and impressive recurring phrase 'Crown Him Lord of all.' "[21] We note its distinctive features:

First, it broadly includes every created being imaginable, from angels whose habitation is heaven, to sinners of every earthly kindred (family) and tribe (nation) who live here "on this terrestrial ball"; from Jews to Gentiles (everyone not a Jew!); from those of the past (martyrs, now at His altar), to those of us in the present (we who fall at His feet).

Second, there is the universality of the Lordship of Jesus Christ: over time and eternity, over matter and mind, over men and angels—over all He is enthroned,[22] and willingly!

Third, the language throughout is massively picturesque; one can see the various groups as they are called on to add their offerings to His praise; the imperative verbs are striking, compelling us to do something as well as be-

lieve something; as Routley points out regarding the enthronement of Christ
as King,

> this does not mean to ascribe to Him irresponsible and dictatorial pow-
> ers; [rather, it does mean] to make Him the focal point of thought, action
> and hope, to regard nothing as complete without Him.[23]

Fourth, this is rich in biblical images, with a large number of passages
lying behind each stanza; thus, the angels (Philippians 2:9–11; Hebrews 2:9);
the martyrs (Revelation 6:9–10); the Rod of Jesse (Isaiah 11:1); the seed of
Israel, which of course is the church (Romans 9; Isaiah 45:25, Galatians
3:29); sinners (Lamentations 3:19; Romans 3:23; Revelation 4:4, 10); and hu-
mankind (Revelation 7:9–12; 5:11–13).

Fifth, there are notes of hope and encouragement here: for the martyrs,
their deaths were not in vain, since they are now "near His altar," in His presence; Israel's seed has experienced His saving grace; sinners, remembering
their bitter past, are not experiencing judgment from God, but forgiveness,
His love calling forth theirs; and all the rest, who are enabled to recognize
and properly respond to His majesty!

Routley's suggestive comparison of this with the coronation of Queen
Elizabeth II in June 1953 is instructive:

> . . . the very literary texture of this hymn suggests pageantry and proces-
> sion. It thunders along on its majestic ground-bass . . . each verse saying
> the same thing but with a variation; each verse, bringing in a new sacred
> community, urges it to praise. All these cohorts of cheering and praising
> people suggest irresistibly the many-coloured regiments and orders who
> gathered for their coronation. The Queen knelt before the priest, the
> priest knelt before the Queen; she took her coronation oath, the people
> said 'God save the Queen.' In humility and splendour, it was thus a pointer
> to Christ.[24]

And after he quotes these familiar lines from the Messiah,

> Hallelujah, for the Lord God Omnipotent reigneth. The kingdoms of this
> world are become the kingdoms of our God and of His Christ, and He
> shall reign, forever and ever

he goes on to ask the crucial question:

> What human truth, what human achievement, what human hope can be
> complete, or even sane without taking account of that?[25]

Perronet, as he lay on his deathbed, repeated these as his last words:

Glory to God in the height of His divinity!
Glory to God in the depth of His humanity!
Glory to God in His all-sufficiency!
And into His hands I commend my spirit.[26]

Notes

1. Hostetler, *op. cit.*, p. 3.
2. McCutchan, *Our Hymnody*, pp. 208–209.
3. Stulken, *op. cit.*, p. 385.
4. Covert and Laufer, *op. cit.*, p. 208.
5. *Ibid.*
6. Brown and Butterworth, *op. cit.*, p. 28.
7. Covert and Laufer, *op. cit.*, p. 208.
8. Brown and Butterworth, *op. cit.*, p. 29.
9. Moffatt and Patrick, *op. cit.*, p. 497.
10. Covert and Laufer, *op. cit.*, p. 209.
11. Smith, *Lyric Religion*, p. 20.
12. Bailey, *op. cit.*, p. 122.
13. Moffatt and Patrick, *op. cit.*, p. 458.
14. McCutchan, *op. cit.*, p. 207.
15. Duffield, *op. cit.*, pp. 17–18.
16. Julian, *op. cit.*, p. 890.
17. *Ibid.*
18. *Ibid.*, p. 964.
19. *Ibid.*
20. *Ibid.*
21. Breed, *op. cit.*, p. 141.
22. *Ibid.*
23. Routley, *Hymns and the Faith*, p. 278.
24. *Ibid.*, pp. 276–277.
25. *Ibid.*, p. 279.
26. Duffield, *op. cit.*, p. 16.

Title/Date	*"Come, Ye Thankful People, Come"* *(1844, 1867)*
Author	*Henry Alford*
Composer/Tune	*Sir George J. Elvey "St. George's Windsor" (1859)*
Scriptural Basis	*Matthew 13:24–30, 36–43*

Henry Alford (1810–1871) was one of the most gifted men of his day, serving his generation—as well as succeeding generations—as theologian and scholar, poet and artist, author and musician; certainly much of the inspiration that undergirded this man and the use he made of his many gifts, abilities, and talents was his deeply spiritual commitment—a commitment he inscribed in his Bible on his sixteenth birthday when he wrote:

> I do this day, in the presence of God and my own soul, renew my covenant with God, and solemnly determine henceforth to become his and do his work as far as in me lies.[1]

All his life he was a strenuous worker, never idle; at the end of a hard day's work, he would stand up, much as we do returning thanks for our meals, and thank God for what he had been enabled to accomplish that day. Moreover, "he was catholic-spirited, and a staunch supporter of the Evangelical Alliance, maintaining throughout his life cordial relations with Nonconformists";[2] his disposition was amiable, and he was noted to be absolutely fair in his judgments on controversial issues, making him a deservedly popular pastoral leader. On one occasion when he was in southern England, he stopped to worship in a small chapel where the preacher was a woman; in her sermon she "called it like she saw it," declaring boldly,

> some men tell us they are the only authorized dealers in truth, when they themselves have never understood it; they sing their prayers and chant their psalms, while they have no more of the spirit of either than the organs in their steeplehouses.[3]

The harvest is the end of the world; and the reapers are the angels. Matt. 13:39

ST. GEORGE'S, WINDSOR 7. 7. 7. 7. D.

Henry Alford, 1844, text of 1867   Sir George J. Elvey, 1859

1. Come, ye thank-ful peo-ple, come, Raise the song of har-vest-home:
2. All the world is God's own field, Fruit un-to his praise to yield;
3. For the Lord our God shall come, And shall take his har-vest home;
4. E-ven so, Lord, quick-ly come To thy fi-nal har-vest-home;

All is safe-ly gath-ered in, Ere the win-ter storms be-gin;
Wheat and tares to-geth-er sown, Un-to joy or sor-row grown:
From his field shall in that day All of-fenc-es purge a-way;
Gath-er thou thy peo-ple in, Free from sor-row, free from sin;

God, our Mak-er, doth pro-vide For our wants to be sup-plied:
First the blade, and then the ear, Then the full corn shall ap-pear:
Give his an-gels charge at last In the fire the tares to cast,
There for ev-er pur-i-fied, In thy pres-ence to a-bide:

Come to God's own tem-ple, come, Raise the song of har-vest-home.
Lord of har-vest, grant that we Whole-some grain and pure may be.
But the fruit-ful ears to store In his gar-ner ev-er-more.
Come, with all thine an-gels, come, Raise the glo-rious har-vest-home. A-MEN.

While he told of this experience with good humor, there is no record as to whether she ever realized who the distinguished visitor to her chapel was that day!

Alford—a precocious child, who wrote a life of Paul when he was six years old and whose college career at Trinity, Cambridge, was distinguished—took Holy Orders in 1833, and served several parishes until he was made dean of Canterbury Cathedral in 1857. He held this post until his untimely death in 1871, brought on principally by overwork—he simply wore out his body. Among his fifty published works, probably the greatest was his critical study of the *Greek New Testament,* to which he gave twenty years of labor, publishing it in four volumes between 1849 and 1861. In addition to this standard work, which promoted New Testament scholarship over the next century, he also served on the committee that revised the New Testament in 1881; he wrote poetry, translated Greek literary masterpieces like the *Odyssey,* and authored many hymns, including one of the greatest on the second coming of Christ, "Ten Thousand Times Ten Thousand." He not only published these and other works, but also founded and edited the influential *Contemporary Review* for many years.[4] His one unfulfilled desire was to visit the Holy Land; this unrealized longing suggested the beautiful inscription on his tombstone, which he requested:

> When I am gone, and a tomb is to be put up, let there be, besides any indication of who is lying below, these words, and these only "THE INN OF A PILGRIM TRAVELING TO JERUSALEM."[5]

Sir George Elvey (1816–1893) was a superb musician, three of whose hymn tunes, "Diademata," "St. Crispin," and "St. George's Windsor," possibly written especially for this hymn,[6] are to be found in all first-class hymnals to this day, according to Haeussler.[7] Chosen, when he was only nineteen, to serve as organist and master of the Boys' Choir at St. George's Chapel, Windsor, he held that position for forty-seven years! Moreover, as the organist of the Royal Family's church, it was his honor to play for several weddings of royalty during his tenure, and for his outstanding service he was knighted in 1871.

He apparently enjoyed the married state, for he was a widower three times and lived close to a half century with his four wives, the last of whom—much younger than he was—published his *Life and Reminiscences* a year after his death.

Of his philosophy of church music one writes:

> he believed that the music of the Church should be as stately, uplifting and inspiring as the soaring arches and most exquisite stained glass windows of cathedrals . . . suggestive of the sublime music of heaven. The architecture and music, the physical and aesthetic setting of worship should be integrated parts of a complete pattern, designed to lift the soul of the worshipper to the heights.[8]

This tune, "St. George's Windsor," was named after his place of service, and first appeared with this hymn in *Hymns Ancient and Modern,* published in 1861; whether or not it was intended originally to grace this, Alford's most popular hymn, it certainly does for this hymn what "Diademata" does for Bridges' "Crown Him with Many Crowns"; as a "forceful tune, it progresses to a splendid climax in the last line and moves strongly throughout, lending itself readily to antiphonal singing."[9]

Let us now turn to an examination of "Come, Ye Thankful People, Come," a hymn that "sweeps broadly through the whole regime of God's grace manifest in his present worldly blessings and in his eternal salvation."[10]

Stanza One: Alford begins with an invitation or an exhortation to us who are enjoying God's bountiful provision for our material needs ("needs," probably rather than "wants" in the sense of "desires") to express our gratitude to Him; and we do so, properly, as we come into His own temple, His sanctuary, where His presence is eternally manifested! This is, quite appropriately, a hymn for special celebrations like Thanksgiving, when indeed the harvest has been safely brought into the barn, silo, root cellar, or, in these modern days, the freezer—stored for its eventual usage. God's ongoing providential care is recognized—as Our Maker, and the Maker of the crops, He is rightly to be lauded!

Stanza Two: Here Alford expounds the familiar parable of the wheat (true believers) and the tares (pseudo-believers), beginning with the faith statement that since all the world is God's *own* field, its obvious response to Him should be genuine praise. Using the metaphor of an ear of corn, which represents the wheat (and why he mixes them I do not know!), he parallels that with us, the believers, and prays that we may be pure and wholesome grain, rather than tares (or weeds) that are noxious and good for nothing.

Stanza Three: Following hard on this theme, the awesome fate of the tares is declared, that they be cast into the fire and burned up, while the good grain (or ears of corn) is to be stored up in His garner, heaven. Moreover, while the angels have destroyed the tares, He Himself personally "harvests" the good grain, and thus leaves His fields free of "all offences," a phrase that seems to me to need further elucidation!

Stanza Four: Here is a prayer to God to bring His angels and gather His own into His presence, where there can be "nothing that defiles"; therefore, His people must be free from sin and purified; thereby they will also be free from sorrow—for what is it in our human experience that is the occasion of much of our grief, but sin? That final harvest-home, that final act of God that completes the process that begins with our justification, continues through our sanctification, and culminates in our glorification will indeed be a glorious harvest-home. Hopefully, the occasions we sing this grand hymn will extend beyond one Thanksgiving service a year!

Notes

   1. McCutchan, *Our Hymnody,* p. 514.
   2. Moffatt and Patrick, *op. cit.,* p. 251.

3. Duffield, *op. cit.*, pp. 120–121.
4. Haeussler, *op. cit.*, pp. 525–526.
5. Moffatt and Patrick, *op. cit.*, p. 251.
6. Covert and Laufer, *op. cit.*, pp. 125–126.
7. Haeussler, *op. cit.*, p. 646.
8. *Ibid.*
9. Covert and Laufer, *op. cit.*, p. 126.
10. *Ibid.*, p. 472.

Title/Date	*"Fight the Good Fight with All Thy Might . . ." (1863)*
Author	*John S. B. Monsell*
Composer/Tune	*Mozart "Mozart"*
	(arranged from the kyrie in the Twelfth Mass)
	William Boyd "Pentecost" (1868)
Scriptural Basis	*I Timothy 6:12; Ephesians 3:14; 4:17–32;*
	II Timothy 4:7–8; I Corinthians 9:24, 26

John S. B. Monsell (1811–1875) was an Irishman, born in Londonderry, educated at Trinity College, Dublin, and ordained in 1834; he served a number of parishes, including some in England. His passionate love of his native land was exceeded only by his earnest faith and his love for his God, a love expressed in his many hymns; on one occasion he wrote:

> We are, alas, too distant and reserved in our praises. We sing not as if our hearts were on fire with the flame of divine love and joy, as we should sing to Him, and of Him, Who is Chief among ten thousand, and altogether lovely. If we loved Him as we ought to do, we could not be so cold.[1]

A man of genial spirit and sunny disposition, he gave himself unstintingly to his parish work and to his preaching; of this aspect of his calling Edwin Hodder has given his estimate in these generous lines:

> Many a time have I listed to the words of life from his lips. Standing there in the pulpit, with a small Bible in his hand, unencumbered with notes or sermon-book, the preacher has held his audience (!) spellbound, while in plain, simple language, yet full of tender poetic thought, he has told them the sweet story of eternal love.[2]

His poetic gifts, which filled eleven published volumes, included some three hundred hymns; of these Julian comments, appreciatively, that "they are, as a whole, bright, joyous and musical," but then he adds that "they lack massiveness, concentration of thought, and strong emotion";[3] while I would

Fight the good fight of faith . . . I Tim. 6:12

MOZART L. M.
Arr. from the *Kyrie* in the *Twelfth Mass,*
attributed to Mozart

John S. B. Monsell, 1863

1. Fight the good fight With all thy might; Christ is thy
2. Run the straight race Through God's good grace, Lift up thine
3. Cast care a - side; Up - on thy Guide Lean, and his
4. Faint not, nor fear, His arms are near; He chang - eth

Strength, and Christ thy Right: Lay hold on life, and
eyes, and seek his face; Life with its way be -
mer - cy will pro - vide; Lean, and the trust - ing
not, and thou art dear; On - ly be - lieve, and

it shall be Thy joy and crown e - ter - nal - ly.
fore us lies, Christ is the Path, and Christ the Prize.
soul shall prove, Christ is its Life, and Christ its Love.
thou shalt see That Christ is all in all to thee. A - MEN.

not presume to enter into the hymnological lists with such an eminent scholar, I would point to Monsell's hymn "My Sins, My Sins, My Saviour" (*Trinity Hymnal,* p. 464) as an illustration of strong emotion, hardly surpassed by any writer! And I would cite W. Garrett Horder's high regard for Monsell's work, when he says,

> His deep [piety], his tenderness of spirit, his lyric nature all combined to give the Church verses which have done much, and will probably do more, to express and deepen her worshipping emotion.[4]

Monsell's ministry, moreover, was not limited to serving just his parish, or even the "wider parish" touched by his hymns; he also apparently believed that one's faith should be demonstrated in one's home! One of the many visitors entertained in their rectory at his last parish, St. Nicholas' Church, Guildford, said that it was "an ideal household, full of the beauty of holiness, with genial brightness and gaiety playing like sunshine over all the troubles of life."[5] Tragically, his death came there as a result of an injury he sustained while he watched some workmen making repairs to the church roof. And ironically, in a hymn he had previously written to help raise funds for this project, he had *included* these lines:

> Dear body, thou and I must part;
> thy busy head, thy throbbing heart,
> Must cease to work, and to cease to play,
> For me at no far distant day![6]

This hymn of Monsell certainly demonstrates his dictum, that "hymns for corporate singing should be fervent and spontaneous,"[7] and in my judgment the tune "Pentecost" is a better match for these lyrics than the choice made by the *Trinity Hymnal*'s editors! That tune, arranged from Mozart, is not only very hard to sing, but it does not have the strength and vigor of the other! "Pentecost" (*Trinity Hymnal*, p. 496), written by William Boyd (1847–1928), was a tune sung at most English confirmations, "including those of the Royal family; Lord Kitchner told Boyd, 'It is the most moving hymn I know!'"[8] Originally written at the request of Sabine Baring-Gould for one of his hymns, it was first sung at a large meeting of Yorkshire coal miners[9] and soon became very popular as a tune. When Boyd was asked how it came to be associated with this hymn, he recounted this incident:

> Ah, that is a funny thing. One day as I was walking along Regent Street I felt a slap on my back and turning around saw my dear friend Arthur Sullivan. "My dear Bill . . . I've seen a tune of yours which I must have" [for *Church Hymns,* soon to be published]; I responded "All right; send me a cheque and I agree." No copy of the book, much less a proof, was sent me, and when I saw the tune I was horrified to find that Sullivan had assigned it to [that hymn]. We had a regular fisticuffs about it, but judging from the favor with which the tune has been received, I feel that Sullivan was right in so mating words and music.[10]

And as I said earlier, so do I!

This "Billy" Boyd, born in Jamaica, was said to have come "from an old Scots stock of lowland Border thieves"![11] Always interested in music, he began to compose when he was but ten; tutored as a youth by Sabine Baring-Gould, he later graduated from Oxford, where he had studied organ and had been organ scholar of his college; he then was ordained a priest in the Anglican Communion in 1882. His most fruitful pastoral charge was the Church of All Saints, London, where he served effectively for over twenty-five years; his interest in hymns and good congregational singing was aided by the service in his parish of two excellent organists, Edward Bairstow and William Wolstenhome, in succession.[12] Bairstow, for example, was both a music professor at Durham University and an author of numerous music textbooks, whose contributions to that mode of artistic expression were considerable enough for him to be honored by knighthood at the insistence of King George V.[13]

The tune "Mozart," found in the *Trinity Hymnal,* is a theme from the kyrie of the "Twelfth Mass," published in 1821; this Mass has been the subject of considerable argument, and there are some music scholars who question its alleged Mozartian source.[14]

Monsell originally had called this hymn "The Fight for Faith," and had based it on Ephesians 4:17–32, the Epistle lesson for that Sunday in the liturgical calendar. In that passage Paul reminds believers that faith in Christ calls them to "put off the old man, and put on the new man," to experience a thoroughgoing transformation of character, demonstrated in their daily lifestyles. So this hymn, stressing the fulness of Christ's availability and the absoluteness of His necessity, is filled with imperatives—calls to vigorous action! As Erik Routley points out:

> Treated as human aspirations, they are all commonplace, and could be found in a heathen, selfish life. . . . But with Christ as the context, human courage, for example, is lifted up and assimilated with the royal courage of the Captain of our salvation.[15]

Some of its distinctive features are as follows.

First, its thoroughgoing emphasis on Christ, and on Him as the source of every gift and grace that the believer needs in order to meet life's challenges and demands. Thus Christ is our strength, enabling us to "lay hold on life . . . ," but He is also our right to do so; there thus is clear legitimacy in what we are empowered to do.

Moreover, as I travel on the right path, I discover that He *is* that path—"I am the Way . . ."; as I seek for life, I discover *He* is the prize that I'm really seeking.

Second, its emphasis on the absolute necessity for me to do something, but ever as a response to what He has already done; so, I use my might, but in reality it is His might (or strength) I draw upon; *I* run the race—on a straight path, but I run it by His grace and with my eyes on Him as the goal; the surest way to lose any race is to turn around to see where your competition is!

Third, I am exhorted to be dependent on Him even in my vigorous efforts to attain the goal. So we are twice urged to *lean* on Him, without worrying or being anxious; we are not to be fearful or faint-hearted, but rather we are to recognize that His arms are ready to enfold us, for we are dear to Him—"tender" words, along with words denoting power, strength, and might. Moreover, we are assured that He is unchanging, and so we do not need to worry that if we falter, stumble, or even fail on occasion, He will give up on us—for He will not! This is a powerful reminder, similar to what the evangelist D. L. Moody used to say: "Pray as if everything depends on God, and work as if everything depends on you," another way of stressing the priority of faith, but the necessity of human response and a faith demonstrated by obedience! The fact, incidentally, that of these 116 words, only ten are more than one syllable, adds to the thrust on action, for short, action words predominate!

This is a good hymn to teach children; its words are simple, and its easily understood commands can be deeply ingrained in their memories, to stand them in good stead throughout the turbulent years that lie ahead of them.

Notes

1. Duffield, *op. cit.,* p. 135.
2. Smith, *Lyric Religion,* p. 325.
3. Julian, *op. cit.,* p. 763.
4. McCutchan, *Our Hymnody,* p. 147.
5. Haeussler, *op. cit.,* p. 802.
6. Smith, *op. cit.,* p. 325.
7. Covert and Laufer, *op. cit.,* p. 10.
8. McCutchan, *op. cit.,* p. 320.
9. *Ibid.*
10. *Ibid.*
11. *Ibid.*
12. Covert and Laufer, *op. cit.,* p. 293.
13. Wienandt and Young, *op. cit.,* pp. 364–365.
14. Covert and Laufer, *op. cit.,* p. 263.
15. Routley, *Hymns and the Faith,* p. 205.

Title/Date	*"God Moves in a Mysterious Way . . ."* *(1774)*
Author	*William Cowper*
Composer/Tune	*Lowell Mason "Hermon" (1832)* *Scottish Psalter "Dundee" (1615/1621)*
Scriptural Basis	*John 13:7; Psalm 77:19; Psalm 107:23–31; Isaiah 54:7–8; Job 37:23; Romans 8:28; II Corinthians 4:17*

Along with James Montgomery, William Cowper (1731–1800) is the other greatest English hymn-writer who was not a clergyman; yet that is not the whole story, since Montgomery had been raised by parents who died serving as Moravian missionaries, and their influence on his life and faith was considerable; and Cowper's father had been a minister and chaplain to King George II, and his devout mother, who died when he was but six years old, was a descendant of the saintly John Donne,[1] lending some credence to Duffield's observation that "grace runs in the blood."[2]

Cowper's life has been variously interpreted, but it is clear that he was a shy and timid child, bullied in his first formal schooling and deeply affected by his mother's death; his health was never robust, and he was forced to live on the fringes of a more active life because of frequent bouts with melancholia, or in today's terms, mental depression. Moreover, while some writers blame his religious convictions for this troubled state of mind, the fact is that it was during his first hospitalization in the asylum at St. Albans in 1764 that—through the witness of his brother—he experienced a genuine conversion,[3] realizing the forgiveness of his sins through personal faith in Jesus Christ. And in the years that followed, some of which were most sunny and productive, it was his faith that kept him on an even keel; as Percy Dearmer notes:

> Indeed, as long as he was not pressed too hard, his religion seems to have been the ultimate source of whatever inward peace and happiness he ever knew, and it was his bouts with insanity that created his belief that he was a lost soul.[4]

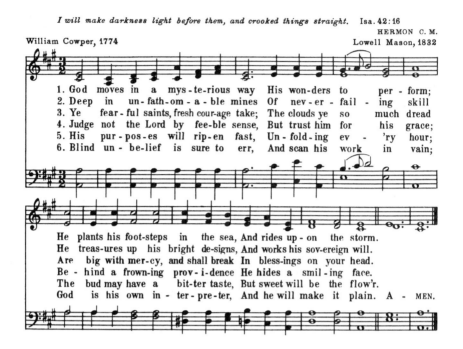

I will make darkness light before them, and crooked things straight. Isa. 42:16

HERMON C. M.

William Cowper, 1774   Lowell Mason, 1832

1. God moves in a mys-te-rious way His won-ders to per-form;
2. Deep in un-fath-om-a-ble mines Of nev-er-fail-ing skill
3. Ye fear-ful saints, fresh cour-age take; The clouds ye so much dread
4. Judge not the Lord by fee-ble sense, But trust him for his grace;
5. His pur-pos-es will rip-en fast, Un-fold-ing ev-'ry hour;
6. Blind un-be-lief is sure to err, And scan his work in vain;

He plants his foot-steps in the sea, And rides up-on the storm.
He treas-ures up his bright de-signs, And works his sov-ereign will.
Are big with mer-cy, and shall break In bless-ings on your head.
Be-hind a frown-ing prov-i-dence He hides a smil-ing face.
The bud may have a bit-ter taste, But sweet will be the flow'r.
God is his own in-ter-pre-ter, And he will make it plain. A-MEN.

Originally destined for the legal profession, he was made a barrister in 1754; during these years he had fallen in love with his cousin Theodora, but her father opposed their marriage, primarily on the grounds that they were too closely related. In 1759, he received an appointment as Commissioner of Bankrupts, and in 1763, as Clerk of the Journals in the House of Lords. It was his dread of facing this House for his first formal appearance that unbalanced his mind and led him to attempt suicide; that, in turn, led to his hospitalization mentioned earlier. After his release, with limited income and few prospects for earning a living—for his poetic gifts had not yet begun to really blossom—he met the Rev. and Mrs. Morley Unwin at Huntington and became a boarder in their happy home for several years until Mr. Unwin's accidental death precipitated another crisis. Happily, however, John Newton, the curate at Olney, came to call in their home and persuaded Cowper and Unwin's widow, Mary, to move to a house near his vicarage. There Cowper came under the caring influence of Newton's friendship, and developed an interest in all manner of things, from gardening and carpentry, raising rabbits, and bird-watching to helping Newton in some of his pastoral duties—conducting prayer-meetings, visiting the poor and the sick, distributing alms provided by a wealthy friend of Newton,[5] and, most important of all, sharing with him in the preparation of a hymnbook for the Olney congregation, which was published in 1779 as *Olney Hymns.*

Meanwhile, Cowper had become engaged to Mary Unwin,[6] but a return of "the dark night of his soul" left him in despair, even of his salvation,[7] and their marriage never took place. Nursed back to health by her care and Newton's steady influence—after another attempt at suicide—he finally recovered and enjoyed some twenty years of comparatively good health, during which he wrote his secular works that have secured his place in English literature, and won him, in 1794, an annual pension of £300. His last years were spent in caring for Mary, who had become a helpless invalid; she died in 1796, and this plunged him once again into despair, but of this kind of experience he could write, in his more lucid moments:

> I have never met, either in books or conversation, with an experience at all similar to mine. More than a twelve month has passed since I began to hope that, having walked the whole breadth of the bottom of the Red Sea, I was beginning to climb the opposite shore, and I proposed to sing the song of Moses. But I have been disappointed. . . . Yet, "I love Thee, even now, more than many who see Thee daily."[8]

For this oft-tortured, sensitive soul—whose hymns are "touchingly beautiful, and reflect the gleam of light which from time to time irradiated his troubled spirit"[9]—death meant his release; Bishop Handley G. C. Moule has given us this rather dramatic portrayal of that event:

> Shortly before he died his face, sad and hopeless of expression, suddenly lighted up with a look of wonder and inexpressible delight. It was as if he saw his Saviour . . . and realized the blessed fact, "I am not shut out of heaven after all." This look of holy surprise and of joyful adoration remained until he passed away, and even . . . in his coffin the expression was still there," as witnessed one who saw him in that state, composure and calm reflected in his face.[10]

To complete our brief consideration of Cowper's life, it remains to cite Mrs. Browning's noble lines quoted on his grave:

> O Poets! from a maniac's tongue was poured the deathless singing!
> O Christians, at your cross of hope a hopeless hand was clinging!
> O men, this man in brotherhood your weary paths beguiling,
> Groaned only while he taught you peace, and died while ye were smiling!
> And now, what time ye all may read through dimming tears his story!
> How discord on the music fell, and darkness on the glory,
> And how when, one by one, sweet sounds and wandering lights departed,
> He wore no less a loving face because so broken-hearted.[11]

While there is some question as to precisely when Cowper wrote this hymn, which is regarded by many critics as the "finest hymn on God's providence ever written,"[12] it was probably written shortly after his troubled period of 1773, perhaps mid-1774; it was entitled originally "Light shining out of darkness," and is apparently the last hymn he ever wrote.

"Hermon," the tune used with it in the *Trinity Hymnal,* was written by Lowell Mason, whom we have discussed in previous studies. In the case of this hymn, I would again promote the use of a different tune, the popular "Dundee," from the Scottish psalter, used in the *Trinity Hymnal* with several other hymns—which may be why it was not chosen for this one.

In any event, this was originally one of the twelve tunes with common meter published by A. Hart in *The CL Psalms of David,* in Edinburgh in 1615, and it was published a few years later in Ravenscroft's *Whole Booke of Psalmes* under the name "Dundy," and indexed among the Scottish tunes. It probably was an adaptation of a secular melody, cast into the psalter tune form by some Protestant composer.[13] In its present form it is notable for its "smooth, flowing style, moving almost step by step in a melody which rises to its highest point in the third line and comes to a substantial and dignified cadence at the close."[14]

Erik Routley, writing of this hymn, tells us that Cowper had written these words of our Lord above it—"What I do thou knowest not now, but will know hereafter" (John 13:7)—pointing out that Cowper's intention is to present God in His "Mystery," but in such a way that our confidence in Him is strengthened, not shattered, or even shaken. Further, Routley writes:

> God holds the secrets of life and unlocks them at His own discretion, not at our request. . . . The very darkness, and the withholding of light and clear guidance are themselves a sign of God's grace and power. [Then he quotes King George VI's statement in World War II.] "Put your hand into the hand of God: that shall be better than a light, and safer than a known way"; for God acts in history with a royal gentleness.[15]

Let us examine this, "one of the most widely known hymns in English speaking countries,"[16] following Hodson's twofold division:

First, the way of the wonder-working God (Stanzas One, Two). The focus here is on God's ability to accomplish what He wants done, making even our trials channels of His love to us (Romans 8:28), thus causing the painful, dark side of life to manifest a "bright design"; further, they are *His* wonders, and it is *His* will that will be sovereignly realized. As any Christian knows, the ways God has of bringing something good out of a devastating human experience are legion—and this, true of our temporal affairs, is also true of spiritual concerns, where He even brings those "dead in trespasses and sins" to life by His grace and power (Ephesians 2:1–10). Bushnell once wrote:

Every human soul has a complete and perfect plan cherished for it in the heart of God, a divine biography marked out which it enters into life to live; great in its conception, great in the divine skill by which it is shaped, great in its glorious issue.[17]

[Gerhardt added:] When thou arisest Lord, what shall thy work withstand? What'ere thy children want, Thou givest, and who shall stay thy hand?[18]

Second, the way of the Suffering Saint (Stanzas Three, Four, Five, and Six). Here Cowper's autobiography can almost be detailed: the fears he has had about his being a lost reprobate, fears that rolled over him like ocean waves again and again, threatening to drown him; and the black clouds of depression that hid the sun of God's love for months on end from him—these are not destructive storm clouds but hold the promise of being refreshing rain clouds that will rain "blessings on our heads"; thus clouds of trials often pour down benedictions on the child of God.

Next he reminds himself that we do not do well to judge God by our own superficial criteria: His ways are not our ways, and we do not think like He does; therefore when clouds (those in Stanza Three?) veil His presence, we are not to assume He is not still there, and we do not let the "frown" on our Father's face convince us that He no longer cares! As Cowper wrote elsewhere "sometimes a light surprises the Christian while he sings . . . ," and, as quoted earlier, he said to God on another dismal occasion, "I love Thee, even now, more than many who see Thee daily"[19]—that is *faith*!

In Stanza Five he shares another important truth, that God's purposes for human growth and maturation are comparable to flowers whose budding and unfolding occur on God's time-table, with unfailing regularity as long as someone else doesn't try to hasten the process. So our lives—and His purposes for them—need to be given over to His "gardening" oversight. But, alas, even though we know that, we get anxious, and do not "let patience have her perfect work" (James 1:4); we forget that it is "moment by moment [that] we are kept in His love."

Finally, an important truth for apologetics is detailed in Stanza Six. The one who does not believe will never see God in nature, or in any of His activity, since he is blind to the clues that *are* there! And even the Christian, when he chooses to ignore the signs or signals from the Lord, will also err, and find himself frustrated, and perhaps make the whole distressing situation much more complicated than it needs to be. As Francis Ridley Havergal, another devout and earnest Christian sufferer, wrote:

Light after darkness, gain after loss,
Strength after suffering, Crown after cross
Sweet after bitter, song after sigh

Home after wandering, praise after cry.
Near after distant, gleam after gloom,
Love after loneliness, Life after tomb.
After long agony, rapture of bliss
Right was the pathway leading to this.[20]

Although they were worlds apart theologically, John Henry Newman also experienced times when "the heavens seemed as brass," and when he searched and yearned for a clear sign of God's direction for his life; one indication of this is to be found in his hymn "Lead kindly light, amid the encircling gloom, lead thou me on . . ."; another is in this prayer that he composed:

> O my God, Thou and Thou alone art all-wise and all knowing! I believe that Thou knowest just what is best for me. I believe that Thou lovest me better than I love myself, that Thou art all-wise in Thy providence and all-powerful in Thy protection. I thank Thee, with all my heart, that Thou hast taken me out of my own keeping, and hast bidden me to put myself in Thy hands. I can ask nothing better than this, to be in Thy care, not my own. O my Lord, through Thy grace, I will follow Thee whithersoever Thou goest, and will not lead the way. I will wait on Thee for Thy guidance, and, on obtaining it, I will act in simplicity and without fear. And I promise that I will not be impatient, if at any time I am kept by Thee in darkness and perplexity: nor will I complain or fret if I come into any misfortune or anxiety.[21]

It is comforting to know that times of uncertainty, and doubt, and even despair have come to God's choicest servants in the past, especially when you are going through deep waters; it is even more encouraging to know that they were preserved, intact, through them, and so will you be; so hang on, "trusting as you tremble," and keep your eyes on Him!

Notes

1. Moffatt and Patrick, *op. cit.,* p. 309.
2. Duffield, *op. cit.,* p. 368.
3. Bailey, *op. cit.,* p. 131.
4. Phillips, *op. cit.,* p. 190.
5. Bailey, *op. cit.,* pp. 131–132.
6. Haeussler, *op. cit.,* p. 609.
7. Julian, *op. cit.,* p. 265.
8. Duffield, *op. cit.,* p. 180.

9. Moffatt and Patrick, *op. cit.,* p. 309.

10. Haeussler, *op. cit.,* p. 610.

11. Smith, *Lyric Religion,* pp. 446–447.

12. Haeussler, *op. cit.,* p. 610.

13. Covert and Laufer, *op. cit.,* p. 113.

14. *Ibid.*

15. Routley, *Hymns and the Faith,* pp. 39–42.

16. Julian, *op. cit.,* p. 433.

17. Hodson, *op. cit.,* p. 92.

18. *Ibid.,* p. 93.

19. Duffield, *op. cit.,* p. 180.

20. Hodson, *op. cit.,* p. 98.

21. *Ibid.*

Title/Date	*"I Heard the Voice of Jesus Say..."* *(1846)*
Author	*Horatius Bonar*
Composer/Tune	*John B. Dykes "Vox Dilecti" (1868)*
Scriptural Basis	*John 1:16; 4:14; 8:12; Matthew 11:28*

The prince of Scottish hymn-writers, one of her greatest preachers, and a man whose pastoral care for his congregation was legendary, Horatius Bonar (1808–1889) also loved children, and wrote many of his earliest hymns for them to sing in their Sabbath Schools, loving music and the Lord who inspired it as he did. Preaching on the text "the Spirit and the Bride say, Come"—the last invitation in the Bible—he paused and directly addressed the Sunday School children who sat by themselves on one side of the pulpit. And the visitor to his church, who was describing this scene, concluded by saying,

> With one of the most winning faces I ever saw he closed his sermon by saying "Whosoever—that includes *you;* whosoever *will*—does *that* include you?"[1]

This godly and vigorous man, born in Edinburgh into a family that had given many sons to the ministry of the Church of Scotland, aggregating 364 years of service among them, was educated there in its university under the theological tutelage of the renowned Thomas Chalmers. His first charge after his ordination was at Kelso, where he met his future wife Jane Lundie, daughter of its incumbent, whom he eventually succeeded there; they married in 1843,[2] the same year that he joined his mentor and 472 other pastors in withdrawing from the state church and forming the Free Church of Scotland. Of their several legitimate grievances, one, the rights of patronage, was eventually abolished in 1874. This split, while lamentable in some ways, did lead to an increase of zeal and attendant growth in the Church of Scotland.[3]

Bonar, a tireless worker, maintained his growing parish at Kelso; he also wrote scores of evangelical tracts and devotional books, which were widely circulated and read, and one of which, "Believe and Live," sold over a million

Come unto me, all ye that labour and are heavy laden, and I will give you rest. Matt. 11:28

VOX DILECTI C. M. D.

Horatius Bonar, 1846

John B. Dykes, 1868

1. I heard the voice of Je - sus say, "Come un - to me and rest;
2. I heard the voice of Je - sus say, "Be - hold, I free - ly give
3. I heard the voice of Je - sus say, "I am this dark world's Light;

Lay down, thou wea - ry one, lay down Thy head up - on my breast."
The liv - ing wa - ter; thirst - y one, Stoop down and drink, and live."
Look un - to me, thy morn shall rise, And all thy day be bright."

I came to Je - sus as I was, Wea - ry and worn and sad,
I came to Je - sus, and I drank Of that life - giv - ing stream;
I looked to Je - sus, and I found In him my Star, my Sun;

I found in him a rest - ing - place, And he has made me glad.
My thirst was quenched, my soul re - vived, And now I live in him.
And in that light of life I'll walk, Till trav'l - ling days are done. A - MEN.

copies.[4] For over a quarter century he edited the *Quarterly Journal of Prophecy*, furthering his own interest in premillennial eschatology and leading him to travel and study for a year in the Holy Land. He also wrote hymns, over six hundred in his lifetime, many of which are still widely used and "the best of

which rank with the classics, with one or two having been acclaimed by ex-
acting judges to be the best hymns ever written";[5] these mostly arose out of
his pastoral visiting and listening to the heart beats of his people as they and
he together faced life's varied experiences. Of him, a remarkably devout and
earnest man,

> one said that he was always visiting, another
> said that he was always preaching, another
> said that he was always writing, and another
> said that he was always praying.[6]

And pray he did, fervently in his study for hours on end for himself, his family, his congregation and his servants; in fact, one of his servants, a young
woman, owed her conversion to his prayers on her behalf, saying, "If *he*
needs to pray so much, what shall become of me if I do not pray?"[7]

Others laud him for his wide scholarship; his cultural awareness, probably
increased by his vast correspondence—generated through his varied writings—with an incredible number and variety of people from all walks of life
and from all over the world; his mind that, saturated with Scripture, could
aptly relate it to the needs of all, including children; and for the "far broader
faith in his heart than the Calvinistic creed to which his intellect gave assent."[8] Bonar himself once expressed his own working creed in these characteristically simple lines:

> Think truly, and thy thoughts shall the world's famine feed;
> Speak truly, and each word of Thine shall be a fruitful seed;
> Live truly, and thy life shall be a great and noble creed.[9]

While he fully intended to serve his congregation at Kelso until his re-
tirement, after almost thirty years there he was called to the Chalmers'
Memorial Church in Edinburgh, and partly out of gratitude for his prede-
cessor's ministry to him while studying theology at Edinburgh years before,
he reluctantly accepted the call as from God, serving in that wider sphere for
over two decades until his death in 1889. One of the greatest honors he received from his Church was election as the moderator of its General Assem-
bly in 1883, a post he filled, as he did everything else, most admirably. Of
him and his hymns Julian offers this balanced judgment:

> His scholarship is thorough and extensive, and his poems display the grace
> of style and wealth of allusion which are the fruit of ripe culture. His
> hymns satisfy the fastidious by their instinctive good taste; they mirror the
> life of Christ in the soul . . . with vivid accuracy; they win the heart by

their tone of tender sympathy; they sing the truth of God in ringing notes; and a singularly large number of them have been stamped with approval, both in literary circles and by the Church.[10]

Not without reason has he been considered by many the peer of Watts and Wesley!

"Vox Dilecti" was written especially for this hymn by John Dykes (1823–1876), of whom we have written extensively in several previous studies. Dykes, an eminent composer who never exhibited any prima donna characteristics, did write hymn tunes for many hymns, and attempted to do so whenever he felt a hymn was "unworthily set." On one occasion he wrote to William Monk, music editor of the most widely used hymnal ever published, *Hymns Ancient and Modern,* this, his reason for so doing:

> You, and Stainer, and Sir Henry [Baker] laughed at me the other day for apologizing for setting so many hymns. And I really feel it still needs an explanation. . . . I know so well the teaching power of hymns, if they are happily wedded, that I am anxious to do my best (as far as God is pleased to help me) to add to the number of those useful and felicitous unions. God forbid that I should make these attempts from any unworthy desire to thrust myself forward. I earnestly pray that this reason may never, never actuate me. My one desire is this—that each hymn should be so set to music (by whomsoever God wills to select for that purpose) that its power of influencing and teaching may be best brought out. All other considerations must be subordinate to that.[11]

This tune carries out in a striking manner the intent of Bonar's hymn; thus in each stanza, the music for the Master's invitation is written in G minor, and should be sung quietly, softly, and, above all else, invitingly; the music announcing joyous acceptance of the invitation is written in G major, a strong contrast, and should "mount to exultant high tones in the last bar, properly emphasizing 'found,' 'resting place,' 'glad,' 'light of life,' and 'live in him.'"[12] Moreover, this crescendo should be sustained to the very end, so that this part of the hymn becomes a paean of praise.

Now let us consider this hymn, "so beautiful in its simplicity,"[13] written at Kelso, probably for a children's service originally; its distinctive features need to be carefully examined:

First, it is aptly entitled "The Voice from Galilee," for Bonar has woven together three of our Lord's sayings, dealing with one in each stanza; so Matthew's "Come unto Me all ye who labor and are heavy laden and I will give you rest" (Stanza One); John's "Whosoever drinks of the water that I shall give him shall never thirst" (Stanza Two); and John's "I am the light of the world; he who follows Me shall not walk in darkness but shall have the light of life" (Stanza Three). Breed makes the point that even when Bonar urges activity, as he does here "Come unto Me," "stoop down and drink," "look unto Me," it's not so much a "call to duty as it is an encouragement" to the hearer.[14]

Second, the emphasis throughout these stanzas of dialogue is very personal: "*I* heard, *I* came, *I* found"—the personal pronoun occurs seventeen times herein as relating to the speaker, the one to whom Jesus seeks to minister. And Jesus refers to Himself also in the first person five times. As De Tocqueville says, "The Almighty does not generalize," and as Bishop Warburton affirms, "the care of Christianity is for particulars."[15]

Third, these are all very commonplace concerns in the lives of people regardless of their age, gender, station, or circumstances: at times we all get tired to the point of being worn out, and that does in fact sadden us, even at times depress us (vs. 1); we all have experienced thirst, both for physical refreshment and for spiritual "watering" in particularly dry seasons (vs. 2); we all have found ourselves alone, on an unknown path, or trail, or highway, in the dark, and we can appreciate the sense of being lost, or at least uncertain of our direction (vs. 3). But the Lord's Name be praised, for when we come to Him in our fatigue, He gives us rest and gladdens our hearts—as often is the case after a good, peaceful night's deep sleep (vs. 1). He quenches our thirst, revives our spirit, and continuously provides for our lives (vs. 2); and He is, Himself, our Star, by which we can make our nighttime journey lead to the right destination, or our Sun to give us guidance in the daylight hours, that we might ever walk in peace and safety (vs. 3).

As Bailey says,

> It is all so direct and simple: . . . a transcript of Christian experience which the wayfaring man, though a fool, can understand and appropriate.[16]

Notes

1. Duffield, *op. cit.*, p. 169.
2. Julian, *op. cit.*, p. 162.
3. Haeussler, *op. cit.*, p. 555.
4. Temple, *op. cit.*, p. 120.
5. Covert and Laufer, *op. cit.*, p. 73.
6. Moffatt and Patrick, *op. cit.*, p. 273.
7. *Ibid.*
8. *Ibid.*, pp. 273–274.
9. Temple, *op. cit.*, p. 121.
10. Julian, *op. cit.*, p. 161.

11. Smith, *Lyric Religion,* p. 155.

12. *Ibid.*

13. McCutchan, *Our Hymnody,* p. 257.

14. Breed, *op. cit.,* p. 226.

15. Duffield, *op. cit.,* pp. 238–239.

16. Bailey, *op. cit.,* p. 454.

Title/Date	*"It Came upon the Midnight Clear..."* *(1850)*
Author	*Edmund H. Sears*
Composer/Tune	*R. Storrs Willis "Carol" (1850)*
Scriptural Basis	*Luke 2:9, 13–14; Isaiah 1:18–19; 2:4; Romans 12:21*

In his significant study, *English Hymns,* Samuel Duffield expresses this estimate of several of the greatest American hymns:

> If "My faith looks up to Thee" can claim to be the most spiritual, and "Stand up, stand up for Jesus," the most stirring, this one "It came upon the midnight clear" may surely be classed as the most lovely; wedded to [Storrs'] tune, it almost sings itself; . . . as poetry it outranks almost anything else of its kind and day.[1]

Usually classed as a Christmas hymn or carol, it is at the same time more than just a recital of the events surrounding the birth of the Savior; in fact, it presents very clearly the social implications of the message of the angels heard on that night so long ago and far away. While this is evident, especially in Stanzas Three and Four, it was stressed even more forcefully in its original third stanza, rarely if ever found in any of our more modern hymnals; that omitted stanza reads:

> Yet with the woes of sin and strife
> The world has suffered long:
> Beneath the angel's strain have rolled
> Two thousand years of wrong;
> And man, at war with man, hears not
> The love-song which they bring;
> Oh hush the noise, ye men of strife,
> And hear the angels sing![2]

While in an earlier period, English Evangelicals were strongly exercised about ministering to the needs of the downtrodden and the forgotten of

286

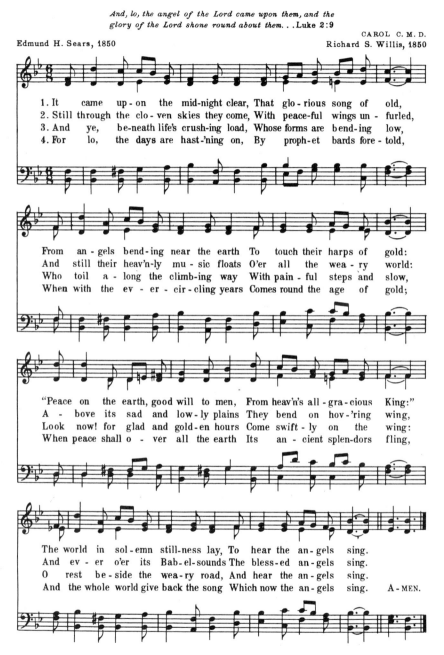

*And, lo, the angel of the Lord came upon them, and the
glory of the Lord shone round about them. . .Luke 2:9*

CAROL C. M. D.

Edmund H. Sears, 1850

Richard S. Willis, 1850

1. It came up-on the mid-night clear, That glo-rious song of old,
2. Still through the clo-ven skies they come, With peace-ful wings un-furled,
3. And ye, be-neath life's crush-ing load, Whose forms are bend-ing low,
4. For lo, the days are hast-'ning on, By proph-et bards fore-told,

From an-gels bend-ing near the earth To touch their harps of gold:
And still their heav'n-ly mu-sic floats O'er all the wea-ry world:
Who toil a-long the climb-ing way With pain-ful steps and slow,
When with the ev-er-cir-cling years Comes round the age of gold;

"Peace on the earth, good will to men, From heav'n's all-gra-cious King:"
A-bove its sad and low-ly plains They bend on hov-'ring wing,
Look now! for glad and gold-en hours Come swift-ly on the wing:
When peace shall o-ver all the earth Its an-cient splen-dors fling,

The world in sol-emn still-ness lay, To hear the an-gels sing.
And ev-er o'er its Bab-el-sounds The bless-ed an-gels sing.
O rest be-side the wea-ry road, And hear the an-gels sing.
And the whole world give back the song Which now the an-gels sing. A-MEN.

society, during the nineteenth century this emphasis had been championed
by men like Charles Kingsley and F. D. Maurice, but by few others. In New
England, similar concern for these issues was part of the Unitarian agenda,
and their chief theological impact came through Harvard Divinity School.

So, the fact that American hymn-writers who were educated there became proponents of such causes, and incorporated them into their hymns should not surprise readers. This hymn, and its author Edmund Hamilton Sears (1810–1876), is one of the best illustrations of a felicitous blending of the two; moreover, it is significant that Sears, while a Unitarian, wrote to Bishop Bickersteth averring, "I believe and preach the divinity of Christ."[3] Others have pointed to his deeply spiritual teaching[4] and to the strong christological position consistently maintained in his works.[5]

Moreover, and I believe quite importantly, his attitude and approach to his ministry gave evidence that he drank deeply of the spirit of genuine humility that characterized both our Lord Jesus and His most faithful servants through the ages. Looking back on the time of his graduation from Harvard, he said that he felt thus:

> When we left the school some of my classmates sought metropolitan positions; and their names have become somewhat celebrated. I had no other ambition then to lead such a quiet pastorate as Goldsmith describes in his *Deserted Village*.[6]

And this, several pastorates in small Massachusetts communities, was the extent of his ministry. He served three within a short distance of each other for close to forty years; but he served with such energy that several of those years were spent farming, recuperating from overwork, and writing a number of his best devotional works, which have been described as "scholarly, couched in rich and poetic language, and moving on a high level of spiritual thought."[7]

It was Sears' love for music, however, which led him to write the hymns that have made his name immortal; of his two greatest, "ranking among the best on that holy season in the English language,"[8] the earlier one, "Calm on the Listening Ear of Night," is still occasionally used. But "It Came upon the Midnight Clear" is easily among the most beloved of all those still used at Christmas. Its first American publisher wrote of it:

> I always feel that, however poor my Christmas sermon may be, the reading and singing of this hymn are enough to make up for all [my] deficiencies![9]

This comment, which stresses the hymn's worth in the service of worship, to "make up for" a poor sermon, is interesting, but should not encourage sloth in sermon preparation! More to the point is Sears' own view:

> In our church service the sermon consummates in the hymn, or sacred song, which makes the heart lyrical with the truth it sets forth. . . . The

song, or hymn, should be a summing up of the sermon, helping us to take home its truth, and so carry it with us to fill our daily life with its melodies.[10]

To which this author says Amen!

As Dykes' "Nicea" is a perfect match for Heber's "Holy, Holy, Holy," so is the tune "Carol" by Richard Storrs Willis (1819–1900) perfectly suited for this Christmas gem, and they were wedded when they first appeared in print in an 1850 edition of the *Monthly Religious Magazine,* which Sears co-edited for many years.[11] As an essentially modern carol tune,

> it should be sung at a moderate speed, smoothly and without undue emphasis on the first and fourth beats of the measure, and always with due regard for the full value of the shorter notes.[12]

Its composer, Richard Storrs Willis, was born in Boston, the son of Deacon Nathaniel Willis, founder of *The Youth's Companion.* He graduated from Yale, where he wrote some music for the college choir; later, while studying in Germany, he was befriended by Felix Mendelssohn, who took an interest in his musical compositions, revising some and encouraging him.[13] Returning home, he taught German at Yale; then, encouraged to enter the field of journalism he did, editing a number of important music journals for many years and publishing a biography in English of his friend Mendelssohn and a volume entitled *Our Church Music.* He also was a composer, his works including church chorales, student songs, hymn tunes, and harmonizations, including the melody "Schoenster Herr Jesu" made famous through its use with the folk hymn "Fairest Lord Jesus."[14]

Now let us examine this hymn, which "reflects the universal unrest prevailing in the 1850*ties,* through revolutions in France and Germany, the Chartist Movement in Britain, and in America, the passing of the Fugitive Slave Law."[15]

Stanza One: Here we have a vivid word-picture of that first Christmas night: like the dramatic event it portrayed, there was the *music,* glorious in its rhythm and message, sung by an angelic chorus, accompanying themselves on gold harps; there was the *message,* sent from the throne of God, the message of peace that He would give to men of good will—still an important qualifier! And there was the *mood,* one of hushed silence, as the world lay in solemn stillness—what a contrast to the raucous noise that bombards our ears today on every hand and that even then was part of the wider world around Bethlehem—which was, in its quietness, like an oasis in a desert!

Stanza Two: The emphasis here should be placed on the word "still" and its significance; for Sears is reminding us that those blessed messengers of God—ministering spirits—do not just belong to the past, but to every age, wherever men and women seek peace, for they bring peace and quietness, rather than the usual Babel sounds, the discordant messages that bring a weariness to the world and pain and sadness in their wake.

Stanza Three: Here the shift is to the personal: to those "who find the burden of life heavy—victims of poverty, disease, and social injustice,"[16] the message is heartening; for better times are coming—indeed "glad and golden hours" are not only coming but are coming swiftly. Therefore such are encouraged to take time out from the crush, the toil, and the painful in life to rest and listen to that same song! Smith brings it home to us when he writes:

> How many there are, in our modern, machine-dominated civilization who toil along the [steep] way with bent [backs] and minds deadened by the crushing loads of life, loads which today seem to be increasingly more devastating to every aspect of our humanity![17]

Stanza Four: Here is stressed that eternal hope which Christians especially have reason to anticipate, for Christ born in that manger is "the reason for the hope that is within us," since He *is* our hope! So here, past (foretold by prophet bards), present (epitomized in the current song of the angels, which we can hear if we can get quiet enough), and future (the "age of gold," the golden years ahead) are all drawn together; and we are reminded that "when the earth is filled with the knowledge of God as the waters fill the seas," then peace will cover the earth and the angels' song will be returned, perhaps even antiphonally, by our entire human family! One has said of this magnificent vision of the angel chorus as it proclaims peace on earth:

> this calm and lovely scene in which heaven draws near to earth is in striking contrast to the marching legions of Rome, the clashing armies, the clamor for blood and power which dominated the era. The world weariness, the mute appeal of accusing hands of dead soldiers, the silent sorrows of mothers of every generation, the restless fears of nations cry out for Him who alone is able to heal the hurt of the nations. The sound of strife dies away. Eternal triumph belongs to the Child of Bethlehem who is King of Kings, and Lord of Lords and who shall reign forever and forever![18]

Notes

1. Duffield, *op. cit.,* p. 264.
2. Haeussler, *op. cit.,* p. 156.
3. *Ibid.,* p. 901.

4. Moffatt and Patrick, *op. cit.*, p. 494.

5. Haeussler, *op. cit.*, p. 901.

6. *Ibid.*

7. *Ibid.*, p. 902.

8. Julian, *op. cit.*, p. 1036.

9. McCutchan, *Our Hymnody*, p. 127.

10. Haeussler, *op. cit.*, p. 902.

11. McCutchan, *op. cit.*, p. 127.

12. Covert and Laufer, *op. cit.*, p. 145.

13. Haeussler, *op. cit.*, p. 987.

14. *Ibid.*, p. 235.

15. Moffatt and Patrick, *op. cit.*, p. 21.

16. Bailey, *op. cit.*, p. 518.

17. Smith, *Lyric Religion*, p. 184.

18. Covert and Laufer, *op. cit.*, p. 145.

Title/Date	*"Jerusalem the Golden" (12th century)*
Author	*Bernard of Cluny*
	John Mason Neale, trans. (1851)
Composer/Tune	*Alexander Ewing "Ewing" (1853)*
Scriptural Basis	*Revelation 21:18; 22:3–4, 14*

We have already met one of the two great Bernards of the Middle Ages, St. Bernard of Clairvaux. Now we meet the other, St. Bernard of Cluny, who lived during the twelfth century. Unfortunately, accurate details about his life are difficult to obtain. We know that his parents were English, and that he was born either at Morlaix, in Brittany, or at Morlas, in the Pyrenees,[1] and that his entire ministry was spent in the abbey of Cluny, under the direction of Peter the Venerable, a man of superlative ability and character.[2]

The monastery at Cluny had been founded in A.D. 910, on a very modest parcel of hunting grounds; but within less than two centuries it had grown into a world-influencing religious center, with its abbot controlling several hundred—some said two thousand—other Cluniac monasteries throughout France, Italy, Germany, England, Scotland, and Poland,[3] under the principle of the centralization of authority. This principle Bernard of Clairvaux was to later reject, so that his Cistercian Order insisted on the local autonomy of each of its monasteries, preventing the amassing of power and wealth! Of this monastery at Cluny one writes that it was the

> head of an international system . . . [with] a new and famous school of architecture; . . . the Church of St. Peter, the admiration and wonder of the world; . . . the most famous musical center of Europe; . . . a monastery so extensive in size that St. Louis of France and his courtiers could stay there without one of the monks having to leave his cell . . . ; it was an international meeting-place better known than Paris itself;[4] . . . its wealth was enormous, its abbot lived as a prince, its furnishings were luxurious, its table incomparable.[5]

However, the world outside its walls was in desperate condition, with endless wars, disease, poverty, ignorance, superstition, political oppression, and considerable ecclesiastical corruption—indeed, it "was openly said that

And the city was pure gold, like unto clear glass. Rev. 21:18

Bernard of Cluny, 12th century
Tr. by John Mason Neale, 1851; alt.

EWING 7. 6. 7. 6. D.
Alexander Ewing, 1853

1. Je - ru - sa - lem the gold - en, With milk and hon - ey blest,
2. They stand, those halls of Zi - on, All ju - bi - lant with song,
3. There is the throne of Da - vid; And there, from care re - leased,
4. O sweet and bless - ed coun - try, The home of God's e - lect!

Be - neath thy con - tem - pla - tion Sink heart and voice op - pressed.
And bright with man - y an an - gel, And all the mar - tyr throng.
The song of them that tri - umph, The shout of them that feast;
O sweet and bless - ed coun - try That ea - ger hearts ex - pect!

I know not, O I know not, What joys a - wait us there;
The Prince is ev - er in them, The day - light is se - rene;
And they who with their Lead - er Have con - quered in the fight,
Je - sus, in mer - cy bring us To that dear land of rest;

What ra - dian - cy of glo - ry, What bliss be - yond com - pare.
The pas - tures of the bless - ed Are decked in glo - rious sheen.
For ev - er and for ev - er Are clad in robes of white.
Who art, with God the Fa - ther And Spir - it, ev - er blest. A - MEN.

Christ and his Saints wept."[6] So it was that Bernard, a Cluniac monk, knowing the veracity of these accusations, penned a bitter satire about the moral apostasy of his generation, both without and within the walls of his monastery; the poem, "De Contemptu Mundi," extended to some three thousand lines written in "the dactylic hexameter, with a leonine and tailed rhyme"[7] (six rhymes in every two lines), exceedingly difficult to translate as well as to write! Indeed, Bernard himself with characteristic humility says of his labors,

> And I said: Lord, to what end may my heart think, . . . my pen write . . . my mouth set forth thy praise . . . And He said, Open thy mouth. Which He straightway filled with the spirit of Wisdom and Understanding, that by one I might speak truly, by the other perspicuously. And I say it . . . with all humility . . . : that unless the Spirit of Wisdom and Understanding had been with me and flowed in upon so difficult a metre, I could not have compassed so long a work.[8]

This great poem is really in three sections; in it Bernard, in a spirit of awe-stricken self-abasement, reviews the vices of his age in sharp and biting sarcasm, announces God's judgments on the awful reprobates, and then contemplates, with rhapsody, the joys and glories of heaven, the celestial country. Thus, properly interpreted, as Julian points out,

> the prevailing sentiment of the poem [is] of an awful apprehension of the joys of heaven, the enormity of sin, and the terrors of hell;[9] [it is] not a rhapsody on heaven; rather, it is hot with the fires of hell.[10]

John Mason Neale (1818–1866), without question one of the greatest translators of the ancient Greek and Latin poems and hymns, has been earlier discussed. A scholar who could read, write, and think in twenty-one languages and a poet, he also was

> a man of action . . . and enthusiastic champion of the religious life for women, who successfully founded the well-known Sisterhood of Margaret . . . in the teeth of bitter popular prejudice and opposition, which on one occasion nearly cost him his life.[11]

Further, in his concerns for the poor and downtrodden, he also founded an orphanage, a school for middle-class girls, and a home for the reclamation of "fallen women," which was, alas, short-lived because of unfair opposition![12]

Neale never copyrighted his hymns, believing them to be the common property of Christendom; on his coffin was inscribed "a poor and unworthy priest, resting under the sign of the cross,"[13] reflecting his High Church convictions. But one who knew him well said of him,

Of all his teachings, the one most edifying to my own soul was when I saw him in his last illness laying in the dust all his works and all his talents, and casting himself as a little child only on the atoning work of Jesus Christ.[14]

The tune "Ewing," written originally for another hymn translated from Bernard's poem, soon became the standard tune for this hymn by Neale; of it Neale once said that it was "the earliest written, the best known, and with children the most popular, no small proof in my estimation of [its worth]."[15]

Alexander Ewing (1830–1895), a native of Aberdeen, Scotland, originally studied law, but developed a special love for music, which he studied in Heidelberg, Germany, becoming a proficient instrumentalist and composer; he was an enthusiastic member of both the Haydn Society and the renowned Harmonic Choir of Aberdeen.[16] One evening in the course of this choir's rehearsal, he asked the director to try a hymn tune he had written; they sang it, and it began its life as "Ewing," soon attached to "Jerusalem the Golden." Originally the tune had been in triple time, but it was changed to common time for this hymn, a change to which Ewing never gave his assent; on one occasion he said, "they have vulgarized my little tune; it now seems to me a good deal like a polka; I hate to hear it."[17] It was sung at his funeral, a fitting tribute to his popularity and its significance,[18] being at that time one of England's ten greatest hymns.[19]

Ewing, held in high regard as an amateur musician, also served in the British army as a paymaster, attaining the rank of colonel and being decorated for valor.[20] He later married Juliana Scott-Gatty, daughter of Lord Nelson's chaplain and private secretary; she was a well-known author of children's books, some of which became classics.

It remains for us to examine this "graceful and melodic" paraphrase through which Neale has opened up the richness of Bernard's refined Latin literary style, a style "characterized by such obvious accent and musical rhythm that even one ignorant of the language can pronounce it, and catch its rhymes."[21] This hymn focuses on the halls of heaven, the glories of the celestial country, the vision of hope that comes when one turns his gaze from the abominations of this world's wicked conditions to the world "wherein dwelleth righteousness"—for God is there, and He bids us welcome! As Neale himself says,

As a contrast to the misery and pollution of earth the poem opens with a description of the peace and glory of heaven of such rare beauty as not easily to be matched by any medieval composition on the same subject.[22]

Erik Routley speaks of a survey taken of some two hundred Englishmen in which they were asked about their religious views; though fewer than half had any connection with either Christianity or a church, many of them clung to some hope of a future life; then he asks the question of them "what is reality? squalor? or the love of God?" and quotes Bernard's lines,

> Brief life is here our portion, brief sorrow, short-lived care;
> The life that knows no ending, the tearless life is there.
> The miserable pleasures of the body shall decay;
> The bland and flattering struggles of the flesh shall pass away;
> And none shall there be jealous, and none shall there contend;
> Fraud, clamor, guile—what say I? All ill, all ill shall end.[23]

Again, hear William Blake regarding the importance of a clear, scriptural view of heaven if one wants to be an effective reformer of the ills and corruption found all too prevailingly in this world; he says, "You will not find many effective Christian reformers in any field who did not have a very clear doctrine of heaven!"[24] What, then, was Bernard's view?

Stanza One: He begins by comparing Jerusalem the Golden, the heavenly city, with Canaan, the "land of milk and honey," which the Israelites conquered to be their homeland. He recognizes that our contemplations of the precise nature of that city are ever shrouded in mystery; the biblical images are, at best, pointers to a reality about which we know but little. Yet the expectation is all positive: joys, radiant glory, incomparable bliss—and because of that, we eagerly expect and anticipate it.

Stanza Two: Here we are struck with a mixture of pictures: the angels, the martyrs, and Jesus the Prince are there, and the halls ring with jubilant singing; serenity characterizes its mood; light pervades the scene within the halls/walls of Zion; and then, as a natural setting, verdant pastures—where the blessed live? or romp? or sit and meditate, drinking in the beauty of the world of nature—"are decked in glorious sheen."

Stanza Three: The Prince (vs. 2) becomes their leader in this stanza; the throne of David, the messianic King, is there in Jerusalem, symbolizing not only God's power but also His redemption; and around that throne is the throng of delivered martyrs—clad in white robes—who can sing, and shout, and feast because they have conquered all their enemies—the world, the flesh, the devil, hell, and all of its terrors; they have overcome them "by the blood of the Lamb, slain before the foundation of the world"! And that is *victory,* ultimate and final! As Katharine Hinkson writes,

> They come with shining faces to the house of the Lord;
> The broken hearts and weary, that life has racked and scored,
> They come hurrying and singing, to sit down at His board,
> They are young and they are joyful in the House of the Lord.[25]

Stanza Four: Here is a prayer—a simple prayer with which we can all identify—that Jesus, our merciful Redeemer, will bring us to that country, that land about which we've heard so much and to which we yearn to go! For that is our home, as His elect children, chosen in Him as we have been from eternity past (Ephesians 1:3–14); naturally, children always want to go home, especially if home has a welcoming tone about it! Finally, Bernard reminds us that our Prince is not simply an earthly prince, or our leader not merely one whom we have chosen or even elected; He is Jesus, the Savior, ever one with God the Father and God the Holy Spirit—a solid conviction of Trinitarian theology.

Routley draws together the "there and then" and the "here and now" aspects of our life in Him when he writes,

> Jesus' Life opens life to a newness now; we go "home" even before we go "Home"; heaven is sociable: free, frank, friendly conversation between friends; no more jealousy, ignorance, suspicion, hurt feelings, misunderstandings . . . ; heaven is *there*, but it is God's will that heaven, in exactly the same sense *that* heaven—bought by Jesus' cheerful, willing and loving death, and the denial of all dark, satanic things—shall be here also![26]

Notes

1. Bailey, *op. cit.*, p. 256.
2. *Ibid.*
3. *Ibid.*
4. *Ibid.*, p. 255.
5. Smith, *Lyric Religion*, p. 186.
6. *Ibid.*
7. Haeussler, *op. cit.*, p. 432.
8. Bailey, *op. cit.*, p. 257.
9. Julian *op. cit.*, p. 137.
10. Moffatt and Patrick, *op. cit.*, p. 208.
11. Phillips, *op. cit.*, pp. 207–208.
12. Moffatt and Patrick, *op. cit.*, pp. 441–442.
13. *Ibid.*
14. *Ibid.*
15. Lightwood, *op. cit.*, p. 379.
16. McCutchan, *op. cit.*, pp. 513–514.
17. Metcalf, *op. cit.*, p. 71.
18. Covert and Laufer, *op. cit.*, p. 449.
19. Duffield, *op. cit.*, p. 272.
20. Haeussler, *op. cit.*, p. 648.
21. Brown and Butterworth, *op. cit.*, p. 510.

22. Haeussler, *op. cit.*, p. 433.
23. Routley, *op. cit.*, pp. 295–296.
24. *Ibid.*, p. 297.
25. *Ibid.*, p. 300.
26. *Ibid.*

Title/Date	*"Like a River Glorious . . ."* (1878)
Author	*Frances Ridley Havergal*
Composer/Tune	*James Mountain "Like a River"* *(c. 1876)*
Scriptural Basis	*Isaiah 48:18; 26:3–4*

In order to understand the biblical concept of peace, it may be helpful to compare it with the popular notion. In this conception peace can be likened to a pond covered with a thick layer of green algae in the middle of summer; throw a stone into it and it simply goes "klung," with nary a ripple to disturb its surface. That kind of peace prevails when nothing untoward happens to disturb one's tranquility—no problems, no questions to answer, no distressing situations to deal with, nothing but tranquility!

Biblical peace, by contrast, can be compared to a mighty river that moves along in its course, steady in its purpose and direction; on the surface there are wind-whipped waves a plenty, and it is anything but tranquil; but down underneath, the river courses steadily on, staying in its channel, unmoved by the haphazard events on the surface. That is what the Bible understands as peace; peace in the midst of all of life's tumult; peace in spite of problems, challenges, frustrations, even tragedies; and that peace is possible to God's child as he stays his heart on the One who is indeed and alone the Giver of peace. And this is the peace—the "peace that does pass all human understanding," the peace that Jesus Himself possessed, epitomized, and promised to all who would trust Him for it, the peace that our hymn celebrates, for its author possessed it in abundant measure.

Frances Ridley Havergal (1836–1879), "the best loved hymn-writer of the Evangelical Anglicans, whose hymns reveal her supreme devotion to the spiritual life,"[1] began writing poetry at the age of seven, and continued to write books, verses, and tracts of a devotional nature all her life, in addition to carrying on a considerable correspondence with those who had been touched through this, which she considered—and rightly so—to be her God-given talent and ministry.

But these gifts were not just hers, for her heritage needs to be remembered: her father William was an eminent musician, an authority on church music and psalmody who had refused a professor's chair in music at Oxford

Behold, I will extend peace . . . like a river. Isa. 66:12

LIKE A RIVER 6. 5. 6. 5. D. and refrain

Frances R. Havergal, 1878

James Mountain, 1844-1933

1. Like a riv - er glo - rious Is God's per - fect peace,
2. Hid - den in the hol - low Of his bless - ed hand,
3. Ev - 'ry joy or tri - al Fall - eth from a - bove,

O - ver all vic - to - rious In its bright in - crease; Per-fect, yet it
Nev - er foe can fol - low, Nev-er trait-or stand; Not a surge of
Traced up-on our di - al By the Sun of Love. We may trust him

flow - eth Full - er ev - 'ry day,— Per - fect, yet it grow - eth
wor - ry, Not a shade of care, Not a blast of hur - ry,
ful - ly All for us to do; They who trust him whol - ly

REFRAIN

Deep - er all the way.
Touch the spir - it there. Stayed up-on Je - ho - vah, Hearts are full - y
Find him whol - ly true.

blest, Find - ing, as he prom - ised, Per - fect peace and rest. A - MEN.

because he believed his calling from God was to the ministry of the gospel,[2] a ministry he exercised faithfully in several parishes in the Church of England, including the Worcester Cathedral where, incidentally, Frances was confirmed in 1853. Writing of this experience she said:

> I was the fourth or fifth on whom the Bishop laid his hands. . . . I felt alone—alone with God and his chief minister. My feelings when his hands were placed on my head I cannot describe, they were too confused; but when the words "Defend, O Lord, this thy child with thy heavenly grace, that she may continue thine forever, and daily increase in the Holy Spirit more and more, until she comes into thy everlasting kingdom," were solemnly pronounced, if ever my heart followed a prayer, it did then; if ever it thrilled, with earnest and longing, not unmixed with joy, it did at the words "Thine forever."[3] [And she often told others, simply] I committed my soul to my Saviour, and earth and heaven seemed brighter from that moment.[4]

A prolific author and writer, William published several worthy volumes on psalmody and other subjects, plus writing over one hundred hymns and many hymn tunes. But his primary concern was to "raise the standards of church music which at that time had sunk to a low level in England,"[5] a task in which he was ably assisted by his oldest son and by Frances.

Moreover, Frances also gloried in her middle name, "Ridley," bearing it as she did as a descendant of the godly and learned bishop who had suffered martyrdom, being burned at the stake with Hugh Latimer many generations earlier. Thus she was well prepared for the life she lived, a life that began bright with promise in every way—for she had climbed the Alps in her student days on the Continent, and gloried in her strength,[6] and which ended after many years of suffering as an invalid. Consider her early accomplishments:

> Possessed of a remarkable musical talent, not only as a singer and pianist, but also as a composer, in her mid-twenties she considered . . . music as a profession, [encouraged to do so] by Hiller . . . ; she had a good working knowledge of Latin, Hebrew and Greek, and could speak French, German and Italian. She could play all of Handel, and much of Beethoven and Mendelssohn without notes;[7] [moreover,] with her prodigious memory she had committed the entire New Testament, the Psalms, Isaiah and the minor prophets to memory![8]

Moreover, she was a sunny woman, with a brightness and charm about her that drew people, naturally, to her side. As one who had the joy of meeting her once wrote:

In a few seconds Miss Frances, carolling like a bird, flashed into the room!
Flashed! yes, I say the word advisedly, flashed in like a burst of sunshine
. . . and stood before us, her bright eyes dancing, and her fresh sweet voice
ringing through the room. I shall never forget that afternoon, never! I sat
perfectly spellbound as she sang chant and hymn with marvelous sweetness
and then played two or three pieces of Handel, which thrilled me through
and through![9]

Her writings reveal a heart that was set on following God, and as such
they are introspective, mystical—in the best sense of that word—and other-
worldly; she was not bothered by intellectual difficulties, and considered even
her long-term illness a vehicle by which God could use her. Yet, for all of her
subjectivity, she was not "addicted to the use of the perpendicular pronoun";[10] she attracted people from all walks of life, and insisted, even from
her sickbed, on answering all correspondence; she was also an active worker
in the Sunday School, the Church Missionary Society, and various Aid societies. Always concerned about the needs of the poor, she not only gave
Bible readings in the servants' halls, but also encouraged those, poor through
intemperate use of alcohol, to sign a total abstinence pledge![11] As a woman
whose life was joyfully consecrated to Christ, she requested, before her
death—which occurred when she was in the prime of life—that her tombstone read "The blood of Jesus Christ His Son cleanseth us from all sin"
(I John 1:7).

One has suggested that her active, buoyant temperament enabled her "to
skim any waves when she was not under them,"[12] and her own attitude toward the deep trials she endured with her health was best seen in her own
expression, "Thy will be done is not a sigh, but only a song"![13] At the time
of her death, she and her sister were in South Wales; in spite of having in-
flammation in her lungs, she sang a number of hymns, her own and others,
some to tunes she had also composed; then, said her sister,

> she looked up steadfastly, as if she saw the Lord; and nothing less heavenly
> could have reflected such a glorious radiance upon her face. For ten min-
> utes we watched that almost visible meeting with her King, and her coun-
> tenance was so glad, as if she were already talking to Him! Then she tried
> to sing, but after one sweet, high note her voice failed, and as her brother
> commended her soul into her Redeemer's hand, she passed away.[14]

This hymn, "Like a River Glorious," first appeared in her *Loyal Responses,*
published in 1878; the tune, sometimes known as "Wye Valley," but in the
Trinity Hymnal as "Like a River," was composed by James Mountain
(1844–1933), originally educated for the Congregational ministry, both in

England and on the Continent; after brief pastoral service, his health broke, and he spent a two-year period of recuperation in Switzerland. Then he returned to England, where he was greatly influenced by the revival ministry that Moody and Sankey carried on there briefly. In fact, he spent the next eight years in mission preaching in England, and then seven more traveling around the world, conducting evangelistic meetings; upon his return to England, he served two churches for some twenty years.

Mountain always maintained a strong orthodox theology, and was prominent in a movement for "Bible defense";[15] he also edited several religious magazines and a hymnbook, *Hymns of Consecration and Faith* (c. 1876), which contained several hymns by writers of the Keswick School, in addition to many of the "gospel song" model.[16] Honored with a D.D. degree by Ewing College, in Illinois, he died an elderly man, "full of faith and good deeds." In addition to this beautiful and forceful hymn tune, he also composed the tune "Resting," which graces Jean Pigott's marvelous hymn "Jesus, I Am Resting, Resting in the Joy of What Thou Art . . ." (*Trinity Hymnal,* p. 139).

Now let us turn to an examination of the distinctive features of this hymn, one of Havergal's finest, of the more than sixty that she authored.[17]

First, there is everywhere here a note of quiet but clear, no-nonsense assertion: God's peace is perfect, yet it grows fuller and deeper to the trusting soul who experiences it every single day! God's child, "hidden in the hollow of His blessed hand," is absolutely safe and secure, and nothing—neither person nor circumstance—can disturb his well-being, *ever!* Furthermore, whatever of trial as well as of joy that comes to the believer comes ultimately not from our foes, nor from traitors to God, nor from untoward circumstances, but from His hand! That bespeaks confidence in the ultimate sovereignty of God, but in a touchingly personal way.

Second, her adjectives are heaped up, as if to underline the qualities of which she writes; so a "glorious" river, a "perfect" peace, "bright" increase, "every" day, "all" the way, "blessed" hand, "fully" blest, "perfect" peace and rest.

Third, the experiences dealt with are the common ones of life, to which we are all exposed at one time or another: the opposition of personal enemies; the treachery of those who are traitors to a cause or a country; things that make us worry or fret, harried or anxious; trials that create difficulty or heartache—understood or mysterious; for these all of us need the ongoing assurance of God's presence, power, and peace in our lives.

Fourth, there is the universal assurance herein: His peace is *perfect,* lacking nothing; it can "conquer" *any*thing and *every*thing, for *every*one—"over *all* victorious"; foes can *never* trouble us, *never* stand against us; not even *one* "surge of worry," *nor one* "shade of care," *nor one* "blast of hurry" can touch us as we are "hidden" within His hand's hollow. Further, it is *every* joy and trial that He "traces on our dial," and since He will do *all* for us, we may trust Him *fully*, or *completely*—as we "stay our hearts on Him." And that is the key: We are to stay our hearts upon Him; literally, our hearts are to stand firm upon Him, in a settled state; then nothing can shake us up, or destroy that "peace that passes all human understanding," for it will keep watch over our hearts like a sentinel on guard duty (Philippians 4:7) who protects his camp at the risk of his own life! That indeed is blessing, that indeed is perfect peace!

Notes

1. Benson, *The English Hymn*, p. 519.
2. Houghton, *Christian Hymn Writers*, p. 245.
3. Smith, *Lyric Religion*, p. 380.
4. Marks, *op. cit.*, p. 166.
5. Haeussler, *op. cit.*, p. 708.
6. Smith, *op. cit.*, p. 378.
7. Colquhoun, *Hymns That Live*, pp. 266–267.
8. Haeussler, *op. cit.*, p. 706.
9. Houghton, *op. cit.*, p. 243.
10. Haeussler, *op. cit.*, p. 707.
11. *Ibid.*
12. Duffield, *op. cit.*, p. 189.
13. *Ibid.*, p. 190.
14. *Ibid.*
15. Covert and Laufer, *op. cit.*, p. 349.
16. Benson, *op. cit.*, p. 520.
17. Julian, *op. cit.*, p. 497.

Title/Date	*"Now Thank We All Our God . . ."* *(1636, 1647)*
Author	*Martin Rinkart*
	Catherine Winkworth, trans. (1858)
Composer/Tune	*Johann Crüger "Nun Danket Alle Gott"* *(1648)*
Scriptural Basis	*Ecclesiasticus 50:22–24, 29–32;* *I Chronicles 29:13; Psalm 103:1, 2, 4*

According to C. S. Lewis, the kind of tragedy that causes some men to question the very existence of God—let alone His mercy and love—drives others into a sense of deeper trust in His love and compassion. That apologetic was certainly borne out in the Thirty Years' War (1618–1648), which devastated Central Europe; about that period Temple wrote:

> It was a time when men's hearts failed them for fear. . . . Those who fell not in battle perished before the still deadlier scourges of plague and famine. The very abomination of desolation seemed to be set up: rapine and pillage, outrage and slaughter reigned unchecked. . . . In vain, to all outward appearances did the saints cry: how long? Yet of their cries and tears, and of the amazing tenacity of their faith, the hymns they have left us bear irrefragable witness.[1]

The hymn before us, "Now Thank We All Our God," by Martin Rinkart (1586–1649), is a superlative illustration of this truth—that tragedy drove men and women to God! For it was written during those years, probably in 1635, since it was included in the original edition of his *Jesu-Hertz-Beuchein,* published in Leipzig in 1636 under the caption "Tish-Gebetlein" (Grace at Table).[2] Therefore, the story that it was sung when the Peace of Westphalia was signed in 1648 is not without plausibility, and as the German "Te Deum" it holds the place that Old Hundredth held in England, being sung on many occasions of national rejoicing in Germany, such as the completion of the cathedral at Cologne (1880) as well as in honor of the Diamond Jubilee Celebration of Queen Victoria (1897).[3]

Now therefore, our God, we thank thee, and praise thy glorious name. I Chron. 29:13

Martin Rinkart, c. 1636   NUN DANKET 6.7.6.7.6.6.6.6.
Tr. by Catherine Winkworth, 1858   Johann Crüger, 1647

1. Now thank we all our God With heart and hands and voic - es,
2. O may this boun - teous God Through all our life be near us,
3. All praise and thanks to God, The Fa - ther, now be giv - en,

Who won-drous things hath done, In whom his world re - joic - es;
With ev - er joy - ful hearts And bless-ed peace to cheer us;
The Son, and Him who reigns With them in high - est heav - en,

Who from our moth - ers' arms, Hath blessed us on our way
And keep us in his grace, And guide us when per - plexed,
The One E - ter - nal God Whom earth and heav'n a - dore;

With count - less gifts of love, And still is ours to - day.
And free us from all ills In this world and the next.
For thus it was, is now, And shall be ev - er - more. A - MEN.

Martin Rinkart, the son of a poor cooper (barrel maker), attended the Latin school in his birthplace of Eilenberg, and then went to the University of Leipzig, where he studied theology, supporting himself as a musician and eventually graduating. Meanwhile he also taught in the gymnasium in

Eisleben, and served as the cantor of St. Nicholas Church there; two small pastorates followed until he took his M.A. in 1616, and was called as archdeacon in the Eilenberg church in 1617,[4] where he spent the rest of his productive, dedicated life and ministry. Since Eilenberg was a walled city, offering some protection during the horrors of the war, it became overcrowded and unsanitary, the site of pestilence and famine. Eventually Rinkart was the only clergyman there—having buried four others himself, and read the burial service over forty to fifty persons daily, some 4,480 in all, including his first wife, in an epidemic that claimed a total of over eight thousand victims in 1637. Famine followed (1637–1639), which reduced the citizens to "fighting in the open streets for a dead cat or a crow."[5] Then, to top it all off, the conquering Swedish general demanded a ransom of some thirty thousand thalers; Rickart's pleadings with him to reduce the amount went unheeded, whereupon Rickart said to those with him, "Come, my children, we can find no mercy with men, let us take refuge with God";[6] and his prayer was so fervent that the general relented and lowered his demands, first to eight thousand thalers, and finally to two thousand thalers, which the desperate people were still hard-pressed to raise. Rickart, although in incredibly straitened circumstances, gave himself unsparingly to his—for the most part—ungrateful and unappreciative fellow citizens; to make amends Eilenberg later fixed a memorial tablet in his memory to his family home, on Easter Monday 1886,[7] a more than fitting tribute to a man treated with such gross injustice. But Rinkart's greatest memorial is in his devotional writings, which are considerable, his seven dramas, his music, and especially his hymns—some sixty-six in all. Of his hymns, this one has gained universal acceptance throughout the English-speaking world,[8] chiefly through the marvelous translation made by Catherine Winkworth, without peer[9] as the translator of Germany's finest hymns. Of his hymns Julian says,

> The best of them are characterized by a true patriotism, a childlike devotion to God, and a firm confidence in God's mercy, and His promised help and grace.[10]

Catherine Winkworth (1829–1878), of whom we have written briefly in an earlier study, was the finest of several Englishwomen who sought to popularize Germany's great hymns in nineteenth-century England; of her work as a translator Martineau wrote:

> Her translations are invariably faithful, . . . terse and delicate; and an admirable art is applied to the management of complex and difficult versification. They have not quite the fire of John Wesley's Moravian hymns, . . .

but if less flowing they are more conscientious . . . and attain results as poetical as severe exactitude admits, being only a little short of "native music."[11]

Winkworth, who devoted much of her energies to the Clifton Association for the Higher Education of Women, was lauded by its headmaster, who paid her this tribute:

> She was a person of remarkable intellect and social gifts . . . ; but what specially distinguished her was her combination of rare ability and great knowledge with a certain tender and sympathetic refinement which constitutes the special charm of the womanly character.[12]

But her chief claim to fame lies in her hymn translations, including this one, which first appeared in her *Lyra Germanica* (1858),[13] preserving as it does the "spirit and stateliness of Rinkart's original."[14]

"Nun Danket Alle Gott," the tune with which this hymn has always been associated, taking its very name from the hymn's first line—a German custom for naming chorales[15]—first appeared in Johann Crüger's *Praxis Pietatis Melica,* published originally in 1636.[16] Crüger (1598–1662) was a celebrated composer of chorales, which "constituted the main streams of Lutheran hymnody in the mid-17*th* century,"[17] and an eminent music editor.

After studying theology at Wittenberg, he became the cantor of St. Nicholas Church in Berlin and a private tutor there for some forty years. A strong advocate of congregational singing, he encouraged instrumental accompaniment with it, and his tunes were widely used, even by Roman Catholic hymnals; his own published hymn collection numbered five in all, and included close to two thousand hymns—some twenty of which are still in use; one of these collections went through forty-four editions in less than a century![18] His own spirit was illustrated, aptly, in the title he chose for his first work, *Praxis Pietatis Melica,* which means "Tune of Devotion, Sweet as Honey,"[19] as for him devotion to God was something pleasant and desirable!

Now let us examine this hymn, written originally as a table grace, to be read or sung at mealtime, probably at first within his own family; it is also used, fittingly, in many German churches at services on New Year's Eve.[20] There are two passages from Ecclesiasticus 50, which various authorities cite as the basis for the first two verses of this hymn; the third verse—according to another writer—is Rickart's paraphrase of an ancient "Gloria Patri," composed in Greek in the first century, and later translated into Latin and then the various European Protestant vernaculars;[21] those two passages are:

> Now, therefore, bless ye the God of all, which only doeth wondrous things everywhere, which exalteth our days from the womb, and deals with us

according to His mercy. May He grant us joyfulness of heart, and peace
in our days in Israel forever; that He would confirm (entrust) His mercy
with us, and deliver us at His time.[22] (50:22–24)

And now let us all praise God, Who hath done great things, Who hath glorified our days, and dealeth with us according to His loving-kindness. He
giveth us the joy of our hearts, that we may find peace in Israel as in the
days of yore, thus He lets his loving-kindness remain with us, and He will
redeem us in our day.[23] (50:29–32)

(Incidentally, Routley says if he could add one book to the canon of Sacred
Scripture it would be Ecclesiasticus, calling this section of it, chapters 44–50,
a "larger edition of Hebrews 11.")[24]

Stanza One: As I sit here writing about this hymn, the record I have on
is playing it, replete with brass accompaniment and a full choir—quite an inspiration! Rinkart, both in this verse and throughout the hymn, calls on us to
affirm our faith in our God with our whole being: heart—our emotions;
hands—what we do, of work or play, and how we do it; and voices—expressing, for others to hear, what we can see that God has done for us, so that
we can indeed rejoice in Him and in His wondrous works on our behalf.
And what are those works? From infancy He has blessed us on the paths our
lives have taken with *countless* gifts of love; and that past blessing, chiefly His
presence with us, is still a reality today!

Stanza Two: Here Rinkart expresses both a hope, not in the sense of a
wish, but of an assured expectation, and a prayer for this bounteous God—
imagine using that expression in a time of famine!—to be near us, with His
presence to give us encouragement, peace, guidance in our times of per-
plexity, healing in our times of sickness, grace—yea, grace abundant, which
can keep us steady in every circumstance of life! And his prayer for all of this
encompasses both time ("this world") and eternity ("the next world"); as
Routley points out, this wasn't written at a time when gratitude came easily;
it wasn't "when the country church was decorated with corn, and flowers,
and fruit, . . . but in a time of plague and bereavement and slaughter and
famine."[25]

Stanza Three: Here the call to thanksgiving has a more theological focus as
we center on the Triune God: Father, Son, and Holy Spirit—"Him who
reigns with them in highest heaven"; He is three, but He is also "the One
Eternal God," object of the adoration of the entire universe, and so for all
time: past, present, and future. Thus it is an ongoing call to gratitude; to gratitude as more than a duty—though it *is* a duty; to gratitude "as the very
breath of the Christian's life," as a pleasure "but also as a fortifying discipline."[26] Sing it and rejoice because you have reasons to do so, but sing it also
even if you are hard pressed to find such reasons!

Notes

1. Reynolds, *op. cit.*, p. 22.
2. Haeussler, *op. cit.*, p. 123.
3. Stulken, *op. cit.*, p. 543.
4. Julian, *op. cit.*, p. 962.
5. Duffield, *op. cit.*, p. 393.
6. *Ibid.*
7. Julian, *op. cit.*, p. 962.
8. Bailey, *op. cit.*, p. 323.
9. Haeussler, *op. cit.*, p. 988.
10. Julian, *op. cit.*, p. 963.
11. Haeussler, *op. cit.*, p. 988.
12. *Ibid.*, p. 989.
13. Julian, *op. cit.*, p. 963.
14. Haeussler, *op. cit.*, p. 123.
15. McCutchan, *Our Hymnody*, p. 30.
16. Julian, *op. cit.*, p. 963.
17. Moffatt and Patrick, *op. cit.*, p. 312.
18. Haeussler, *op. cit.*, p. 616.
19. Smith, *Lyric Religion*, p. 269.
20. Covert and Laufer, *op. cit.*, p. 471.
21. Bailey, *op. cit.*, p. 323.
22. Temple, *op. cit.*, p. 41.
23. Haeussler, *op. cit.*, p. 123.
24. Routley, *Hymns and the Faith*, p. 30.
25. *Ibid.*, p. 33.
26. *Ibid.*, p. 32.

Title/Date	*"O Come, All Ye Faithful . . ." (1841)*
Author	*Anonymous Latin Hymn*
	Frederick Oakeley, trans. (1841)
Composer/Tune	*Unknown "Adeste Fideles"*
Scriptural Basis	*Luke 2:15, 20; John 1:1, 14*

It is interesting that this Christmas hymn, whose popularity in the English-speaking world is unquestioned and is indeed "a testimony to its genuine worth,"[1] and which has been translated into well over a hundred other languages,[2] is still—after much research by eminent hymnologists of the past and present—considered anonymous as to its origins. Neither the author of the lyrics nor the composer of the beautiful tune that graces it—a tune that has been *its* tune for as far back as it can be traced—can be identified with any degree of assurance. Once ascribed to the saintly Bonaventure, it has never been found in any of his extant writings;[3] Julian speaks of it as "most probably a hymn of the 17*th* or 18*th* century, and of French or German authorship."[4] Manuscripts of it in Latin go back to the mid-1750s, and Yeats-Edwards refers to a study done by a Dominican, John Stephen, in which he

> proved beyond reasonable doubt, on MSS evidence, that both the words
> and the music were the work of John Francis Wade, in 1751, and can be
> seen in a volume preserved at Stoneyhurst College, Lancashire.[5]

The problem with this suggested proof is that Wade, a pensioner in the employ of Nicholas King, copied three melodies, "Adeste Fideles" among them, for use in their private chapel—a common custom—and published them in a collection called *Cantus Diversi;*[6] there is no evidence, however, that he wrote either words or tune, in spite of Bailey's assertion that he had done so in 1744, using some musical phrases from Handel.[7] We do know, however, that it was sung in England, in 1797, at the Chapel of the Portuguese embassy in London, and that the tune, heard there by the Duke of Leeds, was later introduced at his Ancient Concerts by the title "Portuguese Hymn," a title that has persisted in use since then.[8] Thus, the story that it was written by, and took its name from, the Portuguese operatic composer

*Let us now go even unto Bethlehem, and see this
thing which is come to pass . . . Luke 2 : 15*

Anon., Latin, 18th century
Tr. by Frederick Oakeley, 1841
St. 1, lines 1 and 2, alt.

ADESTE FIDELES irregular
Unknown: probably 18th century

1. O come, all ye faith - ful, Joy - ful and tri - um - phant,
2. God of God, Light of Light;
3. Sing, choirs of an - gels; Sing in ex - ul - ta - tion,
4. Yea, Lord, we greet thee, Born this hap - py morn - ing:

O come ye, O come ye to Beth - le - hem;
Lo, he ab - hors not the Vir - gin's womb:
Sing, all ye cit - i - zens of heav'n a - bove;
Je - sus, to thee be glo - ry giv'n;

Come and be-hold him Born the King of an-gels;
Ver - y God, Be - got-ten, not cre-at - ed;
Glo - ry to God In the high-est;
Word of the Fa - ther, Late in flesh ap-pear-ing;

O come, let us a - dore him,

O come, let us a-dore him, O come, let us a - dore him, Christ the Lord. A - MEN.

Marcos Antonio Portogallo cannot be substantiated, though he may have
actually composed the tune and had someone adapt it for use in a church
setting.[9]

Furthermore, Julian lists some thirty-eight different translations of it into English,[10] pointing out that they differ, considerably, in how they render the Latin lines "Deum de Deo, Lumen de Lumine," saying that "the majority of the translators had the Nicene Creed and not 'Adeste Fideles' in their minds as they wrote"![11] Of all these, and a dozen other translations, the best and by far most widely used is the one by Frederick Oakeley (1802–1880), made originally to be sung in London's Margaret Street Chapel in 1841, which he served as rector; and later, slightly altered, it was published in Murray's *Hymnal* in 1852.[12]

Oakeley, whose father Sir Charles was at one time governor of Madras, India, was born in England and educated at Christ Church, Oxford, where he won a prize for a Latin essay and was elected a fellow of Balliol. He took Holy Orders in 1832, and served several posts, all of which he resigned in 1845 to follow John Henry Newman and others into the Church of Rome. This decision had been brewing for many years, as he had been interested and active in the Oxford Movement from about 1827;[13] he finally asserted publicly his right "to hold, as distinct from teaching, all Roman doctrine,"[14] and when proceedings were taken against him, he resigned rather than recant such views. As a Roman Catholic priest and later a canon in Westminster, he served and worked among the poor of his district for a quarter century.[15] Always interested in the arts, he published several works, including a theological one on our Lord's passion, a drama about the early Christian martyrs, and a liturgical book of verses.[16] In one of his parishes, St. Margaret's, Richard Redhead served as his organist and co-edited with him a Gregorian Psalter, *Laudes Diurnae;* of Redhead one has written "as an accompanist of devotional spirit his extemporizing seemed inspired by his faith."[17]

Now let us consider this hymn, whose popularity "is due to its measure, its lilt, and its fine tune";[18] another adds, "its focus is on the incarnation—not as a theological argument—but as a theme to be sung in glorious triumph, with dignified but jubilant imagery,"[19] calling on the angelic choirs to echo their praises throughout the highest vaults of heaven!

Stanza One: The author begins this hymn of exhortation with a call to the faithful who are both full of joy and victorious—presumably because they are overcomers—to come to Bethlehem, the ancient city in Judea where a miracle has occurred; that miracle, the miracle of all miracles, is the incarnation, God-become-human and dwelling among His people! Moreover, He is not only the sovereign over human life; He is even the King of the angelic host—an idea that does not occur very often in hymnody; and we are exhorted to adore Him, Christ (Messiah, Savior) and Lord!

Stanza Two: This stanza, which, incidentally, is not easy to sing and is omitted from most hymnals, is clearly a reflection of the Nicene Creed, which reads, almost identically, "God of God; Light of Light; Very God of

Very God; Begotten, not made," and does not lend itself to much of spiritual warmth or devotion. The phrase "Lo, he abhors not the Virgin's womb" may have been included to answer the charge made originally by the Docetics, that Jesus only seemed to be human, that He really was not so. That idea, thoroughly rejected by the early church councils, was promulgated because of a false view of the human body, that the body in and of itself was evil, and as such could not have "housed" the pure and perfect God! Biblical creation was good—in all of its aspects; therefore since God Himself had made "male and female" and had pronounced them "very good" (Genesis 1:27, 31), the flesh should not be looked upon as evil, or even as an "unworthy" vehicle for God's incarnation. Thus again we are called upon to adore Him, Very God of Very God!

Stanza Three: Here, added to the choirs of angels who are to sing His praises exultantly, are all the citizens of heaven—the human believers, including those martyred for their faith; giving thus glory to God, they join us in our adoration, which again focuses on Christ—the Messiah, our Lord.

Stanza Four: Here the author exhorts all of us collectively to address the Lord directly and to greet Him, "born this happy morning"—on Christmas "Day"—as Jesus, Savior, the Incarnate Word of God, who has finally come to be among us. The phrase "late in flesh appearing" is often translated "late in time appearing," which may reflect the fact that His people, Israel, anxiously awaited His coming for centuries; then, of course, even after He had come, most of them refused to recognize who He was! Again, we are to ascribe all glory, honor, and blessing to Him, adoring Him as Lord!

The way He is designated is striking: King of angels (vs. 1), God of God, Light of Light, Very God (vs. 2), God (vs. 3), Lord, Jesus, Word of the Father (vs. 4), and Christ, the Lord (chorus). Where else in a hymn of similar length, or even longer, could one find so many exalted titles, names, and descriptions of that "Infant lowly," born that night in a Bethlehem cattle-shed? It is appropriate, indeed, that we come and adore Him! Bailey's comment is to the point:

> This is all so simple, so vivid in imagery, so sincere in emotion, that [except for] a few theological phrases, a child can understand it and enter sympathetically into the experience of worship and joy.[20]

Notes

1. Bailey, *op. cit.,* p. 279.
2. Marks, *op. cit.,* p. 44.
3. Haeussler, *op. cit.,* p. 166.

4. Julian, *op. cit.*, p. 20.

5. Yeats-Edwards, *op. cit.*, p. 151.

6. Covert and Laufer, *op. cit.*, pp. 133–134.

7. Bailey, *op. cit.*, p. 279.

8. Haeussler, *op. cit.*, pp. 166–167.

9. Covert and Laufer, *op. cit.*, p. 134.

10. Julian, *op. cit.*, pp. 20–22.

11. *Ibid.*, p. 21.

12. *Ibid.*, pp. 20–21.

13. *Ibid.*, p. 855.

14. Haeussler, *op. cit.*, pp. 829–830.

15. Moffatt and Patrick, *op. cit.*, p. 450.

16. Julian, *op. cit.*, p. 855.

17. Haeussler, *op. cit.*, p. 870.

18. McCutchan, *Our Hymnody*, p. 131.

19. Covert and Laufer, *op. cit.*, p. 133.

20. Bailey, *op. cit.*, p. 279.

Title/Date	*"Onward, Christian Soldiers..."* *(1865)*
Author	*Sabine Baring-Gould*
Composer/Tune	*Sir Arthur Sullivan "St. Gertrude"* *(1871)*
Scriptural Basis	*Matthew 16:18; Revelation 11:15; 12:10*

Recently a major Protestant denomination decided to leave this and several other hymns with similar "bellicose" themes out of its proposed new hymnal on the general grounds that the idea of fighting and warfare should not be encouraged and does not belong in a hymnal dedicated to the peaceful solution to the problems of humanity. But this "military" image, though scorned by some, has been understood more broadly in the sense of the supernatural warfare in which each of us as Christians has been called to participate; this is the thrust of St. Paul's counsel regarding spiritual warfare, and the whole armor of God in his letter to the Ephesians (6:10–20). In this vein one author writes:

> This hymn will live . . . because it transfigures the warring spirit . . . [for] the victories of peace cannot be won save by a heroism and sacrifice surpassing that of soldiers forced to fight . . . These . . . words can be transformed, as under . . . Paul's inspired pen the ancient soldier's equipment became . . . the whole armor of God. And if marching soldiers, intoxicated by martial music, go forth with passion to their cruel task, how much more should Christian soldiers, their feet "shod . . . with the preparation of the gospel of peace" march to the noblest and most inspiring of all militant rhythms.[1]

Actually, this popular children's hymn was originally written for the parish children of Horbury Bridge, in Yorkshire, England, by their young curate, Sabine Baring-Gould (1834–1924), to sing as they marched to the neighboring village as part of a school festival. Baring-Gould, whose grandfather was an English admiral and whose aristocratic family had owned a huge estate for over three centuries, was

I will build my church; and the gates of hell shall not prevail against it. Matt. 16:18

ST. GERTRUDE 6. 5. 6. 5. D. with refrain
Sabine Baring-Gould, 1865
Sir Arthur S. Sullivan, 1871

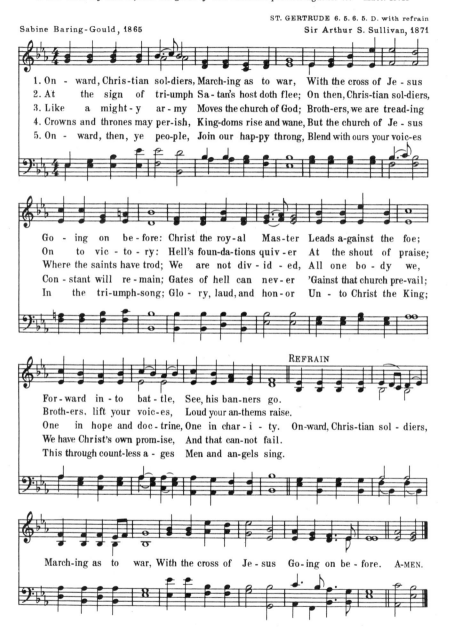

1. On - ward, Chris-tian sol-diers, March-ing as to war, With the cross of Je - sus
2. At the sign of tri-umph Sa - tan's host doth flee; On then, Chris-tian sol-diers,
3. Like a might - y ar - my Moves the church of God; Broth-ers, we are tread-ing
4. Crowns and thrones may per-ish, King-doms rise and wane, But the church of Je - sus
5. On - ward, then, ye peo-ple, Join our hap-py throng, Blend with ours your voic-es

Go - ing on be - fore: Christ the roy-al Mas-ter Leads a-gainst the foe;
On to vic - to - ry: Hell's foun-da-tions quiv-er At the shout of praise;
Where the saints have trod; We are not div - id - ed, All one bo - dy we,
Con - stant will re - main; Gates of hell can nev-er 'Gainst that church pre-vail;
In the tri-umph-song; Glo - ry, laud, and hon-or Un - to Christ the King;

REFRAIN

For - ward in - to bat - tle, See, his ban-ners go.
Broth-ers, lift your voic-es, Loud your an-thems raise.
One in hope and doc-trine, One in char-i - ty. On-ward, Chris-tian sol - diers,
We have Christ's own prom-ise, And that can-not fail.
This through count-less a - ges Men and an-gels sing.

March-ing as to war, With the cross of Je - sus Go-ing on be - fore. A-MEN.

one of the most versatile, energetic and industrious of all modern Englishmen; a clergyman, lord of the family manor, prose and fiction writer,
poet, composer of hymn texts and tunes, editor and translator![2]

Although much of his early schooling was in France and Germany, he received both his B.A. and M.A. from Cambridge University; in 1864, he took Holy Orders and secured his first appointment at Horbury, a small mining and factory town whose people had long been neglected spiritually, "even by the dissenters"![3] Throwing himself into his work, he rented a small two-room apartment, which he used for night-school classes that met every evening and for Sunday worship services. Soon the congregation, a motley crowd, was bulging out the walls; their singing left much room for improvement, and their deportment was anything but aristocratic! But he persevered, and had the assistance of a huge wool-comber who would meet rowdies

> at the door, and cracking a couple of walnuts in his fist, he'd bellow at them "if you don't take care and be peaceable, I'll crack your heads like I did these here walnuts."[4]

One other event in Horbury deserves mention; during one of the frequent floods of the Calder, he saved Grace Taylor, a beautiful young mill-worker of excellent character; he fell in love with her and, obtaining her parents' permission, sent her to be educated at a school in York, and then married her in 1868, shortly after he had been transferred to another parish. Deeply devoted to each other, their marriage of close to fifty years was ideally happy; they had fifteen children. Toward the end of Grace's life she became crippled and was under constant medical care; on her tombstone he had inscribed "Dimidim Animae Meae"—here is "Half of my Soul."[5]

In 1872, upon the death of his father, he became the Lord of Lew-Trenchard, the family estate, and a few years later, the rector of its parish church; while its income was negligible, the opportunity to preach regularly and to guide the spiritual development of its three hundred souls challenged him, and he served them faithfully. A diligent and tireless man, he published some ninety-three books on a wide variety of subjects, including religion, travel, folklore, mythology, history, fiction, and sermons; he also edited a quarterly review of ecclesiastical literature and art, wrote hymns, and composed several hymn tunes, one of which, "Eudoxia," is still used. He also collected folksongs and translated Danish hymns and Walloon carols. He was truly a man of wide interests and gifts. Of his literary output, his *Lives of the Saints* (15 volumes), *Study of St. Paul, The Book of Were-Wolves,* and his folk song collections were widely used for many decades, and the latter was an influence on the eminent folk song researcher, Cecil H. Sharpe.[6] It is claimed that he was

> probably the most prolific of all English authors, the literary catalogue of the British Museum listing more titles by him than by any other British writer of his time.[7]

As a deeply religious man, whose High Church views were sometimes stated rather bluntly, he was widely loved and respected; when queried as to how he managed to accomplish so much, he said,

> My secret is simply that I stick to a task when I begin it. . . . It would never do to wait from day to day for some moments which might seem favorable for work![8]

In other words, his success was "ten percent inspiration and ninety percent perspiration!"

But for all this enormous literary output, he is chiefly remembered for two of his hymns, the gentle "Now the Day Is Over" (*Trinity Hymnal,* p. 666) and this robust one, which owes at least some of its popularity to Sir Arthur Sullivan's stirring tune, "St. Gertrude," which he wrote expressly for it, as it was to be included in *The Hymnary* in 1872. Sullivan dedicated this to his friend and hostess, Gertrude Clay-Ker-Seymer; regarding its composition she wrote:

> I believe it was written at Hanford, my home in Dorsetshire while Sir Arthur was staying there. . . . I do remember . . . that we sang it in the private chapel attached to the house, [he] playing the harmonium, and taught us the tune as we had not the music. . . . I am proud to be the sponsor of this tune which now has a world-wide reputation.[9]

Sir Arthur Sullivan (1842–1900), D.Mus., was a musical child prodigy who, by the age of eight, could play practically every kind of wind instrument and had composed "By the Waters of Babylon"; winning a place in the Chapel Royal, he counted among his teachers the eminent choirmaster, Thomas Helmore; he attracted notice with his anthem "O Israel," composed at age thirteen; and at age fourteen he won the Mendelssohn Scholarship at the Royal Academy of Music, where he studied under superb musicians, including Sir John Goss. These studies took him next to Leipzig, where he decided on music composition as his life's work; he recounts:

> I was ready to undertake everything that came in my way. Symphonic overtures, ballets, anthems, hymn tunes, part-songs and eventually comic and light operas—nothing came amiss to me.[10]
>
> [And of the fact that he excelled in each of these fields another writes,] The reason for his success is not far to seek, for he was essentially a master of melody, with a genius for orchestration.[11]

For Sullivan "music was bound up with daily life and was a necessity of existence";[12] thus he poured his energies into composing, and while he is best known for his popular, comic operas, including the "H.M.S. Pinafore," done in collaboration with Sir W. S. Gilbert, he was and wanted to be considered a serious musician. As such, he composed seven oratorios, including "The Prodigal Son" and "The Light of the World," his famous "The Lost Chord," and many cantatas, anthems, and symphonic pieces. He also excelled as an organist, winning the post at St. Michael's over stiff competition; and he composed hymn tunes, some twenty-six in all, the last one for the Queen's Diamond Jubilee in 1897. His tunes "are characterized by sturdy, diatonic harmony and a smooth melodiousness, which make them most singable."[13] For his magnificent achievements, he was knighted in 1883 by Queen Victoria; and upon his early death at only fifty-eight, he was buried in St. Paul's Cathedral.

As I indicated earlier, Baring-Gould was wont to state his firmly held opinions rather strongly on occasion; in one instance a bishop, who did not favor the choir processional as a liturgical form, refused to begin the service until they put aside their processional cross; they apparently retaliated by singing the lines

> Onward Christian soldiers, marching as to war
> With the Cross of Jesus LEFT BEHIND THE DOOR![14]

Moreover, one stanza of his original six is rarely, if ever, included in the hymnals; his strong views that the apostolic message would always find acceptance in his own Communion are apparently behind these lines:

> What the saints established, that I hold for true,
> What the saints believed, that believe I too;
> Long as earth endureth, men that faith will hold,
> Kingdoms, nations, empires in destruction rolled.[15]

While we who hold to the apostolic faith, by the grace of God and in a humble spirit, can surely agree with Baring-Gould, it is obvious that many would agree with Bailey, that the "theological revolution going on at that time was destined to reinterpret or supplant many of the tenets he believed";[16] at least they were honest enough not to sing what they did not believe. May we believe the truth—the "old old story"—and sing it, with much conviction!

Before we examine the hymn, let us ponder an incident Temple describes as taking place on August 10, 1941, on the British battleship, the *Prince of Wales,* at anchor in Newfoundland. With both Winston Churchill and Franklin Delano Roosevelt on deck, there was a service held, which included the singing of "Eternal Father, Strong to Save," "Our God, Our Help in Ages Past," and "Onward, Christian Soldiers." Then they signed the Atlantic Charter; later Churchill told his people:

> We sang "Onward Christian Soldiers" and indeed I felt that this was no vain presumption but that we had the right to feel we were serving a cause for the sake of which a trumpet had sounded from on high. When I looked upon that densely packed congregation of fighting men of the same language, of the same faith, of the same fundamental laws, of the same ideals . . . it swept across me that here was the only hope, but also the sure hope, of saving the world from measureless degradation.[17]

Stanza One: There is no doubt that this hymn, from the first stanza to the last, has an optimistic spirit, fed and sustained by his deep convictions, based upon the Scriptures and focused in the Matthean text, "I *will* build My Church, and the gates of hell will *not* prevail against it!" (Matthew 16:18). With that confidence, he can exhort us, soldiers in the Lord's employ, to move into battle with our divine General leading the charge and His cross our standard. May he not have had Constantine in mind here, who was allegedly given a vision of a cross and told "in this sign, conquer"—and whose subsequent victory led to the "Christianizing" of the entire Roman Empire!

Stanza Two: Again, the images are vivid; here spiritual hosts are the fleeing enemies, rather than human armies; both Satan, the deceiver of men, and the foundations of hell are not only challenged by the Christians as an "army," but will be bested; another biblical incident that comes to mind is Joshua's capture of Jericho, where the city's walls quivered and then collapsed "at the shout of praise" (Joshua 6:20).

Stanza Three: Note here the simile "like," even as the simile "as" occurs elsewhere; the reminder of history is emphasized: we are walking in the way earlier believers have walked. The next sentence "We are not divided, all one body we" was changed by the editors of *Hymns Ancient and Modern* (1868) to read "Though divisions harass," emphasizing the fact that the body of Christ is divided by many matters major and minor, doctrinal, methodological, and ecclesiastical; and Baring-Gould was not ignorant of these, for he himself had written:

> How is it that England teems with sects? Simply because the Established Church does not meet every religious [need] of Christians. . . . True wisdom would seek to make her bands elastic, and vary her methods to embrace and to satisfy all, and not seek to stamp and stiffen and solidify her, as the martyr Geronimo was kneaded into a bed of concrete! Much better to endow the Church of England with centripetal than with centrifugal

force; allow both . . . objective worship and subjective mysticism; give to those who lack on either side with full hand, instead of measuring to each in grudged pinches.[18]

But there are at least two other ways this can be understood rather than as glossing over our "scandalous division"; it may be that the author, who himself never dreamed that it would have such wide appeal outside his little village, simply intended to express the truth that two groups of little children, who had been taught in common the Apostles' Creed, the Catechism, and other similar truths were now "one body," marching to their "mother-church on the hill."[19] Or, it may seek to reflect a truth that this author has experienced in his own multidimensional ministry of over thirty-five years, that there *is* much unity and commonality of hope, doctrine, and love among all who are committed to Christ—the Nicene "God of Gods . . . ," the Scripture as the fully inspired and authoritative Word of God, and the church as, essentially, the worldwide and age-old body of believers—those who have been "washed in the blood of the Lamb" and who "love the Lord Jesus in sincerity and truth." We—whatever our labels, sexes, ages, racial origins, economic statuses, educational attainments, social graces, heights, weights, whatever—are ONE BODY!

Stanza Four: The fleeting nature of human conquest, organizations, ruling houses is contrasted here, and rightly shown to be impermanent when compared with the great church of Jesus Christ; again, he now makes explicit the Matthean text, to which we can all respond with a hearty Amen! But constant doesn't mean static or boring; the church of Jesus faces new challenges each day, and around every corner of human experience, so she must be "ever Reformed, ever reforming"!

Stanza Five: Here is an invitation to all of us to join the children in their march; as children always are when "on a holiday" from their usual routines, they are here described as "a happy throng"; again, the note of victory is emphasized, and the call to praise is urged: "Glory, laud, and honor," to the Christ who is the King, not only of humanity but also throughout the ages! This is indeed a stirring series of convictions, and a tune that conveys the same thrust, musically; no wonder it is one of the favorites of children, once they learn it.

Finally, let me cite an incident mentioned by Harvey Marks that happened in his ministry. Giving a series of Lenten services in a church in Rhode Island, he shared the story of this hymn; at the end of the evening an elderly lady stepped up and told him that she had known Sabine Baring-Gould, for she was one of those children who had marched in that procession![20]

Notes

1. Covert and Laufer, *op. cit.,* p. 385.
2. Haeussler, *op. cit.,* p. 542.
3. Bailey, *op. cit.,* p. 370.
4. *Ibid.,* p. 372.
5. Haeussler, *op. cit.,* p. 542.
6. McCutchan, *Our Hymnody,* p. 82.
7. Haeussler, *op. cit.,* p. 542.
8. Smith, *Lyric Religion,* p. 330.
9. McCutchan, *op. cit.,* p. 316.
10. Haeussler, *op. cit.,* p. 928.
11. *Ibid.*
12. Smith, *op. cit.,* p. 331.
13. Haeussler, *op. cit.,* p. 929.
14. Ellinwood, *op. cit.,* p. 85.
15. Bailey, *op. cit.,* p. 373.
16. *Ibid.*
17. Temple, *op. cit.,* pp. 155–156.
18. Smith, *op. cit.,* p. 331.
19. Bailey, *op. cit.,* p. 373.
20. Marks, *op. cit.,* p. 171.

Title/Date	*"The Church's One Foundation" (1866)*
Author	*Samuel Stone*
Composer/Tune	*Samuel Sebastian Wesley "Aurelia" (1864)*
Scriptural Basis	*Ephesians 1:22–23; 2:19–20; 4:4–6*

As we have seen in our previous studies, hymn-writers and hymn tune-composers have come from a large variety of interesting backgrounds, differing economic and social strata, wide-ranging ecclesiastical perspectives, and varied personal spiritual convictions—all of which have molded their hymnody in delightful as well as in profound ways. And this magnificent hymn is no exception, owing to the colorful lives and deeply held convictions of both its writer and its tune's composer.

Whenever theological heresy raises its banner, there are always those who are quick to condemn the heretic and those who are equally quick to defend his right to "freedom of thought and expression"—which often really means that he should not be bound by the confessional standards of his church, the standards he pledged to teach and uphold at the time he took his ordination vows. This hymn was written in such a context.

In 1863,[1] Anglican Bishop John Colenso, of Natal, South Africa, published a book in which he espoused the rationalistic views of the higher critics, including a denial of the historical accuracy and reliability of the Pentateuch. Nearly every Anglican bishop called on him to resign, since his views clearly opposed those of his Communion. When he refused, he was tried for heresy, condemned, deposed, and prohibited from exercising any divine office; he disregarded the sentence and was excommunicated, but appealed to the Crown and had his case considered by the Privy Council's judicial commission—even though it was a theological issue. The entire sequence of events distressed the Church and created schism, with people choosing up sides as though watching a rugby match!

Among those who were so troubled was Samuel J. Stone (1839–1900), who was a curate at Windsor, a mission chapel on the outskirts of the town, where he worked among the poorer classes of the people. In fact, while one of his concerns in writing this and his other hymns was to champion the apostolic faith—which he does, admirably, in his hymns[2]—he also had

Jesus Christ himself being the chief corner stone. Eph. 2:20

AURELIA 7. 6. 7. 6. D.

Samuel J. Stone, 1866

Samuel S. Wesley, 1864

1. The church-'s one Foun - da - tion Is Je - sus Christ her Lord;
2. E - lect from ev - 'ry na - tion, Yet one o'er all the earth,
3. Though with a scorn-ful won - der Men see her sore op - pressed,
4. The church shall nev - er per - ish! Her dear Lord to de - fend,
5. 'Mid toil and trib - u - la - tion, And tu - mult of her war,
6. Yet she on earth hath u - nion With God the Three in One,

She is his new cre - a - tion By wa - ter and the Word:
Her char - ter of sal - va - tion One Lord, one faith, one birth;
By schi - sms rent as - un - der, By her - e - sies dis - tressed,
To guide, sus - tain and cher - ish, Is with her to the end;
She waits the con - sum - ma - tion Of peace for ev - er - more;
And mys - tic sweet com - mun - ion With those whose rest is won:

From heav'n he came and sought her To be his ho - ly bride;
One ho - ly Name she bless - es, Par - takes one ho - ly food,
Yet saints their watch are keep - ing, Their cry goes up, "How long?"
Though there be those that hate her, And false sons in her pale,
Till with the vi - sion glo - rious Her long - ing eyes are blest,
O hap - py ones and ho - ly! Lord, give us grace that we,

With his own blood he bought her, And for her life he died.
And to one hope she press - es, With ev - 'ry grace en - dued.
And soon the night of weep - ing Shall be the morn of song.
A - gainst or foe or trait - or She ev - er shall pre - vail.
And the great church vic - to - rious Shall be the church at rest.
Like them, the meek and low - ly, On high may dwell with thee. A - MEN.

observed that his parishioners, faithful in their use of the Creed in their devotions and prayers, had nonetheless, little understanding of its meaning. So
his goal was twofold: to teach them what the Creed meant, in common, vigorous language they could grasp, and to "assist Bishop Gray in his steadfast
defense of the Faith against the heresies of Colenso."[3] In its original form,
this hymn had seven stanzas and was an exposition of the ninth article of the
Apostles' Creed, affirming belief in the "Holy Catholic Church";[4] actually,
Stone wrote twelve hymns in all, expounding the various statements of that
Creed, and published them in 1866 as *Lyra Fidelium,* which he designed for
use in either private devotions or public worship. Of that series this is the
only one that is still universally sung. Julian says that his hymns

> vary considerably in metre and subject, presenting a pleasing variety. . . .
> His best [ones] are well designed and clearly expressed, their tone . . .
> hopeful, [with] a masterly condensation of Scripture facts and church
> teaching given tersely and with great vigor. . . . His rhythm . . . is rarely
> at fault, and his rhyme is usually perfect. While some of his hymns are
> plaintive . . . the greater part are strongly outspoken utterances of a manly
> faith, where dogma, prayer and praise are interwoven with much skill.
> Usually the key-note of his song is Hope.[5]

Stone, who was early educated at the Charterhouse, earned both a B.A.
and an M.A. from Oxford University, where he distinguished himself in ath-
letics, captaining his college's crew, and intending upon graduation to enter
military service. However, a persistent call to the ministry finally prevailed,
and he took Holy Orders in 1862, followed by eight years of service in the
aforementioned poor parish at Windsor, where he wrote his now-famous
hymn. In 1870, he joined his father at St. Paul's Haggerston, a poor East End
parish in London, which had no school, no church, and no vicarage, but
which they developed into "a fully-equipped, well-cultivated and fruitful
field"[6] during his twenty years of service there.

Samuel was an interesting study in contrasts: on the one hand a fine poet,
with several published volumes, he was described as

> emotional, excitable, with an active brain and a tender heart; a churchman
> rather than a missionary, a shepherd rather than an evangelist, with St.
> Paul's church the door of the sheepfold.[7]

But he was also described as having "the muscles of a prize-fighter," and on
one occasion, at least, he put them to good use! Seeing three hoodlums at-
tacking a poor girl walking alone, he rushed to her defense, knocked out the
first man with one blow, trounced the second until he begged for mercy, and

regretted that the third ran off before he could dispose of him, too; later he told a friend he'd learned to use his fists at Charterhouse, and thanked God for the "lessons"![8] His muscles got further use as he used a tricycle to make his pastoral calls, and won the parish with both his vigor and his kindly pastoral concern for each of his charges. Of him his biographer writes, with perhaps a touch of overstatement,

> So brave of heart was he as to make possible for us the courage of a Coeur de Lion, so knightly of nature as to make possible the honor of an Arthur or a Galahad, so nearly stainless in the standard he set himself, and in the standard he attained as to come . . . almost to making possible the purity of the Christ.[9]

His last parish, which he served for some ten years until his death, was All Hallows, London, an "inner-city" area of businesses and offices, teeming with ten thousand people by day, but nearly abandoned by night. Seeing an opportunity for ministry here, he had the old church building renovated— largely at his own expense—and opened it at 6:30 A.M. as a place of rest, comfort, and meditation for the office workers and factory girls who rode the early, cheap trains in from their homes;[10] here they could attend services, read, sew, or just relax until time for their work to begin—a kind gesture, much appreciated by all involved. Worn out from his energetic labors, he died at age sixty-one, beloved and greatly mourned by his largely commuter flock.

"Aurelia," the tune that has become inseparably wedded to this fine hymn, was originally composed for a wedding hymn written by John Keble; it was also associated with "Jerusalem the Golden," whence its name, meaning "golden";[11] but it came into its own when it appeared as the setting for this hymn in the Appendix to *Hymns Ancient and Modern* in 1868. Some years later it was sung in St. Paul's Cathedral at a service of thanksgiving for the recovery of the Prince of Wales from a serious illness. Henry John Gauntlett wrote an article in *The Choir* criticizing it as "inartistic, not fulfilling the conditions of a hymn-tune" and as "secular twaddle";[12] it remained unscathed, however, and its great popularity shows that his judgment has not been accepted by posterity!

Samuel Sebastian Wesley (1810–1876), its composer, has been the subject of an earlier study. Regarded by some as the "Anglican composer par excellence" and recognized as an exceptionally fine organist, serving five parish churches and four cathedrals over a span of fifty years, he was a fine extemporizer; of this ability one in attendance wrote:

> Dr. Wesley played on the great organ, beginning with a long fantasia, in the course of which almost every effect [possible] on this enormous instrument

was developed by [his] masterful skill. Most interesting was the enormous fugue, extemporaneous, with which it concluded . . . [his] performance was greeted with uproarious applause. Even while he was playing, orchestra and chorus crowded around the organ, anxious to obtain a view of his flying fingers and feet.[13]

He had been called a "colorful personality," and he indeed was; an avid fisherman, he at one time was close to resigning as organist at Leeds for a church in Tavistock, knowing of the reputation of the Tavy for fine fishing![14] But this may have helped him maintain his sanity at a time when the standards for church music were at a low ebb in England; he was constantly irritated by—and probably an irritant to—those who could have made positive changes, and financed them, but who wouldn't; their lack of interest and sympathy, coupled with the inadequacy of facilities, frustrated him, and would have stifled his growth in musicianship, had he allowed it to do so, but he did not. For

> he was true to his ideals, and those who knew him well could not fail to appreciate his idealism, and his kindness and sympathy in spite of his reserved, retiring—and at times, even eccentric manner.[15]

And it was his ability to combine in his hymn tunes ease of singing and churchly dignity that enabled his musical contributions to be an uplifting factor in the music sung by the masses of Englishmen, both in his day and in ongoing eras.

Now let us examine this hymn—"whose tune is tops in melody, stride, and infectious musical charm"[16]—chosen for use as the processional at the services held at three of England's greatest cathedrals, Canterbury, Westminster, and St. Paul's in 1888, for the Lambeth Conference, the gathering of the leaders of the worldwide Anglican Communion; so profoundly was New Zealand's Bishop Nelson affected by these stirring words and its martial tune that he paid their author this tribute:

> Bard of the Church, in these divided days
> For words of harmony to thee be praise;
> Of love and oneness thou dost strike the chords,
> And set our thoughts and prayers to tuneful words.
> The Church's one Foundation thou didst sing,
> Beauty and Bands to her thy numbers bring.
> Through church and chancel, aisle and transept deep,
> In fullest melody thy watch-notes sweep;
> Now in the desert, now upon the main,
> In mine and forest, and on cited plain;

From Lambeth towers to far New Zealand's coast
Bard of the Church, thy blast inspires the host.[17]

And inspire the host he has, for this hymn is used worldwide; Archbishop Temple once commented that in every country parish he ever visited he could be sure of two things: "cold chicken and 'The Church's One Foundation'—and both had merits almost above criticism"![18]

Stanza One: Stone begins his description of the church at the beginning—with her divine origin. She is founded on Jesus the Christ; created by Him, by the water of baptism (the symbol of cleansing from sin) and by the Word (His creative Word that originally called the world into being and now calls Her into being as well, when believers respond to that preached Word and receive it by faith). Moreover, she is His bride, bought by the precious blood He shed, as the bride-price(?), and given life through His willing death in her behalf! (See I Corinthians 3:11 and Ephesians 5:26–27.)

Stanza Two: Here we are reminded of the universality of the church ("elect from every nation") as well as of its unity ("yet one . . ."); salvation is dependent upon, but also guaranteed by, chartered by, one Lord—Jesus Christ, the Jehovah of the Old Testament dispensation; one faith—faith that works through love, faith without which it is impossible to please Him"; one birth—new birth, which occurs from above, by the power of God's grace; one Holy Name—the Name of Jesus, is blessed; one holy food—the "bread of the world, in mercy broken," the manna from on high, freely given to all who receive it in a humble, thankful spirit; one hope—the hope of eternal life, "the blessed hope, and glorious appearing of our great God, and the Father of Jesus Christ," a hope to which His people ever do rightly aspire! (See I Peter 1:1–2; Ephesians 4:4–5; Philippians 2:10; II Corinthians 9:8.)

Stanza Three: This is the most frequently omitted stanza, speaking frankly as it does of the schisms of Stone's day; Routley comments that "it is a brave verse, which few modern editors dare print in their hymnals, for it states the fact of schism, and calls the Church to repentance."[19] For there is an orthodox theology, and heresies, promulgated by whatever name or in whatever guise, are still heresies; the skeptics and the enemies of the truth do scorn the church and her stance on orthodox doctrine; but the believers, distressed by such disloyalty to truth and to her confessions, watch, and pray, and weep, for schism does threaten to rip her heart out and hold her up as a laughingstock! Again, Routley observes,

> The seeds of [schism] which is wholly displeasing to God . . . are not organizational difficulties or technical disputes, but the ancient sins to which all men are heirs: pride, wrath, greed, fear of the truth, fear of losing face, self-love,[20] much of which sin is deliberate sin!

But schism is not the winner, for the truth will be held inviolate by some and the song of those who ever champion the truth will continue to be sung, with every breath—including the last—that they take! (See II Peter 2:1; Luke 12:37; Revelation 6:10.)

Stanza Four: Again we are reminded, that for all our loyalty to the truth and for all our courage we cannot take the credit; no, for our Lord Jesus, who is Truth Incarnate ("I AM THE . . . TRUTH"), will continue to defend, sustain, guide, and cherish us, and we as the church will never be destroyed, nor shall the "gates of hell ever prevail against us"! Wounded as we may be by false sons in our midst—even "familiar friends, with whom we walked God's pleasant paths"—we need not fear even these, for they, foes and traitors alike, shall also eventually be the losers.

Stanza Five: But heresy and schism are not the church's only enemies; she also faces toil, just plain hard work, in a myriad of ways; and she faces tribulation, with all the noise and clamor of warfare, physical and spiritual! But the day will come when the guns have been silenced and the weapons laid down—or better yet, beaten into pruning-hooks—and peace, with its attendant restfulness, will be accomplished. Then the Church Militant, necessary now in this sin-cursed world, will be the Church Triumphant, and the Beatific Vision will be the common possession of all who wait upon Him—for "blessed are the pure in heart, for they shall see God"! (See Revelation 7:14.)

Stanza Six: Here Stone reaffirms the apostolic truth that the true body of Christ is not rent asunder by schism; rather, believers on earth are united to their glorious Head, and so "have union with the Triune God"; moreover, they have communion with "all those who have gone on ahead of them"—who "rest from their labors, and whose works do follow them." Now comes the concluding prayer. From affirmation about God to seeking Him, from the objective to the subjective; so we do ask that "we may dwell with Thee," on High—in Thy presence, "with these our brothers and sisters who even now behold Thy face in unbroken light, in unclouded day"! And that surely is the reason why they are "happy and holy, meek and lowly"—who wouldn't be, in such glorious circumstances and such precious company as that!

Truly this is a magnificent hymn, as Julian said so long ago!

Notes

1. Bailey, *op. cit.,* p. 378.
2. Julian, *op. cit.,* p. 1096.
3. Smith, *Lyric Religion,* p. 384.
4. Covert and Laufer, *op. cit.,* p. 354.

5. Julian, *op. cit.*, p. 1096.
6. Moffatt and Patrick, *op. cit.*, p. 510.
7. Smith, *op. cit.*, pp. 382–383.
8. *Ibid.*, p. 383.
9. *Ibid.*
10. Bailey, *op. cit.*, p. 376.
11. Haeussler, *op. cit.*, p. 360.
12. Lightwood, *op. cit.*, p. 401.
13. Haeussler, *op. cit.*, p. 977.
14. *Ibid.*, p. 976.
15. McCutchan, *Our Hymnody*, p. 349.
16. Smith, *op. cit.*, p. 385.
17. McCutchan, *op. cit.*, pp. 400–401.
18. Smith, *op. cit.*, p. 385.
19. Routley, *Hymns and the Faith*, p. 244.
20. *Ibid.*, p. 245.

Title/Date	*"There Is a Green Hill Far Away..."* *(1848)*
Author	*Cecil Frances Alexander*
Composer/Tune	*John H. Gower "Meditation" (1890)*
Scriptural Basis	*Hebrews 13:12–13; John 19:17; Romans 5:8*

Is it an accident of arrangement or is it possibly providential that this hymn, regarded by the French composer Charles Gounod as "the most perfect hymn in the English language—a hymn which set itself to music,"[1] was also written as an exposition of one of the phrases in the Apostles' Creed, as was our previous hymn by Samuel John Stone? And the similarity does not end there, for Cecil Frances Alexander (1823–1895), its author, whose early years were spent in the Evangelical wing of the Anglican Church and whose heart was warmed by a deeply devotional life, became greatly interested in the Oxford Movement[2] and was profoundly influenced by John Keble's illustrious *Christian Year*. In fact, Miss Humphreys (her maiden name), who had written creditable poetry while still a child and as a young woman had become actively involved in the Christian education of children, had written and published her first book of hymns and verses—*Verses for Holy Seasons*—which was intended to explain the teaching of the Creed and the Prayer Book, in 1846, and had modeled this on Keble's work.[3] Two years later, in 1848, came her *Hymns for Little Children*,[4] for which John Keble himself had written the Preface; this work contained three of her best-known children's hymns—"There Is a Green Hill Far Away," "Once in David's Royal City," and "All Things Bright and Beautiful"—hymns that not only charm and instruct children, but also have "the power to speak to the child in the heart of a man."[5] Julian's high estimate of her hymns is clear:

> They are charmingly simple and tender, clear in dogma, and of poetic beauty, combining the plainness of Watts with the feeling for childhood of Jane Taylor, and uniting with both the liturgical associations of the English Prayer Book, they remain unequalled and unapproachable.[6]

*Jesus . . . suffered without the gate. Let us go forth therefore
unto him without the camp, bearing his reproach.* Heb. 13:12-13

MEDITATION C. M.

Cecil Frances Alexander, 1848

John H. Gower, 1890

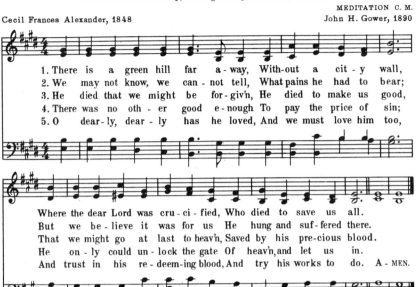

1. There is a green hill far a-way, With-out a cit-y wall,
2. We may not know, we can-not tell, What pains he had to bear;
3. He died that we might be for-giv'n, He died to make us good,
4. There was no oth-er good e-nough To pay the price of sin;
5. O dear-ly, dear-ly has he loved, And we must love him too,

Where the dear Lord was cru-ci-fied, Who died to save us all.
But we be-lieve it was for us He hung and suf-fered there.
That we might go at last to heav'n, Saved by his pre-cious blood.
He on-ly could un-lock the gate Of heav'n, and let us in.
And trust in his re-deem-ing blood, And try his works to do. A-MEN.

And another has noted that "few women of her time understood the psychology of childhood as well as she,"[7] which may in part account for the little short of phenomenal reception many of her over four hundred hymns received; in fact, *Hymns for Little Children* passed through sixty-nine editions before the end of the nineteenth century![8]

Born in Ireland, daughter of a distinguished major in the Royal Marines, she published many volumes, and her works include poetry and devotional writings as well as hymns; her greatest poem, "The Burial of Moses," was elegant enough for Alfred Lord Tennyson to exclaim: "I wish I might have been its author."[9] When in her mid-twenties she married a brilliant, devout, and capable young clergyman, William Alexander, an Oxford graduate and a fine poet in his own right,[10] and it proved to be an excellent match, a happy union—productive for God and the church for some forty-five years. Louis Benson describes her, appreciatively:

She was admirably fitted to be a pastor's wife. She was [never] the dreamy, ineffectual . . . poet . . . never posed, detested gush and sentimentality, had a direct tongue and decisive speech, . . . and a vigilant eye for [their] home, garden and farm. Keeping her devotional life largely hidden in her heart, she was a strict "Prayer Book Christian," worshipping daily and

communing weekly. Beyond that her days were given over to errands of
charity and helpfulness, going from one poor Irish home to another, from
one sick-bed to another, from one house of sorrow to another, no matter
how remote. She knew and loved all her neighbors. When her husband
became Bishop of Derry and Raphoe in 1867, and she was brought more
into contact with society and large institutions, she became the hostess of
many distinguished people, and shared her husband's publicity. But she was
ever as much at home in the back streets of Londonderry as in the Bishop's
Palace. It was in the Palace she died, and for her funeral a great throng
gathered, from England as well as from Ireland, paying a spontaneous tribute to her noble life.[11]

The author is reminded of the portrait of the noble and worthy life in
Proverbs 31:10–31: "The heart of her husband does safely trust in her, and
she does him good, and not evil, all the days of her life"! Moreover, he also
had many words of commendation for her; in 1896, the year after her death,
he was elected Archbishop of Armagh and Primate of all Ireland; he described her and their early years together as they shared their ministry with
some fifteen hundred persons, scattered widely over the bogs and mountains:

> Her elastic step brushed the heath in all weathers and not seldom she
> walked several miles to meet [me] returning from some distant [trip]; she
> was intensely practical and devoted to all the minutiae of our garden and
> farm; often have I said upon returning something of this sort: "Have you
> sold the cow? Have you shown the gardener how to prune the roses? Have
> you given orders to feed the pigs properly? Have you finished that poem?
> Yes? Then let us come into the study. Read me what you have written,
> and I will criticize it ferociously!"[12]

Moreover, he goes on to tell us of her aversion to publicity, and even to
praise for her poetic efforts; possibly the only poet who has ever lived that
really did not like to hear her poems praised, her husband says,

> Again and again I have read to her words of lofty, almost impassioned
> commendation from men of genius or holiness, or rank and position. She
> listens without a remark and looks up with a frown.[13]

The one exception was when he read her a tract, in which an English Nonconformist pastor told the story of a man whose worldly life had been profoundly changed after—and as a direct result of—hearing one of her hymns
sung; with that she sprang to her feet and joyfully exclaimed, "Thank God!
I do like to hear that!"[14]

As a humble and devout woman, Alexander had wide contact with many eminent Christian leaders of her day, including Bishop Wilberforce, the ardent antislavery champion, High Churchman Dean Stanley, the poet Matthew Arnold, and historian William Lecky; she became indignant when shallow criticism was voiced of them and their views; she also counted many Nonconformists, especially among the Presbyterians(!),[15] as her friends and fellow travelers on the King's Highway. Another outreach to which she gave of her time and energies was the institution named *The Home for Fallen Women;*[16] her no-nonsense approach to human sin and her compassionate concern for the needs of the disadvantaged combined so that she was able to influence many into lives reclaimed for healthy and godly purposes.

While this hymn, though intended for children, has become one of the greatest of those dealing with the doctrine of the atonement, and as such is used by all ages, it has never been identified with a single tune. "Meditation," the tune in the *Trinity Hymnal,* although written originally for another hymn, has become wedded to it, especially in British hymnals, expressing as it does the hymn's message "with feeling and felicity."[17] Its young composer was John Henry Gower (1855–1922). Born in Rugby, England, he earned his B.Mus. and D.Mus. degrees from Oxford University, and became an excellent organist and composer; he served as music professor at Trent College, University of Nottingham, and conductor of the Long Eaton Philharmonic Society; he also gave organ recitals, and served his country as a captain in the Volunteer Battalion of the Derbyshire Regiment. However, he moved about midcareer to Denver, Colorado, where he became involved in a mining interest, although he continued his musical career as organist and choirmaster in various Denver churches.[18] He numbered among his compositions not only hymn tunes and part-songs, but a cantata, "The Good Shepherd," as well.

Now let us examine this hymn, written to explain the Creed and to answer the question put to children in the Catechism, "Why did Jesus Christ die"? And while she paints a picture with her descriptive phrase "a green hill far away outside a city wall" (i.e., Golgotha, outside Jerusalem), her description is obviously inaccurate, for Golgotha, "the place of the skull" was a barren, rocky hill; actually, Dearmer tells us

> when she went shopping in Derry, she had to drive by a little grassy hill near the road, and she tells us that she used to fancy that this was like Calvary.[19]

One other negative note, this one theological: Obviously Bailey does not share the view of the atonement as set forth by St. Anselm—the ransom theory—and represented in this hymn, for after noting the hymn's popularity and clarity, he says, "one can only regret that it perpetuates an outworn theology."[20] Does it? Does it, indeed?

Stanza One: The simple statements herein declare a historical fact, that at a specific time in the past Jesus was crucified on a cross on a hill, far away from Ireland; to those facts is added an interpretation, a doctrine of vicarious atonement, "He died to save us all," which of course includes the little children whom she was teaching in the catechism classes as well as the teacher herself.

Stanza Two: Suffering is always easier to see than it is to explain, and easier to explain than it is to justify—especially the suffering of the innocent! So, while we don't—indeed, can't—know *what* He suffered in His agony on the cross, we do know *why* He suffered, and again, its vicarious nature is implied.

Stanza Three: Why, then, did He die? And here is a twofold answer: both that we might experience forgiveness and that we might be made good, justified or sanctified. As the late C. Stacy Woods, pioneer general-secretary of InterVarsity Christian Fellowship, used to say, "the first without the second would be immoral"; forgiveness wipes out the ugly past, and makes possible a glorious future as we "grow in grace, and in the knowledge of Christ"! We are sinners, by nature and by choice, so we are not good, but He died to make us good! Moreover, that goodness is not simply for our lives in this world—though it does affect this world; it is also that we might be fitted for life in His unclouded presence in heaven!

Stanza Four: Since only God can restore the broken relationship between Himself and His lost, wayward, and rebellious human creation, He did so! He died that we might experience fellowship with Him again—to unlock the barred gates of heaven and give us access, a reiteration of the truth in the previous stanza. An interesting point is her choice of the word "good"; why didn't she say "strong" enough to unlock heaven's gates, rather than "good" enough? Perhaps because the demands of justice can only be met by a perfect, sinless "lamb" as the atoning sacrifice; a strong, blemished, imperfect ram would never do!

Stanza Five: Love is the ultimate piece of the puzzle that makes it all fit together; His love for us—"dearly, dearly"—could she mean at great expense? His love for us calls forth from us a responding love for Him, since "we love Him because He first loved us." And finally, love is demonstrated when we trust that His death is indeed efficacious for us, and when we do our best to "work the works of Him who has called us, while it is yet day"; simple faith, a profoundly simple plan, or scheme, and simple, genuine attention to carrying out in daily life His patterns for that life!

It is indeed fitting that this hymn—clear, simple, and uncluttered with fancy words and high-sounding phrases—serves as our final study. May we ever revel in its truth, knowing His redemptive love, and seeking to share it in life's everyday routines, made more meaningful by that love.

Notes

1. McCutchan, *Our Hymnody,* p. 169.
2. Covert and Laufer, *op. cit.,* p. 173.
3. Smith, *Lyric Religion,* p. 402.
4. Julian, *op. cit.,* p. 38.
5. McCutchan, *op. cit.,* p. 169.
6. Smith, *op. cit.,* p. 402.
7. Haeussler, *op. cit.,* pp. 523–524.
8. *Ibid.,* p. 523.
9. *Ibid.,* p. 524.
10. Julian, *op. cit.,* p. 39.
11. Bailey, *op. cit.,* p. 352.
12. Haeussler, *op. cit.,* p. 523.
13. Smith, *op. cit.,* p. 402.
14. Marks, *op. cit.,* p. 158.
15. *Ibid.*
16. Haeussler, *op. cit.,* p. 523.
17. Covert and Laufer, *op. cit.,* p. 174.
18. Haeussler, *op. cit.,* pp. 682–683.
19. Bailey, *op. cit.,* p. 353.
20. *Ibid.*

Conclusion

The saintly Puritan Divine Richard Baxter (1615–1691) not only wrote hymns, but also was the early leader of the movement to introduce hymn-singing into Presbyterian churches;[1] as its champion he said,

> I have made a psalm of praise in the holy assembly the chief delightful exercise of my religion and my life, and have helped to bear down all the objections which I have heard against Church music.[2]

After a trial characterized as "one of the most infamous in the whole history of English court procedure,"[3] he was sentenced to prison until a sizable fine was paid in his behalf; eighteen months later he was released, and the fine remitted. The last few years of his life were filled with peace and honor—though not without pain, for his health, often fragile, had been weakened by his prison ordeal. In his *Preface to Version of the Psalms,* published posthumously in 1692, he declared:

> There is no exercise that I had rather live and dye in, than singing praises to our Redeemer and Jehovah, while I might in the Holy Assemblies, and now when I may not, as Paul and Silas in my Bonds, and in my dying pains, which are far heavier than my Bonds. Lord Jesus receive my Praise and Supplications first, and lastly, my departing Soul. Amen.[4]

As I draw this book to a close, I might well comment in a similar fashion, that there is no exercise I had rather live and die in—in addition to singing the praises of our Redeemer—than the study of the lives of these godly men and women, and the examination of their marvelous hymns, as I have been privileged to do "lo these many, many months." For, as I have been researching and then writing this study, and through the more than three decades since I was first encouraged to make hymns a part of my fare in my daily quiet time, I can attest to the spiritual nourishment this practice and this study have provided.

It has indeed blessed my heart to be able to walk with these hymn-writers and composers in their times of challenge, suffering, and sorrow—through the reversal of their fortunes, the loss of their health, the death of their loved ones, and just the petty troublings of life—and to see them emerge with a deepened sense of the reality of God that they have been enabled to put into song. And on other occasions, to enter into the joys and deep delights that they have also been enabled to celebrate through song. Thus, whether the major or the minor chords have best interpreted their experiences, in both cases they have been instruments in the hands of God, and have enriched this world through their soul-searching words and lovely, stirring melodies. And is not this, after all, the highest purpose for music, as a "gift of the bountiful Creator to bring out the best in men, and to bring them together in love for one another,"[5] and the praise of their Maker!

Notes

1. Benson, *The English Hymn,* p. 84.
2. McCutchan, *Our Hymnody,* p. 499.
3. *Ibid.*
4. Duffield, *op. cit.,* p. 624.
5. Pike, *A Theology of Music,* p. 73.

Bibliography

A. Works on Hymnology

Abba, Raymond. *Principles of Christian Worship*. London: Oxford University Press, 1957.

Bailey, Albert E. *The Gospel in Hymns*. New York: Charles Scribners' Sons, 1952.

Barrett, William A. *English Church Composers*. London: Sampson, Low, Marsten, c. 1900 (1882).

Beattie, David J. *The Romance of Sacred Song*. London: Marshall, Morgan and Scott, 1931 (1960).

Benson, Louis F. *The English Hymn*. Richmond: John Knox, 1962 (1915).

Berglund, Robert. *A Philosophy of Church Music*. Chicago: Moody, 1985.

Blume, Friedrich. *Protestant Church Music*. New York: W. W. Norton, 1974.

Breed, David R. *The History and Use of Hymns and Hymn Tunes*. New York: Revell, 1903.

Brown, Theron, and Hezekiah Butterworth. *The Story of the Hymns and Tunes*. New York: American Tract Society, 1906.

Colquhoun, Frank. *Hymns That Live*. Downers Grove: InterVarsity, 1980.

Covert, W. C., and Calvin W. Laufer, eds. *Handbook to the Hymnal (1933)*. Chicago: Presbyterian Board of Christian Education, 1935.

Davison, A. T. *Church Music*. Cambridge: Harvard University Press, 1952.

Dearmer, Percy. *Songs of Praise Discussed*. London: Oxford University Press, 1933.

Dickinson, Edward. *Music in the History of the Western Church*. New York: Charles Scribners' Sons, 1953.

Douglas, Winfred. *Church Music in History and Practice*. New York: Charles Scribners' Sons, 1962.

Duffield, Samuel W. *English Hymns: Their Authors and History*. New York: Funk and Wagnalls, 1888 (1886).

Ellinwood, Leonard. *The History of American Church Music*. New York: Da Capo, 1970.

Ellsworth, Donald P. *Christian Music in Contemporary Witness*. Grand Rapids: Baker, 1979.

Emurian, Ernest K. *Stories of Christmas Carols.* Boston: W. A. Wilde, 1958.

Gardner, George, and Sydney Nicholson, eds. *A Manual of English Church Music.* London: SPCK, 1923.

Haeussler, Armin. *The Story of Our Hymns.* St. Louis: Eden, 1952.

Hodson, J. H. *Hymn Studies.* London: H. R. Allenson, n.d.

Hostetler, Lester. *Handbook to the Mennonite Hymnary.* Elgin: Brethren Publishing House, 1949.

Hughes, Charles. *American Hymns Old and New.* New York: Columbia University Press, 1980.

Hustad, Donald P. *Jubilate: Church Music in the Evangelical Tradition.* Carol Stream: Hope, 1980.

Julian, John A., ed. *Dictionary of Hymnology.* New York: Charles Scribners' Sons, 1882.

Lamb, John A. *The Psalms in Christian Worship.* London: The Faith Press, 1962.

Lang, Paul Henry. *Music in Western Civilization.* New York: W. W. Norton, 1941.

Liemohn, Edwin. *The Singing Church.* Columbus: Wartburg, 1959.

Lightwood, James T. *The Music of the Methodist Hymn-Book.* London: Epworth, 1935.

Long, Kenneth R. *The Music of the English Church.* New York: St. Martin's, 1971.

McCutchan, Robert G. *Hymns in the Lives of Men.* Nashville: Abingdon-Cokesbury, 1945.

———. *Our Hymnody.* 2nd ed. Nashville: Abingdon, 1942.

Marks, Harvey B. *The Rise and Growth of English Hymnody.* New York: Revell, 1938.

Metcalf, Frank J. *Stories of Hymn Tunes.* New York: Abingdon, 1928.

Moffatt, James, and Millar Patrick, eds. *Handbook to the Church Hymnary.* London: Oxford University Press, 1927.

Osbeck, Kenneth W. *Singing with Understanding.* Grand Rapids: Kregel, 1979.

Patrick, Millar. *Four Centuries of Scottish Psalmody.* London: Oxford University Press, 1949.

Phillips, C. S. *Hymnody Past and Present.* London: SPCK, 1937.

Pike, Alfred. *A Theology of Music.* Toledo: The Gregorian Institute of America, 1953.

Price, Carl F. *One Hundred and One Hymn Stories.* Cincinnati: Abingdon, 1923.

Reynolds, William J. *A Survey of Christian Hymnody.* New York: Holt, Rinehart and Winston, 1963.

Rice, William C. *A Concise History of Church Music.* Nashville: Abingdon, 1964.

Routley, Erik. *A Short History of English Church Music.* London: Mowbrays, 1977.

———. *Christian Hymns Observed.* Princeton: Prestige, 1982.

———. *Church Music and Theology.* Philadelphia: Muhlenburg, 1959.

———. *The English Carol.* London: Herbert Jenkins, 1958.

————. *Hymns and the Faith.* Greenwich, Conn.: Seabury, 1956.

————. *The Music of Christian Hymns.* Chicago: GIA, 1981.

————. *The Musical Wesleys, 1703–1876.* New York: Oxford University Press, 1968.

————. *Twentieth Century Church Music.* New York: Oxford University Press, 1964.

————. *Words, Music and the Church.* London: Herbert Jenkins, 1969.

Smith, H. A. *Lyric Religion.* New York: Century, 1931.

Smith, Jane S., and Betty Carlson. *A Gift of Music.* Westchester: Cornerstone Books, 1979.

Steere, Dwight. *Music in Protestant Worship.* Richmond: John Knox, 1960.

Stevenson, Robert Nurrell. *Patterns of Protestant Church Music.* London: Cambridge University Press, 1953.

Stewart, G. W. *Music in Church Worship.* London: Hodder and Stoughton, n.d.

Stulken, Marilyn Kay. *Hymnal Companion to the Lutheran Book of Worship.* Philadelphia: Fortress, 1981.

Sydnor, James R. *The Hymn and Congregational Singing.* Richmond: John Knox, 1960.

Temple, Arthur. *Hymns We Love.* London: Lutterworth, 1954.

Topp, Dale. *Music in the Christian Community.* Grand Rapids: Eerdmans, 1976.

Werner, Eric. *The Sacred Bridge.* New York: Columbia University Press, 1959.

Wesley, S. S. *A Few Words on Cathedral Music.* London: Hinrichsen Edition, 1966 (1849, original edition).

Wienandt, Elwyn A. *Choral Music of the Church.* New York: The Free Press, 1965.

Wienandt, Elwyn A., and Robert H. Young. *The Anthem in England and America.* New York: The Free Press, 1970.

Yeats-Edwards, Paul. *English Church Music—A Bibliography.* London: White Lion, 1975.

B. Works in Related Areas

Cowman, Lydia. *Streams in the Desert.* Grand Rapids: Zondervan, 1925 (1970).

Maxwell, William D. *A History of Christian Worship.* Grand Rapids: Baker, 1936 (1982).

Rayburn, Robert G. *Oh Come, Let Us Worship.* Grand Rapids: Baker, 1984.

C. Bible Commentaries

Carson, Herbert M. *The Epistles of Paul to the Colossians and to Philemon.* Grand Rapids: Eerdmans, 1966.

Clark, Gordon H. *Colossians.* Phillipsburg: Presbyterian and Reformed, 1979.

Guthrie, Donald, and J. A. Motyer, eds. *The New Bible Commentary, Revised.* Grand Rapids: Eerdmans, 1970.

Kidner, Derek. *Psalms, Tyndale Old Testament Commentary.* 2 vols. London: Inter-Varsity, 1973.

Leslie, Elmer A. *The Psalms.* Nashville: Abingdon, 1949.

Lightfoot, J. B. *St. Paul's Epistle to the Colossians and to Philemon.* Grand Rapids: Zondervan, 1961 (1869).

Parker, T. H. L., trans. *Calvin's New Testament Commentaries: Galatians, Ephesians, Philippians and Colossians.* Grand Rapids: Eerdmans, 1965.

Simpson, E. K., and F. F. Bruce. *The Epistles to the Ephesians and Colossians.* Grand Rapids: Eerdmans, 1957.

Weiser, Artur. *The Psalms.* Philadelphia: Westminster, 1962.

D. Reference Works

————. *Greek-English New Testament.* Washington: Christianity Today, 1975.

————. *The Holy Bible: New International Version.* Grand Rapids: Zondervan, 1978.

————. *New American Standard Bible.* Carol Stream: Creation House, 1961.

————. *Trinity Hymnal.* Philadelphia: The Orthodox Presbyterian Church, 1961.

Arndt, William F., and F. Wilbur Gingrich. *A Greek-English Lexicon of the New Testament and Other Early Christian Literature.* 4th rev. ed. Chicago: University of Chicago Press, 1952.

Cook, Paul E. G., and Graham Harrison, eds. *Christian Hymns.* Bryntirion: The Evangelical Movement of Wales, 1977.

Douglas, J. D., ed. *The New Bible Dictionary.* Grand Rapids: Eerdmans, 1962.

Index

Abelard, Peter, 192
"Aberystwyth," 178, 183
"Abide with Me, Fast Falls . . . ," 88, 117, 120–25
Abraham, 246
"*Adeste Fideles*," 187, 311, 312, 313
Adolphus, Gustavus, 47
Advent hymns, 214
Agape feast, 7, 29
"Age of gold," 290
"Ajalon," 237, 241
Albany, New York, 193
Albert, prince of Wales, 160, 238
Aldersgate experience, 139
Alexander
    Archibald, 229
    Cecil Frances, 21, 254, 332–37
    James Waddell, 226, 227, 229–30
    William, 333
Alford
    Dean, 21
    Henry, 263–66
Alfred the Great, 114
All
    "Glory, Laud and Honor," 127–30, 214, 252
    "Hail the Power of Jesus' Name," 256–62
    Hallows parish, 327
    "Praise to Thee, My God, This Night," 49–52
    Saints Day, 155
    "Things Bright and Beautiful," 332
"Alleluia," 93
Alpha and Omega, 206
Ambrose, 7, 10, 21, 22, 226, 246
Ambrosian scale, 20, 247
Ancient Concerts, 311

Angels, 224, 235, 266, 286, 289, 296, 313, 314
    "from the Realms of Glory," 176
Anglican Church. *See* Church of England
Anne, Queen, 83
Anselm, 335–36
"Antioch," 73, 74, 75
Antiphonal singing, 6, 7–8, 74, 290
Apologetics, 277
Apostles' Creed, 155, 322, 326, 332
Arian hymns, 7
Arius, 166
Armenian martyrs, 237
Arminianism, 18, 240
Arnold, Matthew, 244, 335
"Art Thou Weary, Art Thou Languid," 21
Assurance, 303–4
Athanasius, 166
Atlantic Charter, 321
Atonement, 209–10, 212, 230–31, 235, 239, 241, 242, 244, 336
Attitude in worship, 35–36
Augustine, 10, 40, 116
"Aurelia," 63, 64, 324, 325, 327
"Austrian Hymn," 54, 55, 56, 91
"Awake, My Soul and With the Sun," 49

Babylonian exile, 217
Bach, J. S., 25, 32, 129, 160, 226, 227, 230
Baker, Henry W., 21, 111–14, 147–48, 191, 192, 193, 283
Ban on public singing, 8, 56
Baptist Cymanfaoedd Canu, 61
Baring-Gould, Sabine, 21, 270, 31622
Barnabas, 152

Barnby, Joseph, 152, 153, 154, 249, 250–51
Baxter, Richard, 12, 339
Beckwith, Paul, 1
Beecher
    Henry Ward, 76, 180, 207
    Lyman, 76
"Beecher," 203, 207
"Benedictus," 28, 111
Bernard
    of Clairvaux, 21, 93, 171, 186–90, 191–94, 292, 226–31
    of Cluny, 21, 292–97
Berridge, John, 19
"Bethel," 139
Bethlehem
    birthplace of Jesus, 222–23, 224, 313, 314
    Hospital, 205
Bickersteth, Edward, 21, 118, 182, 194, 288
Birde, William. See Byrd, William
Blood of Christ, 200–1
Bodleian Library, 191
Bohemian Brethren, 8
Bonar, Horatius, 136, 254, 280–84
Bonaventure, 311
Book of Common Prayer, 20, 73, 131, 158
Book of Were-Wolves, The (Baring-Gould), 318
Boston Academy of Music, 76
Bowring, John, 3
Boyd, William, 268, 270
Bradbury
    Thomas, 83
    William Batchelder, 74, 196, 197, 199
Brady, Nicholas, 12
Bremen, Germany, 96
Bride of Christ, 329
Bridges, Matthew, 147–50
"Brightest and Best of the Sons of the Morning," 131–35
Broad church Anglicans, 106
Brooks, Phillips, 219–25
Browning, Elizabeth Barrett, 275
"Burial of Moses, The," 333
Bushnell, Horace, 276–77
"By the Waters of Babylon," 319

Byrd, William, 37
Byron, George Gordon, 114

Calkin, J. Baptiste, 122
"Calm on the Listening Ear of Night," 288
Calvin, John, 9–10, 28
Calvinism, 18, 19
Canaan, spiritual, 296
"Cantate Domino," 73
Canterbury Cathedral, 264
Cantors, 7–8
Cantus Diversi, 311
Cardiff Festival, 251
Carey, William, 711
"Carol," 286, 287, 289
Caswall, Edward, 21, 20, 154–55, 186, 187, 189, 191, 249–50
Catholic Encyclopedia, The, 187
Cennick, John, 19
Chalmers, Thomas, 280, 242
Change, expectation of, 200
Chant, 78
    antiphonal, 6
    Gregorian, 217
Chants de Sion (Malan), 198
Charlemagne, 7–8, 127
Charles
    II, 50
    V, 44, 46
"Cheerful Light," 7
Child's Catechism, 168
Children, songs for, 14–15, 91, 168, 272, 295, 316–22, 332, 335
Choir, The, 327
Choral Society of Nantwich, 106
Christ
    in Song, 187
    "the Lord Is Risen Today," 136–40
    "Whose Glory Fills the Skies," 142–46
    "word of," 26–27
    worship, 7
Christian
    Century, 143
    "Dost Thou See Them?" 21
    "Greeting, A," 251
    Lyre, 177

Observer, 131
Year (Keble), 101–2, 216, 332
Christmas hymns, 66, 160–61, 219,
    286–90, 311–14. *See also* Advent
    hymns
Chrysostom, 40
Church
    of England, 15, 19–20, 106, 112, 189,
        144, 324, 259
    Hymns (How), 154
    Hymns and Tunes (Sullivan), 109, 270
    militant, 155, 330
    Missionary Society, 196
    of the Nativity, 223
    of Scotland, 22
    singing in early, 6–7
    Triumphant, 156
    year, 106
"Church's One Foundation . . . , The,"
    21, 254, 324–30
Cistercian order, 188, 292
CL Psalms of David, The (Hart), 276
Clapham Sect, 196
"Clara Vallis," 188
Clark
    Gordon H., 27
    of Canterbury, 74
Clarke, Adam, 66
Clay-Ker-Seymour, Gertrude, 319
Clement
    VII, 46
    of Alexandria, 28
Clerk of the Journals, House of Lords,
    274
Cluniac monasteries, 292
Colenso, John, 324, 326
Collection of Hymns for the Use . . . , A
    (Wesley), 18
Collection of Psalms and Hymns (Madan),
    19
Come
    "Thou Everlasting Lord," 204
    "Ye Thankful People, Come," 263–66
Communion, 29. *See also* Lord's Supper
Comprehensive Rippon, Rippon, 260
Confessional standards of church, 324,
    326
Confidence in God, 121

Connection. *See* Lady Huntington
Constance, Council of, 8
Constantine, 321
Contemporary Review, 265
Controversial hymns, 18
Conventions, singing, 76
Conyers, Richard, 19
Coram, Thomas, 91
"Coronation," 256, 257–58
Coterill, Thomas, 20, 186
Courage, 182–83
Court of the Queen's Bench, 234
Coverdale, Miles, 44
Cowper, William, 19, 20, 22, 56, 170,
    254, 273–78
Creation, 78–79, 94, 99
"Creation, The," 57
Croft, William, 81, 82, 84
Cross of Christ. *See* Atonement
"Crown Him with Many Crowns,"
    147–50, 265
"Crucifer," 173, 174, 176
"CWM Rhondda," 59–61
Crüger, Johann, 305, 306, 308
Crusades, 188–89
Cummings, William Hayman, 158, 159,
    160

Dartmouth, Lord, 54, 77
David, King, 5, 12, 29, 40, 114, 130,
    218
Day
    "of Resurrection, The," 21
    "Thou Gavest, Lord Is Ended, The,"
        106–10
"*De Contemptu Mundi*," 293–94
Death
    in Christ, 231, 335–36
    victory over, 140, 155, 235, 296
Dependence upon God, 26, 121
Depression/despair, 175, 182, 197, 212,
    273–76, 277–78, 295–96
Deserted Village (Goldsmith), 288
Devotional value of hymnody, 1
"Diadem," 256
"Diademata," 147, 148, 265
Dictionary of Hymnology (Julian), 3
Didactic hymnody, 21, 27, 254

Didymus, 40
"Disciple," 177
Discipleship, 271–72
Divine
  and Moral Songs, 81
  Songs . . . for the Use of Children
    (Watts), 14–15
Doddridge, Philip, 22
Dominican order, 188
"Dominus Regit Me," 111, 112
Douglas, Winfred, 1, 41
Doxology, 252
Duffield, George, 180
"Duke Street," 68, 70
"Dundee," 273, 276
Durant, Will, 171–72
Dusseldorf, Germany, 96–98, 99
Dvorak, Antonin, 154
Dwight, Timothy, 258
Dykes, John B., 22, 111, 112, 118, 163,
    164, 166, 184, 186, 187, 190,
    193, 232, 233, 234, 280, 281,
    283, 289

East
  India Company, 77
  London, Parish, 152
"Easter Hymn," 136
Ecclesiasticus, 308, 309
Education
  music, 36, 74–76, 199, 240, 257
  music in, 9
"Ein Feste Burg," 187
El Shaddai, 61
"Elijah," 160
Elizabeth
  I, 13
  II, 88, 261
Eller, James, 256
Ellerton, John, 21, 63, 106–10
"Ellesdie," 176
Elliott, Charlotte, 196–201
Elvey, George J., 22, 147, 148, 149, 263,
    264, 265
Emmanuel, Christ the, 161, 217
Emotion
  in music, 70, 198, 210, 240, 255, 309
  in worship, 41, 117, 268

English church hymnody, 11–22
English Hymns (Duffield), 286
"Eternal Father, Strong to Save," 167,
    320
"Eudoxia," 318
Eusebius, 28
Evangelical
  Alliance, 263
  Anglicans, 86, 106, 299
  impulse, 17, 106–9, 303
  Party, 19, 20
Evening hymn, 50, 51
"Eventide," 120, 121, 123–24
Ewald, Georg, 234
Ewing, Alexander, 292, 293, 295
"Ewing," 292, 293, 295
Exhortative songs, 254

"Faben," 91, 92
"Fairest Lord Jesus," 289
Faith, 194, 212
Faithfulness of God, 77, 88
Family Prayers for the Use. . . , Baker, 112
Famine, 305, 307, 309
Fatherhood of God, 88
"Faust," 145
Fear, 271–72, 277
"Fight the Good Fight with All Thy
    Might," 254, 268–72
Florence, Italy, 127l
"For All the Saints, Who from Their
    Labors Rest," 152–56
Forgiveness, 239, 336
Forsyth, P. T., 108
Foundation in Christ, 329
Foundling hospitals, 17, 91, 294
Francis of Assisi, 216
Franciscan order, 188
Frederick Wilhelm I, 229, 230
Free Church of Scotland, 280, 282
Freedom in Christ, 217
French
  Psalter, 109
  Reformed Church, 198

"Geneva Jigs," 13
George
  I, 83

V, 271
VI, 276
Samoan king, 71
Gerhardt, Paul, 16, 226, 227, 277
Gibbon, Edward, 233
Gilbert, W. S., 109, 320
Gilmore, Patrick S., 44
Gladstone, William, 238
"Gloria Patri," 41, 252, 308–9
"Glorious Things of Thee Are Spoken,"
    54–57
Glory
    of Christ, 145, 245
    of God, 26, 30, 31, 240, 262
Goldsmith, Oliver, 288
"God Moves in a Mysterious Way," 254,
    273–78
Good Shepherd, Christ as, 112, 114
"Good Shepherd, The," 335
Gordon, A. J., 125
Gospel Magazine, The, 239, 258
Gospel song, 254
Goss, John, 21, 86, 87, 89–90, 319
Gounod, Charles F., 142, 143, 145–46,
    332
Gower, John H., 332, 333, 335
Grace of God, 88, 200, 203, 205, 231,
    271, 278
Graham, Billy, 196
Grant, Robert, 77–80
Greek
    New Testament, 264
    scale, 247
Gregorian chant, 217, 247, 313
Gregory I, 214, 247
Grimm, Jacob, 251
"Guide Me, O Thou Great Jehovah,"
    59–62

"Hail to the Lord's Anointed," 63–66
"Hamburg," 244, 245, 247
Handel
    George Frideric, 57, 71, 74, 75, 91,
        302
    and the Haydn Society, 71, 76
Harding, James P., 131, 132, 133
"Hark, the Herald Angels Sing," 158–61
Harmonic Choir of Aberdeen, 295

Harris, Howell, 59
Hassler, Hans Leo von, 226, 227, 230
Hastings, Thomas, 36, 74, 238, 240
Hatton, John, 68
Havergal
    Frances Ridley, 21, 277, 299–304
    William, 299–301
Haydn
    Franz Josef, 25, 54, 55, 56–57, 79, 91
    Johann Michael, 57, 77, 78, 79–80
    Society, 295
"He Leadeth Me," 199
Heaven, 294, 295
Heber, Reginald, 20, 71–72, 131–35,
    163–67, 232
Helmore, Thomas, 214, 215, 217, 319
Help from God, 83
Henry VIII, 51
Herberger, Valerius, 129
Heresy, 324, 329, 330
"Hermon," 272, 273, 276
"Hesperus." See "Quebec"
Hill
    Rowland, 59
    Sumner, 199
History of the Jews (Milman), 232–33
Holden, Oliver, 256, 257–58
Holiness
    God's, 165i
    personal, 207
"Hollingside," 184
Holmes, Oliver Wendell, 221–22
Holy
    Club, 142
    "Holy, Holy," 30, 118, 163–67, 289
    Spirit, 6, 27, 47, 127
Home for Fallen Women, 335
Hope in Christ, 176, 231, 261, 309, 326
Horbury Bridge parish, 316–17
How, William Walsham, 21, 152–56
"How Sweet the Name of Jesus
    Sounds," 168–72, 186
Hughes, John, 59–62
Huguenots, 259
Huntington, Lady, 18, 196, 258, 260
"Hursley," 101
Hus, John, 8
"Hyfrydol," 91, 93

Hymn
    definition, 116, 189, 194
    "of Praise," 160
    use, 1, 3–4, 116–18
Hymn Society of America, 116
Hymnal
    of the Episcopal Church, 223
    by Murray, 313
    Noted, The (Helmore), 217
Hymnary, The (Sullivan), 319
Hymns
    Ancient and Modern (Baker, Monk),
        21, 103, 107, 111, 112, 113,
        123, 147, 154, 184, 234, 250,
        265, 321, 327
    of Consecration and Faith (Mountain),
        303
    of the Heart, 147
    by InterVarsity, 1
    for Little Children (Alexander), 332,
        333
    and Psalms, 15
    and Sacred Poems (Wesley), 17
    and Spiritual Songs, 68
    of the Week, 198
    *Written and Adapted to the Weekly
        Service . . . ,* 131

"I Heard the Voice of Jesus Say . . . ,"
        254, 280–84
"In the Cross of Christ I Glory"
        (Bowring), 3
Immanuel. *See* Emmanuel
Incarnation, 313
Infinity of God, 79
Ingersoll, Robert, 221
Inner-city ministry, 327
Instruments, musical, 5
InterVarsity
    Christian Fellowship, 336
    Urbana Missionary Conference, 256
Invitation to salvation, 280, 283–84
"It Came upon the Midnight
        Clear . . . ," 286–90

Jacob of Misi, 8
James I, 114
Jerusalem, 188–89
    "the Golden," 292–97, 327

Jesu
    "dulcis, memoria," 186, 191
    "Hertz-Beuchein" (Rinkart), 305
Jesus
    "Christ Is Risen Today," 139
    "Loves Me," 199
    "I Am Resting, Resting . . . ," 303
    "I My Cross Have Taken," 88, 89,
        173–77
    "Lover of My Soul," 117, 178–84
    name of, 329
    reign of, 70, 73–74
    "Shall Reign Where'er the Sun . . . ,"
        42, 68–72
    singing of, 6
    "Thou Joy of Loving Hearts,"
        191–94, 209
    "the Very Thought of Thee . . . ,"
        186–90
Jews, emancipation of English, 77
John the Deacon, 7–8
Journal (Charles Wesley), 181
Joy, 205, 252, 296
    "to the World, the Lord is Come,"
        73–76
"Joyful (Jubilee) Rhythm of St. Bernard,
        on the Name of Jesus, The," 186,
        187, 189, 191
"Jubilee Rhythm." *See* "Joyful (Jubilee)
        Rhythm of St. Bernard . . . ,
        The"
Judgment of God, 266, 294
"Just As I Am, Without One Plea . . . ,"
        196–201
Justification, 266
Juvenile Music Festivals, 199

Kaiser, Leonard, 44
Katholisches Gesangbuch, 101, 102, 249
Keble, John, 20, 21, 101–4, 106, 117,
        194, 216, 327, 332
Keller, Helen, 222
Ken, Thomas, 49–52
"King of Love My Shepherd Is, The,"
        111–14
Kingdom of God, 78–79, 237

Lambeth Conference, 328–29
Latimer, Hugh, 301

Latin
  Christianity (Milman), 233
  hymnody, 20
  Hymns, 191
Laudes
  "*Diurnae*" (Oakeley, Redhead), 313
  "*Domini,*" 154–55, 249, 250, 250
Le Jeune, George, 203, 204
"Lead, Kindly Light, . . . , 278
Lecky, William, 335
Leeds
  Duke of, 311
  Festival, 251
Lewis, C. S., 305
Liberty for oppressed, 66
Liddon, Henry P., 252
Life and Reminiscences, 265
Light
  of life, Christ the, 134
  "Shining out of Darkness," 276
  "of the World, The," 320
Lightfoot, J. B., 28
"Llanfair," 136, 137, 139
"Lyons," 57, 77, 78
Lightwood, James, 8, 74, 122
"Like a River Glorious . . . ," 299–304,
     299, 300, 302
Liturgical hymns, 20
Lives of the Saints (Baring-Gould), 318
Livingstone, David, 191
"*Lobe den Herren*," 96, 97, 98–99
Lock Hospital, 17
London
  Bible Society, 147
  bishop of, 54
London, H. M. S., disaster, 237
Long-Eaton Philharmonic Society, 335
Lord's supper, 114, 194
Lordship of Christ, 260
"Lost Chord, The," 320
Louis
  IX, 292
  the Pious, 127
Love
  for Christ, 189
  of Christ, 178, 183, 228, 336–37
  "Divine, All Loves Excelling," 203–8
  of God, 79, 112, 113, 203, 205

God's gifts of, 309
  human, 203–5
Loyal Responses (Havergal), 302
Luther, Martin, 8–9, 44–47, 191, 235,
     251–52, 255
  hymn philosophy, 4
  musicianship, 8, 10–11
  philosophy of music, 32, 33
  at Wartburg, 46
"*Lux Prima,*" 142, 143, 145
Lyra
  Fidelium (Stone), 326
  Germanica (Winkworth), 308
Lyric poetry, 116–17
Lyte, Henry Francis, 42, 86–90, 106,
     117, 120–25, 173–77

Macauley, Lord, 77
Madan, Martin, 19, 139
"*Magnificat,*" 28, 116
Majesty
  of Christ, 261
  of God, 242
Manual of Prayers (Ken), 49
Marcion, 40–41
Marot, Clement, 109
Marsh, Simon B., 178, 179, 184
Martial hymns, 316, 330
"Martyn," 178, 179, 184
Mason, Lowell, 36, 73, 74, 75, 76, 131,
     167, 199, 209, 210, 211, 240,
     244, 245, 272, 273, 276
Mass, singing in, 7
Massachusetts, bishop of, 222
Maurice, F. D., 287
Mechanics Institute, 106
"Meditation," 332, 333, 335
"Melita," 167
Memorial Church, Edinburgh, 282
Mendelssohn, Moses, 160
"Mendelssohn," 158, 159
Mendelssohn-Bartholdy, Felix, 25, 160,
     289
Mercy of God, 99, 307
Message of hymnody, 1
"Messiah, The," 91, 261
Messiah-King, Christ the, 130, 161,
     235, 245, 296, 314

Methodist
  beginnings, 96
  Hymn Book, The, 18
  hymnody, 16–19
Metrical Psalms, 12, 13
"Mighty Fortress Is Our God, A," 30,
    44–47, 237
Milan, 226
"Miles Lane," 256, 258
Milman, Henry Hart, 232–35
Milton, John, 22, 69, 114
Missionary vision, 133
Mitre, The, 259
Monk, William Henry, 22, 103, 120,
    121, 123–24, 283
Monsell, John S. B., 21, 254, 268–72
Montgomery, James, 49, 63–66, 71–72,
    77
Moody, Dwight L., 272, 303
Moravians, 16, 22, 63, 139, 307–8
Morning hymns, 50
"Morning Star," 131, 132, 133
Morris, James, 239
Moses, 5, 241
Moule, Handley, G. C., 21, 275
Mountain, James, 299, 300, 302–3
Mozart, Wolfgang Amadeus, 176, 268,
    269, 270
"Mozart," 268, 269, 271
Music, emotion in. *See* Emotion, in
    music
Music education, 19, 36, 74–76, 199,
    240, 257
My
  "Faith Looks up to Thee," 209–13,
    286
  "Sins, My Sins, My Saviour," 269
Mystery of God, 276

Name of Jesus, 171, 190
Nature, praise in, 73–74
Neale, John Mason, 20–21, 127, 128,
    129, 214–17, 249, 292, 294
Neander, Joachim,. 96–99
Nelson, Horatio, 295
New Version of the Psalms of David, A
    (Tate and Brady). *See New Version*
    Psalter
New Version Psalter, 12–13, 15, 16, 42

Newman, John Henry, 20, 21, 189, 278,
    313
Newton, John, 20, 54–57, 168–72, 186,
    274
"Nicea," 118, 163, 164, 166, 289
Nicene Creed, 166, 313–14, 322
Normandy invasion, 83
Now
  "the Day Is Over," 319
  "Thank We All Our God . . . ," 305–9
"Nun Danket Alle Gott," 305, 306, 308

O
  "Come, All Ye Faithful, . . . ," 241,
    254, 311–14
  "Come, O Come, Emmanuel . . . ,"
    214–18
  "Gladsome Light," 7
  "Israel," 319
  "Little Town of Bethlehem," 219–25
  "Sacred Head, Now Wounded,"
    226–31
  "Worship the King, All Glorious
    Above," 57, 77–80
Oakeley, Frederick, 21, 241, 311, 312,
    313
"Odes of Solomon," 28
Odyssey, 265
Office hymn, 13
Oglethorpe, James Edward, 138, 139
Oh
  "for a Closer Walk with God," 170
  "for a Thousand Tongues," 139
Old
  "Hundredth," 71, 305
  "Rugged Cross, The," 10
Old Version Psalter, 11–12, 13, 16, 41
"Olivet," 209, 210, 211–12
Olney Hymns (Cowper, Newton), 19,
    56, 131, 169, 274
Omnipotence of God, 261
"Once in Royal David's City," 332
"Onward Christian Soldiers . . . ," 109,
    316–22
Orleans, France, 127
Osler, Edward, 21, 91–92, 93, 94
"Our God, Our Help in Ages Past,"
    81–84, 117, 244, 320–21
Oxford Movement, 19, 20, 216, 313, 332

Palestrina, Giovanni, 51
Palm Sunday hymns, 129–30, 232, 235
Palmer, Ray, 191, 192, 193, 209–13
"Park Street," 68, 69, 70
Parry, Joseph, 178, 183
"Parsifal," 154
"Passion Chorale," 226, 227, 230
Passover, 6
Paul, apostle, 1, 6, 8, 25–26, 28, 40, 246, 254, 271, 316, 339
Peace
  announcing, 66
  in God, 299, 303–4
  "Perfect Peace," 21
  victory of, 316
Penitential
  hymns, 196
  use of psalms, 40
Penny Post, 194
Pentateuch, 324
"Pentecost," 268, 270
Perfectionist movement, 207
Perronet, Edward, 256–62
Pestalozzi, Johann Heinrich, 76
Peter the Venerable, 292
Philharmonic Society, 251
Philip, Duke of Edinburgh, 88
Philo, 28
Phos Hilaron, 7
Pigott, Jean, 303
Pilgrim's Progress, The (Bunyan), 212
Pilgrimage of life, 176
Plague, 305, 307, 309
Pliny, 7, 28
Plymouth Collection, The (Zundel and Jones), 207
Poetic
  imagery, 69–70
  style, 13–14
Portogallo, Marcos Antonio, 311–12
Power of music, 5
Praise
  to Christ, 155, 252, 260
  to God, 88, 251, 252, 308–9, 340
  "God from Whom All Blessings Flow," 49, 93. *See also* Doxology
  "the Lord, Ye Heavens Adore Him," 91–94

"to the Lord, the Almighty, the King . . .," 96–99
"My Soul, the King of Heaven," 42, 86–90, 117, 174–75
  in music, 8–9, 30
  in nature, 73–74
  Songs of, 25
Praxis Pietatis Melica (Crueger), 99, 308
Prayer, 282
Preciousness of Jesus, 168
Preface to Version of the Psalms (Baxter), 339
Premillennialism, 281
Prescott, 104
Prince of glory, 245
Prince of Wales, H. M. S., 320–21
Pritchard, Rowland, 91, 93
Privy Council, 324
"Prodigal Son, The," 320
Promises of God, 176
Prophecy in Psalms, 70
Protection by God, 102, 266
Providence of God, 266, 276
Psalms
  of David Imitated, The (Watts), 14, 83
  Hymns, and Anthems of the Foundling Hospital, 92
  hymns, and spiritual songs, 6–7, 12, 26–28, 40
Psalter
  English, 11
  French, 109
  Gregorian, 313
  Jewish, 6, 40, 41
  metrical, 7, 10–12, 13, 34, 41
  New Version, 12–13, 16
  Old Version, 11–12, 13, 16
  penitential use of, 40
  Scottish, 111, 273
  use of, 28–30
Purcell
  Henry, 32
  Society, 160
Puritans, 22
Purpose, God's eternal, 790

Quarterly
  Journal of Prophecy, 281
  Review, The, 131

"Quebec," 191, 192, 193

Redemption. *See* Salvation
"Redemption, The," 145–46
Redhead, Richard, 22, 237, 241, 313
Redner, Lewis H., 219, 220, 223
Reformation, 11, 44–47
Reformed Church in Germany, 97–98
Refuge in God, 184
"Regent Square," 176
Reign
    of Christ, 149–50, 156, 245, 261, 290
    of God, 78–79, 88, 99, 108
Reinagle, Alexander R., 22., 168, 169,
    170
Renan, Joseph, 234
Rest in Jesus, 171
Resurrection of Christ, 140
"*Rhythmica Oratio*," 228
"Ride On, Ride On in Majesty . . . ,"
    232–35
Ridley, Nicholas, 301
Righteousness, establishing, 66
Rinkart, Martin, 305–9
Rippon, John, 260
Ritschl, Albrecht, 230, 231
"Rock of Ages," 237–43
Roman Catholic Church, 189, 247, 313
Roman Empire under Constantine the Great
    (Bridges), 147
Rossetti, Christina, 242
Rous, Francis, 111
Royal
    Academy of Music, 71, 89, 184, 251,
        319
    Choral Society, 154
Rudiments of Music, The, 160
"Rules for Methodist Singers," 37
Rutherford, Samuel, 182
Ryle, J. C., 21

Sacrifice
    call to, 316
    of Christ, 173
St.
    "Agnes," 186, 187, 190
    "Anne," 81, 82, 84
    "Clement," 106, 107

    "Crispin," 265
    "Drostane," 232, 233, 234
    Gaudens, Augustus, 219
    "George's Windsor," 263, 264, 265
    "Gertrude," 316, 317, 319
    "John's Passion," 129
    "Louis," 219, 220, 223
    Mary's Woolworth Parish, 168
    "Matthew's Passion," 160, 230
    Nicholas, Church of, Berlin, 229
    Nicholas's Parish, 269
    Oswald's parish, 234
    "Paul," 160
    Paul's Cathedral, 234, 251, 320
    Paul's Haggerston parish, 326
    "Peter," 168, 169, 170
    "Theodulph," 127, 128, 252. *See also*
        Theodulph of Orleans
Salvation, 94, 140, 200–1, 217, 224–25,
    297
"Samson," 71
Sanctification, 266, 336–37
Sankey, Ira, 303
"Sarum," 152, 153, 155
Satan, 46
Savior, Jesus as, 189
"Saviour, Like a Shepherd Lead Us," 199
Schaff, Philip, 187, 228
Schism, 329, 330
Schoefield, Clement Cotterill, 109
"*Schoenster Herr Jesu,*" 289
Schola Cantorum, 247
Scholefield, Clement C., 106, 107
Schoolmen, 192
Schubert, Franz Peter, 80, 142
Schwartz, Christian, 230
Scottish Psalter, 111, 273
Scripture
    music in, 5, 25–30, 31
    proclaiming in hymns, 4
    versification of, 7, 10, 12–13
Sears, Edmund H., 118, 286–90
"Seasons, The," 57
Security in God, 51, 57, 84, 231, 241,
    242, 303–4
Selection (Perronet), 260
Selection of Psalms and Hymns (Cotterill),
    20

Sermon on the Mount, 259
Shakleton, Lord, 124
Sheffield Register/Iris, 63, 77
Shelley, Harry Rowe, 111
Shrubsole, William, 256, 258
Silas, 40, 339
Sin, original, 73
Singer's Friend, The (Pritchard), 93
Singing
    antiphonal, 6, 7–8, 74, 290
    ease of, 35
    conventions, 76
    in the early church, 6–7
    in the Roman Catholic Church, 7
    popularity of, 34–35
    schools, 257
    in worship, 1, 3–4, 116–18, 336, 339
Sisterhood of St. Margaret, 216, 294
Slavery, abolition of, 17, 174, 196, 205,
    207
Smart, Henry, 173, 174, 176, 258–59
Social reform, 17, 63, 91, 205, 286–87,
    290, 292–94
Society for Promoting Christian
    Knowledge, 93
Solace in Christ, 178, 182
Solomon, 40
"Sometimes a Light Surprises . . . ,"
    277
Sorrow, victory over. *See*
    Depression/despair
South Wales, 61
Southey, 164, 232
Sovereignty of God, 70, 84, 99
Speier, Diet of, 96
"Spem in alium non habui," 51
Spener, Philipp, 96
Spiritual
    songs, 254
    warfare, 316
Spurgeon, Charles, 178
"Stabat Mater," 154
Stainer, John, 89, 283
"Stand Up, Stand Up for Jesus," 180,
    286
*Sternhold and Hopkins Psalter. See Old
    Version Psalter*
Stone, Samuel, 21, 254, 324–30, 332

Stowe, Harriet Beecher, 76
Strauss, David, 234
Stuart, J. E. B., 237
Study of St. Paul (Baring-Gould), 318
Style, worship, 31–35
Suffering
    saint, 277
    Savior, 150, 245, 336
Sullivan, Arthur, 109, 270, 316, 317
"Sun of My Soul, Thou Savior Dear,"
    101–4, 117, 194
"Sweet Hour of Prayer," 199
Swansea Eisteddfod, 183
System of Praise (Watts), 14

Tallis, Thomas, 49, 50, 51
"Tallis' Evening Hymn," 49, 50
Tate, Nahum, 12
"Te Deum," 259
    (German), 305
Teignmouth, Lord, 77
Ten Commandments, 10, 109, 217–18
Tennyson, Alfred, 163, 333
Tertullian, 7, 28, 29
Teschner, Melchior, 127, 128, 129
Testimony songs, 254
Thankfulness, 27
Thanksgiving songs, 266, 308–9
Theodulph of Orleans, 127–30
Theology of hymns, 1–2, 8–9, 18
There
    "Is a Green Hill Far Away . . . ," 254,
        332–37
    "Is a Land of Pure Delight," 69
Thirty Years' War, 229, 305
Thomas à Kempis, 183
Thring, Geoffrey, 149, 150
"'Tis Midnight, and on Olive's Brow,"
    199
"Tish-Gebetlein," 305
Titanic, H. M. S., disaster, 124
Tocqueville, Alexis de, 284
Toplady, Augustus M., 19, 237–43,
    258
"Toplady," 237, 240
Tractarian Movement, 21, 189
Trajan, 7
Tranquillity, 299

Trench, Richard Chevenix, 28, 187
Trials, overcoming, 299, 303–4
Tribulation, 330
Trinity, 297, 309
Triumph over death, 181–82
Triune God, worship of, 165–66
Trust in Christ, 177, 336
Truth Incarnate, 330
"Twelfth Mass," 268, 269, 271

Unitarianism, 287–88
Unity of the church, 321–22, 329
Universality of psalms, 42

"*Veni Emmanuel*," 214, 215, 217
Venn, Henry, 196
Venua, Frederick M. A., 68, 69, 71
Verses for Holy Seasons (Humphreys-
    Alexander), 332
Versification of Scripture, 7
Victoria, 108, 154, 160, 222, 238, 251,
    305, 320
Victory
    of Christ, 322
    over death, 125, 140, 245
Virgin birth, 314
"*Vox Dilecti*," 280, 281, 283

Wagner, Richard, 154
Walloons, 318
Walton, Izaak, 49
Wartburg, Luther at, 46
Watson, John, 244
Watts, Isaac, 13–16, 18, 22, 41, 136
    appearance, 81
    hymns for children, 14–15, 168
    "Jesus Shall Reign," 68–72
    "Joy to the World," 73–76
    letter to, 15
    metrical psalms and, 42
    "Our God, Our Help," 81–84, 117
    philosophy of psalmody, 14, 29, 68–70
    poetic style of, 14, 19, 332
    psalm paraphrases, 42, 68, 70
    scholarship of, 81
    use of hymns, 56, 68, 70
    "When I Survey . . . ," 244–47
    world vision of, 71–72

Wellington, Duke of, 138
Welsh Calvinistic Methodist Church, 59
"Wesley," 131
Wesley, 71–72, 96, 196
    Charles
        "Christ the Lord Is Risen Today,"
            136–40
        Christ, Whose Glory Fills the
            Skies," 142–46
        conversion, 17
        "Hark, the Herald Angels Sing,"
            158–61
        as hymn writer, 29, 93, 117
        "Jesus, Lover of My Soul," 178–84,
            186
        "Love Divine, All Loves Excelling,"
            203–8
        Moravian influence on, 16, 22
    John, 138, 142, 144, 158
        as controversialist, 18, 240
        as hymn translator, 16, 307–8
        Moravian influence on, 16, 22
        Newton and, 54
        Perronet and, 259–60
        rules for singing, 19, 37
        views on hymns, 16–17
    Samuel, 16, 138
    Samuel Sebastian, 63, 64, 65–66, 324,
        325, 327
    Susannah, 138
Western Recorder, The, 240
Westminster Abbey, 222, 238
Westminster Catechism, 168
Westphalia, Peace of, 305
"When I Survey the Wondrous
    Cross . . . ," 69, 83, 244–47
"When Morning Gilds the Skies . . . ,"
    154–55, 249–55
Whitefield, George, 18, 54, 196
Whole Booke of Psalmes, The (Ravens-
    croft), 276
Whole Book of Psalmes . . . , The (Starn-
    hold and Hopkins). *See Old
    Version Psalter*
Whytehead, Thomas, 52
Wilberforce, William, 56, 77, 174, 196,
    335
Wilderness analogies, 61

Willcox, John H. 91, 92
William III, 12
Williams
    Robert, 136, 137, 139
    William, 59–62
Willis, Richard Storrs, 192, 286, 287, 289
Winkworth, Catherine, 96, 97, 98, 229,
        249, 305, 306, 307–8
"Woodworth," 196, 197, 199
"Word of Christ," 26–27
World
    evangelism, 70–72
    War II, 83, 124, 276

Worship
    ancient, 5–6
    attitude, 35–36
    emotions during, 25, 117
    in heaven, 165
    purpose, 30–31
    singing in, 1, 3–4, 116–18, 336, 339

York, Archbishop of, 20
Youth's Companion, The, 289

Zinzendorf, Ludwig von, 22
Zundel, John, 203, 207